CONCISE HISTORY OF AUSTRALIA

Russel Ward was born in South Australia in 1914. After graduating with an MA in English and History from Adelaide University, he taught in schools, served with the AIF and held a number of academic positions. His political activity made him a controversial figure in his early career, causing him to be passed over for key appointments. From 1967 until 1979 he held the Chair of History at the University of New England, where he is now Emeritus Professor. His publications include *The Australian Legend, A Nation for a Continent: The History of Australia 1901-1975, Australia Since the Coming of Man,* and *Finding Australia*.

In 1983 he was awarded a DLitt from the University of New England for his published work, and in 1986 was made a Member of the Order of Australia for services to literature, particularly in the field of Australian history.

RUSSEL WARD

CONCISE HISTORY OF AUSTRALIA

Maps, Diagrams and Drawings by Mark Ward

University of Queensland Press

First published 1965
This revised edition published 1992 by University of Queensland Press
Box 42, St Lucia, Queensland 4067 Australia

© Russel Ward 1965, 1979, 1982, 1987, 1992

Typeset by University of Queensland Press
Printed in Australia by The Book Printer, Victoria

Distributed in the USA and Canada by
International Specialized Book Services, Inc.,
5602 N.E. Hassalo Street, Portland, Oregon 97213-3640

Cataloguing in Publication Data
National Library of Australia

Ward, Russel, 1914-   .
    A concise history of Australia.

    New ed.
    Bibliography.
    Includes index.

    1. Australia — History. I. Ward, Russel, 1914-   , Australia since the
    coming of man. II. Title. III. Title: Australia since the coming of man.

994

ISBN 0 7022 2386 7

Contents

Preface to 1992 Edition

A Concise History of Australia is an entirely new and revised edition published by the University of Queensland Press. That is not to disguise the fact that it is basically the same book as *Australia Since the Coming of Man*, but to emphasise that much new material has been added, especially to chapters 1 and 8.

Russel Ward
Armidale
1992

Preface to 1987 Edition

This book outlines the experience of humanity in Australia since its arrival here at least 40 000 years ago. It sketches the conflicts, and occasional co-operation, between people of the different racial, cultural, religious, sex and class backgrounds which make up our history, and it seeks to explain why all of these groups are only now beginning to form one Australian nation.

It is a revised updated version of *Australia Since the Coming of Man* published in 1982. This volume differs in three ways from most existing general histories of Australia. It keeps in view, necessarily by cursory glances at illustrative incidents, three themes which are barely mentioned in other general works — the doings of Aborigines, of explorers and of the female half of the Australian people — and it examines the relationship of each group with the dominant white, male establishment.

In the introduction to one of his books, my old friend and mentor, the late Brian Fitzpatrick, quoted Othello's dying speech to sum up his own practice as a historian: "Speak of the dead as they were; nothing extenuate, nor set down aught in malice." Every historian worthy of the name strives to write such fair, "objective" history while knowing that he or she can never wholly succeed. The very questions a historian asks of his documents will inevitably be coloured, if not completely determined, by his or her own sympathies, prejudices and beliefs, both conscious and unconscious. Good history, I think, springs from this continuous dialectical tension between the writer's will and the intractable nature of his material: good history, but not impartial or objective history — something which exists only in the minds of a few bad historians and readers ingenuous enough to be taken in by them.

Try as I may, I do not flatter myself that I have been able to stifle or disguise my own biases in this volume. I am for the weak not the strong, the poor not the rich, the exploited many not the select few. I believe reason has done more for mankind than religion; and that reformist and radical political paries have done more for Australia than conservative ones, if only because they are habitually more concerned than their opponents with Australian national interests and less with British or 'allied' ones. I hate particularly self-styled conservatives who smash constitutional traditions instead of jealously guarding them.

There is only one major change in this 1987 revised edition. Recent research by Dr W.A.R. Richardson and others has convinced me that a sixteenth-century Portuguese discovery of our east coast is less likely than it seemed five years ago and I have toned down the section dealing with this accordingly.

Acknowledgments

I am very grateful to the following friends and colleagues who helped by checking the manuscript of this book, offering suggestions for its improvement and freely sharing with me their expert knowledge of certain themes and periods: Miss Alison Affleck, Professor Graham Connah, Dr Stephen Ellis, Professor W.G. Hoddinott, Mr Klaus Loewald, Dr Harry Lourandos, Professor Cliff Ollier, Dr H.G. Royle, Dr Carl Bridge and Associate Professor A.T. Yarwood.

I must thank also the University of New England for giving me an honorary fellowship, and the Australian Research Grants Commission for the travel grant which enabled me to do much of the research on which this book is based.

Figures and Tables

Tables

Drawings and Sketches

Illustrations And Sketches

Illustrations

Soldier tends a wounded comrade
Makeshift homes resulting from housing shortages
Aboriginal shanty dwellers
Australian volunteer troops
Mrs Petrov
Moonie oil field
The new affluence and technological changes of the 1960s
Sydney Opera House
Christmas week crush on Bondi Beach
"Aboriginal Embassy"
President Johnson in Australia
Young radicals
Vietnam War demonstration
The Springboks visit Australia
Equal rights for women demonstration
Vietnamese ceremony in Hyde Park
Aborigines vote for National Aboriginal Consultative
    Council
R.J. Hawke addresses House of Representatives

1 Black and white discoverers

c. 60 000 B.P. – A.D. 1770

Black Australians' progenitors were the first human beings to cross oceanic depths between continents. When Cro-Magnon people were creating their magnificent cave art in southern France and northern Spain about fifteen thousand years ago, the first Australians had been living – and painting – here for at least thirty-five millennia. On present evidence, men and women first entered the Americas about twenty-five thousand years ago and Australia at least 50 000 B.P. (i.e. before the present (time), as archaeologists say). In 1989 Rhys Jones and others excavated two ancient Aboriginal campsites at the foot of the western escarpment of the Arnhem Land plateau. Using both thermo-luminescent and radio carbon dating techniques, they established that men and women had first occupied the sites between 60 000 and 50 000 B.P.[1] Less ancient but more detailed evidence of how the first Australians lived comes from the shores of the long dried-up bed of Lake Mungo in western New South Wales. The most exciting find was the skeleton of a graceful young woman who had been cremated, the first instance of human cremation found so far anywhere in the world. There J.M. Bowler and his colleagues established the fact of continuous human occupation from at least 32 750 to 24 000 B.P., a period when the 25-kilometre-long lake teemed with fish and bird life, for the earth's climate and sea-levels have changed vastly over the ages.[2]

During the long cold spells, millions of tonnes of ice accu-

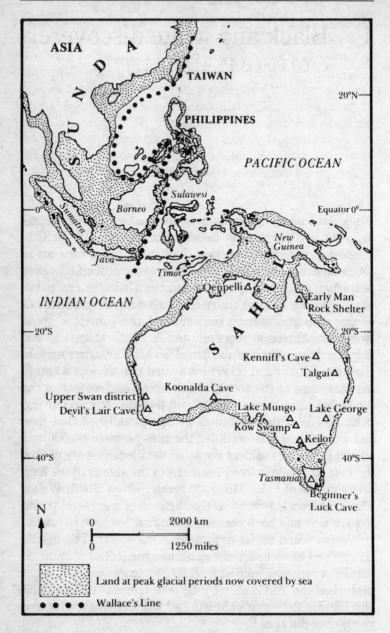

Figure 1 Sahul and Sunda — continents at peak glaciation periods

mulated around the poles and on continental highlands. As nearly all of this ice came ultimately from the evaporation of salt water, sea levels fell and shore lines extended outwards − for many hundreds of kilometres in some places. At those times the world's land masses extended roughly to the edge of the present continental shelves, where today the oceans are about 180 metres deep. Australia, New Guinea and Tasmania constituted one large continent known to historical geographers as Sahul. A sub-continent known as Sunda jutted southeast from Asia, taking in present day Burma, Indo-China, Malaysia, Sumatra, Java, Bali, Borneo and the seas between and around them. Sunda was bounded on the east by Wallace's Line, a narrow strip of deep ocean named after the great nineteenth-century British naturalist, Robert Wallace, who first noted that Asian fauna and flora predominated in islands west of the Line while Australian plants and animals flourished to its east. Between the two ancient continents there stretched chains of islands − the Celebes, Moluccas, Timor and others, somewhat larger than they are today.[3]

Perhaps human beings first reached Sahul during a glacial period when it was possible to walk most, though not all, of the way? But even at periods of peak ice-age cold, there was one sea crossing of about 90 kilometres and several of 30 kilometres or so to be negotiated. We may never know exactly how or when men and women first discovered Australia. Did they cross the water purposefully in dugout or bark canoes or on log rafts, or were the first landfalls made accidentally by fisherfolk blown to the new land by storms? Probably both kinds of voyage were made, for it is very unlikely that the colonisation of Sahul was a unique event.[4] To the question "when?" we can answer only "before 50 000 B.P.", but how long before? The date 60 000 B.P. falls long before the last ice age, at a time of quite high sea levels, but this does not prove that a crossing could *not* have been made. Not the least puzzling aspect of this discussion is that there is little agreement among prehistoric geographers and geologists as to just when glacial periods, prior to the last one, took place. There is, nevertheless, some consensus that a minor glacial

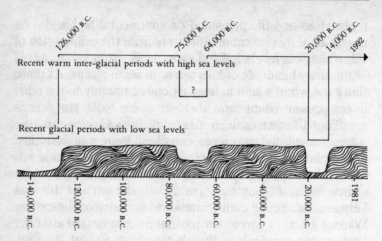

Figure 2   Probable high and low glaciation periods

peak occurred at about 70 000 B.P., and that another ice age ended at about 120 000 B.P. as shown in Figure 2. On the face of it, this last seems the most likely date for humanity's arrival in Australia, and work by botanical historians provides cogent supporting evidence that people may have reached Sahul near the end of the antepenultimate ice age.

By the shore of Lake George near Canberra, scientists in 1978 bored a hole 8.6 metres deep in the sedimentary deposits and then analysed the core, at regular intervals, for fossilised pollens and charcoal. They were able to determine quite precisely the number of years B.P. represented by each layer of the core's contents: the surface centimetre held the detritus of the last century or so, while the bottom layer held that of 350 000 B.P. The percentage of fossil pollen from different kinds of plants found at each level gave a picture of how some species had flourished while others had wilted at different periods. The percentage of carbon found at successive levels in the core showed how bushfires had waxed and waned over the whole span of time. The duration of each glacial age was also indicated partly by the relative scarcity of carbon remains. Fossil pollen analysis and carbon counting both suggest that there have been five ice ages in the Southern Hemisphere since about 350 000 B.P. The first, extending back for an unknown time, ended at about 347 000 B.P. The second seems to have lasted from about 297 000 to 251 000 B.P., the third from about 195 000 to 120 000 B.P., the fourth from about 75 000 to 64 000 B.P., and the last or most recent from about 20 000 to 8000 B.P.

There is a marked correlation between the quantity of carbon remains and the prevalence of different species of plants at successive periods. During all five ice ages, traces of carbon almost disappear from the core, as does pollen shed by eucalypts and other fire-resistant plants, while at the same time pollen from cool-temperate, fire-sensitive plants becomes more plentiful. During the long inter-glacial periods the carbon count increases, as does the abundance of both dry and cool-temperate kinds of vegetation, but a great change in the pattern occurs at the end of the third or antepenultimate ice age, about 120 000 B.P. To that time, fire-sensitive plants like casuarina grew prolifically while eucalypts were only sparsely represented, as were signs of bushfires. Thereafter bushfires raged more furiously than ever before and continued to do so up to the present. It is hardly surprising that gum trees have flourished with forest fires. Some botanists hold that eucalypts do not merely tolerate fire well but require it to grow their best.[5] But why did bushfires and eucalypts proliferate so mightily from about 120 000 B.P. onwards? To that question no one has yet been able to suggest a plausible answer other than the explanation that human beings carrying fire sticks may have first reached this country at that time.[6]

Later evidence supports this. In 1986 R.V.S. Wright re-examined the Lake George core materials which had been radio-carbon dated. It is well known that dating by this method rapidly becomes increasingly less reliable before about 20 000 B.P. On the other hand, Wright showed that plotting an age–depth curve on the core-material back until that time gave an almost perfect correlation. Extrapolation of this curve back beyond 20 000 B.P. gives something in the order of 120 000 B.P. as the time when newly raging bushfires began to produce the ubiquitous eucalypt vegetation which has been so familiar ever since to all Australians. On the other hand, as Rhys Jones observes, other archaeological evidence makes 60 000 B.P. a much "more believable date" for the arrival of fire-stick bearing people in Australia.[7]

Where did these pioneering explorers come from and who were they? The only safe answer to the first question is a rather vague one — from Southeast Asia. The earliest stone tools, lost or discarded by the first Australians, conform to a certain type known to many archaeologists as the "core tool and scraper tradition". Some artefacts of similar type and antiquity have been excavated in the Philippines, in many places in the eastern Indonesian islands and, more remotely, in Indo-China, south China and even Japan. However, this is rather tenuous evidence. From finds in Arnhem Land we know that edge-ground stone axe-heads were hafted there long before this technique was used anywhere else in the world, except possibly in Japan. So we can really say little more than that the first Australians most probably came from some region or regions of Southeast Asia, though *their* progenitors may well have taken a coastal path thither from the cradle of humanity in Africa.[8]

It is less difficult to answer clearly the question of who they were. Anthropologists hold that people from two distinct racial stocks, Australoid and Mongoloid, were the first human occupants of the Pacific Islands, including New Guinea, Australia, Tasmania and New Zealand. Archaeological evidence shows that the first named group colonised New Guinea, Australia and most of Melanesia before — for the most part, long before — about 10 000 B.P. Then Mongoloids, emanating perhaps from southern China and Taiwan, spread through Micronesia and Polynesia, surrounding and mingling to varying degrees with the earlier Australoid populations of New Guinea and Melanesia, but not, to any considerable extent, of Australia. Thus black Australians are probably the "purest" living representatives of the Australoid race. Their skin is dark chocolate brown to black in colour, but their body hair tends, as with Caucasoids, to grow more luxuriantly than in other races. Head hair may be

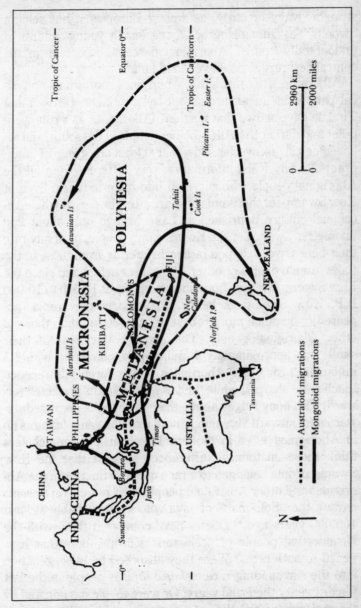

Figure 3 Australoid migrations, beginning at least 60 000 B.C.; Mongoloid migrations, beginning not earlier than about 10 000 B.C.

straight, wavy or curly, as among Europeans, but seldom "woolly", as among Negroes. Occasionally young children of undoubtedly "pure" Aboriginal descent, especially in the central desert regions, have blond hair.[9]

All this does not mean that Aborigines conform to a physical pattern identical throughout the continent. Birdsell and Tindale have shown that northern Aborigines as a rule were taller and darker than the stockier people in the south, and archaeological discoveries show that at least one group of immigrants, in physical conformation very different from all the Aboriginal people who survived into historic times, lived at Kow Swamp for thousands of years after the period when Aboriginal culture flourished at Lake Mungo only about 250 kilometres away. Yet the Kow Swamp people, or at any rate their bones, were shaped rather differently from those of the Lake Mungo people or other Aborigines before and since the Kow Swamp dwellers flourished from about 14 000 to 10 000 B.P. Kow Swamp skeletons, particularly the crania, appeared to be much more robust or "primitive" than those of other Aboriginal people. The average thickness of their skulls was approximately 4 millimetres, compared with 2.5 millimetres for other Aborigines. Their foreheads receded much more sharply, while the jaws and mouths projected forward. The bony ridges above their eye stocks projected upward and outward very much more than the same features do in Aborigines – or in modern Europeans. Some scholars think these anatomical differences suggest that the Kow Swamp people belonged to a race quite distinct from the Aborigines and other Australoid peoples and more akin to *homo erectus*, the "Solo man" of Java who lived probably at least 100 000 years ago.[10] Others have compared them with the Neanderthal people of prehistoric Europe, but what happened to both races? Were they absorbed by miscegenation into the surrounding race of *homo sapiens* people in the last ten or twenty thousand years? Or were they exterminated by the majority group? We may never know, but the apparent absence of wounds in the remains of the first forty Kow

Swamp people excavated perhaps makes assimilation more likely.[11]

Despite the Kow Swamp data, it is clear that the Aborigines were essentially one people, descended from perhaps several waves of settlers, not all of them necessarily Australoid. Of course, there were very considerable differences between tribes in different areas and at different times. Linguists have identified well over two hundred separate languages, for example. Some tribes were ignorant of the boomerang. Some practised circumcision, some sub-incision and some neither operation. However, the basic elements of Aboriginal culture were common to all mainland tribes, though possibly not to the Tasmanians. A linguistic map of Aboriginal Australia emphasises the point.

The 250-odd languages, mutually unintelligible though many of them were, all belonged to one linguistic stock. Within this stock there are twenty-eight families of languages, twenty-seven of them spoken by tribes living very close to each other in the Kimberley district of Western Australia and the "top end" of the Northern Territory. The twenty-eighth family, comprising more than 150 different languages, covers the rest of mainland Australia. So it seems at least likely that the people, like the languages they spoke, all derived from a common stock, though this stock was itself the result of an earlier mingling of at least two populations.[12]

It now seems clear that the extinct Tasmanian languages also belonged to the mainland Australian linguistic family. Though few words seem related to words used on the mainland, the structure and sounds of Tasmanian languages show that they almost certainly belonged to the general Australian group.[13] Can the same be said of the black Tasmanian people? Probably. Archaeologists have long agreed that the first Tasmanians walked to the island about 21 000 B.P., soon after the onset of the last ice age.[14] Tasmanian technological and cultural equipment included a great many artefacts which were common on the mainland before about 6000 B.C., but none of the many new elements which were common in Australia after that date. One very important aid to living which

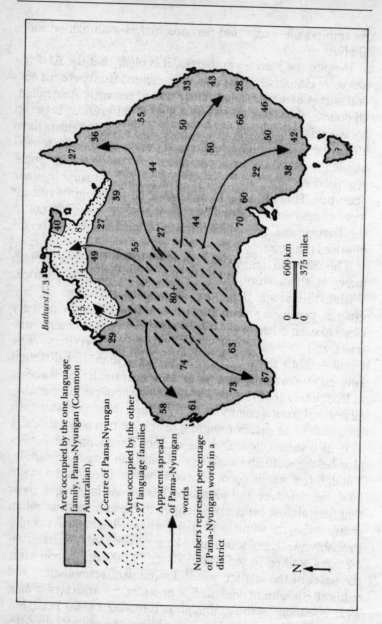

Figure 4 Distribution of Australian languages from about 5000 B.C.

the Tasmanians − and the early Australians − did not possess was the dingo. Intensive excavation has so far failed to turn up any sign of this invaluable hunting dog before about 5000 B.P., or to find any conclusive signs of where its ancestors must have lived in Asia. About that time the dingo turned up in Australia, perhaps with a new wave of migrants from the old world, and over the next few thousand years it no doubt helped to exterminate on the mainland the thylacine, or Tasmanian wolf, and the Tasmanian devil. That these animals continued to flourish in Tasmania until the arrival of Europeans is one of the surest proofs that Tasmania must have been settled long before the dingo's arrival in Australia.

A great many other interesting things occurred at about that time. Indeed, we might almost speak of a kind of prehistoric renaissance in Australian life during the fifth and sixth millennia B.P. Up until then, excavation has revealed only a relatively simple and limited armoury of implements belonging to the "core tool and scraper" tradition. There is reason to suppose that these early Australians possessed, with only one exception, the same implements as the Tasmanians: simple (but not crude) hand-held axes and hammer-stones made from cores and struck off flakes, trimmed on one side to make scrapers. The exception, already mentioned, is the discovery from at least 20 000 B.P. in Arnhem Land of edge-ground axes which look as though they were made to be hafted to wooden handles; however, there is so far no evidence that edge-grinding or hafting spread early to the rest of Australia, or that hafting of stone knives, spear heads or other implements was practised long ago, even in Arnhem Land. It seems likely that until about the fifth millennium B.P., as in Tasmania at the time of white contact, there were no edge-ground stone, or bone-tipped spears, but only pointed wooden ones, no spear-throwers, no boomerangs, no dogs and no small, deftly made stone implements or microliths.

These things all appear fairly suddenly in the archaeological record from about 5000 B.P. onwards. Together they brought about a technological revolution in Australian life. The geographical pattern and time sequence of the very scattered finds made so far suggest that the new techniques may have spread outwards from the central northwest to the east and south of the continent. The language map of Australia is consistent with this possibility. The northwestern desert languages contain by far the greatest number of "common Australian" words, which become fewer and fewer in other languages roughly in proportion to their distance from the central northwestern area occupied by the Pintubi. It is difficult to account for the dingo's arrival at this time unless we suppose it was brought here by human beings. Perhaps a new wave of Australoid immigrants landed on the northwest coast bearing with them the new technology, dingoes and their own variant of the Australian languages – and perhaps not. Most scholars think that, despite the puzzle of the dingo's genesis, new techniques, new ideas, and not new people, were diffused. Within one or two thousand years, new ways spread all over the mainland to improve a culture, variegated in detail but the same everywhere in essentials, that endured until the British invasion of 1788.[15]

The Aborigines lived, as did all other human beings until about 9000 B.P., entirely by hunting and gathering food from nature. Consequently, white observers for a long time assumed them to have been ignorant of the arts of agriculture and animal husbandry. However, we now know that agriculture, based on extensive terraced irrigation works, was practised in the New Guinea Highlands (then part of Sahul) at least as long ago as 9000 B.P.[16] So the first Australians *chose* to live as hunter-gatherers. Over a century ago, the American anthropologist Morgan, followed by Engels, V. Gordon Childe and others, characterised the people of such societies as "savages" or "primitive communists". To think of them in this light is still the best way to understand them today, and particularly to understand why the new white Australians and the old black ones in the eighteenth and nineteenth centuries could seldom begin to understand each other. The white invaders' society was based on the sanctity of private property. The white invasion of Australia was launched in the first place to punish those who stole private property. The ancient black societies were based equally firmly on the sanctity of communal or public property. In 1688, exactly a century before the "First Fleet" discharged white immigrants on the shores of Sydney Cove, William Dampier, the English pirate, spent about nine weeks careening his ship on the northwest coast near where Broome now stands. His description of Aboriginal life was so misleading in many ways that few have noticed how accurate it was in others. He saw clearly that all members of a horde shared equitably, as far as they were able, in the work of finding food and in the pleasure of eating it:

> They live in companies – twenty or thirty men, women and children together. Their only food is a small sort of fish, which they get by making weirs of stone across little coves or branches of the sea . . . In other places at low water they seek for cockles, mussels and periwinkles . . . At their places of abode the old people and infants await their return; and what providence has bestowed on them they presently broil on the coals and eat it in common. Whether it be much or little every one has his share. When they have eaten they lie down till the next low water, and then all that are able march out. Be it night or day, rain or shine, 'tis all one; they must attend the weirs or else they must fast . . .[17]

In all Aboriginal societies everyone shared in the work of food-gathering and everyone was entitled to an equitable (though not of course an equal) share in the products of this social labour. The implements used for food-gathering – spears, spear-throwers and boomerangs for the men, digging-sticks, coolamons and such like for the women – seem generally to have been regarded as personal property, though a given tool or weapon was often made by the co-operative labour of several individuals.[18] Larger implements such as bark or dug-out canoes seem to have been both made and used co-operatively and to have been regarded as group or tribal property. Above all, the fountainhead of life, the land itself (and the adjacent sea and inland water) was regarded as communal property. That a large piece of country should belong to any individual, or even that it could be held in some sense by a chief or head-man on behalf of the tribe, was inconceivable to an Aborigine. The land belonged to the whole tribe but no more firmly than the whole tribe belonged to its land. Mervyn Meggitt has expressed perfectly the relationship between Aboriginal individuals, their tribe and their land (nature) thus:

[Their] view of the universe . . . regarded man, society and nature as interlocking and interacting elements in a larger, functionally integrated totality. According to Aboriginal belief, each variable in the system had an eternal, moral commitment to maintain itself unchanged for the benefit of the others and to contribute to the proper functioning of the system as a whole.[19]

The tribe, its people and its territory belonged to each other so completely that Aboriginal Australians saw the three as one entity, just as Christians conceive of the Holy Trinity.

At the time of white contact there were about 600 tribes in Australia. Every tribe had its own kinship system, its own distinctive ceremonial life, and its own language, though often some elements of the culture, particularly the language, of neighbouring tribes might be very similar or even identical. Tribes ranged in size from one or two hundred to one or two thousand people, varying of course with the extent of the tribal territory and the natural resources it contained. Perhaps the average size of a tribe was about five hundred. Within each tribal area, extended family groups, or "clans", moved about searching for food, usually in their own part of the terrain, but coming together with other clans at certain times to participate in initiation ceremonies and the like. Each clan might number twenty, thirty or more people.

The fact that Aboriginal economic life was based entirely on hunting, fishing and gathering wild plants and insects had important consequences for tribal organisation. Food gathered from nature, particularly in the hot Australian climate, must be eaten promptly. Though Aborigines did store some foods for short periods, they did so rarely, because in a communal or "sharing" society there is no point in hoarding things, and very few things are of a kind which can be hoarded. In farming societies, the existence of storable wealth inevitably meant that some individuals became richer and more powerful than others. People counted their sheep and cattle and their quantities of grain. Richer or stronger individuals became head-men, or chiefs, or medicine-men, or priests, or kings. Men began to specialise in different tasks, including the tasks of ruling and being ruled. Classes and "government" came into existence. In Aboriginal societies, because there was no storable wealth, none of these developments had taken place. As W.E.H. Stanner wrote:

> The Blacks did not fight over land. There were no wars or invasions to seize territory. They did not enslave each other. There is no master-servant relation. There is no class division. There is no property or income inequality. The result is a homeostasis, far reaching and stable.[20]

There were no chiefs, hereditary or elected, in any Aboriginal tribe and no classes except two — males and females. In all tribes the male lords of creation hunted larger animals and birds while the exploited women were forced to do the much more laborious work of gathering edible vegetable matter, insects, roots and so on. One early white male observer wrote:

> The men walk along with a proud and majestic air; behind them, crouching like slaves, and bearing heavy burdens on their backs, with their little ones astride on their shoulders, come the despised and degraded women. They are the drudges in all heavy work; and after their lords have finished the repast which the women have prepared for them, these despised creatures contentedly sit at a distance, and gather up the bones and fragments, which the men throw to them across their shoulders, just as we should throw meat to a dog.[21]

Of course, some men were naturally better spearmen than others, some better "witch doctors", some more skilled in corroborees, and so on; but all men were expected to do everything proper to their sex for themselves, as were all women. No individual lived solely by performing a specialised task and no one grew rich or "different" from or "superior" to his fellows.[22] The best proof of the reality of this egalitarian, classless society is that no Aboriginal language had words for any numbers beyond two or three. If there is no private property, there is no need to count its worth and no one felt the need of words to do so. Some tribes,

"King" Bungaree of the Broken Bay tribe, wearing his breastplate and other "gifts" of the early Europeans (Source: *Bungaree, King of the Broken Bay Tribe* 1823–32 by C. Rodius, Mitchell Library, State Library of New South Wales)

when they engaged in trade with "Macassar men" from the Indonesian archipelago, or with Europeans, quickly developed a system of numerals.[23]

During the last century, most white invaders simply could not conceive of a human society in which there were no kings, priests, chiefs, nor any other kind of formal authority structure. Usually they decided that the man who seemed the most influential and charismatic individual in a clan or a tribe *must* be its chief, and accordingly hung around his neck a brass plate inscribed "King Billy" or some such European nickname; but William Buckley, who lived with the Port Phillip

Aborigines for over thirty years, knew better. In fact, the only kind of "government" or leadership was completely informal and was seen by the tribesmen as "natural".[24] Males generally dominated and exploited the females. Older, more experienced men, especially those learned in tribal lore, were listened to more respectfully than younger men when a group was coming to a consensus by informal discussion of a question; but it would be just as true to say that the function of these elders was to apply the immemorial custom or law of the tribe as to lead or guide it. In particular circumstances leadership was exercised by different persons according to "custom". For instance, all Aboriginal tribes had extremely complex kinship systems with strict rules governing the classes of persons whom an individual might marry. The rules were broken at least as often as in modern European societies, but the penalty was much more severe — usually death. The man who led such a revenge, or "pay back", or execution party was not necessarily one of the most influential people in the group or even one of the best warriors, but the man who stood in a certain relationship to the wronged person.[25]

Transgression of marriage rules was by no means the only way in which an Aborigine might incur punishment or death at the hands of his fellows. Aborigines believed, for instance, that a person never died from "natural" causes. Not illness, but malign sorcery, was the cause of death, and honour demanded that certain of the deceased's relatives should wreak vengeance on the sorcerer or his relatives. A great many Aborigines died in these blood feuds, probably more than were killed as infants by their parents. Infanticide and other forms of "birth control" also tended to keep the population at a level where the number of tribespeople rarely outstripped the natural resources of the territory. Yet most of the murder and mayhem took place within the tribe, and this violence seems more akin to what civilised people call the administration of justice than to warfare. Often justice was administered to members of neighbouring tribes, and people who entered another tribe's territory without invitation or excuse were often killed, but there is very little evidence to suggest that Aborigines ever engaged in what "more advanced" people call warfare. No Aboriginal tribe ever seems to have conceived the notion of exterminating or enslaving another, or of stealing any part of its collective property or territory.

Of course, the British invaders could no more conceive of a human society without war than they could imagine one without chiefs or war-leaders. Early accounts frequently refer to inter-tribal wars and battles, but these bloody clashes, like the "chiefs" who fought in them, were creations of the white men's imagination. Eyewitness accounts differ in detail according to the tribes concerned, but all agree that few if any people were killed in these meetings, though a great deal of hostility was expressed in ritualised ways. Here is an account, typical of many, of an inter-tribal "battle" which took place in the Bathurst district in 1831:

> When about to fight, the contending parties, except where treachery is employed (which I believe is not very often practised), encamp opposite each other. At dawn of the following day two young men, one from each side, advance in front of their respective friends, and, after using the most opprobrious epithets to each other, mutually throw a spear, and then retire to procure others, which are thrown in the same manner. If neither is wounded, they then commence a battle with the club, using sometimes an eleman, or shield, made of wood; while the women, particularly those advanced in years, who are, probably, more crabbed than the younger ones, excite them to the utmost. When one is worsted, another advances to succour him, and others to aid his adversary, until a general melee takes place, and broken heads, and sometimes bad spear wounds, are the result; but the latter do not occur as often as might be expected. The conquered are allowed to depart without molestation; and they will even frequently join the victors, so that a person would not know that there had been any animosity between them. There is certainly more talking than fighting in their battles, and it is, therefore, to be hoped they will some day send over a few of their people as missionaries, to convince civilised nations that it is far worse to cut the throat of a man while alive, than to eat his body when dead![26]

Such meetings are reminiscent of international football matches or other sporting contests, rather than of wars between civilised nations. Aboriginal tribes were simply not organised to fight defensive or other wars. Without any form of hierarchical social structure, they had no representative person or body to lead them against the whites in war, or to negotiate with them in peace. Tribal social structure was ideally suited to Aboriginal life for scores of thousands of years, but it was just as big a handicap in resisting the European invasion as was the inferior armoury of Aboriginal weapons.

All tribes were not equally unwarlike however. They differed in martial prowess just as they did in other aspects of their culture. Generally speaking, Aboriginal bellicosity increased from south to north. There is a good deal of evidence to show that the Tasmanian tribes, though perhaps the bravest, were certainly equipped with the worst weapons and were the least warlike in outlook. Consequently, almost all the Tasmanians were slaughtered within forty years of the first permanent white settlement at Risdon Cove in 1803. The most warlike tribes, conversely, were those nearest the northern Australian coasts in Queensland, the Northern Territory and the Kimberley. There resistance was bloodiest and lasted longest — naturally, because it was there that most pre-European invaders, including Australian immigrants themselves, first entered the continent.

We now know that "Macassar men" had fished for trepang along the northern coasts for at least one or two hundred years before the British invasion.[27] Chinese and other visitors may have preceded them, at least transiently, to say nothing of thousands of years of sporadic contact with aggressive New Guinea tribes which *had* practised the arts of agriculture, husbandry and warfare. It would have been astonishing if these north coastal tribes, and some inland groups in contact with them, had not quickly learnt to fight more effectively in defence of their ancient culture, just as some of them who traded with the Indonesian trepang fishers had quickly learnt to count. That warlike skill among the tribes increased as one went north was obvious to white observers a hundred years ago and more, though it seems to have escaped the notice of some modern scholars. In 1849 an English student of early Aboriginal–white contacts wrote:

> In examining carefully the reports of those observers, on whom . . . the greatest confidence may be placed, the general conclusion is, that the inhabitants of Australia are naturally of an unoffending and pacific disposition. In every place where there has been reason to conclude that the visit of Europeans was a first one, and the conduct of the visitor was kind, or even equitable, there is no evidence of primary aggression on the part of the natives . . . [but] the man who had been plundered, or had seen his brother or countryman carried off captive, by strangers whom he had never offended, would teach his children vengeance for the wrong, and hatred for whatever strangers might arrive . . . In like manner, the nearer the region of the Malays is approached, the more do the Australians seem disposed to attack, and, generally speaking, the better are they provided with weapons. From what is known of the natives of New Guinea, they seem to be of the same family with those of New Holland and Van Diemen's Land; and they are so disposed to be hostile, that no foreign race, probably not even the Malays, have settled in their country.[28]

The first non-Australoid visitors to Australia may have been Chinese. Ancient records state that between 1405 and 1433 the eunuch, Ch'eng Ho, made seven voyages to the south with a huge fleet of junks. It is certain that Chinese merchants reached East Africa during the fourteenth century and that some settled in Indonesia to exploit the sandalwood forests in Timor.[29] That some of the Ming emperor's ships may have visited Australia is suggested by the discovery in 1879 of a small Chinese statuette, embedded in the roots of a banyan tree more than a metre underground in Darwin, and in 1948 of a shard of Chinese pottery on the beach at Winchelsea Island in the Gulf of Carpentaria. Both the little soapstone statuette of Shou Lao, the god of Long Life, and the piece of blue and white pottery are said by experts to belong to the Ming period, but they *could* have been brought to Australia by Macassan trepang fishers or modern Chinese visitors.[30]

When Ch'eng Ho's fleets first visited the Indonesian archipelago, Arab sailors and the Muslim religion had been estab-

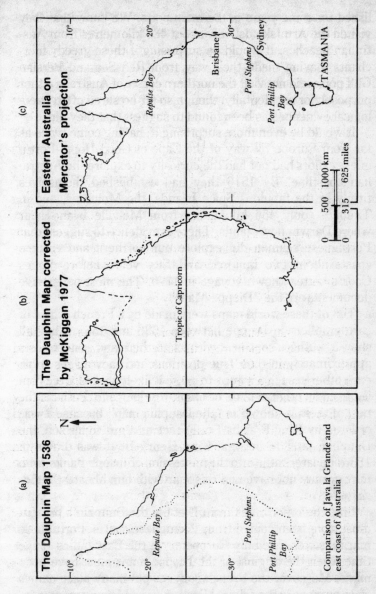

Figure 5 (a) The Dauphin Map 1536 (b) The Dauphin Map corrected by McKiggan 1977 (c) Eastern Australia on Mercator's projection

lished for some years in the main ports. We know that they visited the Aru Islands, only about 480 kilometres from Australian beaches. It would be surprising if these greedy merchants, having made their way from Red Sea and Persian Gulf ports, did not visit the northern coasts of Australia either purposely or accidentally, though so far no shred of archaeological evidence has been found to suggest that they did.

It would be even more surprising if, having come twice as far from Europe by way of the Cape of Good Hope, Portuguese sailors had not had the curiosity to explore the Australian coastline. By 1516 they had established themselves firmly in the fabulous Spice Islands, the Moluccas, and in Timor — only 456 kilometres from Melville Island near where Darwin now stands. There is evidence to suggest that Portuguese seamen did explore our northern and eastern coasts about two hundred and fifty years before James Cook's better known voyage in 1770. The most persuasive documents are the "Dieppe Maps".

Ten of these world maps were made by a French school of cartographers in Dieppe between 1536 and 1567. They all show a southern continent with its northern and eastern costs approximately in their true positions and they all resemble each other in such a way as to make it likely that all were copied from an original map, or maps, lost long ago. Perhaps the best of them is known as "the Dauphin map" because it was ordered by King Francis I of France as a gift to his son, the Dauphin, later to become King Henry II. It was drawn in 1536 and later came into the possession of Joseph Banks, who may or may not have had this map with him aboard the *Endeavour*.[31]

Like the other maps from Dieppe, the Dauphin's present must have been copied from Portuguese charts. Portuguese mariners were the only Europeans in the East Indies at the time when the original of the Dieppe maps must have been made. Moreover the French copyists put many place names on their maps in the original Portuguese and many more in incorrect Portuguese. Anyone who has seen the outline of Australia in a school atlas will find familiar the representation of the east coast of Australia on the Dauphin map. From Cape York to Nelson's Bay in New South Wales the "Dieppe" and modern coastlines correspond quite closely. From there south and west again to the region of Port Fairy the line of the coast is distorted by a great sweep to the east, though Port Phillip Bay seems to be marked in its correct position.

The distortion may spring from the Old Portuguese method of calculating longitude and also from the fact that the Dieppe maps are not drawn on Mercator's projection or any other projection ever seen by a modern reader. It is possible for skilled mathematicians to correct the distortion in the Dauphin's map and carefully to calculate exactly what it would look like if "transposed" to Mercator's projection. When this is done, the Dauphin's map looks like a very good map indeed of the eastern Australian coast and one that strongly suggests that Portuguese mariners charted it at least some years before 1536.[32]

K.G. McIntyre, who has studied the matter closely, believes that the whole eastern coast round to Port Fairy was charted between 1521 and 1523 by three ships commanded by Cristoval de Mendonca. It may be true, but it seems at least that *some* Portuguese ships visited the Kimberley coast and also Port Phillip, which appears on the Dauphin maps as "Gouffre", before Cook's great voyage. In July 1916 a landing party from HMAS *Encounter* discovered two bronze cannon on an unnamed island in the entrance to Napier Broome Bay at the northernmost part of the Kimberley district. It has been claimed that one cannon was embossed with the "rose and crown of Portugal" and that both were made at Seville in Spain in the late fifteenth or early sixteenth century. In 1982, alas for Lusitanophiles, both cannon were proved to be of Asian manufacture not earlier than the late eighteenth century. They were possibly left *in situ* by Macassan Trepang fishers not long before Cook charted the eastern coast.[33]

The Port Phillip evidence is more prosaic. In August 1847, at Corio Bay, a workman discovered a bunch of keys in a hole he was digging for shells to make lime. The keys were found at a depth of 4.5 metres and about 12 metres inland from the

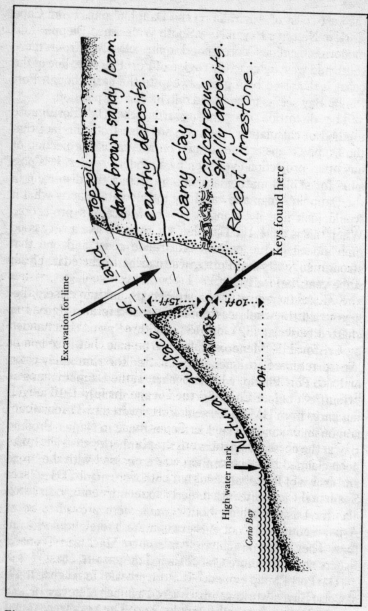

Figure 6   A direct copy of Superintendent La Trobe's sketch of the position of the old keys found buried in the sand at Corio Bay, near Geelong, in 1847

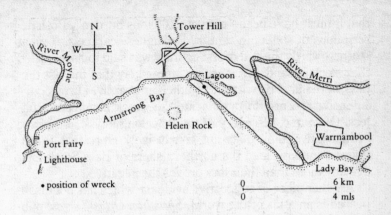

Figure 7 Location of the Mahogany Ship

shoreline. Next day the superintendent of the Port Phillip District, Charles Joseph La Trobe, a keen geologist, visited the site. He obtained three of the keys and wrote a detailed account of the find accompanied by a diagram. He had no doubt that they were old European keys "just of the description still used for a box or trunk or seaman's chest". When La Trobe returned to Britain he left the keys for safekeeping with the Melbourne Mechanics' Institute, which lost them when it went bankrupt. All the Dieppe maps end effectively in the vicinity of the present Port Fairy and Warrambool, about 120 kilometres west of Cape Otway.

Perhaps the original cartographer, whoever he was, turned back at this point. He could have been forced to do so because one of his ships was wrecked there. In 1836 two sealers found the wreck of an old-fashioned ship on this part of the coast lying in a hollow between the first and second line of sandhills. Hundreds of other people must have seen it in the last century, for there are extant reliable records of twenty-seven who did so and most of these left descriptions of it. For instance, Mrs T.C. Manifold wrote that in 1860, when she saw it, "the sides, or bulwarks, [were built] after the fashion of a pannelled door, with mouldings (as in a door) stout and strong". Captain John Mason, a practical seaman, estimated that it must have been "of about 100 tons burden". Both descriptions fit sixteenth-century Portuguese caravels. A great storm towards the end of last century was said to have buried the wreck in sand, but it seems more likely that the last timbers were burnt by whalers or others in search of firewood.[34] Intensive recent efforts to locate the wreck have been fruitless. Of course, discovery of the "Geelong keys" and of the "Mahogany Ship" does not conclusively *prove* that Portuguese seamen visited the northern shore of Bass Strait long ago any more than their loss proves the negative.

Another piece of suggestive evidence which has not disappeared is an atlas of the world, *Speculum Orbis Terrae*, published in 1578 by Cornelis de Jode in Flanders. The charts in this work derive ultimately from the "Dieppe Maps". On the title page, a large engraving of a horse is positioned, apparently to symbolise Europe, a camel Asia, a lion Africa and a kangaroo with two "joeys" in its pouch Australia. The weird looking marsupial could have been drawn only from a description by someone who had seen a kangaroo at least thirty years before the first recorded Dutch landing in Australia.

If Portuguese explorers discovered and mapped much of the Australian coast in the first quarter of the sixteenth century, why did they not proclaim their achievements to the world? The reason may be simple. At that time, and for long afterwards, any discovery of new lands was regarded as a trade secret, to be jealously guarded by the government of the country whose seamen made it. Spain and Portugal were the first European powers to be engaged in an imperialist struggle for possession of the newly discovered East and West Indies and America. To contain the strife, the two kingdoms concluded in 1494 the Treaty of Tordesillas, which divided the planet between them. Everything to the west of what we now call the fifty-first meridian of longitude west of Greenwich was to be Spanish territory and everything to the east of it Portuguese. Thus Spain was to exploit all of the Pacific and America except Brazil, which fell to Portugal along with Africa and Asia. On the other side of the world the demarcation line was determined by continuing longitude 51^0W

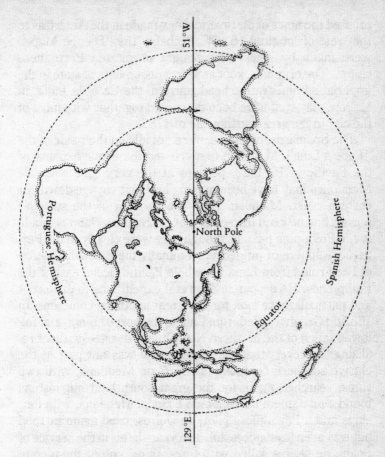

Figure 8 The "Pope's Line", 1494

through the north and south poles where it becomes longitude 129⁰E. This "Pope's Line", as it came to be called, runs through the Moluccas and now forms the boundary of Western Australia. Since Portugal was a very much weaker power than Spain, it paid her to make much of the treaty and to observe its provisions scrupulously. Any voyages made east of longitude 129⁰E were flagrant violations of the treaty and so had to be kept secret. There is good evidence that the Portuguese, at the same period and for the same reason, suppressed the news of discoveries they made in the Americas to the west of longitude 51°W. Probably the "Dieppe Maps" were made by spies from bought or pirated Portuguese charts. The originals, kept as secret documents of state in the imperial administrative headquarters, the Casa da India, in Lisbon, may well have been destroyed together with most of the city in the great earthquake of 1755.

The Spaniards, of course, were not idle on their side of the "Pope's Line". Magellan first crossed the whole expanse of the Pacific in 1521–23, perhaps at the very time when de Mendonca may have been making his illicit voyage down our eastern coast. Magellan, with the backing of the stronger power, had no need to keep secret the Spanish claim he made to the Philippine Islands, though they were clearly in the Portuguese sphere of influence. Nominally the Spanish Viceroy of Peru ruled from Lima the whole Pacific Ocean east of the Philippines. He despatched several expeditions to explore it and particularly to look for the great southern continent. In 1537 de Grijalva sailed from Callao, the port of Lima, and followed much of the northern New Guinea coast – without realising, however, that the land he saw was not part of the elusive southern continent. In 1567 de Mendana, with two ships, searched again for the great south land but instead found, and named, the Solomon Islands. Mendana, with four ships and a Portuguese pilot, de Quiros, tried again in 1595 but was even less successful. Ten years later, in the service of Spain, de Quiros sailed with three ships, one of them commanded by Luis Vaez de Torres, said to have been a fellow Portuguese by birth. They discovered and landed on one of the islands later to be named the New Hebrides by James Cook. De Quiros believed he had found the great south land at last and, with much ceremony, named it *La Austrialia del Espiritu Santo,* Australia of the Holy Ghost, and claimed it for the holy Catholic Church and His Most Christian Majesty, King Philip III of Spain.

While the expedition was exploring the new land, Torres' ship and another were separated from de Quiros. Convinced that the new land was not part of a continent, Torres sailed southwest to continue the search but turned north when not very far from the Great Barrier Reef. In August 1606 he sailed to Manila through the shallow straits that bear his name, passing over what had been continental soil where some of the first Australians had lived thousands of years before. He sighted some islands and the Australian mainland. He seems also, like his Portuguese predecessors in those parts, to have kept his discovery secret. There is no evidence that Dutch or other sailors knew of the existence of Torres Strait until 1762 when a copy of Torres' report to King Philip III was found in the archives at Manila by a British raiding party.[35] Six months before Torres passed through the Strait, the first European landing of which fully authenticated records survive was made nearby on the northwestern coast of Cape York Peninsula in March 1606.

The date is significant. Throughout the sixteenth century the Portuguese had dominated the rich trade between Europe and the Far East. From their bases at Goa, Malacca and Bantam, and at Ternate and Tidore in the Moluccas, they dominated the Indian Ocean and the East Indies. Throughout the seventeenth century the same areas were dominated by Dutch merchants organised, from 1602 onwards, in the national, monopolistic Dutch East India Company. Until 1580 the Dutch had been content to gather rich profits by acting as the intermediaries who distributed spices from Portugal through the rest of Europe, but in that year, when Philip II of Spain became King of Portugal too, he closed the port of Lisbon to Dutch ships. For some years the Dutch sought vainly to find a way to the Spice Islands by summer voyages round the north of Asia. Then, from 1595 on, they followed the Portuguese route round the Cape of Good Hope and fought them, not for God or glory, but for trade and profit. By the time of Torres' voyage, they had replaced the Portuguese as the European masters of the Eastern seas.

In 1606 the East India Company despatched from Batavia Captain Willem Jansz in the yacht *Duyfken (Little Dove)* "to discover the land Nova Guinea and other unknown east and south lands". Jansz and his men struck the south coast of

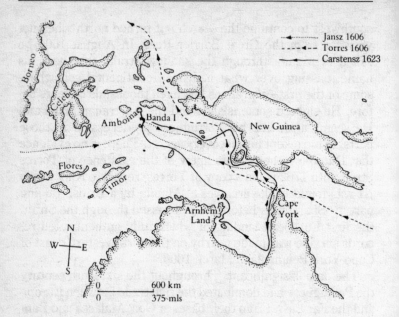

Figure 9 Torres', Jansz's and Carstensz's voyages

New Guinea, sailed across the western end of Torres Strait
and then followed the western coast of Cape York Peninsula
southward to Cape Keerweer (Turnagain). On the return voyage there was a bloody clash with the Aborigines at the
mouth of the Batavia River. J. Carstensz, another Dutch skipper, landed at the same spot in 1623 and noted in his log that
the local people were much more hostile than those who lived
further south and that they also had "knowledge of muskets
whose terrible effects they learned in 1606 from the men of
the *Duyfken*". Jansz thought that the coast he had followed
was part of New Guinea,[36] which raises the question of
whether it is better to discover a new continent without
knowing it, or to discover it and keep it secret, as Cristoval de
Mendonca may have done eighty-three years before.

  At first the Dutch followed the Portuguese route to the Indies – northwards from the Cape of Good Hope along the African coast and then from the northernmost point of
Madagascar almost due east to Sunda Strait. This course

necessitated battling against the southeast trade winds or coping with equatorial calms in the long passage across the Indian Ocean. Hendrik Brouwer, later Governor-General of the Indies, tried a new plan in 1611. He sailed south from the Cape into the path of the prevailing westerly winds and then ran east before them until his ship reached the longitude of Java. Then, turning north, he was able to run before the southeast trades to Sunda Strait. Brouwer's two ships made the voyage in just under six months, compared with the average time of about fifteen months by the old route. Naturally more and more Dutch captains took the new route, until in 1616 the Company ordered all to do so. So a great many ships, running too far eastwards before turning north, sighted the Western Australian coast.

The first to do so was the *Eendracht*, commanded by Dirck Hartog. On 25 October 1616 he landed on the barren island that now bears his name and, before sailing away for Batavia, nailed to a post a pewter dish engraved with a brief record of the event. Subsequently on Dutch maps the extreme northwestern "corner" of the Australian coast was labelled "Eendrachtland". During the next eleven years, at least as many Dutch ships sighted different parts of the coast. Among the more interesting discoveries was that of North West Cape by the *Zeewulf (Seawolf)* and the *Mauritius,* of Houtman's Abrolhos by the *Dordrecht* and the *Amsterdam*, of Cape Leeuwin (lioness) by a ship of that name, and of the south coast of the country to beyond the head of the Great Australian Bight by Pieter Nuyts in the *Gulden Zeepaert (Golden Sealeopard)*.

By 1623 the governors of the East India Company had had enough of accidental discoveries. They despatched two ships, the *Pera* and the *Arnhem,* with orders to explore more fully the southern coast of New Guinea. This Jan Carstenz and his men did but, like Jansz before them, they were attacked so strongly by the Papuans that they crossed Torres Strait and explored more of the coasts of the Gulf of Carpentaria and Arnhem Land, perhaps still under the impression that these areas were part of New Guinea. There were a few other half-

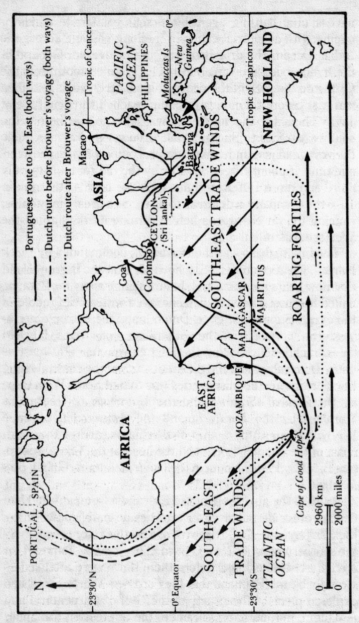

Figure 10   Portuguese and Dutch routes to the Indies

hearted official efforts at exploration, but none achieved very much until Tasman's two voyages of 1642 and 1644.

Tasman's first voyage was the greatest exploring expedition ever mounted by the Dutch, yet it was more remarkable for the discoveries it did not make than for those it did. Tasman was as good a navigator and certainly as great a bully[37] as any other blue-water sailor of his day, but he seems to have entirely lacked the first requisite of a good explorer: curiosity. Perhaps his masters realised this and accordingly gave him unusually specific instructions. Anthony van Diemen, Governor-General of the Dutch Indies, and his Council instructed Tasman to sail from Batavia to Mauritius, there to pick up wood, water and fresh supplies. Thence he should sail south to latitude 52^0 or 54^0 and run eastwards before the prevailing westerlies in search of the great south land. If no land were found, Tasman might sail northwards at about the longitude of the eastern tip of New Guinea to solve the mystery of what lay between the coast discovered by Pieter Nuyts and the western coasts of New Guinea and Cape York already known to the Dutch. Specifically, was there a channel from the Fowlers Bay neighbourhood to the Gulf of Carpentaria?

The *Heemskerk* and the *Zeehaen* took on board at Mauritius wood, fresh water and provisions. Whether the latter included the meat of some still surviving dodos we do not know. They reached 49^0 south, but speedily returned to warmer seas and clearer skies as they sailed eastward between latitudes of 40^0 and 44^0S. On 24 November they sighted the west coast of an unknown country with high mountains inland, two of which are known today as Mount Heemskerk and Mount Zeehan. They also estimated that "the west side of New Guinea must be north of us" and they were not very far wrong. They pursued their voyage to the east, naming the new country Van Diemen's Land and mapping its southern and eastern coasts. They anchored in the lee of Cape Frederick Henry for the first three days of December while shore parties replenished their supplies of wood and water. They saw the footprints of what can only have been a Tasmanian "tiger" and heard human beings in the forest but did not see any. Both animals and people apparently wanted only to be left in peace. Then they sailed north along about two-thirds of Tasmanian's east coast and a council of officers decided to leave the new land and bear away eastwards to the longitude of the Solomon Islands or farther. Why did Tasman not at least pursue the mapping of the Tasmanian coast? He knew the position of Nuyts' Land and of what the Dutch thought was New Guinea, that is, of Cape York Peninsula. Was the new land joined to Nuyts' Land or to Cape York or to both? Van Diemen and his Council were as displeased as we may be puzzled. In a report to their masters in Amsterdam they wrote that Tasman:

> did not employ . . . great . . . eagerness to establish the extent of the lands discovered or the nature of the inhabitants, and regarding the principal issues, left everything open for a more conscientious successor.[38]

Tasman's immense lack of curiosity was demonstrated hardly less impressively in New Zealand, the southwest coast of which he sighted on 13 December and named Staten Land. Cruising northwards he rounded Cape Farewell and anchored in Golden Bay five days later. The local Maoris paddled out in canoes and attacked the Dutchmen so furiously that the latter named the place Murderers' Bay. Then they bore away to the east and spent a few more days wondering whether they were in a large bay of the southern continent they thought they had discovered, or whether there was a strait. Tasman decided on the former and followed the coast of the North Island to Cape Maria van Diemen, its northernmost point. He then left the new land and discovered Tonga and Fiji on his way home to Batavia by way of the north coast of New Guinea. His neglect in completing the mapping of New Zealand meant that he returned thinking the new country to be a promontory of the supposed Great South Land which stretched away eastwards to somewhere south of Cape Horn. Most geographers shared his view until the myth of a southern continent was finally laid to rest by Cook 130 years later.

In January 1644 Tasman set out again in three small ships.

He was enjoined to find out whether there was a passage into the Pacific south of New Guinea and whether there was a passage from the unknown southern end of the Gulf of Carpentaria extending to the neighbourhood of Nuyts' Land and his half-explored Van Diemen's Land. Again he failed completely to carry out the first order. Instead he sailed south across the western side of Torres Strait and reported that it was a "shallow bight" in the continuous land which extended from New Guinea to the coast of the Gulf of Carpentaria. The Portuguese may have known better for over a century. After this characteristic sin of omission, Tasman did succeed in showing that the Gulf of Carpentaria was just that and not the entrance to a strait dividing New Holland from Van Diemen's Land–New Guinea.

Until sail gave way to steam in the late nineteenth century Dutch ships outward bound to the Indies continued to use Brouwer's route. In about 4600 voyages made in the seventeenth and eighteenth centuries, only five ships were wrecked on the coast of New Holland, as the Dutch began to call the new country. In 1696 Willem Vlamingh, on his way to Batavia, was ordered to search for any survivors of one wreck. He found no trace of them but, unlike Tasman, he bettered his instructions. He made the first accurate and detailed map of the Western Australian coastline from the Swan River to the North West Cape, and he landed on and named Rottnest Island and rowed up the Swan River for about 30 kilometres. Like many later visitors, he was not much impressed by anything he saw except the black swans. On Dirck Hartog Island Vlamingh found the pewter dish left there eighty years before. He had the inscription copied on to another pewter plate, which also recorded his own visit, and took the original home with him to Holland.[39]

By the end of the seventeenth century Dutch navigators had produced tolerably accurate charts of the entire coastline of New Holland from Cape York west, south and east to Fowlers Bay, of the southeastern coast of Van Diemen's Land and of the western shores of New Zealand. What lay between these charted shorelines – land or a waste of waters or some of both, or even whether there was a strait between New Guinea and New Holland, remained a mystery to most Europeans for another seventy years.

The eighteenth century in Europe, particularly the latter half of it, is often called the Age of Enlightenment or the Age of Reason. For the first time in human history, large numbers of middle-class people, not bound by the traditional outlook of the nobility or the clergy, became rich, cultivated and influential. Many leading figures in intellectual life, like the great historian of the *Decline and Fall of the Roman Empire*, Edward Gibbon, became agnostics or deists. Sir Isaac Newton and others had shown that the natural world was governed by rational laws. Enlightened people believed that human society should be similarly arranged. The authority of the church and the lingering belief in the innate superiority of royal and aristocratic persons were at a discount. Reason and love of one's fellow man might do more for humanity than the fasting, prayer and preaching of priests or the decrees of kings. Even some Anglican clergy became *de facto* deists, people who saw the Christian God as a sort of almighty clockmaker who had created the universe but who had no interest in the last sparrow to fall, in human suffering or in performance of miracles. It was not surprising that after the French Revolution of 1789 a voluptuous French actress should have been installed in Notre Dame Cathedral, albeit briefly, as the Goddess of Reason.

Throughout Europe, many enlightened people believed in the cult of the "noble savage". South Sea Islanders, North American Indians – indeed, uncivilised people in general – were seen as being more virtuous because they lived simpler, purer lives more in accordance with "natural" laws than the "effete" and sophisticated citizens of London or Paris or Rome. Some of the first white visitors to Australia, like Watkin Tench, Captain of Marines, and Governor Arthur Phillip himself, initially viewed the Aborigines in this romantic way.

Enlightened people believed also in one of the great rallying cries of the French Revolution, which they did so much to bring about: "Careers must be open to talent". Power and place should be conferred on people best able to do the requisite work well, not on those selected by the accident of birth, or the inheritance of wealth, or the weight of ancient traditions. In this respect, daily life in eighteenth century Britain or Holland was much freer than in France or the rest of Europe. In the British Navy, for instance, commissions were not sold as they were in the Army, but were given out by patronage or "influence". Of course, this meant that most of the higher commanders were or aristocrastic or "gentlemanly" stock but (and it is a big "but") most officers of and below the rank of captain were not. The son of an illiterate peasant *could* become a naval officer and a great many common people did. Officers without the benefit of aristocratic, or at least "gentle", birth were known affectionately as "tarpaulins". In order to get on in the service they had, of course, to be a great deal better at their job than their gently-born rivals, and they had also to win somehow or other the patronage of at least one great and powerful friend; but even aristocratic youths, with all the influence the heart of an eighteenth-century sailor could desire, had to serve long years at sea before gaining preferment. This system of promotion by merit seems to have been the main reason why, throughout the wars of the eighteenth century and later, the Royal Navy almost always worsted the French whenever battles were joined.

The greatest "tarpaulin" of his time was James Cook. He was also its greatest explorer, a believer in the "noble savage", in science and in the efficacy of human reason. C.M.H. Clark says that he held religion in such low esteem that "he would never tolerate a parson aboard his ship".[40] Others have observed that it was not customary in the Royal Navy of Cook's day to include a chaplain in the complement of smaller ships such as those Cook sailed in. Perhaps so, but at any rate Cook never did, when in command, have a parson among those at his table and there is no evidence that he had any belief in, or even respect for, divine revelation and its earthly exponents.

The son of a day-labourer, Cook was born on 27 October

1728 at Marton in Yorkshire only about 24 kilometres from the North Sea. He learnt "the three R's" at the village school, his fees being paid by the farmer who employed his father. At the age of 18 he was apprenticed to John Walker, a Quaker, ship-owner and coal merchant of Whitby. Young Cook served his time mostly at sea, carrying coal to other parts of the British coast as well as to Scandinavian and Dutch ports. He must have learnt a good deal about the theoretical side of navigation before he signed on as a seaman with Walker's firm at the end of his apprenticeship. By 1755 he had learnt his trade so well that Walker offered him the captaincy of one of his colliers, the *Friendship*. Instead of jumping at this chance, Cook signed on as an able seaman in the Royal Navy on 17 June. We shall never know why. Everyone knew that the navy was preparing for war with France and that there would be more chances of promotion, prizemoney and loot for brave sailors. We know too that within a month Cook was promoted to the rank of master's mate. Perhaps he was given to understand there would be immediate promotion for a sailor of his proven steadiness and capacity? It is equally likely that the position fell vacant by chance, and that he was obviously the best possible man to fill it. Two years later he was again promoted − to the rank of master.[41]

There is no such rank in the navy today. In the eighteenth century the master of a merchant ship was her captain and usually a man who had worked his way up from the lower deck. In the navy a master might in fact command a small ship but in larger vessels he was, so to speak, the chief petty officer, responsible to the captain for all technical and practical matters pertaining to the working of the ship − for navigation, sails, masts, rigging, taking soundings, bearings and so on. During the Seven Years' War with France, in 1756–63, Cook spent much of his time as master under Captain John Simcoe and much of it in command of his own small craft. In both posts he learnt trigonometry and surveying from an army engineer, Samuel Holland, and he helped to make charts of the St Lawrence River, which did much to make possible Wolfe's victory over Montcalm at Quebec. After the war he was sent to chart the coast of Newfoundland and to observe there an eclipse of the sun. This latter work brought him to the notice of the Royal Society, then a body with very much more influence, though not more prestige, than it has now. When, a few years later, the Society wished to have an observation of the transit of Venus across the face of the sun made from Tahiti, who better could be recommended to command the expedition than James Cook?

The Admiralty concurred and Cook was given commissioned rank as a lieutenant on 25 May 1768. Careful preparations were made for the voyage. In addition to the naval crew, His Majesty's barque *Endeavour* was to carry an excellent astronomer, Mr Green, who was intoxicated perhaps no more often that most Britons of that time. The ship was also to take two of the greatest botanists of the age, Daniel Carl Solander, a pupil of the great Swedish scientist Linnaeus, and the 25-year-old Joseph Banks, already a Fellow of the Royal Society, a young Lincolnshire gentleman who was to be regarded for the rest of his long life as the leading authority on all things Australian. Among Banks' small retinue of servants was Sydney Parkinson, a Quaker and artist whose sketches often tell us more of the *Endeavour*'s discoveries than does the log of her master. Cook was given, by the Admiralty, sealed orders to be opened after the astronomical work at Tahiti had been completed. They instructed him to sail south, then west in search of the mythical great southern continent and to chart and take possession of New Zealand.

The *Endeavour* left Plymouth on 25 August 1768 and left Tahiti, her scientific mission accomplished, in the same month of 1769. Sailing south as instructed, Cook satisfied himself that the great southern continent − unless it was situated in the polar regions − was a chimera. He turned west and spent six months exploring New Zealand far more thoroughly than Tasman had dreamed of doing. This done, he was free to sail home. His orders said merely that he was to return "either round the Cape of Good Hope, or Cape Horn, as from Circumstances you may judge the Most Eligible way".[42] Cook did neither, or rather, he sailed home round the

Cape of Good Hope by way of a route that had never occurred to Tasman or to the Lords of the Admiralty who had issued his orders. This decision constitutes perhaps his greatest claim to fame. He called a council of the officers and, we must conclude, led it to resolve that they should steer "westward till we fall in with the East Coast of New Holland and then to follow the deriction of that Coast to the northward or what other direction it may take until we arrive at its northern extremity".[43]

So the *Endeavour* left New Zealand on the last day of March 1770. Cook's second lieutenant, Zachary Hicks, a Londoner, sighted land on the morning of 19 April. Cook named the place Point Hicks, but it has since been renamed Cape Everard. Coasting northwards he entered a fine sheltered bay on 28 April and anchored the *Endeavour* close to the beach inside its southern headland. The Britons were as puzzled by the behaviour of the Aborigines as previous European observers had been. Some people spearing fish from bark canoes off the headland seemed to ignore the invaders. Another group of Aborigines ran off into the bush as soon as the British party made for the shore, but two warriors stayed to menace it with spears until they were driven off by a few volleys of small shot.

The white men spent a week exploring the surrounding country, most of which, before it was buried under the concrete jungle of Sydney suburbs, was covered by thin sandy soil with sandstone outcrops or swamp. Cook, the farmer's son, puzzled future settlers and historians by writing that some of the land was "as fine meadow as ever was seen".[44] For Banks and Solander the week was a dream of delight. Never before or since have naturalists found or collected in such a short time such a vast range of plant, animal and bird specimens previously unknown to science. The sailors ate their fill of fresh fish and, consequently, Cook first named the place Stingray Harbour. Later he changed this to Botany Bay in deference to the more refined enjoyment experienced there by the two scientists.

Coasting northwards again, Cook noticed what appeared

to be the entrance to a fine harbour which he named Port Jackson. On 22 May they replenished the water casks and shot a fine wild turkey at the place still marked on maps as Bustard Bay, but Cook's even temper was deeply disturbed by what he called in his log "a very extra-ordinary affair". On the previous night, while the *Endeavour* lay at anchor, Richard Orton, the captain's clerk, had fallen into his bunk dead drunk. While he lay senseless, "some Malicious person or persons in the Ship" cut off all the clothes from his back and a piece of both his ears. Cook was so furious that, at Batavia on the way home months later, he offered a reward of fifteen guineas and fifteen gallons of arrack to anyone who would inform him of the prankster's name. No one would or could, but Cook suspected one of the midshipmen, Mr James Magra or Matra, a native of New York whom Cook considered "one of those gentlemen, frequently found on board Kings Ships, that can very well be spared, or to speake more planer good for nothing".[45] The incident shows us something of Cook's stern discipline and, equally, something of his care for the well-being of his crew. It also shows his low opinion of Mr Matra, who was destined to become, after Banks, the most influential of the *Endeavour*'s complement in lobbying the British government about founding a colony at Botany Bay.

While, as a mark of the captain's displeasure, Matra was still suspended from duties, the barque nosed into the labyrinth of coral islands, shoals, rocks and lee shores which the world now knows as the Great Barrier Reef. It was almost too much for the greatest navigator of the age. At about eleven o'clock, at high tide on the night of Sunday 11 June, the *Endeavour* struck the reef. Thanks to Cook's superb seamanship, and to the splendid morale he had fostered in his crew, the ship got off at high tide the following night. Banks was surprised that the seamen did not refuse duty and plunder the ship as, he believed, was customary in the eighteenth century whenever a craft was in a desperate situation. Instead, he wrote that "the Seamen worked with surprizing chearfulness and alacrity; no grumbling or growling was to be heard throughout the ship, not even an oath (tho the ship in general was as well furnishd with them as most in his majesties service)." [46]

The ship was beached for repairs near the mouth of the Endeavour River where Cooktown now stands. The botanists enjoyed their month in the tropics at least as much as they had their week at Botany Bay. They collected hundreds of new plants, fish, birds, reptiles and animals, including their first kangaroos and turtles — enough and to spare for all hands to eat their fill of fresh food. Small wonder that the crew's morale was so high. Their commander was probably the only one of that time in the Royal Navy who could write unselfconsciously in his log book:

> Whatever refreshment we got that would bear a division I caused to be equally divided amongest the whole company generally by weight, the meanest person in the Ship had an equal share with my self or any one on board, and this method every commander of a Ship on such a Voyage as this ought ever to observe.

No doubt Cook's men concurred with their commander's views. Some at least realised that his care for their diet saved them from scurvy and other diseases that usually decimated eighteenth-century crews. T. Perry, a sailor in HMS *Resolution* on Cook's third voyage, wrote a song in praise of his paternal care for their health:

> We were all hearty seamen, no colds did we fear,
> And we have from all sickness entirely kept clear.
> Thanks be to our Captain, he has proved so good
> Amongst all the Islands to give us fresh food.[47]

At Endeavour River occurred an incident with "the Indians" which graphically illustrated the total inability of the two races to understand each other. The local Aborigines were shy and timid, like their brethren at Botany Bay, but after three weeks some of the men approached the ship in a friendly manner. They showed no interest in the trinkets offered them but, on leaving, they started to carry off two of the turtles which were lying on the deck. They were outraged by the Englishmen's greed and ignorance of the laws of hospitality and sharing when the crew stopped them from taking away some of their own communal property — property which, from the Aboriginal viewpoint, the white man had already stolen from the black men without so much as a "by your leave" or a "thank you". To mark their displeasure, the Aborigines set fire to the bush and some ship's stores on the river bank. "I had little idea," wrote Banks, "of the fury with which the grass burnt in this hot climate, nor of the difficulty of extinguishing it when once lighted."[48]

On the evening of 22 August 1770, Cook landed on and named Possession Island off the tip of Cape York. He also had the British colours hoisted and formally laid claim to the whole of eastern Australia from Point Hicks to their then position under "the name of *New South Wales*". In the *Endeavour*'s log he wrote that he was confident the whole area "was never seen or viseted by any European before us."[49] As we have seen, this was one of the few instances in which Cook was possibly mistaken, but any evidence there might have been of an earlier visit by Europeans had been destroyed in the terrible Lisbon earthquake just fifteen years before. So the *Endeavour* steered westward for Batavia, the Cape of Good Hope and home. While she was crossing the Gulf of Carpentaria, Cook committed to his journal his ideas on the land and the people they had discovered. Both, he reported, were a great deal more attractive than Dampier had found on the west coast of New Holland.

The eastern coast had many splendid harbours and was reasonably well watered. The native plants and trees seemed of little use to civilised people, though much of the fauna, particularly kangaroos and green turtles, made good eating. However he added, prophetically, that fruits, vegetables and grain crops would flourish if introduced and that there was ample fodder for more domestic animals "than ever could be brought into the country". He then launched into a panegyric on the Aborigines, consciously contrasting his perception of them with Dampier's:

From what I have said of the Natives of New-Holland, they may appear to some to be the most wretched people upon Earth, but in reality they are far more happier than we Europeans; being wholly unacquainted not only with the superfluous but the necessary Conveniencies so much sought after in Europe, they are happy in not knowing the use of them. They live in a Tranquillity which is not disturb'd by the Inequality of Condition: the Earth and sea of their own accord furnishes them with all things necessary for life.

... In short they seem'd to set no Value upon anything we gave them, nor would they ever part with any thing of their own for any one article we could offer them; this in my opinion argues that they think themselves provided with all the necessarys of Life and that they have no superfluities.[50]

This passage has become the classic statement of the nature of the "noble savage" seen through the eyes of the man who must surely be considered the noblest-natured son of the enlightenment in the European Age of Reason. The decription is highly romantic, even sentimental. Most readers now, or then, they may take leave to doubt whether eighteenth-century Aborigines were in general *happier* than Europeans of the same era. Yet the passage shows too that Cook understood the nature of Aboriginal society better than almost any other European observer for well over a century afterwards. He saw that the black people lived entirely by hunting and gathering food direct from nature, that they shared it according to need, and that consequently their lives were "not disturb'd by any Inequality of Condition". They were free of class conflict because classes standing in a different relationship to the means of production had not developed any more than had chiefs, sorcerers, priests, kings, police or other specialists in the mean art of imposing their will on their fellows. A few more white people with James Cook's kind of "enlightenment" might have ameliorated the murderous conflict between blacks and whites which was to darken the history of the next two hundred years in New South Wales, New Holland and Van Diemen's Land.

"Nothing in his life became him like the leaving it", wrote Shakespeare. Cook died like a hero of ancient Greek tragedy, brought down by *hubris* – that sense of overweening pride in one's own prowess which is said to anger the gods and presage a fall. On his third great voyage of discovery in 1779, when his name and fame had already become legendary throughout the Pacific, he was felled by the daggers and clubs of some Hawaiian Islanders. A party of natives had carried off one of HMS *Discovery*'s boats and it was felt that nothing less than Cook's personal *mana* would suffice to get it back. Accordingly he led the landing party and retrieved the boat – as was his custom, without bloodshed. Then as they were returning to their boat, one of the sailors, without orders, fired on an Hawaiian canoe and killed a great chief. The infuriated islanders rushed on the landing party just as they were about to get back into their boats. The Englishmen turned to defend themselves or ran as best they could through the sea for safety, but their commander's tremendous sense of his own status, and of the dignity of a human being, allowed him to do neither. Certain, seemingly, that no Polynesian would dare attack him, Cook unhurriedly turned his back on the islanders in order to gesture the men in the boats close inshore. He fell immediately under a rain of blows.[51]

2 Empire, convicts and currency

c. 1771–1820

In his thirties, James Cook had played a notable part in securing the empire of the world, particularly of North America and India, to Britain in her Seven Years' War with France (1756-63). When he was killed in 1779, in what his European contemporaries called the Sandwich Islands, Britain was in the midst of another and less successful war with France. When it had ended in 1783, Britain had won Canada from the French but lost her own settlements in North America. The thirteen colonies on the Atlantic seaboard from New England to Georgia had federated to form a new nation, the United States of America. The Peace of Versailles left British statesmen with one major problem – how to preserve what was left of the Empire, principally India – and one minor one – what to do with her surplus criminals now that the North American colonies would no longer take them. William Pitt, who first became prime minister in December 1783, saw his first task as the "uniting and connecting" of a "shattered" empire.[1]

His father, William Pitt the elder, Earl of Chatham, had done much to create the empire when he inspired the country and the government during the Seven Years' War. His great-grandfather had founded the family's fame and fortune during the years when he governed Madras for the British East India Company – in an age when corruption was universal and, under the name of "mercantilism", even those with the cleanest hands innocently proclaimed that colonies should exist for the benefit of the merchants of the mother country. With such a background it is not surprising that the younger

Pitt saw the fostering of British rule in India and the East as the principal part of his task. To it he brought those unmatched abilities which had made him prime minister at the age of 24 only two years after he entered parliament. At a time when many English gentlemen drank port every night until stupefaction set in, it was said that Pitt was seen drunk in the House of Commons only once − and then he had the *sang-froid* to retire behind the speaker's chair to vomit. The least talented person in the government was probably Thomas Townshend, Viscount Sydney, Secretary of State. To him fell the less important but more pressing task of finding a place suitable for the reception of Britain's felons.[2]

The matter was urgent because, as it seemed to contemporaries, crime and criminals had been multiplying at an alarming rate. Throughout the eighteenth century the "agricultural revolution" transformed the face of the English countryside. More and more enclosure acts were passed through parliament by and for the landed gentry and their friends − for large "capitalist" farms, run on scientific lines, produced much more food for sale, and profit for their owners, than the traditional kind of land use. As the change proceeded, thousands of small tenant farmers, poor labourers and their families with ancient traditional rights to some forms of land use found themselves expropriated. Most of them moved to the growing industrial towns, as did Henry Parkes' family to Birmingham in the early years of the nineteenth century,[3] but much was lost even by those who found work in the new factories driven by water or steam power. They left, perforce, a settled life in a village community made secure by friendship and traditionally sanctioned relationships involving mutual obligations with squire and parson. They became, often, "hands" in an impersonal factory, living among strangers in jerry-built terrace houses, working for inhumanly long hours at low wages and bereft of all sense of belonging or personal worth − and these were the lucky ones. Those who could not find work often had to steal or starve.[4]

Citizens with property worth stealing naturally worried mightily about the increasing criminality of those to whom they referred as "the lower orders". But their ideas for stemming the flood of larceny, mayhem and murder were limited. The British governing classes, those whom G.A. Wood called "the men who plundered their country in habitual political robbery",[5] thought only of terrifying potential malefactors by hanging more and more of the few who were caught. Thus in the century between 1688, when Dampier's pirates were careening the *Cygnet* on a New Holland beach, and 1788 when the First Fleet landed the first white Australians in Sydney Cove, the number of capital crimes in the English statute books rose from about fifty to two hundred. For instance, by the end of the eighteenth century hanging crimes included picking pockets of goods worth more than one shilling, shoplifting of goods worth more than five shillings, and cutting down trees in an avenue or garden.[6]

Alas for the property-holders, neither the preachings of the clergy nor fear of the scaffold deterred many poor people from following the paths of wickedness in which they had been trained by desperate or demoralised parents. This was partly because police forces were so ineffecient that wrongdoers had an excellent chance of escaping scot free, and partly because the very severity of the laws defeated their purpose. When the penalty for stealing goods of or above the value of a shilling was death, juries often found the value to be less – despite the most cogent evidence to the contrary. Even magistrates and judges frequently sentenced to transportation people who should legally have been "turned off" by the hangman. But these temperings of justice with mercy merely exacerbated the problem of what was to be done with the hordes of criminals unlucky enough to be caught.

Until 1776 most of them had been shipped to the American colonies, where their services, for the term of their sentences, were sold to planters and other employers by the contractors who took them off the hands of the British government. In that year Adam Smith published his classic statement of capitalist economics, *The Wealth of Nations*, and the American colonists, some of whom in time were to become the world's most ardent capitalists, published their Declaration of Independence, proclaiming "life, liberty and the pursuit of happiness" to be the inalienable rights of all. Few at that time troubled their heads much about the rights of women, but the founding fathers of the United States of America did think it beneath the dignity of the new nation to continue receiving British gaolbirds. Illogically, or perhaps logically, they made up for the deficiency of cheap labour by buying more Negro slaves, many of whom were brought from West Africa in British ships. There were not enough gaols in the British Isles to hold those sentenced to transportation and so, as a temporary expedient, the government confined them in old hulks, generally moored in naval ports where the prisoners' labour could be used in building docks and other harbour facilities. Meanwhile successive Secretaries of State for Home Affairs sought suitable places of exile.

In 1782 a few hundred felons were drafted into the army and sent to Cape Coast Castle on the West African "Slave Coast", but those who survived the fever deserted and fought with a nearby Dutch force against their British masters. Later in the year Gambia was suggested for the first time as a receptacle for the ungrateful wretches. In the following year Cook's old shipmate, James Mario Matra, first pressed on the government the surpassing advantages of Botany Bay. He felt that this place would make an ideal prison for the convicts, offered many commercial and strategic advantages and, in addition, would make a splendid home for thousands of dispossessed United Empire loyalists – people who, like Matra himself, had declared for the mother country when the American colonies rebelled. The government was not much impressed, nor was Viscount Sydney when he returned to the Secretary of State's desk in December 1783.

During the next three years Matra, the "loyal" New Yorker, and Banks, his patron, were only two of the multitude of people who lobbied the government with conflicting ideas for the transportation of convicts. Among the places considered more or less seriously were the Canadian maritime provinces, British Honduras, the island of St Thomas in the Gulf of Guinea, New Zealand, New Caledonia, Norfolk Island, points on the coast of Madagascar, Lemain (an island about 700 kilometres up the Gambia River in West Africa), Das Voltas Bay and several other points on the African coastline, and the islands of Tristan da Cunha, Diego Garcia and the Andamans. The claims of Botany Bay were agitated more often than those of any other place because Cook had sung the praises of *phormium tenax*, a flax plant, and of splendid-looking straight pine trees, both of which flourished on Norfolk Island.[7]

In the eighteenth century, naval power and world dominion depended on ample and assured supplies of timber for ship-building and flax for sails and cordage, just as later navies depended successively on coal and oil; but England drew uncertain supplies of these strategic commodities from Russia and other Baltic areas and, worse from Pitt's point of view, all British ships in the Indian Ocean depended completely on these Baltic supplies shipped to the east with vast difficulty and at great expense. Alan Frost has shown that from 1784 onwards decisions about Home and Colonial Affairs were not made by Sydney, but by the prime minister, Pitt.[8] As we have seen, he was deeply concerned with the security of the Indian trade, after the loss of North America the greatest source of imperial wealth and of his own family's fortune. Perhaps a settlement on the east coast of New Holland, close to the supposed naval supplies of Norfolk Island, would buttress Britain's strategic position throughout the Indian and Pacific Ocean areas, forestall the French, secure to the Honourable East India Company the lion's share of the "Eastern" trade, and at the same time furnish a suitably remote dumping-ground for the denizens of the hulks whose presence at home had embarrassed successive governments for so long. Besides, empty convict transport ships might bring home cargoes of China tea to quench the latest British thirst.

At last in 1787 the King's speech to parliament announced that a plan had been formed "for transporting a number of convicts in order to remove the inconvenience which arose from the crowded state of the gaols in different parts of the kingdom".[9] A new empire and a new receptacle for unwanted criminals was to replace the lost American colonies. It was symbolic that the first human being to be hanged at "Botany Bay", Thomas Barrett, was transported for the crime of having returned to England before the end of the fourteen years for which he had been exiled to America for stealing a watch.[10]

In May of the same year, the First Fleet of eleven storeships and transports set sail for Botany Bay. Most of its complement of something more than a thousand felons and their gaolers disembarked in the virgin bush at Sydney Cove eight months later, on 26 January 1788. It had been — for the period — a slow but more than usually healthy voyage.

The first governor and commander-in-chief was Arthur Phillip, a sensible and, by contemporary standards, unusually humane naval captain. A typical man of the Age of Reason, he gave formal assent to the doctrines of the Church of England, which body he regarded as a useful buttress of state power rather than as one concerned with supernatural revelations or the calling of sinners to repentance. He probably owed his appointment to his friendship with George Rose, Secretary to the Treasury, or with Sir Evan Nepean, Under-Secretary to the Home Office, both of whom were friends and confidants of Pitt himself. All three knew of Phillip's abilities, for they had despatched him on a secret and successful mission to France in 1784 to spy on war preparations in Toulon and other ports.[11] Doubtless Phillip knew too that the government saw the new settlement as a "strategic outlier" to imperial interests in Asia as well as a conveniently remote convict depot. This would account for his being almost the only person in the First Fleet who foresaw the time when the miserable little gaol might become a prosperous and civilised country, but the immediate struggle for survival taxed his strength to the limit.

His human cargo had been dumped on the shore where Sydney now stands. About three-quarters of them were convicts, men, women, and children; many were aged or infirm, and nearly all unwilling to work. The remainder were mainly

Marine Corps officers and men, sent out as a guard; but from the moment of landing, the officers manifested a keen appreciation of their station in life. They refused to compromise what they regarded as their dignity by supervising the work of felons, except in the case of those who had been assigned to them personally as servants. Thus the best-behaved – or most sycophantic – convicts had to be made constables and placed in other positions of some responsibility. Most of the colonists were criminals from the slums of London and other great cities. There was hardly a gardener or farmer among them. Seeds refused to sprout in the alien soil, and for the first two years the colony was threatened with famine. With something of Cook's nobility, Phillip placed his private stock of food in the communal store and decreed the same scale of rations for bond and free. The "starving time" had passed by the time he sailed for England in December 1792, and the day when the colony would be self-supporting seemed not quite as far off as before. There was one convict in the First Fleet who had been bred to farming, James Ruse. Phillip gave him every encouragement and in April 1791 title to the first 40 acres (16 hectares) of land ever granted by the British Crown on the Australian continent. By that time Ruse had succeeded in producing enough to keep himself and his family.[12]

Only about one convict in every four in the First Fleet was female. This gross imbalance between the sexes generally increased throughout the whole period of transportation. When the last "exile" landed in Western Australia in 1868, about 162 000 had been transported, of whom about 25 000, or one in every six or seven, were women.[13] The scarcity of women in the early days disfigured Australian life for long afterwards, creating a much cruder, male-dominated, "frontier" society than developed in most other colonies where Europeans settled in the nineteenth century. Surprisingly, the reasonable men in the British government, who drafted Phillip's commissions, recognised the danger and sought to provide against it. Phillip was to order the commanders of any ship visiting islands in the south seas "to take on board any of the women who may be disposed to accompany them to

Sydney", providing that no deception or compulsion was employed.[14] Possibly because he feared that the Polynesian women would in fact be brutally kidnapped if the scheme were put into effect, the man of the enlightenment ignored the proposal. No women were present when the officers and marines hoisted the Union Jack and "christened" Sydney Town about noon on 26 January 1788, at the spot in the bush where the obelisk now stands in Macquarie Place. When the female convicts landed on a Sunday eleven days later, most un-Sabbath-like scenes ensued. As darkness fell, men and women, convicts and marines joined in an orgy of rum and fornication. A tropical storm poured down on the revellers, seemingly lashing them on to fulfil the Biblical command to Noah and his sons to be fruitful, to multiply and to replenish the earth.[15]

Contemporary observers, whether male or female, agreed that the women convicts were even more profligate, vicious and irredeemable than the men, but recent research shows that all have been tarred with the sins of a minority.[16] At least one woman in every five was a prostitute at the time of her arrest.[17] In the early years of the system, most others were forced into prostitution on the transport ships, where they lived promiscuously with the sailors or took a protector from among them. Those whose "innocence" survived until their arrival at Port Jackson or Hobart Town were almost always forced into prostitution in the new country, if only because prisoners had to find their own board and lodging. Only the luckier or more attractive women were able to cohabit with only one man, at least for a time. As late as 1811, as soon as female convicts disembarked, officers, non-commissioned officers, privates and free settlers took it in turns to have women assigned to them "not only as servants but as avowed objects of intercourse, which is without even the plea of the slightest previous attachment as an excuse, rendering the whole colony little less than an extensive brothel".[18]

Up until about the same date, women were sometimes flogged for real or imagined misbehaviour, but this rarely or never happened later on. After about 1820, recalcitrant or spirited female prisoners were punished only by having their heads shaved, by serving a sentence on the treadmill, by solitary confinement or by imprisonment at the Female Factory at Parramatta or at The Cascades outside Hobart Town.[19] To these places were sometimes sent also those female prisoners unlucky (or lucky) enough not to have been assigned to a settler. Hardened old harridans and at least relatively innocent new arrivals were all put to work weaving rough cloth for "Government". Yet the life of a Factory woman was not one of unrelieved hard labour and boredom. Because of the scarcity of white women, and because the authorities believed that embracing holy matrimony improved the character of both spouses, a sort of marriage bureau was conducted at Parramatta every Monday morning. The best behaved women were paraded by the matron. Dressed in whatever finery they could muster, they conversed with free but unmarried men in search of a helpmeet. Any couple who fancied each other was then given a special licence and married, often by Reverend Samuel Marsden. The bridegroom was usually an emancipist farmer or "dungaree settler" like the bushranger Ben Hall's father, who was married "out of the Factory" in this way. James F. O'Connell gives a vivid account, that at least rings true, of one such wedding. The happy couple sets out on their long journey to the farm in a bullock-dray in which the "stringy-bark" settler has "previously deposited something hardly less beloved . . . than his wife − a five-gallon keg of Cooper's gin". After the wedding party has disposed of tea, mutton and damper served on dishes made of "rounds of logs, sawed off thin", the keg is broached, pipes and tobacco produced, and

> an edifying conversation commences between the new wife and her female visitors − an exchange of experiences, in which each details how cruelly she was "lagged" on suspicion; all innocent as the fifteenth generation yet to be born, of the crime for which the magistrates had the tyranny to convict her; the dirty vagabonds of witnesses cruelly swearing her life away.[20]

Yet despite the profligacy and drunkenness forced on them by a crude and massively male-dominated society, the

A drawing by Juan Revenet of New South Wales in 1793 shows a convict woman. The numerical imbalance of the sexes in the colony forced most unattached women into prostitution. (Source: *Inhabitants of New Holland* 1793 by J. Revenet, Mitchell Library, State Library of New South Wales)

majority of women convicts did improve vastly in morals, if not necessarily in manners. The most cogent proof of this is that they bore and brought up the first two generations of native-born, white Australians, people whom even the sternest moralists proclaimed to be ethically superior in every way to their parents and, more often than not, to the generality of free immigrants.[21]

Phillip's instructions also enjoined him to "open an intercourse with the natives, and to conciliate their affections, enjoying all our subjects to live in amity and kindness with them".[22] No one could have tried harder to carry out this order. On 15 May 1788 in his first despatch to his master, Lord Sydney, Phillip wrote "it was my determination from my first landing that nothing less than the most absolute necesity should ever make me fire upon them".[23] Two years later he was still better than his word. On 7 September 1790 at Manly Cove, displaying, as a later generation of Australians might say, "more guts than Ned Kelly", but not more than Cook had shown at his death, the unarmed governor of New South Wales walked along the beach holding out both hands in a gesture of peace towards an armed Aborigine. For answer the black man hurled his spear so forcefully that the barbed point transfixed Phillip's right shoulder. The butt-end of the 3 metre-long spear kept striking the ground as this gentleman of the age of enlightenment returned painfully to his boat. No serious efforts were made to punish the offender.[24]

The captain-general could not, however, control the passions of his white subjects as he could his own. From the very first day of contact many convicts and marines stole from the Aborigines their fishing and hunting tackle, their women and sometimes their lives, just as the British government, in the person of Arthur Phillip, had already stolen their land. The first-comers fought back as well as they could. In the first three years up to December 1790 they had killed or wounded seventeen whites. When Phillip's gamekeeper, M'Entire, was killed in that month, the governor's stock of calm reason came to an end. He despatched two punitive expeditions with orders to bring back in bags the severed heads of six Aborigines from what was thought to be the offending tribe. Both expeditions failed even to make contact with the Aboriginal enemy,[25] but from that time onwards no one set in authority over white Australians made such efforts as Phillip had done to see that they lived "in amity and kindness" with black ones, and few indeed tried so hard to understand them.

The abyss of incomprehension which separated the two races was graphically illustrated in May 1791. Phillip decided to make an example of a convict caught in the act of stealing fishing tackle from Dar-in-ga, the wife of Colbee. The man was severely flogged in the presence of many Aborigines who had been made to understand the reason for his punishment, but "there was not one of them that did not testify strong abhorrence of the punishment, and equal sympathy with the sufferer".[26] Aborigines never could understand people who, in cold blood, deliberately inflicted pain on a fellow human being. Unlike nearly all other people on the earth, they never engaged in any form of cold-blooded torture. As the eyewitness, Tench, put it, the fiasco showed that the Aborigines were "not of a sanguinary and implacable temper. Quick indeed of resentment, but not unforgiving of injury."[27] Their

A marine. Drawing by Juan Revenet in 1793. (Source: *Inhabitants of New Holland* 1793 by J. Revenet, Mitchell Library, State Library of New South Wales)

humane and conciliatory temper, like their social organisation and the inferiority of their weapons, remained a fatal weakness in their efforts to resist the implacable and bloodthirsty European invaders. The temper of North American Indians, for instance, was very different and their resistance to white conquest correspondingly more sustained and somewhat more successful.

Thus with relatively slight pressure toward closing their ranks against the black natives, white Australian pioneers had ample scope for falling out with each other. The historian may doubt whether there was any more quarrelsome society in the world than that of early New South Wales, though even at this period quarrels were usually fought out in law courts, drawing rooms and grog shops with words and fists rather than with more lethal weapons. Naturally, indeed inevitably, the traditionally hallowed class distinctions of England tended to be reproduced in the Antipodes. In some ways, conditions even accentuated them. For many years after the first white settlement — up until at least 1840 — the vast majority of working people were convicts, or ex-convicts, or people who associated familiarly with these groups and their children.

Thus a visiting ship's captain wrote in 1805:

> The circumstances under which the colony was settled, and the very
> purpose of the settlement, has had a very visible effect upon the gen-
> eral manners, or what may be called the national character, of Bot-
> any Bay. The free settlers are not without something of the
> contagion . . . From upwards of a hundred families who have been
> sent out from England, there are not above eight or ten between
> whom and the convicts the smallest degree of discrimination could
> be drawn.[28]

Under these conditions it was not surprising that the colonial "gentry", at first nearly all naval or military or civilian
government officers, should have drawn their spiritual skirts
closely about them in an effort to fix between themselves and
the "felonry" an even greater gulf than existed between the
gentry and the "lower orders" in contemporary Britain.[29]
The two parties early came to be known as "exclusionists"
and "emancipists", the former because they sought to exclude from polite society ex-convicts and all other low fellows, the latter because they were emancipated prisoners or
friends, associates or descendants of such people. John Hood
hardly exaggerated when he wrote as late as 1843: "Caste in
Hindostan is not more rigidly regarded than it is in Australia:
the bond and free, emancipist and exclusionist, seldom associate together familiarly." [30]

This deep and bitter class feeling was sharpened too by the
fact that there were relatively few middle-class people to serve
as any kind of bridge between the masses, tainted with the
stigma of felonry, and those who considered themselves the
colonial gentry. As late as 1841 the New South Wales census
listed 4477 squatters (large-scale graziers), merchant-import-
ers, bankers, and professional men, and 50 158 craftsmen,
labourers, servants and so on. Between these upper and lower
millstones there were only 1774 shopkeepers and other retail
dealers. In the foundation years the absence of any middle
order of people was, as we have seen, even more marked. As
David Collins, the colony's first judge-advocate, noted:

> It was to have been wished, that a watch . . had been formed of free
> people . . . But there was not any choice. The military had their line

of duty marked out for them, and between them and the convict there was no description of people from whom overseers or watchmen could be provided.[31]

Yet, despite these factors, the gulf between the two classes was never as unbridgeable as those who came to be ironically termed "pure merinos" (rigid exclusionists) wished to make it.[32] From the beginning there were other, and even more powerful, levelling influences at work. First, the very intensity of the exclusionists' emphasis on their gentility betrayed the precariousness of their position. The British class structure could not in the nature of things survive, without modification, transplantation to an antipodean wilderness — especially with its vital middle component missing. If the colonial working people were heavily tainted by convictism, so were their self-appointed betters by the part they played in "the system". As the celebrated naturalist, Charles Darwin, who visited Sydney in 1836, put it:

> How thoroughly odious to every feeling, to be waited on by a man who the day before, perhaps, was flogged from your representation, for some trifling misdemeanour. The female servants are of course much worse; hence children learn the vilest expressions, and it is fortunate if not equally vile ideas.[33]

Moreover, though a few of the squatters and other "pure merinos", especially after about 1820, came from families recognised in Britain as gentry, the great majority of the exclusionists did not. For the most part, members of the colonial upper class came from the middle or lower middle class in England. Often they were distinguished from the generality of colonists only by their greater wealth — and their greater taste for vulgar display. As the well-bred Hood lamented in 1843:

> If the truth must be told, the fortunes of many of the exclusionists themselves were not acquired by the purest means; close contracts, the gin or rum-shop, embarrassments wilfully created by insidious loans and ejectments, and other crooked paths, were used equally by both parties, bond and free.

Or as the radical Presbyterian parson, Reverend Dr John

Dunmore Lang, put it: "*Very* strange tales are told of gentlemen of New South Wales."

Worse, from the point of view of the traditionalists, was the extreme fluidity of colonial society. Many emancipists like Simeon Lord and Samuel Terry, the "Botany Bay millionaire" who once owned the land on which Sydney's general post office now stands, rapidly became rich, and if they themselves were never quite accepted in polite society, their offspring often were. "Their children are sent to the colleges of England," wrote Hood, "and their daughters' fortunes get them husbands from among the free."

The truth was that the convict system tended to corrupt the manners, if not always the morals, of both the prisoners and their gaolers. Technically the settler acquired a property in the services of the convict, not in his or her person; but in practice, as we have seen, free persons selected female convicts, more or less openly, as mistresses. There were of course honourable and honoured exceptions, men like Governor Phillip and the much-loved Governor Lachlan Macquarie who ruled from 1810 to 1821, but Governor Philip Gidley King (1800–06) had two sons by convict mistresses, one named Norfolk and one Sydney, presumably in honour of their respective birthplaces. David Collins, deputy judge-advocate of New South Wales under Phillip, had two children by Anne Yeates in Sydney and two more by Margaret Eddington when he was Lieutenant-Governor of Van Diemen's Land, where his successor, "Mad Tom Davey", in his official capacity attended divine service with a convict paramour on his arm. True, Davey was dismissed, but when viceroys conducted themselves thus, what was to be expected of the felonry? In fact, at least up to the end of Macquarie's reign, the great majority of all the children born in the colony were illegitimate, being quaintly if prophetically termed in official documents "national children". About nine-tenths were the offspring of convicts or ex-convicts on at least one side of the (often temporary) parental union.[34]

The general debauchery was both sustained and aggravated by the oceanic tide of Bengal rum which was for many

years the principal commodity imported. It was an age of prodigious drinking in which London gin-shops advertised that
customers could get drunk for a penny and dead drunk for
twopence, but the specially selected colonists at Sydney and
Hobart Town outdrank all others. The New South Wales
Corps, recruited for the peculiar service of keeping order at
"Botany Bay", replaced the Marine detachment on Phillip's
departure in 1792. It proved a thorn in the flesh of successive
governors from 1795 until its departure in 1810, earning in
popular usage the sobriquet of the "Rum Corps". During its
existence, and for most of the following decade, coinage was
in such chronically short supply that rum, often used as a ge-
neric term for spirits, became the commonest medium of incentive payments to convicts and the commonest article of
barter, so common that some historians have held that it functioned as the *de facto* currency of the colony during this period. The traditional words of "The Convicts' Rum Song"
give a romanticised, or heroic, picture of the place rum occupied in the community and hint at the reasons for its importance.

> Cut yer name across me backbone,
>   Stretch me skin across a drum,
> Iron me up to Pinchgut Island
>   From today till Kingdom-come!
> I will eat yer Norfolk dumpling
>   Like a juicy Spanish plum,
> Even dance the Newgate Hornpipe
>   If ye'll only gimme RUM!

"Pinchgut Island", originally little more than a barren rock
in Sydney Harbour, served as a place of solitary confinement,
and occasionally of execution, for particularly refractory convicts in the early days. Later officially renamed Fort Denison,
the older term has persisted in popular usage. A "Norfolk
dumpling" symbolised prison conditions at Norfolk Island,
after 1825 the most appalling of all penal settlements for
twice-convicted felons. The "Newgate hornpipe" meant, of
course, the "dance" of death on the gallows. Nevertheless,
legend has exaggerated the quantity, though not the quality,

of brutality inflicted on the "government men" under the convict system. Probably fewer than 15 per cent of all those transported ever saw the inside of such penal hells as Norfolk Island, and probably fewer than half were ever flogged at all. Soldiers in the army, equally subject to the lash, very often committed crimes in Australia because they were convinced that they would be better off as convicts. There were many humane and reasonable men like D'Arcy Wentworth among employers, as well as some sadists. Alexander Harris, one of the most judicious reporters of early Australian life, has left two accounts which together show vividly the worst and the best sides of "the system". The first is an eyewitness account of a flogging, the second a convict's own tale of the brighter side of the picture:

> I saw a man walk across the yard with the blood that had run from his lacerated flesh squashing out of his shoes at every step he took. A dog was licking the blood off the triangles, and the ants were carrying away great pieces of human flesh that the lash had scattered about the ground. The scourger's foot had worn a deep hole in the ground by the violence with which he whirled himself round on it to strike the quivering and wealed back, out of which stuck the sinews, white, ragged and swollen. The infliction was a hundred lashes, at about half-minute time, so as to extend the punishment through nearly an hour . . . They had a pair of scourgers, who gave one another spell and spell about; and they were bespattered with blood like a couple of butchers. I tell you this on the authority of my own eyes. It brought my heart into my mouth.[35]

The narrator of the following story was a convict who had absconded from the penal settlement at Coal River, later Newcastle. He was captured and brought before the bench for sentence:

> Then was my turn; but old Dr Wentworth was on the bench, and you know I had been sent to him for six weeks in harvest directly after I came into the country . . . So, all of a sudden, just as I thought I was going to get my dowry, up jumps the old doctor, stamping as if he was mad, and shaking his fist at me . . . "Gentlemen," says he, "this is one of the most polished scamps in the Colony. I know him well. Two hundred lashes! Pooh, pooh! He'd forget about it by tomorrow morning. I fancy I'd better have him down to my Homebush farm

and see what I can do with him." . . . So it was agreed on, for none of the other magistrates dared say No when D'Arcy Wentworth said Yes . . . So there I was by that night at sundown eating and drinking the best there was in the huts at Homebush; and you heard tell how all the doctor's men live. There I stayed till I got free; and then hired to him. Never got one lash the whole five years I was with him.[36]

The prevalence of rum, like the foundation of Australia itself, also owes something to America. When Phillip, worn out and ill, left for England, no new governor had been appointed. Major Francis Grose, commandant of the New South Wales Corps, became lieutenant-governor. Soon after his assumption of power, the Yankee ship *Hope* sailed through Sydney Heads with a much-needed cargo of general provisions and 7500 gallons (more than 28 000 litres) of rum. Her skipper, Benjamin Page, swore he would not sell his mixed cargo unless every barrel of rum was also purchased. Supplies of all kinds were still desperately short and Page, like other trading skippers, demanded absurdly inflated prices for his goods. In the face of such extortionate demands, the officers of the Corps and their friends decided to form a counter-monopoly of their own. Under the nominal command of Grose, but largely inspired by a forceful young lieutenant called John Macarthur, they combined to purchase, without competition, the whole cargo of the *Hope* − and of most other ships which came to the colony for years afterwards. Soon the soldiers of the Corps found that their wages were being paid partly or wholly in rum or other trade goods, all of which were valued by the officers' junta at absurdly high rates. In this way poor settlers, mostly emancipated or time-expired convicts, and even those still serving their sentences, were also exploited by the monopolists; for it had early been discovered that as an incentive to efficient work, the scourger's cat-o'-nine-tails, no matter how furiously and continually plied, was insufficient. The convicts were therefore allowed to seek private employment in the late afternoons after their "government work" for the day had been done. When Phillip left, the officers of the Corps lost little time in extending this privilege, especially by withdrawing many more convicts altogether from government work and assigning them to themselves and their friends. The officers also began the practice, continued by later governors, of granting large tracts of land to each other. These changes, however discreditable to the officers concerned, did lead to much more efficient farming. The amount of wheat in circulation increased almost as much as the amount of rum. The colony rapidly became self-sufficient in basic foods and the "starving time" a memory.[37]

Three more naval governors, John Hunter, Philip King and William Bligh, tried without avail to break the rum traffic and to mitigate the social and economic evils which it nourished. Instead their own careers were blighted by the entrenched influence of the rum traffickers. Bligh, who governed from 1806 until 1808, was actually deposed in a *coup d'état* carried out by the "Rum Corps" – the very body whose prime function it was to uphold his authority. Fifteen months after the First Fleet reached Sydney Cove in January 1788, Bligh's crew had mutinied in HMS *Bounty* near Tahiti. The story is well known and has caused posterity to think of Bligh as a blustering and brutal bully. True, but the record shows he was a good deal more than that. How else could he have brought safely to Timor, a distance nearly 9000 kilometres, the open boat in which he was set adrift, overloaded as it was with eighteen men and boys who refused to join the mutineers? As governor of New South Wales, Bligh's determined efforts to curb the power of the rum traders rapidly made him very popular with the "little men" of the community, particularly with the struggling emancipist farmers of the Hawkesbury River district some 40 kilometres northwest of Sydney. They made him equally unpopular with the officers of the Corps and the exclusionists, people who were not used to being sworn at in the "tarpaulin's" language Bligh favoured.

Of these, the most influential was John Macarthur. Legend held that he came of an old Jacobite family and had the the ear of powerful friends in England. With his wife and infant son, he arrived in 1790 as a lieutenant of the New South Wales Corps. Though he never became a senior officer, the strength of his character was such that, almost from the beginning, he dominated those who considered themselves gentlemen and, more narrowly, the junta of military and civilian officers which led the rum monopoly. Yet he enriched Australia as well as himself by his obsessive pursuit of wealth, and his dubious claim to have founded the wool industry has been accepted by most historians.[38] Gentle and virtuous in his family life, his overweening pride drove him to quarrel violently with any man who crossed his designs. His critics maddened him with the taunt of "Jack Boddice", implying that his father, a Devon draper, had specialised in selling male corsets to his military customers. One of his many enemies called him "as sharp as a razor and as rapacious as a shark", and Governors Hunter, King and Bligh all denounced him in scarcely less baleful terms as, among other things, "the grand perturbator". Towards the end of his life his turbulent passions ended in madness. At the time of the "Rum Rebellion" he had been thrown into gaol by the courts, formally for a minor breach of the law but in fact more for his obstinate and successful defence of the rum traders' interests. From prison he engineered the junta's bloodless coup, which was actually carried out by Major George Johnston, commander of the Corps and lieutenant-governor of the colony.

In the hot evening of the twentieth anniversary of the first landing, 26 January 1808, with band playing and colours flying, the "Rum Corps" carried out what some cynics have termed its only martial action. Inspired by rum thoughtfully provided by Mr Macarthur, the soldiers lurched across the bridge which spanned the Tank Stream near the present intersection of Pitt and Bridge Streets. To the tune of "The British Grenadiers" they staggered up the hill to Government House where the New South Wales Corps soldiers on guard promptly joined their fellow rebels. No one offered to defend the King's representative except his daughter, Mrs Mary Putland, who invited the drunken troops to stab her to the heart but to respect the life of her father. Major Johnston then "arrested" Bligh, whom it was his first duty to protect against all the King's enemies. A contemporary print shows him being dragged from his hiding place under a bed; but in view of his naval record it seems likely that this was a piece of rebel propaganda.[39] Macarthur's part in these treasonable proceedings may be divined from a hasty note he sent to his wife:

> My Dearest Love,
>
>   I have been deeply engaged all this day in contending for the liberties of this unhappy colony, and I am happy to say I have succeeded beyond what I expected. I am too much exhausted to attempt giving you particulars: therefore I must refer you to Edward [their son] who knows enough to give you a general idea of what has been done. The tyrant is now, no doubt, gnashing his teeth with vexation at his overthrow. May he often have cause to do the like.

Johnston and the junta took over the government, continued to import rum, and proceeded to grant more land to themselves and their friends. After some years Johnston was cashiered by a London court-martial. Macarthur was not allowed to return to Australia for some time, but his wife Elizabeth capably looked after his colonial interests during his absence.

Those who hold that the New South Wales Corps' treasonable deposition of Bligh constituted the only warlike deed in its inglorious history do it a little less than justice. Four years earlier it had carried out a slightly less discreditable action. In 1798 the most recent Irish revolt against their British overlords had been bloodily suppressed at the "Battle" of Vinegar Hill. Shiploads of the defeated rebels were transported to New South Wales where, despite the fact that their lives had been spared, they obstinately continued to hate their masters. Governor King, a devout loyalist and supporter of the Protestant establishment, inquired into rumoured Irish plots to take Sydney in 1800 and 1802. Then in March 1804 the rumours became real. One of the transported rebels, William Johnston, armed a band of convicts, mostly Irish, with stolen muskets and improvised pikes and swords. They marched from Castle Hill towards Windsor, calling on all convicts to join their crusade against the establishment. Informed by an Irish traitor, one Keogh, King ordered Major George Johnston and a detachment of the New South Wales Corps in pursuit. The soldiers overtook the rebels at Vinegar Hill, now known as Rouse Hill, about 7 kilometres short of Windsor. They answered Johnston's demand for their surrender with a defiant shout of "Death or Liberty". Johnston then asked their leaders to come forward to parley with him under an implied promise of safe-conduct. William Johnston and his fellow rebel, Phillip Cunningham, were simple-minded enough to trust the word of a British officer, even one enrolled in the notorious "Rum Corps". After some discussion, George Johnston clapped his pistol at Cunningham's head while an attendant trooper pointed his at William Johnston's. Defeated by what the gentlemen of the Corps doubtless considered a brilliant stratagem, the leaderless and ill-armed convicts ran away. Nine were butchered before they reached Windsor and Cunningham was hanged out of hand there on the staircase of the public store. In the following week those considered to be the ringleaders were punished according to the heinousness of their offences. Three were publicly hanged at Parramatta, three at Castle Hill and two at Sydney. Thirty-five were sent to the penal station at Coal River, renamed Newcastle.[40]

The Reverend Samuel Marsden, ever zealous in his support of the Protestant ascendancy, busied himself in extracting incriminating evidence from witnesses, as he had done after the earlier rumoured revolt of 1800. On that occasion, in his capacity as a magistrate, he had not scrupled to break the laws of God and man by ordering floggings to extort confessions from vaguely suspected persons. In 1804 two such were named Fitzgerald and Galvin, transported for their part in the rebellion of 1798. Their flagellation was described by Joseph Holt, another suspected plotter who, since he was a Protestant and a gentleman, was punished only by being forced to watch the torture of his countrymen. "There was two floggers," wrote Holt,

Richard Rice and John Jonson, the Hangman from Sidney. Rice was a left handed man and Jonson was Right handed so they stood at each side and I never saw two trashers in a barn moove their stroakes more handeyer than those two man killers did . . . as it happened I was to leew'rd of the floggers and I protest, tho' I was two perches from them, the flesh and skin blew in my face as they shooke off of the cats.

Next was tyed up paddy galvin, a young boy about twenty years of age. He was ordered to get three hundred lashes. He got one hundred on the back and you cud see his back bone between his shoulder blades, then the Doctor order him to get another hunder on his bottom. He got it and then his huckles was in such a jelly the Doctor order him to be flog on the Calves of his legs. He got one hunder there and as much as a whimper he never gave. They asked him if he would tell where the pikes was hid, he said he did not now, and if he did he would not tell. "You may as well hang me Now," he says, "for you will never get any musick from me." So they put him in the Cart and sent him to the Hospital.[41]

Australians generally and Irish-Australians in particular remembered the sort of thing that was done to Paddy Galvin and to thousands like him. Folk memory often preserved too the tradition of Galvin's iron will in the face of hopeless odds. "I'll fight but not surrender," said the anonymous, but clearly Irish-Australian, Wild Colonial Boy many years later. Later still, at the time of what contemporaries called the Great War, most Irish-Australians, though very willing to fight for Australia, still hated England, their hereditary enemy, sufficiently to vote "No" in the campaigns for conscription for overseas service.

The "Rum Rebellion" at least prompted His Majesty's ministers, preoccupied with the Napoleonic wars, to give an unwonted modicum of thought to affairs in New South Wales. The system by which naval governors had to depend for their authority on the goodwill of a military force, which distance made semi-autonomous in practice, was abandoned. On New Year's Day 1810 Lieutenant-Colonel Lachlan Macquarie, at the head of his own regiment of 73rd Highlanders, assumed office as governor. For the next twelve years he ruled New South Wales and its dependencies in much the same absolute but paternalistic spirit as some of his ancestors had ruled their Highland clans. Like previous governors, he regarded the Church of England as a body of men whose prime function was to preach obedience to the secular power of the state. He made the leading clergyman in the colony, Reverend Samuel Marsden, a magistrate of whom the convicts said "The Lord have mercy on you, for his reverence has none" and whom Commissioner Bigge found to have ordered floggings far more freely than any of the lay magistrates in the colony.[42] The Church of England in Australia at this time seems to have regarded itself as a kind of moral police officer in the service of government, so much so that many church foundation stones, like those of St Matthew's at Windsor and St James' in Sydney, bear no cross or other Christian symbol but simply a crown, the date and the sufficiently significant inscription, "L. Macquarie Esq., Governor".

During his regime (1810–21), the power of the rum monopolists was broken, not so much because of the loyalty of his regiment or even his own prodigious efforts, as because the rising native-born generation, an increasing trickle of free immigrants and growing export trade in whale oil and sealskins rendered a nearly closed monopolistic system no longer economically viable. He closed scores of licensed taverns while sly-grog shops multiplied, for if the monopoly of rum was ended, the rate of its consumption hardly lessened. He gave to the central Sydney area the basic street plan it has today. He ordered the erection of many fine buildings. Among those still standing are St James' Church in King Street, the adjoining Hyde Park convict barracks and the graceful Georgian building long known as the "Rum Hospital". Only two parts of the last still stand. One serves as the Parliament House of the state of New South Wales. Its name derived from the fact that, in his efforts to stamp out the rum trade, Macquarie at one stage thought to control it by granting to three contractors (not including Macarthur!) an *official* three years' monopoly of the import of spirits. In return they built the hospital. History will never know how much more rum was smuggled into the colony or illicitly distilled there.

Macquarie's chief architect was an emancipist who had been transported for forgery, Francis Greenway, whom later generations have agreed to honour as an artist in brick and stone. The new governor consistently encouraged merit wherever he found it, even inviting deserving emancipists to dine at his table. One of Macquarie's ex-convict friends was William Redfern, a 23-year-old surgeon's mate in the Royal Navy when he was transported in 1797. When the crew of his ship mutinied, he was overheard by a fellow officer to advise them to "be more united among themselves", and thus he became a mutineer and a felon.[43] Not all of Macquarie's emancipist friends were such fine people as Redfern, but a vice-regal invitation to dine with any emancipist was more than most exclusionists could stomach. So two of them, Archibald McNaughton and Phillip Connor, lieutenants in Macquarie's own regiment, pointedly left his table one night early in 1813. A few weeks later in the dusk of a fine June evening, "flown with insolence and wine", and dressed in merry parti-coloured costumes, the two officers took a turn in the lower end of Pitt Street near the waters of Sydney Cove. There they met a young needlewoman, Elizabeth Winch, also taking the air with her lover, "John Brown the Painter". Apparently every emancipist girl knew what to do when confronted with military gentlemen. Elizabeth turned at once and ran for cover to the house of her employer, Mrs Ann Holness, with whom she lived at number 17 a few metres along the road.

Lieutenant Connor gave chase. To protect his sweetheart, Brown ran between them and was beaten about the head by Connor, who then walked some little distance away up the street. McNaughton continued to argue with Brown outside the locked door of number 17, behind which Mrs Holness and her boarder waited anxiously. When Connor returned to support McNaughton, Elizabeth bravely stepped out into the street, but only for long enough to persuade Brown to come back inside the house with her. The gentlemen then began to batter their way inside while the occupants pushed against the door to keep them out. Alerted by the din, Mr William Holness returned from a neighbour's house, which he had been visiting. When he asked what the drunken assailants wanted, they answered that they would have the two women, Ann Holness and Elizabeth Winch, and that they would "do

so and so to them and you too . . . making use of a very indecent expression".

At this the emancipated tradesman, described by several
witnesses as "a remarkably quiet man", replied, "I'll do so to
you", as he put his hand on Connor's chest and pushed him
away from the door. Both gentlemen then battered Holness
to death with sticks, fists, their boots and palings torn from a
nearby fence.

Those whom Macquarie officially named the murderers
were tried by a court presided over by Ellis Bent, the judge-
advocate, and comprising five mess-mates of the accused and
two other officers from the Royal Volunteer Corps. The luckless Holness's body was examined by four medical gentlemen
including D'Arcy Wentworth. They all swore to the opinion
that death had been caused by "an effusion of blood in the
lungs", but said that they could find on the corpse no external
marks of violence sufficiently severe to have caused it. The
fatal effusion, they thought, was much more likely to have
been caused by the very violence of the dead man's passionate anger than by any slight violence inflicted by those who
had sought to rape his spouse. So the honourable military
court was able to find Connor and McNaughton not guilty of
murder but "guilty of Feloniously killing and slaying the said
William Holness" and to impose on each the farcical penalty
of one shilling's fine and six months in Parramatta Gaol.[44]

Small wonder that the new viceroy came to the considered
conclusion that the emancipists, with all their sins upon their
heads, had done more for the prosperity and good order of the
country than those who considered themselves their betters.
During the last two years of his term, the British government
sent out an able lawyer, J.T. Bigge, to report on the colony
and on Macquarie's administration of it. The old viceroy's
view of the factions in New South Wales was made clear in a
letter he wrote to Commissioner Bigge during 1819. Here is
an extract with emphatically muddled syntax and indignantly
explosive capitals, just as it sputtered from his quill.

You already know that Nine-tenths of the population of this Colony
are or have been Convicts, or the Children of Convicts. You have Yet

perhaps to learn that these are the people who have Quietly submitted to the Laws and Regulations of the Colony, altho' informed by the *Free Settlers* and some of the Officers of Government that they were illegal: these are the Men who have tilled the Ground, who have built Houses and Ships, who have made wonderful Efforts, Considering the Disadvantages under which they have Acted, in Agriculture, in Maritime Speculations, and in Manufacturers; these are the Men who, placed in the balance as Character, both Moral and political (at least since their Arrival here) in the opposite Scale to those Free Settlers (who Struggle for their Depression) whom you will find to preponderate.[45]

We have seen that bitter class feelings existed in Australia before Macquarie's time. Perhaps his emancipist policy did something to accentuate them. It certainly did in the opinion of leading exclusionist spokesmen like Macarthur, who successfully obtained the ear of Bigge and decisively influenced the tenor of his official report. More than ever the emancipists and their children felt that Australia, as it was beginning to be called, was *their* country, founded for them and their descendants. Yet Macquarie's period had also instituted profound changes that were to strengthen the influence of the free immigrants even more in the long run.

When he sailed for Britain, New South Wales was no longer primarily a prison farm measuring some 60 kilometres from east to west and from north to south – extensive by British standards, it is true, but still hemmed in between the Blue Mountains and the Pacific. In 1813 a way across the range had been found by a party which included young W.C. Wentworth, son of the old doctor, and one of the first and most illustrious native white Australians. Six years later he wrote, of the western plains stretching away beyond the Great Divide, that they were "admirably suited for the pasture of sheep, the wool of which will without doubt eventually become the principal export of this colony, and may be conveyed across the mountains at an inconsiderable expense".[46] Not everyone at the time shared Wentworth's vision. Nevertheless, almost limitless pastures for the expansion of the wool industry stood waiting. The Bank of New South Wales, which flaunted its contempt for tradition in 1982 by renaming

itself Westpac, was founded in 1817, mainly by some successful emancipists, with the governor's encouragement. Cedar-
cutting in the coastal brushes had joined whaling and sealing
to furnish profitable export commodities. Wholesale importers and traders were firmly established in Sydney and Hobart, and retail trading had begun. Few people still depended
directly on the communal government store, as all had done
in the foundation years and most still did on Macquarie's arrival. Bigge's *Report* to the home government urged that extensive parcels of land, principally for stock raising, should be
granted to respectable free immigrants in proportion to the
amount of capital they brought with them to invest. With
cheap assigned convict labour, the profits to be made in pastoralism were very tempting, and an increasing stream of
well-to-do free immigrants arrived to take advantage of the
new arrangements.

Yet the harvest lay for the most part in the future. Only the
seeds had been planted during Macquarie's regime, some of
them unwittingly. In any case, the old chieftain received little
official credit for his exertions. Bigge's *Report* condemned his
emancipist policy and his "extravagant" building program –
unjustly as it has seemed to posterity. At the same time, the
report recognised economic reality by advocating the development of a large-scale wool industry for the future, thereby
at least tacitly condemning the effort of past governors to
carry out government policy; for, insofar as the Home authorities can be divined to have had an economic policy for the colony, it had been to encourage the development of a large class
of (mainly emancipist) small-holding agriculturalists. Macquarie was given an affectionate farewell by thousands of his
subjects.[47] When he sailed for the last time out of Sydney
Harbour in the *Surry* on 15 February 1822, New South Wales
was considerably more prosperous, and somewhat less turbulent and wicked, than it had been on his arrival.

It was also much more extensive. In pursuance of his instructions, and of the elusive flax plant, Phillip had despatched Philip Gidley King to settle Norfolk Island within a
few weeks of the First Fleet's arrival in Sydney. By 1799 a

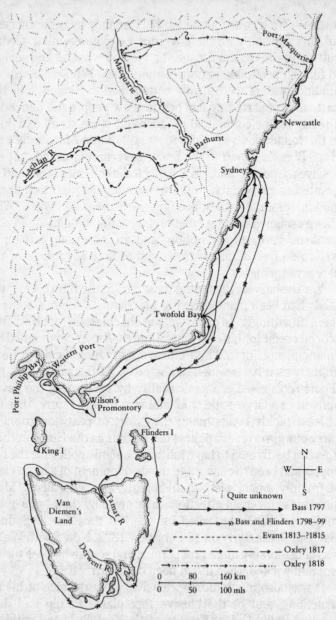

Figure 11 Southeast Australia showing main sea and land exploration until Macquarie's departure in 1821

young naval surgeon, George Bass, had explored the coast-line south of Sydney in some detail, discovered Western Port and circumnavigated Van Diemen's Land, examining *en route* the estuaries of the Tamar and the Derwent. In 1803 he dis-appeared after leaving Sydney on a trading voyage to South America, but his name lived on in Bass Strait.

He had been accompanied on several of his exploratory voyages by another young naval officer, Matthew Flinders, who proved to be second only to Cook as a navigator and hy-drographer. Promoted commander in 1801, he left England in HMS *Investigator* to explore the still unknown coast be-tween Nuyts' Land at the head of the Great Australian Bight and what is now known as the Victorian coast. He thus be-came the first European to see most of the shoreline of South Australia, which he charted accurately. At Encounter Bay opposite Kangaroo Island, on 8 April 1802, he met Captain Nicholas Baudin of the French Navy, who had been following the coast westwards. A month later he dropped anchor in Port Jackson and had the leaky and rotten *Investigator* over-hauled. In July he sailed again on what was to be his greatest achievement, the first circumnavigation of Australia since Tasman's. Unlike the Dutchman, he mapped the coast in de-tail as he proceeded northward. On the Gulf of Carpentaria's shores he was puzzled by numerous indications of recent visits by Asian ships. Finally, at an anchorage off the north-eastern corner of Arnhem Land, which he named Malay Road, the *Investigator* fell in with six Malay proas engaged in fishing for trepang. As the ship's cook was a Malay, Flinders was able to talk easily with Pobassoo, the Malay commander and his captains, who told him there were sixty vessels alto-gether in their fleet. Being Muslims, they exhibited disgust at the sight of pigs but, said Flinders, "had no objection to port wine".[48]

When the *Investigator* returned to Port Jackson in June 1803, relations with France were by no means as cordial as had been his meeting with Baudin in Encounter Bay. Gover-nor King had been alarmed by Baudin's visit to Sydney over a year before and had urged the British government to fore-

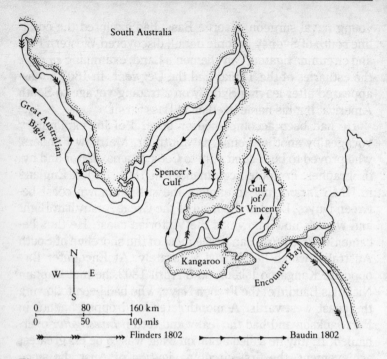

Figure 12   French and English meet in South Australia

stall French designs by planting settlements in the Bass Strait area. He sent a party under Lieutenant John Bowen to settle at Risdon Cove in the Derwent estuary while the erstwhile judge-advocate of New South Wales, Colonel David Collins, sailed from England in charge of 450 marines and convicts to plant the flag in the Port Phillip area. Collins was dismayed by the lack of wood and water on the inner shore of the peninsula near the present site of Sorrento. After only about three months he took his party to the Derwent, where they joined Bowen's smaller band to found Hobart in 1804. In the same year King sent Lieutenant-Colonel Paterson of the New South Wales Corps with seventy-five convicts to found another outpost at Launceston on the Tamar estuary.

Thus began the settlement of Europeans in Van Diemen's Land and the extermination of the original settlers, a process virtually completed within the Biblical span of one man's life-time, three score years and ten. Most of the four or five thousand Tasmanians were killed in the first twenty years of contact with the whites – by the time that the island was made into a separate colony in 1825, administered directly from Britain and no longer responsible to the governor of New South Wales. Many were murdered by white soldiers or police or respectable settlers, but probably many more by assigned convict servants or absconders who had become bushrangers. Many too, especially women, aided in the establishment of white Australia's first major industry – whaling and sealing.

Known to contemporaries as "the fisheries", this industry provided the first "staple" export commodity which flax and ship's timbers failed to furnish. Up until about 1834, whale and seal oil, whale bone and seal skins made up easily the most lucrative part of colonial exports. Only then were "the fisheries" overtaken by wool. American and British whale ships frequently visited Sydney and Hobart Town, especially after the East India Company's monopoly came to an end in 1813, but the industry was largely in the hands of emancipists and native-born people. In Sydney the most prominent firm engaged in "the fisheries" in the 1800s was that of Kable and Underwood, two ex-convicts who had come out with the First Fleet. One of Kable's native-born sons, "Young Kable", became the leading bare-knuckle prize-fighter in the 1820s. People of this sort, for the most part, built the ships of eucalypt hardwoods and provided the finance and the crews. They also kidnapped hundreds of Tasmanian and mainland Aboriginal women to be exploited both as expert seal-hunters and sexual slaves. As James Kelly, a sealing captain of Hobart Town, put it in 1816, "the custom of the sealers in the Straits was that every man should have from two to five of these native women for their own use and benefit, and to select any of them they thought proper to cohabit with as their wives".[49] On one sealing trip in 1816, Kelly circumnavigated Van Diemen's Land in a clockwise direction for the first time. He made great use of female Aboriginal seal-hunters and boasted of the great profit he made on the trip. A surviving portrait shows what later generations of Australians would have called a "flash", bumptious, "two-bob lair" or larrikin. Born in 1791, this "Currency" lad was the son of an Irish convict woman.[50]

Ships often landed parties of men at lonely spots on the south coast, or on islands in Bass Strait, or even far out in the ocean, to collect seals. These people were often left alone for months or years at a time and sometimes, if their "mother ship" was wrecked, until they died. Usually they brutally ill-used Aboriginal women whom they had kidnapped. In South Australia a legend still tells of a beautiful young Aboriginal woman who was snatched away from her child on the mainland and taken to the permanent camp of sealers established on Kangaroo Island from 1804 onwards. She eluded her captors and swam back across Backstairs Passage through 14 kilometres of shark-infested waters to her child and her tribe. Though told with many fanciful embellishments, the story is true down to the unusual comeliness of its heroine.[51] Such things certainly happened hundreds of times. By the end of Macquarie's reign in 1822, most of the southern Australian coasts and islands and even places as far afield as Macquarie Island, halfway to the Antarctic continent, had been visited or lived on by these brutal off-scourings of the convict system, and the population of Aborigines and seals had been reduced by about half. Aborigines living near Sydney had been dispersed and debauched. A contemporary engraving by an American artist, Augustus Earle, shows their state more graphically than volumes of print could do.

Whaling and sealing were the main, but not the only, maritime occupations of early Australians. Until pastoralism surged ahead in the late 1830s, the prevailing odour in white Australia was one of rum and tar, not greasy wool and gum trees. As Alan Frost has shown, the decision to occupy "Botany Bay" in the first place was taken primarily in answer to "a naval question". The first four governors were naval officers. The first settlements at Sydney, Norfolk Island, Hobart, Launceston, Newcastle, Moreton Bay and the rest were virtually island-ports, which communicated with each other and with the rest of the world only by sea. Rum — "Nelson's blood", the preferred drink of British seamen — lubricated the colonial economy, the social intercourse and the dreams and nightmares of the colonists alike. People looked outward to the ocean for inspiration and profit, not inward to the unknown, dry interior of the continent. By the 1830s there were few islands in the Pacific which had not felt the influence, good and bad, of Australian ships and Australian men, most of them convict bolters or Currency people. As early as 1809 King Kamehameha of Hawaii, for instance, employed a convict "bolter", William Stevenson, and seven of his mates as official distillers of rum to the court. To later Australians it may seem ironic that they built their still at Pearl Bay, now known as Pearl Harbor. These men already spoke English with an Australian "accent", as do Fijians and both Maoris and Pakehas in New Zealand to this day.

A Scottish sailor reported the following conversation with "Long William":

> "Sir," he said, "me 'ouse is on a bit of a rise and from me front [veranda] you can see all over your land, and if any of those bloody Indians are loafing on the job you can tell it without stirring a step, and loaf the buggers will, if you let 'em. I've got two of them tending me still, this minute, and iffen I don't look out they'll let the fire out in a jiffy. God strike me pink if they won't, and the mash all spoiled to hell an' gone. You'll find it pays Mr Campbell, to keep an eye cocked and make 'em watch their paces, the easy-going bastids, if you'll pardon me langwidge, sir."
>
> Here was indeed a language which was new to me though not for its oaths. It was like Cockney such as I had heard about the docks in London, but Cockney with a different flavour and with queer turns of speech that those who lived in New Holland or Australia soon acquired.[52]

After whale and seal products the most important commodity in Pacific commerce was timber. The beautiful red cedar wood, which once grew prolifically in the rainforests of coastal New South Wales, was felled and floated down the coastal rivers by old hands and their Currency offspring. From the rivermouths it was taken away in Australian ships more often than not, to Sydney, Hobart and London or other overseas ports.[53] The same colonial ships developed a lucrative trade in sandalwood, carried from Melanesian and Polynesian islands to Chinese and Southeast Asian ports, where it was made into magnificent furniture for the affluent and incense for the religious. Emancipist and Currency merchants shared too in the business which British leaders from Cook to Pitt had hoped would provide the staple commodity for export from New South Wales — timber for shipbuilding.

Most of this, especially wood for masts and spars, came from New Zealand. This meant that it was a dangerous trade, for to the everyday risk of shipwreck was added the chance of being killed, cooked and eaten by Maori or Melanesian warriors who were by no means as backward in the art of warfare as their Aboriginal counterparts. In 1809, for example, the ship *Boyd* sailed for New Zealand to pick up a cargo of spars for London. Among the passengers was Ann Glassop, convict mistress of William Broughton, Deputy Commissary of New South Wales and a magistrate, who had arrived in the First Fleet as a servant to Surgeon White. Ann Glassop was taking her 2-year-old daughter, Elizabeth Isabella Broughton, to England, apparently to visit some of her other children by Broughton who were being educated there. The *Boyd* anchored in the Bay of Islands,[54] that early New Zealand rendezvous of tough Maoris and scoundrelly whites, but was lured away by the promise of spars some 50 kilometres to Whangaroa. In New Zealand, as like as not, massacres were carried out by the first-comers, not the invaders. All the crew and passengers of the *Boyd* were killed and eaten except for a Mrs Morley and her infant, a boy named Thomas Davis and 2-year-old Betsy Broughton. A few months later the survivors were rescued by Alexander Berry, also seeking a cargo of spars, and put ashore in Lima, Peru, where the infant Betsy was looked after for eleven months by a certain Don Gaspar de Rico. She was brought back to her father in Sydney by a passing British ship and lived to marry the nephew and heir of Charles Throsby, the early explorer of the Illawarra and Goulburn districts, Charles Throsby Jnr. By him she had seventeen children, some of whom became the ancestors of many prominent Australians.[55] Betsy Broughton's most illustrious descendant was the commanding officer of the first AIF, Major-General Sir W.T. Bridges who, before he was killed at Gallipoli, ensured that Australian troops would retain their own identity throughout the Great War and not be distributed among British units as they had been in the Boer War fifteen years earlier.

By the end of Macquarie's governorship, white Australian traders had been seen and white Australian voices heard all over the Pacific. On the mainland the mountains had been crossed, as we have seen, and sparse pastoral occupation of the interior had just begun to spread out from Bathurst. To the south, settlement had spread through the Illawarra district and inland to the neighbourhood of the present site of Moss Vale and the Cockbundoon Range. To the north, Governor King had begun the first permanent white settlement at Newcastle as a place of secondary punishment for the rebellious Irish convicts defeated at the "Battle" of Vinegar Hill in 1804. The Hunter Valley and the Illawarra district had been settled, if sparsely, by cedar-getters, coalminers and others.

Much has been written in this chapter of the depravity of early Australian society. It would be misleading to end it without mentioning moral changes for the better which were already becoming visible before Macquarie's departure. Governor Hunter wrote in 1798:

> A more wicked, abandoned, and irreligious set of people have never been brought together in any part of the world . . . order and morality is not the wish of the inhabitants; it interferes with the private views and pursuits of individuals of various descriptions.[56]

The "national children" of the official documents were known popularly as "Currency lads and lasses," originally because, like the makeshift local currency of the early days – Spanish or "Holey" dollars with "dumps" punched out of their centres, traders' tokens, notes-of-hand and so forth – they were a local product not imported from Britain, as were free immigrants, convicts and a trickle of sterling coinage.[57] Some of these Currency children could hardly have known who their parents were. Perhaps they were better off than those who did since, in the eyes of respectable contemporaries, most of their fathers were drunken and demoralised habitual criminals, and most of their mothers equally drunken and demoralised prostitutes. Small wonder that godly people like Reverend Samuel Marsden feared the worst for the thousands of "national children" growing up in these conditions. For the first twenty-five years or so of Australia's history, observers were almost unanimous in expecting that the native-born would reproduce the manners and morals attributed to their progenitors. Yet no such thing happened.

Commissioner Bigge, we have seen, was by no means predisposed to view the convict and emancipist classes favourably. Yet in his *Report on Agriculture and Trade*, issued in 1823, the classic statement on the transformation of their children occurs:

> The class of inhabitants that have been born in the colony affords a remarkable exception to the moral and physical character of their parents: they are generally tall in person, and slender in their limbs, of fair complexion and small features. They are capable of undergoing more fatigue, and are less exhausted by labour than native Europeans; they are active in their habits but remarkably awkward in their movements. In their tempers they are quick and irascible, but not vindictive; and I only repeat the testimony of persons who have had many opportunities of observing them, that they neither inherit the vices nor feelings of their parents.[58]

There is not the slightest doubt that such a reform did take place. Contemporary evidence is practically unanimous. For instance, Peter Cunningham, a hard-headed Scots surgeon, wrote in 1827 of "the open and manly simplicity of character displayed by this part of our population . . . [which] . . . was little tainted by the vices so prominent among their parents . . . Drunkenness is almost unknown to them, and honesty proverbial."[59] And in 1834 even the dour Reverend Lang, whose talent for nosing out human wickedness was possibly unrivalled in the whole continent, wrote:

> I am happy, indeed, to be able to state, as the result of ten years' extensive observation in the colony, that drunkenness is by no means a vice to which the colonial youth of either sex are at all addicted.

Reared in the very midst of scenes of drunkenness of the most revolting description and of daily occurrence, they are almost uniformly temperate: for if there are exceptions, as I do acknowledge there are a few, the wonder, I had almost said the miracle, is that they have not been tenfold more numerous.[60]

The most convincing evidence is probably that of Sir William Burton, a justice of the New South Wales Supreme Court from 1833 until 1844. He was so impressed by the law-abiding nature of the Currency people that he inquired closely into the criminal statistics of the time.[61] From his data it has been shown that the first generation of white natives, as they were called at the time, were, at least in a statistical legal sense, *more* virtuous than any other class in the community including that of the free immigrants. Over the five-year period 1833–37, for instance, the average number of persons tried annually before Burton, per thousand of each of the four classes of people in the colony, was as follows: *Convict*, 3.4; *Emancipist*, 3.2; *Free immigrant*, 1.3; *Currency*, 1.0. Further, none of the crimes committed by Currency people in this period, Burton maintained, was of an atrocious kind punishable by death; and nearly half (thirteen out of thirty) were for stock-stealing, generally known as "cattle-duffing" — an activity not held to be criminal at all by popular Australian opinion until almost the present century. Robert D. Barton, uncle of "Banjo" Paterson and a respectable squatter, as an old man in 1917 could still write, without conscious humour:

The young Australians were, I think, strictly honest as regards money or valuables; you could leave your hut or house with everything open for days, perhaps weeks, and when you returned you would miss nothing, except, perhaps, that someone had made a pot of tea or got a feed, which, of course, they were all entitled to, and never refused. But, from my earliest recollections, the branding of other people's calves was not looked upon as a crime . . . and the killing of cattle for meat on the place was almost invariably done at someone else's expense. However, that condition of things gradually changed, but a great many men never realised the change . . . but continued their depredations, which were then called cattle-stealing.[62]

How did these Currency men and women rise above the in-

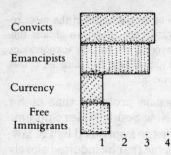

Convicts

Emancipists

Currency

Free
Immigrants

1   2   3   4

Figure 13 Class origin of the persons committed to Sydney Gaol and tried before Burton

fluence of their surroundings? Not by a miracle, as the Reverend Lang was tempted to suppose. The main reason seems to have been that most emancipist parents, though they commonly cohabited without clerical licence or divine blessing, were in other ways reformed and normally decent people, like Ann Glassop, who provided good homes for their offspring. They were not nearly as immoral as they were painted by respectable middle-class observers.[63] Secondly, compared with those in Great Britain at the time, Australian conditions offered a very good living to anyone able and willing to work. There was an almost continuous labour shortage, especially in the bush, partly because in a seemingly limitless wilderness inhabited by very few people the sheer quantity of urgently necessary work also seemed to be limitless, and partly because so much of the labour force was highly inefficient. We have already seen how convicts had to be bribed with incentive payments to improve upon the "government-stroke" which was their preferred, go-slow method of working. Yet most employers found convict labour much more efficient than that of most free immigrants, who were unaccustomed to Australian conditions. Under these conditions, free *and* experienced labour was at such a premium that even children could command good wages — and did. It seems incredible, but contemporary documents abound with evidence of 10- to 15-year-old boys carrying out responsible and sometimes lonely jobs. Thirteen- and 14-year-olds commonly drove bullock-teams on long cross-country journeys; young Albert Wright for many years managed a remote western sheep-station, alone except for one half-mad shepherd. Thus colonial conditions provided the economic opportunity for young people to become precociously self-reliant. The environment was such as to enable and promote the reaction of Currency children away from overtly depraved convict-emancipist characteristics. Thus Bigge's *Report on the State of the Colony* (1822) noted that young Currency men were unwilling to marry convict women, owing "chiefly to a sense of pride in the native-born youths, approaching to contempt for the vices and depravity of the convicts even when manifested in the persons of their own parents".[64]

There were, of course, other convict-emancipist attitudes, not necessarily vicious in themselves — such as group loyalty, or hatred of informers and of affected manners — which the rising generation of young Australians saw no reason to reject. Historians have too long been mesmerised by the horrors of the convict system and the depravity of many of its victims, forgetting the Gospel statement that a person is never defiled by what is done to him or her, but only by the person's own deeds. In this perspective, early Australian history surely gives much cause for pride and little for shame. From the most unpromising possible material there developed in a few short years the self-reliant progenitors of a free and generous people — generous, that is, to all save foreigners and the black people from whom they were taking the country. By 1821 New South Wales had begun to be something much more than the miserable slave farm which had been founded thirty-three years earlier. Not only was a vigorous and self-respecting generation of native-born people growing up, but a new class of respectable free immigrants, not mainly dependent upon the colonial civil or military establishments, had begun to make its appearance.

3 New settlements and new pastures
c. 1821–50

Between 1821 and 1851, important new colonies were founded on remote parts of the Australian coastline, much of the habitable interior was effectively explored and then stolen from the Aborigines by pastoralists and their men, and a distinctively Australian ethos began to take shape — at least among the mass of the population, if not so much among the more cultivated minority. At the same time, the colonies were moving steadily towards self-government. We shall consider these major developments and some of the relationships between them — the planting of new settlements, political reform, the great "squatting rush" to the interior, and the growth of a characteristic outlook. All were strongly influenced in one way or another by the convict system, for the importation of felons to mainland eastern Australia continued until 1840, and to Van Diemen's Land until 1852 (after which the island colony was known as Tasmania). In fact, the great majority of all convicts sent to Australia were transported during these years.

"Botany Bay" had been chosen as the first site for British occupation partly because it offered a suitably remote "dumping ground" for felons. In the same way, many of the first settlement sites beyond Hobart and Sydney were chosen because they were suitably remote from the two colonial capitals, and it was thought that escape from them would be difficult — as it usually was. Thus when Newcastle was settled in 1804, and for at least fourteen years afterwards, there was no possibility of communication with Sydney except by a sea voyage of 160 kilometres. Macquarie Harbour, founded on Van Diemen's Land's west coast by Lieutenant-Governor William Sorell in 1822, was separated from the settled districts by mountains and rainforests so dense that the Aborigines avoided them for 20 000 years and they still resist white occupation today. Such penal stations were established as places of "secondary punishment" — remote gaols for transportees convicted of further crimes or misdemeanours in Australia. Legend has perhaps exaggerated the quantity, but not the severity, of the inhumanly cruel and often illegal tortures inflicted on prisoners at these places. Hundreds of men preferred to die rather than to go on living in them.[1]

As white settlement spread, it tended to make one penal station after another no longer remote enough. Thus when Benjamin Singleton, a Currency lad from Windsor, discovered a passable overland route to the lower Hunter valley and Newcastle in 1818,[2] he greatly reduced the usefulness of "Coal River" as a place of secondary punishment. So another was established in 1821 at Port Macquarie, a further 160 kilometres or more to the north, and yet another three years later, further north still, at "Moreton Bay" on the Brisbane River. Port Macquarie in its heyday was reported to be a comparatively pleasant place of exile, while Moreton Bay under its second commandant, Captain Logan, was believed to be an earthly hell for its inmates. Apparently Logan treated the Aborigines equally harshly, for he was "murdered" by them after only five years in office. According to legend, the black Australians were privily egged on to the deed by the whites, who also suffered under Logan's rule. As the old convict ballad, *Moreton Bay*, has it:

> Like the Egyptians and ancient Hebrews,
>> We were oppressed under Logan's yoke,
> Till a native Black lying hid in ambush
>> Did give our tyrant his mortal stroke.
> My fellow prisoners, be exhilarated
>> That all such monsters such a death may find,
> And when from bondage we are extricated,
>> Our former sufferings shall fade from mind.[3]

Port Curtis 1847

Moreton
Bay 1824

Hastings R

Port Macquarie
1821

Coal R
1804

Newcastle

Sydney

N
W   E
S

0   160   320 km
0   100   200 mls

Figure 14   New penal settlements

The most notorious of all penal stations were Port Arthur in Tasmania and Norfolk Island. The latter, as we have seen, was first occupied a few weeks after the arrival of the First Fleet at Port Jackson, but it was intended as a flax farm, not as a place of secondary punishment. Abandoned in 1813, it was reoccupied as a penal station from 1825 to 1856. For four years from 1840, Norfolk Island men were ruled by Alexander Maconochie, one of the greatest penal reformers and humanitarians of his day. For seven years from 1846 its luckless prisoners were flogged and tortured mercilessly by John Price, one of the most severe disciplinarians ever to disgrace the Queen's uniform. In 1857, as Inspector-General of Prisons in Victoria, he was battered to death with picks and shovels by a group of convicts, which included some of his old charges from Norfolk Island.[4] When the penal establishment was closed in 1856, the island was settled by some of the descendants of the *Bounty* mutineers, for whom there was no longer living space on Pitcairn Island.

Port Arthur was established in 1830 by the newly appointed Governor Sir George Arthur, a devout Anglican who believed with Samuel Marsden that to spare the rod would be to spoil the prisoners in this life and condemn them to hell in the next one. Though only about 100 kilometres from Hobart, the place was deemed suitable because it was situated on a peninsula joined to the mainland by a strip of land only 70 metres wide and known as Eaglehawk Neck. Guards and savage dogs were kept in a line across the Neck and it is said that only four convicts ever escaped from Port Arthur. The peculiarly evil reputation of the place probably derives from the fact that it continued to serve as a purgatory for criminals until 1876, a full twenty-five years after transportation to Tasmania had come to an end.

Beyond the farthest penal stations, other coastal outposts were established, as Sydney had been, partly for strategic and commercial reasons. After the Napoleonic Wars, Britain continued to fear a French *revanche* and to compete with the Dutch for a greater share of the rich trade of the Malay Archipelago. Penang was founded by a British East India man, Francis Light, father of Colonel William Light, the surveyor of Adelaide. In 1824, to support Penang, Fort Dundas was built among sandbanks and mangrove swamps on Melville Island, a little north of the present site of Darwin. Naturally not one Asian ship was seen by the Fort's soldiers and convicts before those who survived scurvy, fever and malnutrition left in 1829. Undaunted, London sent Captain James Stirling in 1827 to found a second trading post at Raffles Bay about 300 kilometres east of Fort Dundas. As Stirling chose a place where the Macassar men clearly came regularly to fish for trepang, Fort Wellington promised succes. In the 1829 trepang season, thirty-four proas, carrying more than 1000 men, visited the fort, but in that very year London, still believing that not one Malay ship had been seen there, ordered its abandonment.[5] Within a decade there was another French scare. To frustrate the desperately clever continentals and also to capture some of the Southeast Asian trade, another outpost was established at Port Essington in 1838. It was abandoned in turn in 1849, a few years after Leichhardt's first expedition had made its way overland from the Moreton Bay district. So the first permanent white settlement was not made until 1868 at Palmerston (Port Darwin), after the territory had been handed over to South Australia by the New South Wales government.

Two other settlements were planted from Sydney in 1826, not so much as trading outposts as to forestall supposed French designs. Early in that year a French expedition under Dumont d'Urville visited Australian and New Zealand waters, reconnoitring, among other places, Shark's Bay on the western edge of Australia and Western Port on the northern shores of Bass Strait. Governor Darling was promptly ordered to despatch soldiers and convicts from Sydney to raise the flag at both places. Western Port was abandoned when the "French scare" receded after only two years and Earl Bathurst, Secretary of State, changed his mind about Shark's Bay almost as soon as his orders had been despatched. Shark's Bay after all had practically no wood, water or fertile soil, but it did have what Englishmen thought a beastly hot climate. King George's Sound near the southern tip of Western Australia had plenty of the desired commodities, was "in the track" of ships to Sydney, had arguably a finer harbour than Port Jackson and also a splendid, or at least reasonably cool, climate. Major Lockyer's garrison hoisted the Union Jack there on Christmas Day 1826.[6]

While these official efforts to attract Asian trade to three north Australian ports all failed abjectly, unofficial trade with the South Seas and with Asia flourished. By 1851 few Melanesian Islands remained unvisited by Australian ships seeking (not always in the gentlest or most honest ways) cargoes of sandalwood for China, and there were few parts of the whole Pacific and Southern Oceans which had not been searched for whales and seals by sailors from Sydney and Hobart Town. One of their most bizarre exploits was carried out by the crew of the Sydney brig *Lady Rowena*. On April Fools' Day 1831, Captain Bourn Russell anchored in a bay on the east coast of Hokkaido, northernmost of the main islands of

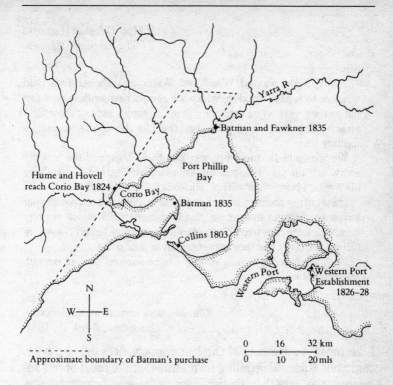

Figure 15 Whites occupy Port Phillip

the Japanese Empire, and opened what could justly be described as undiplomatic relations between Australia and Japan. Going ashore next day the Australians met "a few inotched [innocuous?] creatures, the Aborigines of the land of Tartars." As these Ainu people and their Japanese overlords were less than enthusiastic in supplying the *Lady Rowena* with wood and water, Russell and his crew sacked the local fort, burnt the village, robbed the temple and took prisoner one unlucky samurai who had fallen off his horse. Then, with that stupendous cheek that many thought the distinguishing feature of Currency men, with all the flashness of Captain James Kelly of Hobart Town or that later wild colonial boy, Ned Kelly of Glenrowan, Captain Russell packed the prisoner off to his Emperor bearing a threatening letter:

To his Most Celestial Highness
The Emperor of Japan.

Sir,

. . . We only wanted Wood and Water and shelter from bad weather to repair our ship; which we should have willing paid for; but as they were so inhospitable: as not to supply us; but show fight after waiting many days; I chastised them for their perverseness; by fighting them.

We took one Japanese prisoner and their flags; and the rest ran away! and for presuming to fire on a stranger instead of supplying his wants; I burnt their village, and took what I wanted.

I hope all my countrymen will do the same, burn and destroy all your towns and Villages that refuse, that hospitality which is due to every man; which they are well able to do even in your city Jeddo [Tokyo] un-till [sic] you order that they may enter any of your ports . . .

With all respect you may conceive to be due you without degrading formalities,

I am,
Your obedient servant an Englishman,
Agitana, April, 15, 1831.

Like most Australians of the last century, Russell, we note, could not abide "degrading formalities". Like most of our ancestors, too, whether British-born as he was or not, he was quick, when dealing with those he considered ignorant foreigners, to claim British citizenship. After more voyaging in the South Seas he opened a store in West Maitland in 1835 and became one of the most respectable members of the Australian community – from 1858 to 1880 a life member of the Legislative Council of New South Wales.[7]

Exploration of inland Australia can hardly be said to have begun until the first track across the Blue Mountains was found, more probably by their Aboriginal "guide" than by Blaxland, Wentworth and Lawson in 1813. Thereafter the discovery and mapping of southeastern Australia, the area between Tasmania, southern Queensland and central South Australia where more than three-quarters of all white Australians still live, proceeded apace. John Oxley, surveyor-general of New South Wales and G.W. Evans, his assistant, followed the rivers downstream south, west and northwest from the Bathurst district. Each time, because they were travelling in good seasons, progress ended in "an ocean of reeds". So by 1820 Oxley had fathered the myth of an inland sea into which, he believed, the western rivers must flow. In 1827 Allan Cunningham, a gifted botanist, journeyed from the Hunter Valley north across the Liverpool Plains and the New England Plateau to discover the Darling Downs and to view "Cunningham's Gap" which, he correctly guessed, would give access to the coastal plain and the recently established penal station at Moreton Bay. In 1824–25 a Currency lad named Hamilton Hume joined William Hovell, an immigrant sea-captain, to find an overland route to the northern coast of Bass Strait. The government provided them with a tent and a few pack-saddles, but little else. They reached Corio Bay by a track through the bush, roughly along the line of today's Hume Highway. They discovered and named the mighty river which has, since 1850, formed the boundary between the two most populous Australian colonies. They called it the Hume, but Sturt later renamed it after an undistinguished but gentlemanly Secretary of State for the Colonies, Sir George Murray. Hume and Hovell spent much of the rest of their lives quarrelling over their shares of the credit for their discovery, as they had quarrelled through the journey. They both thought they had reached Western Port, not any part of Port Phillip. Hovell was eleven years older than Hume and a much more respectable person. He was the better navigator while Hume was a better bushman. A reading of the pamphlets they both published makes it clear that Hume thought Hovell a pretentious and impractical "new chum", while Hovell considered Hume a coarse and low colonial.[8]

The myth of an inland sea was finally laid to rest by an English army officer, Captain Charles Sturt. Sent to Sydney in charge of the guard on a convict transport in 1827, he used his influence with Governor Darling to gain command of the next expedition sent to explore the new country to the west of the Blue Mountains. The newly appointed Surveyor-General, T.L. Mitchell, objected vigorously, holding that his position

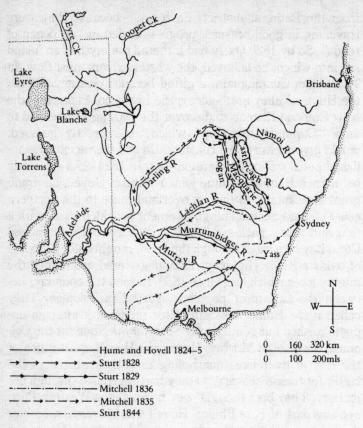

Figure 16   Exploring the southeast of the continent

Legend:
— · · — Hume and Hovell 1824–5
→ → → → Sturt 1828
•—•—•—• Sturt 1829
— · — · — Mitchell 1836
— — → — Mitchell 1835
————— Sturt 1844

0   160   320 km
0   100   200 mls

entitled him to the control of all exploration in the colony. This crusty and quarrelsome Scottish Tory hated Sturt for the rest of his life. Though no less conservative in temperament than Mitchell, Sturt had the wisdom to choose the native-born Hume as second-in-command of his first expedition. They followed the Macquarie River westward and then swung north along the Bogan until it joined "a noble river" which they named after the governor. They followed the Darling downstream for a week, returned to their base and then traced the course of the Castlereagh River northwestwards until it too joined the Darling. A year later, in November 1829, Sturt led a second expedition from a station near Gundagai to trace the course of the Murrumbidgee. At its junction with the Lachlan, the party boarded a small whale-boat and rowed downstream until it joined a "broad and noble river" which Sturt named the Murray. Coming to its junction with the Darling, Sturt rowed northwards far enough to convince himself it was indeed the lower end of the river whose higher reaches he had discovered earlier. Then they rowed on to Lake Alexandrina and gazed sadly at the shifting, narrow channel through which the water of all the western rivers flows to the sea. There was no sign of the ship Sir Ralph Darling had promised to send, and no possibility that it could have approached the shallow, surf-covered shore if he had kept his word. So the convict hands, exhausted and half-starving as they were, rowed back 1500 kilometres against the current to safety.

In 1830 Sturt was sent to command the garrison at Norfolk Island penal station. While there he suppressed a convict rising, but with such humanity as to retain the respect even of the mutineers. After a period of leave in England, where he married the daughter of an old friend, Sturt returned to Sydney, emigrated to the new "province" of South Australia and set out from Adelaide in 1844 on his last journey of exploration. Having done more than anyone else to show that the western rivers flowed into the Southern Ocean, Sturt, oddly, still believed in the existence of an inland sea; and yet not so oddly, as we now know the Diamantina, the Finke, Cooper's Creek and other rivers do drain inland to Lake Eyre. Sturt, like others of the time, was not to know that the rivers and the inland sea to which they flowed were usually bone dry. The expedition struck out northwestwards from the Darling and established a base on permanent water at Depot Glen in the far northwestern corner of the present state of New South Wales. Pinned down there for six months by a terrible drought, Sturt then pushed forward 700 kilometres to the red sand-dunes of what is now known as the Simpson Desert before admitting defeat. The rest is anti-climax. Half-blinded by what our ancestors called "sandy blight", he failed to secure a colonial governorship or any other position to which his achievements and services to the state entitled him. His failure to impress the great people of the world was balanced by the honour in which he was held by subordinates, convict servants, Aborigines and posterity. As we have seen, even mutinous convicts, whom he punished at Norfolk Island, respected the man.[9]

When Governor Darling left New South Wales in 1831, Sturt lost his patron and the cantankerous Mitchell immediately succeeded to the *de facto* position of explorer-in-chief. He led four expeditions into the interior, of which only the last two opened up substantially new areas, respectively what has long been known as the Western District of Victoria and as south-central Queensland — the country around the Warrego, Belyando and Maranoa rivers. Mitchell himself thought his discovery of magnificent grazing and agricultural country between the Murray and the Victorian coast west of Port Phillip was his greatest achievement. He called it Australia Felix. Future generations have agreed to regard this area as the richest pastoral district in Australia, the citadel of wealthy "squatting" families such as that of the Prime Minister from 1975 to 1983, Malcolm Fraser. Contemporaries agreed, and even the faraway Colonial Office recommended that the intrepid Scot be dubbed a knight in 1839. Mitchell thought the country so beautiful that he wrote in his journal a passage which revealed, quite unconsciously, what a different kind of man he was from Sturt.

> The scene was different from anything I had ever before witnessed, either in New South Wales or elsewhere, a land so inviting and still without inhabitants. As I stood, the first intruder on the sublime solitude of those verdant plains as yet untouched by flocks or herds, I felt conscious of being the harbinger of mighty changes there.

Aboriginal "intruders" had inhabited the country for tens of thousands of years but Mitchell's actions, like the above words, showed that he may not have considered them to be fully human. On all his expeditions he treated them like wild animals to be shot or frightened out of his way. In all probability he first used the word "dispersion" as a white Australian euphemism for the murder of Aborigines. At any rate he named the place where the bloodiest affray occurred Mount Dispersion. It cannot be said that Sir Thomas was only a man of his times, no worse, in this respect, than most others. His behaviour was such that in 1836 the Legislative Council of New South Wales, a body not in the least distinguished by its tender regard for Aboriginal rights, was moved to set up an official inquiry into the events at Mount Dispersion. In the time-honoured manner of such bodies before and since, the inquiry white-washed Mitchell, finding merely that he could not be blamed for showing "a want of coolness and presence of mind which it is the lot of few men to possess".[10]

The two most notable explorers, who first traversed new country far beyond the southeastern corner of the continent and the Murray–Darling basin, were E.J. Eyre and Ludwig Leichhardt. Born in an English vicarage, Eyre arrived in Sydney in 1833 at the age of 18 and immediately went "up the country" to gain bush experience. He also gained excellent training for the work of exploration by becoming one of the first "overlanders" in Australia, taking stock from the Liverpool Plains to the Monaro district. Thence he drove another mob to the newly opened Port Phillip district, and in 1838 followed Joseph Hawdon's track along the Murray to become the second overlander to deliver stock to the new Adelaide market. Moving stock between colonies seems to have got into Eyre's blood. He spent the next few years in South Australia searching incessantly for what has never yet been found – a practicable stock-route between that colony and Western Australia. On two probes into the parched north of the province, he discovered Lake Torrens and Lake Eyre and learnt enough to know that in that part of the world the word "Lake" should always be printed in inverted commas. Then, after several probes westwards along the shore of the Great Australian Bight, he set out in 1841 from Fowler's Bay for King George's Sound. About nine weeks later two of the three Aborigines in the party murdered Baxter, Eyre's only white companion, and decamped with most of the supplies and firearms. With Wylie, a King George's Sound Aborigine, Eyre struggled on until they had the incredible luck to find a French whaler, the *Mississippi*, anchored in Thistle Cove near the present site of Esperance. The Frenchmen gave them a few days' rest aboard and a new supply of provisions which enabled them to walk to Albany. The whole journey had taken five months and should have proved that no stock-route from South Australia to the west would ever be found.[11]

Leichhardt was the son of a petty bureaucrat in Prussia. He was also what some later Australians would have called a university "dropout" and "con-man". He studied languages, philosophy and science at the Universities of Göttingen and Berlin, but left both places in 1836 before taking any degree − not, however, before making friends with a wealthy young Englishman on whose generosity he lived for the next few years. He seems indeed to have been supported for most of his life by the subscriptions, gifts, loans or hospitality of the rich and gullible. This is not to say that he was an ignoramus. Though he had no more legitimate claim to the designation of "Doctor" than Ned Kelly later had to that of "Archbishop", the title was thrust upon him by imperfectly lettered Australian colonists who were deeply − and rightly − impressed by his wide-ranging scholarship. Like a few later "dropouts", he was undoubtedly a genuinely learned man. Like more, he also had a genius for charming those on whom he depended for dinners and drinks. One of his Australian hosts described him as "the most amiable of men". It should not be surprising that most of those who depended on him, the men brave enough to accompany him in the field, found him careless, dirty, suspicious, jealous, almost incredibly gluttonous and hopelessly unfitted for the leadership of even a weekend bushwalk.[12] Nevertheless, he led three exploring expeditions, the first to glory, the second to abject failure and the third to mysterious but total disaster.

In 1845 Leichhardt led a party from Moreton Bay to Port Essington near the present site of Darwin. He covered about 3000 kilometres in less than fifteen months and returned by sea to a hero's welcome in Sydney, a government grant of

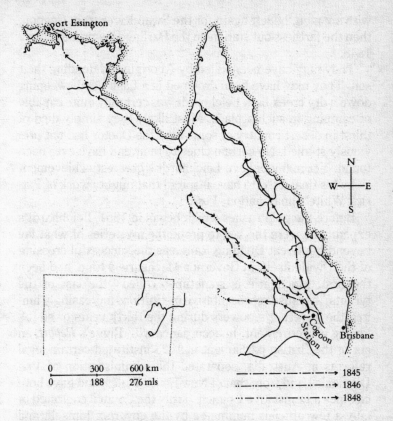

Figure 17 Ludwig Leichhardt's three journeys

£1000, and private gifts amounting to £1500. In the excitement, no one noticed that the whole journey had been made through reasonably well-watered country and that this lavishly equipped expedition had never had to face the problems surmounted by Eyre's much more Spartan band. A year later Leichhardt again set off from the Darling Downs with the grandiose plan of striking across the continent to the west coast and then following it south to the Swan River settlement. In the event he turned back after covering only about 900 kilometres through country quite close to his earlier route in what is now central Queensland. Still thirsting for glory, with six men, he left again for the Swan River from Cogoon, then the farthest-out station on the Darling Downs, on 3 April 1848.

They may have been killed by Aborigines defending their soil. They may have been drowned in a flash flood sweeping down a dry creek bed. Leichhardt was certainly quite capable of camping in such a place. Most likely they simply died of thirst in desert country of some kind the Doctor had not previously studied. No certain clues to their end have ever been found. Yet many believe Leichhardt's greatest achievement is, by his final folly, to have inspired that mighty work of Patrick White's imagination, *Voss*.[13]

Before the gold rushes which began in 1851, Leichhardt's expeditions were the last to probe the mysteries of what lay beyond the Great Dividing Range as the successful crossing of the Divide itself, in Governor Macquarie's time, had been the first. Macquarie is sometimes called "the last of the tyrants" because representative institutions increasingly limited the governor's powers during the thirty years or so following his retirement. In accordance with Bigge's *Report*, an act of the British parliament in 1823 instituted certain legal reforms in Australia, separated the administration of Van Diemen's Land from that of New South Wales, and gave both colonies a Legislative Council. True, the Council consisted of only a few officials nominated by the governor himself, and he could ignore their advice if he thought it wise to do so; but the chief justice now had to certify that every new ordinance was "consistent with the laws of England, so far as the circumstances of the colony will permit". That the governor's powers were no longer absolute was shown in 1827 when a liberal-minded chief justice of New South Wales, Sir Francis Forbes, refused to certify a law which sought to censor the colonial press.[14]

Partly as a result of this squabble, another imperial act of 1828 increased the size of the Council to fifteen. The act also deprived the chief justice of the power of veto. Instead it provided that if all the judges of the Supreme Court considered an act repugnant to English law, the Council must reconsider it. Then, however, the Council could promulgate the new law, if it wished to do so, pending a final decision by the secretary of state in London. All the Council members were still nominated by the governor. Eight of them were to be his chief administrative officials and seven were "unofficial" members, usually in practice leading exclusionists. Since the governor alone could introduce legislation, it is not surprising that disagreements between him and the Council were at first unusual.[15]

This remained the constitutional position until 1842, but throughout the period agitation for a greater measure of self-government increased. Most prominent in the movement was William Charles Wentworth (1790–1872) who, as a young Currency lad, had helped to find a way across the mountain barrier. His father, D'Arcy Wentworth, a connection of Earl Fitzwilliam, after being acquitted at the Old Bailey of highway robbery, had volunteered to join the Second Fleet as a surgeon. In New South Wales bond and free workmen thought him one of the best masters "that ever lived in the world". Young William Charles was educated at Cambridge University where he was runner-up for the Chancellor's Medal for poetry in 1823, but his mother had been a convict girl. By the 1840s he had become the most famous living Australian, yet such was the exaggerated *hauteur* of the exclusionists that as late as 1863, T.S. Mort, a successful Sydney businessman of middle-class but "untainted" background, could speak thus, without intentional humour of Wentworth:

> I have never met him in society as he did not move in the same spheres as myself. Had he visited with the principal families in the colony at that time I must have met him, as I exchanged visits with nearly the whole of them.[16]

Thus, as long as the convict system lasted, the bitter faction strife between emancipists and exclusionists helped to defer the granting of more liberal political institutions. Having already started a newspaper, the *Australian*, Wentworth in 1835 took a leading part in founding the Australian Patriotic Association. Composed mainly of emancipists and their sympathisers, this body yet established an influential lobby in the House of Commons and agitated for a representative leg-islature and other liberal institutions. Led by James Macar-thur, son of the "grand perturbator", the exclusionists lobbied parliament even more effectively. If reform was inev-itable, they wished to limit it, seeking at most extension of the powers of a larger, but still nominated, Council. Both factions desired the continuation of the convict system whcih pro-vided the cheap labour on which their wealth depended, yet the British government remained obstinately of the opinion that free institutions should not be granted to a society whose population still comprised a majority of convicted or emanci-pated felons and their descendants. Some of these who, with a few immigrant artisans, made up the embryonic working class of Sydney, had not much influence on events. When the Patriotic Association declared for the continuance of trans-portation in 1838, most working men withdrew their support. At the same time, the wealthy emancipists and the exclusion-ists began to find more common ground in politics, if not yet in social life.

The impasse was resolved in London rather than Sydney. In 1837–38 a select committee of the House of Commons, under the chairmanship of Sir William Molesworth, heard voluminous evidence and recommended the abolition of transportation to New South Wales.[17] Strongly influenced by Malthusian and Wakefieldian ideas, the committee was much more concerned to provide in New South Wales for the sur-plus population of the United Kingdom than it was with colo-nial self-government, but its recommendations led to the end of transportation to the eastern mainland, as well as to the as-sisted immigration in the 1840s of some 30 000 free immi-grants, many of them paupers from the workhouses and most of them unskilled or semi-skilled workers. The committee's recommendations also prepared the way for a larger measure of representative government. Practically no more convicts were sent to eastern mainland Australia.

In 1842 the membership of the Legislative Council was in-creased to thirty-six, two-thirds of whom were to be elected. Moreover, elected members might introduce topics for debate. However, the franchise was fixed so that only a minority of male citizens could vote, and no one could be elected to the Council unless he owned property worth at least £2000 — equivalent to something like $500 000 in terms of 1990 money values. The governor retained the power of nominating the twelve official members who remained responsible to him, and he retained control of Crown lands and the right, in the last resort, to veto any measure. Thus the new Council was not a very democratic body. Because of its composition, it was often far more conservative in outlook than the Queen's representative himself. It was sometimes termed the "Squatters' Council" because wealthy pastoralists tended to dominate its deliberations and its members spent a disproportionate amount of time wrangling with Governor Sir George Gipps (1838–46) over the conditions under which Crown lands were to be leased to themselves and their friends. It habitually went into recess for the shearing season. Nevertheless, the "Squatters' Council" did provide valuable training in the art of self-government. It acted, to some extent, as a genuine sounding board for public opinion. Its debates were fully reported in the newspapers and discussed, sometimes with passionate interest, by the colonists.[18]

Since convicts could no longer be sent to the mainland, many more – relatively – were shipped to Van Diemen's Land during the 1840s. For a period at the beginning of this decade, New South Wales suffered from a severe labour shortage at the very time when insufficient work could be found for the mass of convict and emancipist labour in Van Diemen's Land. The island colony, since convictism continued, had to remain discontented with its nominated Legislative Council.

In 1840 the territory of New South Wales still included most of eastern Australia – roughly the areas of present-day Queensland, Victoria and the eastern part of the Northern Territory, in addition to that which still constitutes the mother colony; but by that date all the other major colonies had been founded in fact if not in legal form. Oddly enough, Britain laid no formal claim to the western third of New Hol-

Figure 18 Boundary changes and foundation of new colonies

land until nearly forty years after the first settlement at Sydney. Possibly there was a vague feeling that it belonged to the Dutch who, however, continued to show no interest in it. As we have seen, the British government eventually claimed Western Australia in 1826, when it established an outpost at King George's Sound. Albany, as the King George's Sound settlement came to be called, was about 3000 kilometres distant by sea from the nearest white settlement at Hobart. It was even farther by land from the east-coast settlements near Sydney, but until 1917, when the transcontinental railway was built, there was no land communication between Western Australia and the rest of the country. Waterless deserts barred the way to all but a handful of hardy explorers and their camels. No one repeated Eyre's and Wylie's feat. Western Australia's extreme physical isolation is perhaps the main reason why it was developed so much later than all the other colonies. Another was the generally sandy, barren nature of the coastal plain on which the main settlement at Perth was founded three years after the first outpost at King George's Sound. A third handicap was the absence of a "convict establishment" – and of the cheap labour and government investment of capital which convictism brought with it.

In the 1820s the growth of the wool industry in New South Wales was beginning to attract the attention of private British investors. A group of capitalists, of whom the most important was Thomas Peel, a second cousin of the statesman Sir Robert Peel, thought that money might be made in Western Australia. The government was persuaded that the scheme might absorb some of the unemployed in Britain. It agreed to grant capitalists land at the Swan River settlement, at the rate of forty acres for every £3 invested, if they would pay the passages of free labourers. No convicts were to be sent. In return for a promise to land 400 settlers, Thomas Peel was granted 250 000 acres. Most of the land he selected is still worth little today. The government's only role was to pay the civil and military officers. Not surprisingly, many contemporaries thought the establishment of the Swan River colony a "job" – what later generations termed a "racket" – engineered by powerful politicians for their own and their friends' benefit. It probably was, but if so it was also a job contrived for, and partly by, James Stirling, the first governor of Western Australia and son-in-law of a powerful director of the British East India Company.[19] Having set up an outpost of empire at Raffles Bay in 1827, Stirling had the initiative to explore the Swan River area for the first time since Vlamingh's visit 130 years earlier. Unlike the Dutchman, he thought, or persuaded himself, that the country was, like Mitchell's Australia Felix, a veritable garden of Eden.[20]

Back in London, he spent many months impressing upon the government the surpassing virtues of the Swan River and his own fitness for the post of governor of the new colony. He was appointed and became the only governor of any Australian colony to win the dubious distinction of personally leading troops against the Aborigines. On 29 October 1834, a party of about eighty Aborigines was attacked by Stirling and about twenty-five soldiers and police at the so-called Battle of Pinjarra. Though they fought bravely, about half of the Aborigines, including a woman and several children, were killed.[21]

The Swan River settlement long remained a sickly infant. Because the land was almost given away, the few labourers who came to the new colony generally chose to scratch a subsistence from their own blocks rather than to work for increasingly impoverished employers. Most of the latter had no experience of conditions in Australia, and they were too far away from the older settlements to learn very much from earlier colonists. Some of the most able and enterprising immigrants, like the Henty brothers, who pioneered sheep-raising in what was to become Victoria a few years later, moved on to the more prosperous eastern colonies. Under Edward Gibbon Wakefield's influence, land became progressively more expensive after 1831, but the shortage of labour and capital persisted. In the whole of Western Australia, an area of about 2.5 million square kilometres which is mostly desert, there were only 2760 white people in 1841 (twelve years after the first landing), and in 1851 there were only 7186. By that time, however, the colonists themselves had petitioned the Home government to send them convicts. The first shipload reached Fremantle in June 1850, and Western Australia received 10 000 male convicts between that date and 1868, when transportation was finally abandoned. The labour of these men helped to set the colony on its feet, but development continued to be relatively sluggish until the Western Australian gold rush of the 1890s brought a sudden influx of immigrants from the eastern colonies.[22]

The story of white settlement in South Australia is inseparably linked with the name of Wakefield, the leading spirit among the reforming "theoretical colonisers", who considerably influenced British colonial policy at this time. Wakefield was a polished blackguard whose deeds throw a vivid light on the low status of women in nineteenth-century British society. He was also a brilliant publicist who needed money to forward his ambitions for himself and for new British colonies overseas. So in 1816 he married a beautiful young heiress. When she died after he had spent her money, he abducted from a boarding-school in Lancashire a very wealthy 15-year-old-girl, carried her post-haste to the Scottish border and married her at Gretna Green. The child's uncle caught up with the fugitives on the quay at Calais where Wakefield had the effrontery to declare, "Then, sir, you may dispose of your niece as you think proper, but you receive her at my hands as a pure and spotless virgin."[23]

It was too much even for the sexist mores of Regency England, and Wakefield was sentenced to three years' imprisonment. There is no evidence that either his crime or its punishment made most of his male contemporaries think any the less of him. Since he could afford to pay the gaoler for good food and quarters, he passed the time in Newgate pleasantly enough writing his bogously titled *Letters from Sydney*. These newspaper articles, published in 1829 as a book entitled *A Letter from Sydney and Other Writings*, set forth his leading ideas on "systematic colonisation". The blessings of British civilisation must be transferred *in toto* to overseas settlements. To achieve this, land must be sold at a "sufficient price" to ensure that labourers and mechanics could not too readily acquire land of their own. Thus, he argued, due subordination of men to their masters and a proper, or British, relationship between the classes would be maintained. At the same time, the "sufficient price" would prevent that dispersion of settlement which was tending so much to the encouragement of lawlessness in New South Wales, for no man would buy dear land situated far away from towns and markets. Finally, the proceeds of land sales should be used to bring out labourers so that the process should be self-sustaining. Wakefield was too shrewd ever to translate his "sufficient price" into a cash equivalent, and he died holding that his theory had never been given a fair trial in South Australia or later in New Zealand. Nevertheless, his ideas had some effect on policy. The minimum price of Crown lands in New South Wales was raised to five shillings an acre in 1831, to twelve shillings in 1838, and in 1842 to £1 an acre in all the Australian colonies. The extent of Wakefield's influence on South Australia is suggested by the fact that, from the landing of the first settlers there in 1836, the minimum price of land was £1.[24]

In the founding of South Australia, Wakefield notwithstanding, there was a greater measure of idealism than in that of the other Australian colonies. It was not a colony, but a "province", and transportation of convicts was to play no part in its history — facts which many South Australians are still quick to mention today. Radical politicians, systematic colonisers, non-conformist bankers and "reforming" speculators all played a part in its establishment, and some of them settled there. Among the immigrants there were relatively fewer penniless, unskilled labourers, and many fewer Irish people, than among those who shipped to the other colonies. There were relatively many more artisans and other respectable, industrious middle-class people, radical or liberal in politics and piously non-conformist or evangelical Anglican in religion. As with the New England puritans, the passage of time has served only to confirm some of these traits while changing others.[25]

The provincial capital was named after Britain's reigning queen, Adelaide, wife of William IV, generally known to the vulgar as "Silly Billy". It was planned by South Australia's first surveyor-general, Colonel William Light, the bastard son of Francis Light, the founder of that other imperial city, Penang, and a Eurasian woman. At a time when town-planning was little regarded in Britain, Light laid out the most magnificent civic ground-plan the world had yet seen. The city occupied a square mile and was to be surrounded forever by a belt of parklands half a mile wide. Across the northern parklands, which bordered the River Torrens, was another half-square mile of city area also bounded by parks. The city itself was intersected by straight streets, most of them still considered amply wide in the age of motor transport. The main north–south axis was named King William Street after the "sailor King", and the east–west one Wakefield after the kidnapper and propagandist of systematic colonisation. Today Light stands in bronze on an eminence north of the river looking out over the still-beautiful city he created. His own words, engraved on the plinth of the statue justly sum up his achievement:

> The reasons that led me to fix Adelaide where it is I do not expect to be generally understood or calmly judged of at the present. My enemies, however, by disputing their validity in every particular, have done me the good service of fixing the whole of the responsibility upon me. I am perfectly willing to bear it; and I leave it to posterity, and not to them, to decide, whether I am entitled to praise or to blame.[26]

For many years Adelaide was praised by some of its own citizens as "the City of Churches", and sometimes referred to ironically by non-South Australians as "the Holy City": for the material success which often rewarded virtue helped to make South Australians increasingly staid and conservative socially and politically. In South Australia's first decade of responsible government (1856–66), the premiership of the province changed hands thirteen times. For the twenty-six-year span from 1938 to 1965 there was no deviation at all by the electors from Sir Thomas Playford's Liberal–Country Party government. It should be added that this state of affairs owed something also to the most notorious gerrymander up to that time in Australian political history. Playford retired on 5 July 1966. In December 1969 the electoral boundaries were redrawn in such a way as still to favour the Liberal–Country Party League, though less dramatically. After that some Labor governments, led by Mr Don Dunstan, made the state in many ways the most innovatory one in the Commonwealth.

The relative stability of South Australian life probably owes as much to accidents of geography as to the character of her immigrants. Adelaide was built on the southern end of a coastal plain some 250 kilometres long and up to about 80 kilometres wide. Soil and climate were ideally suited to growing wheat as well as vines, olives and other Mediterranean-type crops. Moreover, Spencer's and St Vincent's Gulfs penetrate this area so deeply that they provided cheap sea transport almost from the farmers' boundary fences. Beyond this small area between the Flinders Ranges and the Gulfs, most of the remainder of South Australia is very like the outback parts of New South Wales, Queensland or Western Australia — semi-desert or desert country which can support only a sparse and precarious existence for pastoralists. Conditions in the restricted area between the Flinders Ranges and the Gulfs were far more favourable than in any other part of Australia to the successful application of Wakefield's ideas.

The sage of Newgate denounced the plan, declaring that the £1 per acre was not a "sufficient price". Nevertheless, after initial setbacks caused by delays in the land survey, by speculations, and by a division of control between the governor and the commissioners representing the founding investors and theorisers, the new province prospered steadily if unspectacularly. Unlike the Swan River settlement, it was near enough to the eastern colonies to profit by trading and other contacts with them. "Overlanders" drove thousands of head of stock to the new Adelaide market, and with them came hundreds of "old hands", as experienced ex-convict bushmen were called at the time. Their arrival was deplored by those who wished to keep the province free from the convict "taint", but with their pioneering skills the old hands could command higher wages than the free immigrant labourers could earn, and so most of them stayed on to merge with the general mass of the new colonists.[27] From the outset, most people derived their livelihood directly or indirectly from wheatgrowing, while the discovery in 1841 of rich copper mines at the Burra, Wallaroo and Moonta added to the province's prosperity. By 1851, when the discovery of gold in New South Wales and Victoria brought hundreds of thousands of new immigrants there, South Australia was firmly established as the granary of the whole continent. The relatively sober and industrious character of her citizens may still strike even a casual overseas visitor. To a greater degree than is common elsewhere in Australia, South Australians came to work, to build and to live; they did not come because they had to, or to make a quick pound before moving on. Even their barns and farm outhouses were commonly made of stone or brick, while in other colonies a great many dwelling-houses were built of wood.

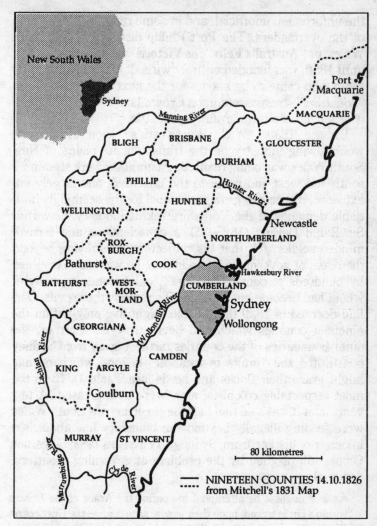

New South Wales

Sydney

Port Macquarie

Manning River

MACQUARIE

BLIGH

BRISBANE

GLOUCESTER

DURHAM

PHILLIP

Hunter River

HUNTER

WELLINGTON

Newcastle

NORTHUMBERLAND

ROX-
BURGH

COOK

Hawkesbury River

Bathurst

CUMBERLAND

BATHURST

WEST-
MOR-
LAND

Sydney

Wollongong

Wollondilly River

GEORGIANA

KING

ARGYLE

CAMDEN

Goulburn

Lachlan River

MURRAY

ST VINCENT

80 kilometres

Murrumbidgee River

Clyde River

—— NINETEEN COUNTIES 14.10.1826
······ from Mitchell's 1831 Map

Table 1 Limits of location

Western Australia and South Australia were conceived, to use a horse-breeding metaphor, out of the British government by English capitalists and theorisers. The latter colony, as we have seen, would not have prospered as it did without the unforeseen, unofficial, and in some respects illegal, help of the overlanders. The Port Phillip district of New South Wales, or "Australia Felix", as Victoria was variously known until 1850, was founded entirely without official sanction by those who came to be known for the next hundred years as "squatters", trespassers upon Crown lands. To understand, we shall have to retrace our steps a little.

By the 1830s, W.C. Wentworth's vision of a great woolgrowing industry on the transmontane plains of New South Wales was being realised. Pastoralists were streaming south and west and north to the unsettled, and largely unexplored, districts to grow more wool for the seemingly insatiable demands of the Yorkshire textile industry. Governor Sir Ralph Darling (1825–31), a conscientious and formal-minded soldier, felt that his subjects were straying beyond the reach of government. In addition, he was much troubled by hundreds of convict "bolters", or absconders, many of whom had become bushrangers. To remedy these evils, Darling decreed in 1829 that people might live only within the nineteen counties which had been surveyed. Further, the outer boundaries of the counties farthest away from Sydney constituted the "limits of location" beyond which no one might graze their flocks and herds (see Table 1). Even the most respectable colonists, alas, were unimpressed. A few years later it was said that half the sheep in New South Wales were feeding illegally beyond the boundary line about 300 kilometres distant from Sydney. Ten years later Governor Gipps, still plagued by the problem of governing squatters, declared:

> As well might it be attempted to confine the Arabs of the Desert within a circle traced, upon their sands, as to confine the Graziers or Woolgrowers of New South Wales within any bounds that can possibly be assigned to them.[28]

Meanwhile, the liberal-minded Governor Sir Richard Bourke (1831–38) had attempted to compromise with reality. In 1836 he had his Legislative Council enact regulations which recognised a squatter's right to temporary occupancy of as much Crown land as he pleased beyond the "boundaries of location", provided he paid £10 annually for a "squatting licence".

While the best grazing land within 500–900 kilometres of Sydney was being taken up in this distressingly unsystematic way, Van Diemen's Land pastoralists were becoming cramped for room in the island colony, much of which was in any case mountainous, heavily forested and unsuitable for pasture. Among them were the Henty brothers, who had tried their luck briefly in the new Swan River settlement before moving on to Van Diemen's Land. In November 1834, Edward Henty, with labourers and stock, crossed Bass Strait and squatted at Portland Bay in the then-almost completely unexplored Port Phillip district.[29] He was followed a few months later by two other parties of Vandiemonians led by John Batman and John Pascoe Fawkner, who settled at Port Phillip Bay itself on the site of the present city of Melbourne. There they were astonished to find living with the Aborigines a "wild white man". His name was William Buckley and he had absconded from a party of convicts which for three months in 1803, under the command of David Collins, had made an abortive attempt to settle at Port Phillip. Most living Australians have never heard of William Buckley, but they still speak of a person's having "Buckley's chance", or merely "having Buckley's", when they mean that the odds against him or her are so heavy as to leave practically no chance at all.[30]

Another member of Collins' visiting party in 1803 had been J.P. Fawkner, one of the two pioneer settlers of Melbourne. As a small boy of 12 he had been brought out with his convict parents in the *Ocean* and had been carried on to Van Diemen's Land with the rest of the party. His childhood experience gave little Johnny Fawkner a lifelong sympathy for underdogs and a carpingly critical attitude towards authority. These traits in his character were deeply ingrained by the scourger's cat-o'-nine-tails in 1814 when, though a 22-year-old free man, he was given 500 lashes and three years' imprisonment for having helped a party of convicts to make an escape attempt from Hobart. He lived on to become an un-

usually vituperative radical politician in Victoria. The other
pioneer of the Port Phillip Bay area was John Batman, a Van
Diemen's Land squatter. Born in Parramatta, this Currency
lad grew up to be a fine bushman endowed with a full measure of the "flashness" of his kind. In 1835 he crossed Bass
Strait and returned triumphantly bearing a treaty, "signed"
by a number of Aboriginal "chiefs", which purported to give
him and his heirs forever outright possession of 600 000 acres
of land contiguous to the Bay. The bare-faced effrontery of
this attempted confidence trick was surpassed only by that of
the first of all Currency lads, William Charles Wentworth,
who five years later claimed to have bought from some Maori
chiefs most of the whole South Island of New Zealand. By
that time Batman had died an agonising death from syphilis.[31]

Meanwhile, officialdom was catching up with events. In
1836 the surveyor-general of New South Wales, Thomas
Mitchell, was astonished to find the Hentys' station already
established when he reached the coast near Portland after
passing through "Australia Felix", and his reports accelerated the rate at which squatters crossed from Van Diemen's
Land to the new settlement, while others overlanded their
flocks south from New South Wales proper. Though Governor Bourke in distant Sydney warned these unlicensed
trespassers on the lands of the Crown, he knew the movement could not be stopped. By the end of the year he had se-
cured London's authorisation of the settlement as a district of
New South Wales and had dispatched to it some government
officials, soldiers and convict servants. Australia Felix
proved as rich a pastoral district as the "first-footers" had
thought. Soon free immigrants began arriving direct from
Britain. Many were hardy Lowland Scots farmers and some
brought capital as well as brawn and brains to invest in the
new settlement. Those whose sobriety and perseverance
were proof against colonial habits profited mightily. By 1850
the human and stock population of the Port Phillip district
considerably surpassed that of South Australia.[32] In the same
year, the Imperial Parliament set up the Port Phillip district
as the new and separate colony of Victoria. Only Western

Australia, where convictism was beginning instead of ending, remained as a Crown colony ruled directly from London.[33] Meanwhile squatters had also moved into the northern part of New South Wales, later to become Queensland.

We have seen that in 1824 a new penal settlement had been established near the mouth of the Brisbane River in Moreton Bay. Remoteness, it was hoped, would give added security to this prison for doubly convicted felons. But by 1840 the first squatters had overlanded their flocks to the rich Darling Downs district on the western slopes of the Great Dividing Range inland from Moreton Bay. Two years later officials in Sydney again bowed to the inevitable and declared the northern district open for settlement. As the northerners grew in number, they agitated, like the inhabitants of the Port Phillip District before them, for separation from New South Wales. Following the example of the Port Phillipians, they chose John Dunmore Lang to represent them in the Sydney legislature. Presbyterian divine, self-righteous moralist, radical politician, newspaper publisher, pamphleteer and republican, Lang was surely one of the most energetic Australians of the last century. Though he probably did more than any other single man to secure separation and self-government for both Victoria and Queensland, his pugnacity made him so many powerful enemies that his name is not widely known today.[34] The new colony of Queensland was proclaimed in 1859. Before thirty years had passed, many observers were agreed that it was certainly the "most Australian", or most nationalistic, of all the colonies. To discover why, we shall have to examine more closely the nature of the great squatting rush which was largely responsible for the creation of the two new colonies to the north and south of the mother colony.

This movement first gathered momentum in the 1830s. By the 1880s few areas capable of supporting one sheep to every 2 hectares or so remained unoccupied, though the occupation was and still is extremely sparse. Even today, over much of this area, a person's nearest neighbour may live 40 or 50 kilometres away. The American historian Frederick Jackson Turner's "frontier thesis" is germane to our understanding of this process. Though his theories have been subjected to searching criticism, the soundness of his basic idea is certainly borne out by Australian history. Adaptation to a strange environment naturally proceeds farthest and fastest on the advancing frontier of settlement, where conditions are most unlike those in Europe whence the settlers or their forefathers came. In the middle of the last century, new attitudes to life, new skills and new manners were acquired far more rapidly by prairie buffalo-skinners, or by stockmen on the dry inland plains of Australia, than they were by relatively newly arrived immigrants in the eastern coastal cities of both continents. The frontier settlers' very lives often depended quite directly upon their capacity for rapid adaptation. As Turner wrote in a famous passage, "the wilderness masters the colonist". On any frontier of settlement, civilised refinements and specialist services of all kinds tend to be scarce. It is far more important to do than to speculate, to make do than to bemoan the absence of proper facilities. Thus in both countries the frontier settlers tended to acquire rough-and-ready manners along with a wide range of practical skills. They became in most ways more self-reliant, more "independent", and more "democratic" than they or their ancestors had been in Europe. At the same time, their life taught them to undervalue, if not actually to scorn, intellectual, spiritual and artistic pursuits. All this does not mean, however, that we should expect frontier conditions to evoke completely identical reactions in the two continents. After all, the two "wildernesses" differed in important ways and so tended to generate different responses.

Turner thought that the two most important effects of the frontier in the United States were to promote national unity and nationalism and to promote democracy. There is abundant evidence that in Australia, too, frontier conditions fostered nationalist sentiment.[35] In both countries in the last century, the proportion of native-born citizens was markedly greater in the "outback" than it was in the urban areas near the coast, and these frontier settlers, mingling together in the wilderness, naturally tended to find that the accident of having been born in different colonies was not as important as it had seemed before they left Boston, New York or Baltimore; Melbourne, Sydney or Adelaide. It is true too that American and Australian frontier settlers both liked to believe that they were the most democratic people on the earth; but the two groups of pioneers, quite unconsciously for the most part, tended to emphasise different, in some ways even mutually incompatible, aspects of the democratic ideal. This basic difference in the two frontier legacies was first clearly indicated by an American visitor to Australia, who wrote in 1928:

> Certainly the United States owes its individualism largely to its small man's frontier; I think it is not fanciful to suggest that Australia owes much of its collectivism to the fact that its frontier was hospitable to the large man instead.[36]

The sparseness of Australia's inland population sprang partly from the land's remoteness from the old world and partly from its aridity. On the one hand the sheer loneliness of Australian bush people placed a high premium on mutual aid; on the other it diminished individualistic tendencies by diminishing competition for the land. This trend toward collectivism was accentuated by the fact that in Australia geography, economics and land legislation, in the first half of the nineteenth century, combined to discourage small-scale agriculture and to encourage large-scale grazing. And from the very beginning, the convict system required heavy emphasis on central government control and even on a sort of state-controlled economic collectivism. In the United States, at least up until about 1870 when settlement reached the eastern edge of the great trans-Mississippi plains, the typical frontier settler was a farmer, working his own land with the help of his family and perhaps of a hired hand or two at harvest time. Moreover, ample rainfall, fertile soil and relatively ready access to markets for produce supported the settler's belief that it was possible to become "independent", if not always rich, by enterprise, thrift and hard work. In Australia, on the other hand, aridity, distance from markets, poor communications and backward farming methods combined to frustrate the petty agriculturalist. Sheep, however, could thrive on the native grasses – given a large enough area to graze over – and walk to the coastal markets. Their wool was so much more valuable by weight than grain that it could be carted profitably, if tediously, over many hundreds of miles of rough bush tracks. Thus large-scale pastoralism became the staple industry of the Australian inland. A sheep or cattle station, covering perhaps more than 200 square kilometres, requires only one resident owner or manager, but many working hands. Since most station work – like shearing, droving or dam-sinking – is seasonal or casual in character, bush-workers received little encouragement to identify their interests with those of their employers. In the 1870s the English novelist, Anthony Trollope, one of whose sons was an Australian station owner, could still write of bush-workers:

> The bulk of the labour is performed by a nomad tribe, who wander in quest of work, and are hired only for a time . . . the squatter seldom knows whether the man he employs be married or single. They come and go, and are known by queer nicknames or are known by no names at all.[37]

Thus the typical Australian frontier settler was not a self-employed farmer, but a landless, itinerant labourer who had little real chance of becoming "independent" – in the financial sense – and who sometimes believed himself to have "Buckley's". For him, freedom to climb to the top of the ladder by his own efforts meant less than freedom to combine with his mates against government restrictions (as the convicts had done), against "those wealthy squatters", and indeed against the overwhelming loneliness which quite often rendered insane habitually solitary bushmen who were known as "hatters". Broadly, we may say that frontier life evoked similar responses in the two continents, if we remember the very large qualification that it tended to foster collectivist attitudes in Australia almost as strongly as it fostered individualistic ones in North America. With this background in mind, let us return to the squatting rush.

When transportation to the mainland ceased in 1840, the movement inland was already in full swing, but the deep-seated emancipist–exclusionist dichotomy of the population broke down only gradually. In the last chapter we noticed that the great majority of native-born Australians in the early years sprang mainly from the convict and emancipist classes. Here we must stress that this group – convict, emancipist and Currency people – were the first white Australians, in the sense that they first came to think of themselves as such, and to feel strongly that they belonged to the country as it did to them. By and large they had less reason to love Britain than did well-to-do exclusionists. Most of them had not sufficient education to read English magazines, to write letters to relatives, or to keep up other connections with "Home". Nor could they afford to send their children there to be educated, or to return there temporarily or permanently themselves, even if they had wished to do so. The wealthier and more cultivated colonists, on the other hand, for long tended to regard themselves as temporarily exiled Britons. The pattern of these contrasting attitudes was indicated by Watkin Tench, captain of Marines in the First Fleet. In 1791 he wrote of the time when:

> the hour of departure to England, for the marine battalion, drew nigh. If I be allowed to speak from my own feelings on the occasion, I will not say that we contemplated its approach with mingled sensations: – we hailed it with rapture and exaltation . . . [Yet] three corporals, one drummer, and 59 privates, accepted of grants of land, to settle at Norfolk Island and Rose Hill . . . [the] majority of them . . . from infatuated affection to female convicts, whose character and habits of life, I am sorry to say, promise from a connection neither honour nor tranquility.[38]

These "other ranks" could, of course, like Tench and his fellow oficers, have returned to Britain with free passages and on full pay. Convicts, emancipists and Currency people could not. Naturally they felt, as a rule, even more firmly attached to the new land. In 1837 James Macarthur complained that these people believed "that the colony was *theirs by right*, and that the emigrant settlers were interlopers upon the soil",[39] and in 1843 John Hood wrote:

> The fact of being a drunkard, or a convict, is not looked upon in this country, amongst the class as any disgrace; on the contrary . . . no

shame whatever is evinced by the very best amongst them; and they look upon all "self-imported devils" as beneath them, and not worth consideration.[40]

Because the convict–emancipist–currency group constituted the great majority of all colonists in the early days, and because they were also the oldest and most thoroughly acclimatised settlers, many free immigrants of working-class background tended rapidly to assimilate their attitudes. Many of these ordinary colonists, feeling themselves thoroughly at home in Australia, naturally joined enthusiastically in the squatting rush to the interior. Because of the loneliness, dangers and hardships associated with it, bush work was easier to get and better paid than work in the cities and towns. As in the United States and other colonies of settlement, newly arrived immigrants tended to prefer life in the relatively "Home-like" cities where they disembarked from Europe, but the bush held few terrors for the old hands and the native-born. Census figures show that, in the decade 1841–51, the proportion of emancipist and Currency people in the population increased directly with distance from Sydney. If we consider convicts, emancipists, and native-born persons as one group and *all* free immigrants as the other, then the ratio of the first to the second in the County of Cumberland during this decade was about one to one.

Cumberland was the first settled area, extending for a radius of about 40 or more kilometres north, west and south of Sydney. Within the nineteen counties (excluding Cumberland) the proportion was about two to one; and beyond them, that is to say in what were sometimes known as "the squatting districts" beyond the erstwhile "limits of location", more than about 300 kilometres from the capital, the proportion was about two-and-a-half to one. Thus the "old Australians", if we may for convenience so call this majority group of mainly lower-class people, tended to concentrate disproportionately on the frontier where conditions were such as to accentuate the distinctive, levelling, nationalist attitudes they had already begun to develop. Table 2 provides a de-

	CONVICTS	'OTHER FREE PERSONS'	BORN IN THE COLONY	TOTAL CONVICTS, EMANCIPISTS & NATIVES	ARRIVED FREE	CONVICT, EMANCIPIST & NATIVE % OF TOTAL POPULATION
County of Cumberland						
1828	8088	5956	7517	21561	5263	80.4
1841	7908	7959	16257	32124	25984	55.3
1851	734	6546	36812	44092	37022	54.4
Other Counties within the boundaries of Location						
1828	6076	1322	952	8350	1017	89.1
1841	13553	7929	11114	32596	14852	68.6
1851	998	12836	35226	49060	29372	62.6
Squatting Districts beyond the boundaries of location						
1828	–	–	–	–	–	*
1841	3028	2360	1210	6598	2447	72.9
1851	961	7247	9353	17561	10136	63.4

Officially no whites beyond boundaries in 1828

Table 2   White Australian population distribution, 1821–51 in and beyond the nineteen counties

tailed picture of white Australian population distribution between 1821 and 1851.[41]

The situation was neatly reflected in literature and the arts. Until the 1880s, writers and painters naturally described the life around them in terms of traditional English literary and artistic conventions, and with a cultivated English audience in mind. The result was that formal literature, even when produced by a really talented native-born son of emancipist parents like Charles Harpur, tended to be little more than a slightly anaemic, provincial reflection of its English exemplar. In Harpur's poetry the setting and the intention are usually Australian, but little else. Quite often native authors felt impelled to write about English life, of which they knew nothing at first-hand, just as the American Fenimore Cooper did in his first novel before turning, in *The Pioneers* (1823), to the frontier theme. Meanwhile, the "old Australians", many of whom were illiterate, produced little or no formal literature; but they did create directly from the raw life around them a considerable body of folk ballads, songs and tales which circulated orally. Enough of these survive to show that the people who composed them had already become spiritually Australianised long before 1851, in a way and to a degree that most of the cultured minority had not. Here, for instance, is the oldest extant chorus of one of the most popular bush songs of the first half of the nineteenth century, "The Old Bullock Dray". Stores were taken up-country to the stations, and wool back to Sydney for export, on ponderous two-wheeled bullock-drays, the drivers of which were almost always old hands or native-born Australians. The chorus emphasises the pride of these men in their familiarity with, and mastery of, the frontier environment. At the same time it underlines one of the most important functions of these folk songs, that of assisting acclimatisation by clothing an initially strange environment and way of life with the familiar garment of homespun myth.[42]

> So it's roll up your blankets, and let's make a push,
> I'll take you up the country and show you the bush;

I'll take you round the stations and learn you how to ride,
And I'll show you how to muster when we cross th' Great Divide!

It is instructive to set against this a stanza from another bullockies' song, reported by a contemporary immigrant *littérateur*, Frank Fowler. Addressing his English audience, Fowler wrote condescendingly of Australian reality:

> The bullock-songs are uncouth snatches generally improvised by the drivers themselves, but not destitute of a wild runic poetry, as the following verses from one of them will show:
>
>   Olle! Heigh ho!
> Blow your horns, blow,
> Blow the Southern Cross down if you will;
> But on you must go,
> Where the fresh gullies flow,
> And the thirsty crane wets his red bill.[43]

Comparison with all other extant "uncouth snatches" makes it appallingly probable that Fowler himself provided what he considered to be the touch of "wild runic poetry" in this stanza.

The same dichotomy between educated persons – with one eye cocked over their shoulders towards Europe – and the masses existed in the United States and other "new countries". Thus in 1839 an acute Austrian traveller, Francis J. Grund, wrote of the Great Republic:

> "And I can assure you," said I, "that in my own heart I have a much higher respect for the common American, who, in his conduct towards strangers is solely guided by his own rude notion of dignity, than for the *educated gentleman*, who measures everything, and himself into the bargain, by the standard of another country."
>
> "Agreed! Agreed!" cried my two companions; "for the one however barbarous, has within him the elements of a national character; while the other, however civilised, is but a mutilated European."[44]

We have seen that in 1839 Grund's remarks would have been at least equally applicable to Australia.

The chorus of "The Old Bullock Dray", cited above, shows how the bush life fostered local, native nationalism. A study of the rest of the song can teach us a great deal more about the nature of early Australian ideas and ideals, in particular about the abysmally low status of women and of Aborigines. With the chorus omitted, the ballad goes like this:

Oh! the shearing is all over
    And the wool is coming down,
And I mean to get a wife my
        boys,
    When I get down to town.
Everything that has two legs
    Presents itself to view,
From the little paddymelon
    To the bucking kangaroo.

Now I've saved up a good cheque
    And I mean to buy a team,
And when I get a wife, boys,
    I'll be all serene:
For calling at the depot,
    They say there's no delay,
To get an offsider
    For the old bullock dray.

I'll teach you the whip,
    And the bullocks how to flog.
You'll be my offsider
    When we're stuck in a bog,
Lashing out both left and right
    And every other way,
Making skin, blood and hair
    Fly round the old bullock dray.

Oh, we'll live like fighting cocks,
    For good living I'm your man.
There'll be leather-jacks,
        johnny-cakes
    And fritters in the pan;
And if you want some fish,
    I'll get you some soon.
We'll bob for barramundis,
    Round the banks of a lagoon.

Oh yes, of beef and damper
    I'll make sure we have
        enough,
And we'll boil in the billy,
    Such a whopper of a duff,
And our friends will dance
    To the honour of the day,
And the music of the bells
    Around the old bullock dray.

We'll have plenty girls,
    We must mind that.
There'll be Buck-jumping
        Maggie,
    And Leather-belly Pat,
There'll be Stringy-bark Peggy,
    And Green-hide Mike;
Yes, my old colonial,
    Just as many as you like.

We'll stop all immigration,
    We won't need it any more.
We'll be making young natives,
    Twins by the score;
And I wonder what the devil
    Jack Robertson would say,
If he saw us promenading
    Round the old bullock dray.

Oh, to tell a lot of lies,
    You know it is a sin;
But I'll go up the country
    And I'll marry a black gin.
"Baalgammon, white feller,"
    This is what she'll say,
"Budgery you,
    And your old bullock dray."

First we notice that the whole song is couched in Australian English. In England, one travels up to London or down to the country. In Australia, in the 1840s when this ballad first became popular, one always went "down to" the city, as in the first verse and "up the country" as in the last. We learn immediately, too, that the wool industry formed the basis of the Australian economy and that country life revolved round the shearing season, just as did the sessions of the Legislative Council in Sydney. The singer then introduces the theme of the whole ballad, which was in fact the basic social problem in nineteenth-century Australia — the effect on society of the great numerical imbalance between the sexes. Obviously the singer could hope to find a wife only in town, and even there he had to be prepared to consider matrimony with any — presumably female — creature "that had two legs". A paddymelon is a very small marsupial of the kangaroo genus.

The "depot" in the second verse was the female immigrant depot in Sydney where, not quite as in the old female convict factory, some newly arrived immigrant girls found shelter, and perhaps a husband, while waiting for a job. A bullock-driver's "offsider" was of course his assistant, usually a younger person who walked along on the off-side of the team. The third verse emphasises the crude brutality of colonial life. The singer's prospective mate must not only put up with the "skin blood and hair" flogged from the tortured beasts, but she must, as a matter of course, learn to flog them herself.

The next two verses stress what was, for most people at the time, the main attraction of Australian life in general and up-country life in particular. Manners might be crude and rude but food, however coarse, was plentiful. In the bush, endless daily quantities of mutton, damper and tea were the unquestioned right of all who remembered, or whose parents remembered, that in the old country working people rarely ate meat once a week — to say nothing of "beef, leatherjacks, johnny-cakes, fritters and barramundi".

At the fantasy wedding in the next verse, the fantasy bride has disappeared altogether, as the singer celebrates the consolations of mateship. He promises his "old colonial" friends that there will be lots of bush whores – or perhaps just friendly Currency lasses – at the nuptial feast. He cannot even imagine white women as anything more than freely available objects of male lust, ingredients of a spree only a little less important than the food and drink.

With its reference to Jack Robertson, the penultimate verse is obviously a later addition to the song. Robertson achieved fame in the 1860s as the author of the *Free Selection Acts* in New South Wales. His opposition to subsidised immigration made him very popular with native-born voters, many of whom shared his freely expressed view that it was the duty of all patriotic Australians to increase the population by their own exertions. The singer strongly endorses the idea, suggesting that the wedding-party should become a general debauch to produce "twins by the score".

The last verse returns to earth with a bump. The idea that any bullock-driver could possibly get a help-meet from the immigrant depot is an impossible dream, and so is the fantasy of a plentiful supply of willing white women to embellish the occasional spree. In fact, the only "wife" a bullock-driver, or any bush worker, was likely to find in the 1840s was an Aboriginal woman, a person infinitely lower in the status hierarchy than "Leatherbelly Pat" and her friends. An Aboriginal female could always be cajoled, bought or kidnapped from the males of her tribe and exploited, then discarded or even murdered by whites. In Aboriginal pidgin English, "baalgammon" meant, in colloquial Australian, "no kidding" and "budgery you", "good on you".

Yet the ballad barely hints at the barbarous brutality of bush life, shown most clearly in the way our ancestors dispossessed and destroyed the Aborigines. Vicious racism was an integral part of the new national identity that was forming most rapidly on the advancing frontier of pastoral settlement. The levelling mateship, which was at the very heart of the new outlook, necessarily connoted hatred of all non-mates, particularly of those who were seen as inferior; and the more nationalist, the more egalitarian, the more "democratic" a white man was in the last century, the more racist he was likely to be in word and deed. The expansion of squatting over most of eastern Australia meant the rapid expropriation and extermination of the Aboriginal tribes. Few living Australians, black or white, have any idea of the scale and duration of the slaughter. It is true that dispossession, disease and despair killed more Aborigines than did white murderers, but premeditated butchery of men, women, children and infants accounted in the aggregate for tens of thousands of black lives. The latest estimate is that when the First Fleet dropped anchor in Sydney Cove in 1788 there were about 750 000 Aborigines in this continent − give or take 50 000 or so. By the time of the white centenary celebrations in 1888, the number had been reduced to about 60 000 fullbloods. From the beginning it is clear that blacks were murdered with impunity by settlers and convicts, in spite of some earnest official efforts to protect them; but it seems that the first officially sanctioned massacre occurred in Van Diemen's Land when a hunting party of about forty was shot down by soldiers in 1804.[45]

In 1838 the most notorious of all such clashes happened on Henry Dangar's Myall Creek Station in northwestern New South Wales. This massacre is remembered not because it was more brutal and bloody than a hundred other similar events − it was not − but because it was better documented and because of what it showed about the values and assumptions of white society at the time.

In the winter of 1838, well before the shearing season, Henry Dangar was in Sydney. His Myall Creek run was being managed by William Hobbs with the help of two assigned convict stockmen, George Anderson and Charles Kilmeister. Early in May a "mob" of forty or fifty Aborigines camped near the stockmen's hut. Friendly relations − including sexual ones between Anderson and Kilmeister and some of the female Aborigines − were established.

Three or four weeks later on Sunday 11 June, eleven armed white men rode up to the hut. All were convicts or ex-convicts save one native-born white, John Fleming, who seems to have led the party. Rumours, but no firm evidence, said they had been busy for some time slaughtering Aborigines further west near Terri Hie Hie, where a white shepherd had been killed.

Fortunately many of the Myall Creek blacks were absent that afternoon with another station manager. Of those in camp, three young boys escaped with the help of Anderson and two beautiful young girls were allowed to live so that they could be raped. The remaining twenty-eight men, women and children were tied together and dragged about half a mile away from the hut. There the eleven men, who had been joined by Kilmeister, shot some but hacked up most of the Aborigines with knives and swords. They spent most of Monday hunting vainly for the black people who had escaped and on Tuesday morning returned to burn the bodies of their victims.

So far there was nothing to distinguish this shambles from so many other earlier and later ones. Then three quite extraordinary things happened. A white man reported the murders. The police arrested the murderers. Some of them were brought to trial and hanged.

On his return to the station Hobbs resolved to report the murders despite Kilmeister's begging him "for Jesus Christ's sake" not to do so. Word was sent to Edward "Denny" Day, the nearest police magistrate at "Mussel Brook" about 350 kilometres away across country. This remarkable officer possessed such zeal and humanity that his name was later honoured in folk tales and ballads as well as in official records. He reported the incident to the governor in Sydney, the newly arrived Sir George Gipps, who ordered him to arrest the culprits. Day rounded up all of them except for the currency lad, John Fleming, whose mates helped him escape justice. Frequently changing his horse along the track, he rode over 500 kilometres in about three days and took a ship to Van Diemen's Land. When the hue and cry ended he returned to the Hawkesbury to become a pillar of respectability – church warden and magistrate in Wilberforce until he died in the odour of sanctity in 1894. On 15 November 1838, Charles Kilmeister, John Johnston, Charles Toulouse,

William Hawkins, James Parry, James Oates, John Russell, Edward Foley, George Pallister, John Blake and Charles Lamb were charged with murder before the Chief Justice, Sir James Dowling.

By then the whole colony was in an uproar – not with horror at the massacre but with sympathy for the murderers. Most white people found intolerable the idea that killing of Aborigines could be regarded as a crime, let alone a capital one. In 1821 a convict "bolter" had been hanged for murdering an Aborigine who had helped to apprehend him. Apart from this, and the punishment of seven of the Myall Creek murderers, it seems that no white man in the colony was ever hanged for killing blacks.

Many landholders and other respectable people signed petitions and, soon after the arrests, a group of rich graziers meeting at Patrick's Plains (now Singleton) pledged £300 to fee the colony's best lawyers for the defence. Their leader was also a magistrate, Robert Scott. He visited the eleven prisoners in gaol and urged them: "not to split among themselves, saying that there was no direct evidence against them, and that, if they were only true to each other, they could not be convicted". For this highly improper action the upright Gipps later removed Scott from the Bench.

However, the prisoners apparently laid his injunction to heart. The jury found them not guilty at the first trial. Four men were then freed in the hope that they would turn Queen's evidence at the second trial of seven. They did not do so. Throughout both hearings the defence rested purely on legal technicalities. The accused never denied their guilt or affirmed it, but simply claimed "they thought it extremely hard that white men should be put to death for killing blacks". At the second trial the "seven unfortunate men" were found guilty and hanged seven days before Christmas.[46] From today's viewpoint what followed was the most horrifying part of the whole story. There were of course some humane and Christian colonists who were sickened by the crime but, to judge from contemporary reports, the majority were incensed by the punishment. A great wave of anti-Aboriginal feeling swept the colony. Massacres — and retaliatory murders by the blacks — became more frequent rather than less. In addition many squatters and their men began handing out to whole bands of Aborigines gifts of poisoned flour or cakes — thus, they believed, making their crime the harder to detect.[47]

Many newspapers deplored the hanging while glossing over the original crime. Some, like the *Sydney Herald* of 5 October 1838, roundly declared that Aborigines were less than human beings and called, in effect, for their extermination:

> We want neither the classic nor the romantic savages here. We have too many of the murderous wretches about us already . . . The whole gang of black animals are not worth the money which the Colonists will have to pay for printing the silly documents upon which we have already wasted too much time.

Even Alexander Harris, perhaps the most humane and percipient of contemporary chroniclers, felt that the seven murderers were punished only for doing what they had always been taught was right by their masters. "From time immemorial," he wrote, "it had been the custom for influential settlers to head parties like this, against the blacks. All former governors had sanctioned this method of proceeding . . ." And Harris recorded too, that after the excitement and alarm occasioned by the hangings had died down, "the matter fell into its true and old form, from which it should never have been disturbed: a simple question of *intimidation* . . . between the musket and the spear".[48]

In other words, white Australian males were tacitly allowed to resume with impunity their destruction of Aboriginal people and culture. Their spoliation of the other despised group, white Australian women, suffered a check at this time at the hands of the greatest champion of womanhood ever to live here. The daughter of a prosperous Northamptonshire farmer, Caroline Jones was brought up in the tradition of Anglican evangelical philanthropy. She showed her mettle first at the age of 22, in 1830, when she married Captain Archibald Chisholm of the British East India Company, on condition that her social work should continue. Continue it manifestly did, possibly on Chisholm's condition that she convert to his Catholic religion — as she did at about this time. In 1838 the Chisholms took their home leave in New South Wales and settled near Windsor. Caroline was immediately struck by the plight of Australian women, particularly of the immigrant girls, who were often forced into prostitution to survive in the colony while they were looking for work. Many were debauched on the voyage out by ships' officers, as so many convict girls had been. On the *Subraon*, which reached Sydney in April 1848, for instance,

> Captain Cawardine had arranged for a constant procession of young girls from a Dublin foundling home to spend the voyage in his cabin . . . Chief Officer Mills seduced a nineteen-year-old orphan girl, who became pregnant, tried to abort herself, and died on board. Third Officer Hill slept constantly with another girl who upon landing was sent to become the inmate of a notorious brothel in Sydney.[49]

Caroline Chisholm sheltered some of these girls in her own home while finding jobs for them, but soon found she could not cope with the numbers who needed help. Undaunted, she persuaded the proprietors of the *Sydney Morning Herald* and the governor himself, Sir George Gipps, to aid her. "I was amazed," Gipps told a friend, "when my aide introduced a handsome, stately young woman who proceeded to reason the question as if she thought her reason and experience, too, worth as much as mine."[50] He gave her use of an old government building, in which she quickly established a temporary shelter for up to ninety-six immigrants at a time, and the only free employment registry office in Sydney. She and her husband raised the necessary money entirely from public subscriptions and she personally conducted many dray-loads of girls "up the country" to jobs she had found them. In 1846 the Chisholms returned to England, where she obtained the support of Earl Grey, James Stephen of the Colonial office and Charles Dickens, among others, for her highly successful Family Colonization Loan Society. Captain Chisholm returned to Australia in 1851 as an unpaid agent looking after the arriving migrants. Caroline came back in 1854 and gained even more recognition as a champion of female immigration and women's rights in Victoria than she had won in New South Wales.

In her lifetime, hostile critics denigrated her with false accusations that she was biased in favour of Irish and Catholic women. Recently she has been damned with faint praise as a conservative and patronising "do-gooder" with thoroughly conformist aims. It is true that she sought to make one generation of working-class girls into the mothers of a later generation of respectable middle-class people, and she was astonishingly successful too. She was brought up as a gentle, conservative middle-class lady, but when she encountered so much indifference and hostility from the rich and officialdom, she plainly proclaimed her commitment to the most radical demands of the day, universal suffrage, vote by ballot and payment of members of parliament. By precept and example she did more than any other single human being to ameliorate, however slightly, the status of Australian women, so crudely figured forth in hundreds of sketches, yarns and folksongs like "The Old Bullock Dray".

The blacks, as we have seen, found no such doughty champion. Missionary efforts to save them from "dispersal" and degradation all failed dismally.[51] Squatters and their employees usually agreed together to "disperse" the blacks as they increasingly came to agree about much else. During the 1840s the old emancipist–exclusionist dichotomy was fast diminishing and for employers and employees alike the acclimatisation process tended to proceed most rapidly on the frontier. In some districts, many of the flock masters were emancipists or Currency lads who, by superior luck, hard work, sobriety or skill in "cattle-duffing", had amassed sufficient capital to stock a "run".[52] In nearly all areas there were a few such squatters, but overall, the majority were free immigrants possessing at least a modicum of education and taste, as well as capital. Some were retired army and navy officers from the old country, and not a few were men of real birth and breeding. Most of these immigrant squatters frankly intended to stay in the barbarous wilderness only long enough to make their fortunes before returning to England to live in comfort and refinement, but as the long years of "roughing it" on the pioneering frontier passed, many of them found to their surprise that they too were becoming Australians. Once such was Patrick Leslie, pioneer squatter of the Darling Downs.

Scottish-born like so many of the early pastoralists, Leslie was 20 years of age when he landed in Sydney in 1835. He went to stay with John Macarthur's nephew, Hannibal, whose daughter he married a few years later. In 1840 he left the last New England out-stations behind him to the south and found rich new country on the western slopes of the Great Divide a hundred kilometres or two inland from the Moreton Bay penal settlement. He became a successful squatter and, as an elected member of the New South Wales Legislative Assembly, did much to secure the separation of Queensland in 1859 — despite differences on other issues with Dr Lang, whom he castigated as "the Reverend Republican". Having made a reasonable fortune, he returned to Scotland but then went to New Zealand for some years. In 1878, however, he returned to Australia and died in Sydney.

Living the frontier life, many such men came to know and love not only the land of their adoption, but also those who had already claimed it for their own. Especially in up-country districts, free immigrants and old hands came increasingly to know and respect each other, and to share many implicit attitudes to life, even if they seldom at this time came to share each other's manners and modes of pronouncing the English language. Of his pioneering journey to the Darling Downs, Leslie wrote afterwards: "We had twenty-two men, all ticket-of-leave or convicts, as good and game a lot of men as ever existed, and who never occasioned us a moment's trouble: worth any forty men I have ever seen since." Of his twenty-two old hands it is recorded that their feelings toward Leslie were such that they swore they would "follow him into hell itself".[53]

We are now in a better position to see why people in the 1880s and since have tended to think of Queensland as the most characteristically Australian of all the colonies. South and Western Australia were settled long after the mother colony of New South Wales, and by free immigrants fresh from Great Britain. Victoria, it is true, was, like Queensland, first unofficially occupied by squatters and old hands from New South Wales and Van Diemen's Land, but, by Australian standards, Victoria occupies only a very small area of well-watered land. This colony was too rich and too cramped for space to remain for long a predominantly pastoral frontier area. Quensland, on the other hand, was the biggest of all the colonies except Western Australia. Most of its land was and remains suitable, but not *too* suitable, for pastoral occupation. As we have seen, it was first settled by convicts and then by graziers and old hands from the mother colony who had already undergone an intensive course of assimilation to Australian conditions. It was, and to a considerable extent has remained, the frontier colony – or state. Climate, as well as area and the accident of late settlement, may have something to do with it. If, compared with Britain, all Australia is hot and dry, Queensland is the hottest and driest part of the continent to be occupied – except on the coast, where it is the hottest and wettest. If characteristically Australian habits and attitudes are apprehended as those which differ most from traditional British ones, we have seen that such reactions were evoked most completely by frontier conditions, and for geographic reasons the traditional Australian tribulations of frontier life – bushfires, droughts, dust storms, floods, poisonous snakes, sharks and insect plagues – prevail in Queensland more than in any other colony.

So does admiration for practical "male" virtues and corresponding contempt for education and the arts, for women, for blacks and indeed all "Southerners". Besides, on the coastal plain, Queenslanders grow sugar cane from which they distil rum for the Commonwealth. Perhaps it is the heat which causes them to drink rather more than their share of it. Certainly the heat has made it much more difficult for them to preserve formal English styles of dress and behaviour. In North Queensland only the most determinedly respectable burghers wear coats in the street. As a visiting Englishman wrote in 1886, "The Englishman in Queensland is, like the sheep, developing into a different species."[54]

Reconciliation between the old exclusionist and emancipist groups and the growth of a sense of Australian national identity were most clearly demonstrated, at a quasi-political level, in the movement against the resumption of transportation at mid-century. In 1847, Earl Grey, the current Secretary of State, proposed to resume transportation to the eastern mainland colonies, something which all colonists thought had ended forever in 1840. To Grey it went without saying that Van Diemen's Land should continue as a receptacle of British criminals, but opposition there was even stronger than in the other colonies. Grey persisted, in spite of colonial rumblings, at least in part because the Legislative Councils in New South Wales, Van Diemen's Land and, after 1850, Victoria, gave him conflicting advice. At that time it still took at least eight months to receive an answer in London to even the most important and official inquiry made of Hobart or Sydney. Grey should not have been expected to understand, from half a world away, that when the squatter-dominated Legislative Councils spoke with divided voices, this meant that virtually all colonists outside the council chambers were united against the proposal.[55]

All employees feared that cheap convict labour would drastically reduce the rate of wages for free men. Since, in the 1830s, convicts had been assigned almost exclusively to up-country squatters, town employers feared that resumption would offer them no benefits, but merely augment what they saw as the privileges of the pastoral class. Almost everyone, including ageing emancipists and even many squatters, opposed transportation also for less selfish reasons. They held passionately that convictism lowered the whole tone of society in the eyes of the mother country and indeed of all the other lands on earth. It also formed the major stumbling block on the path to self-governing institutions. It was felt as an affront to the sense of Australian national identity which was emerging in all the colonies except Western Australia — in the pure province of South Australia as much as in the still "tainted" Van Diemen's Land. Religious people, reformers of all kinds and early Australian nationalists like Charles Harpur,[56] the most considerable poet of the time, joined in 1851 to form the Australasian League for the Prevention of Transportation, whose banner, consisting of the union jack in one quarter and the southern cross, flew in all the eastern colonies and anticipated almost completely the first official national flag of 1901.[57] The League's leading spirit was John West, Congregational parson, historian of Van Diemen's Land and editor of the *Sydney Morning Herald*.[58] Another keen member was the young Henry Parkes, who launched his political career on work for the League, commending it to readers of the *People's Advocate* as "Australia's First National Movement".

When the convict ship *Hashemy* reached Melbourne in April 1849, the superintendent of the Port Phillip District, Charles Joseph La Trobe, prudently ordered her on to Sydney. There she was confronted at Circular Quay by what the superintendent of the Sydney Police sourly described as a mob numbering no more than 700 "composed solely of the working classes". The still-maneless Parkes, who had done more than anyone else to gather the "mob" together in the drenching rain that June morning, estimated 7000 and the *Sydney Morning Herald*'s reporter 5000. The "mob", whatever its size, unanimously passed a resolution, seconded by Parkes, that the *Hashemy*'s "exiles" should be sent back to Britain. To no one's surprise, Governor Sir Charles Fitzroy, a descendant of King Charles II, contemptuously refused. Many up-country squatters, including Wentworth and Henry Dangar, still wanted convict employees.[59] The *Hashemy* landed most of her cargo at Sydney but went on to discharge the rest in the Moreton Bay district where one of the youngest prisoners, 16-year-old William Henry Groom, later lived to become first the colonial and then the Commonwealth member of parliament for Darling Downs. A few more shiploads were sent to Moreton Bay district of New South Wales, but the League's propaganda had won the day.[60]

By mid-century, transportation had been (or in Van

LIST OF THE

Traitors, — Trimmers, — Rose-water Liberals, — and Political Tidewaiters, who voted for MR. WENTWORTH'S ARTFUL DODGE, the adjournment of the Question of NO TRANSPORTATION!!! in the Legislative Council of New South Wales, August 30th, 1850.

W. C. WENTWORTH
J. B. DARVALL
S. A. DONALDSON
COL. SNODGRASS
THE COLONIAL TREASURER
THE AUDITOR GENERAL
THE COLLECTOR OF CUSTOMS
MR. EBDEN
MR· ICELY
MR. MARTIN
MR. JAMES MACARTHUR
MR. WILLIAM MACARTHUR
MR. NICHOLS
C. NICHOLSON, Speaker.

A contemporary broadsheet lampooning W.C. Wentworth and others who favoured the resumption of transportation to New South Wales (Source: Mitchell Library, State Library of New South Wales)

Diemen's Land was on the verge of being) abolished, except in the isolated western colony where it was just beginning. Legislative Councils in New South Wales, Victoria, South Australia and Van Diemen's Land had been invited to devise more fully representative constitutions for approval by the Imperial parliament. Except in the frontier area, which was to become the separate colony of Queensland in 1859, most of the best pastoral land had been occupied, if thinly, by the "shepherd kings" and the "nomad tribe" of bush-workers who were, in an important sense, the first white Australians. The pastoral boom had also drawn from Britain an increasing stream of free immigrants, some of whom were men of substance and culture. The old antagonism between the emancipist and exclusionist factions was diminishing as people in both groups, but especially the former, began to feel at home in the land; yet the colonial middle class had barely come into existence. Retail trade and secondary industry had achieved only a rudimentary stage of development. Even Sydney was still not very much more than an entrepôt centre, siphoning rum and other station stores into, and wool out of, the interior. About 150 000 convicts had been transported, but the total white population of Australia was still only 405 356 in 1851. The discovery of gold in that year led not so much to changes in, as to a rapid acceleraton of, existing trends.

4 Diggers, democracy and urbanisation
c. 1851–85

On 12 February 1851, gold was discovered in Summerhill Creek on the western slopes of the Blue Mountains. Fear of convictism may have had some influence in suppressing news of earlier finds, but by 1851 Australian society had become so open that suppressing the news of Edward Hargraves's discovery would no longer have been practicable. Besides, the gold rush to California in 1849 had enticed away a disquietingly large number of the more enterprising Australian colonists, so that businessmen and some officials rejoiced to see a tide of migration flowing back across the Pacific. The rush to the Turon (New South Wales) diggings had scarcely gathered momentum when the newly separated Victorian government offered a reward for the discovery of a payable goldfield in its territory. Before the end of the year it was obvious that the Victorian fields near Ballarat were even richer than those of the mother colony.

The immediate impact of the discoveries on the placid pastoral society was so great that, for a time, some officials like the normally imperturbable Edward Deas Thomson, Colonial Secretary of New South Wales, feared a breakdown of the social order.[1] Shepherds and other employees, in both country and town, left their jobs *en masse* for the diggings. The draconic provisions of the *Masters and Servants Acts* availed little when so many police constables and other civil servants followed − not to arrest the absconders, but to join them. Governmental difficulties increased from September 1852, when the wave of overseas gold-seekers broke on Melbourne.

Thousands of deserting sailors joined the eager "new chums" in their precipitate trek to the goldfields.

Nevertheless, civil order did not break down. Except for the short-lived Eureka revolt at Ballarat in December 1854, there were few considerable riots and, by Californian standards, a surprising absence of lynch-law and other disorders. Contemporary observers nearly all agreed on the high level of self-discipline and responsibility among the diggers. The goldfields entertainer and satirist, Charles Thatcher, for instance wrote of "the inevitable double-barrelled gun, as if gold was a thing to be shot at and brought down . . . [as the chief among the] other useless trifles [and] usual treasures of a new chum".[2] The adjutant-general of New South Wales, Lieutenant-Colonel Godfrey Charles Mundy, who left for Britain in August 1851, wrote sensibly of the reasons for the relatively orderly life on the fields. In contrast to the Californian situation, he pointed out, gold had been found in areas adjacent to seats of firmly established government, the vast majority of diggers belonged to one national stock – the British – and there was no warlike Aboriginal race and no large bodies of foreigners to cause friction by upsetting traditionally accepted mores.[3] Yet we should not exaggerate the effect of these stabilising factors. The sudden strain on the colonial administrations did result in the only considerably bloody riot in Australia's history.

By 1854 most of the alluvial surface gold had been won. In 1852 the approximate value of gold found per head of population in the Victorian fields was £390. This figure fell to £240 in 1853 and £148 in 1854.[4] All but the luckiest diggers began to find paying a miner's monthly licence fee of thirty shillings irksome. Much more provocative, in the opinion of the diggers, was the inefficient yet brutal way in which the police collected the tax. A tradition of unusually intense hostility between policemen and populace stemmed from convict days, and the "Russian sort of way" in which uniformed, mounted police often rode after diggers in "licence hunts" did nothing to lessen the bitterness. Nearly two years before the Eureka uprising, a respectable and well-educated eyewitness swore that police brutality on the diggings was "creating a spirit that will break out one of these days energetically".[5] As discontent with these very tangible evils grew among all diggers, some of their leaders began speaking of "no taxation without representation" and demanding far-reaching political reforms, including those of the People's Charter which had been drawn up in Britain in 1838 — universal manhood suffrage, vote by ballot, equal electoral districts, annual elections of parliament, abolition of property qualifications and payment of members. In the last weeks of November 1854, the Ballarat Reform League began to organise revolt. Led by an educated, middle-class Irishman, Peter Lalor, the diggers took up arms and built a stockade just outside Ballarat on a hilltop commanding the road to Melbourne. The stockade's defenders then proclaimed the Republic of Victoria, hoisted a blue-and-white Southern Cross flag, and swore by it "to stand truly by each other, and fight to defend [their] rights and liberties".

Thirst was their undoing. On Saturday 2 December, most of the armed diggers sallied forth to the hotels as usual. Troops and police attacked at 4.30 on Sunday morning in the half-light of dawn, and in a few minutes the Eureka Stockade had fallen. Twenty-two diggers and six solders were killed in the fight or died later of wounds. Among the dead diggers, ten were natives of Ireland, two of Germany, two of Canada, one of England, one of Scotland and one of Australia. Two of the remaining five were named Crowe and Fenton, but their birthplaces were unknown. All we know of the last three is that one of them was usually known on the Eureka by the nickname of "Happy Jack". Lalor, who lost an arm in the fight, escaped to Geelong in a cart driven by a certain Tommy Marx,[6] but a number of other alleged ringleaders were soon apprehended by the authorities. Among them were some Americans, but their consul in Melbourne succeeded in having all save one of them released before the trial. The exception was an American negro named John Joseph, about whom the consul does not seem to have concerned himself. He was one of the thirteen men brought to trial for high treason, but public opinion was so overwhelmingly in favour of the diggers that the jury acquitted them. Lalor lived to become the speaker of the Victorian Legislative Assembly. The best, and certainly the liveliest, contemporary account of these events was written by an Italian digger, Raffaello Carboni.[7]

Ever since 1854, Australians have argued about the significance of Eureka. In the last century popular opinion saw it as a fight for liberty, small in scale but great in symbolic significance, which hastened the establishment of full responsible self-government in 1856. This view is reflected by the American writer "Mark Twain", who wrote in his *More Tramps Abroad* (1875) that Eureka was "the finest thing in Australian history . . . It was the barons and John over again . . . It was Concord and Lexington . . . another instance of a victory won by a lost battle." Conservatives tended to dismiss it as a local riot, inspired by Irish and foreign malcontents, which had no appreciable effect on events at large. In this century historians have continued the debate, sometimes with acrimony. In 1923, long after most of the participants were dead, a Ballarat citizens' committee erected a monument to mark the site of the most considerable battle between white men fought on Australian soil. The memorial's inscription reflects nicely the uneasily ambivalent Australian attitude toward the Eureka Stockade: "To the honoured memory of the heroic pioneers who fought and fell, on this sacred spot, in the cause of liberty, and the soldiers who fell at Duty's Call." Similarly, the bullet-torn insurgent flag was long preserved in the Ballarat Art Gallery – not, however, in a prominently placed display case, but under lock and key in the curator's private desk. Increasingly, as the years passed, Eureka and the Eureka flag came to be seen as a potent symbol of radical nationalism. Communist, trade-union, Labor Party, republican and other politico-cultural organisations made much of the Eureka legend and often adopted its flag as their own.[8] Thus no commemorative postage-stamp to stir up dangerous thoughts was issued by the Liberal government of the Commonwealth in 1954, but soon after the election of a Labor government in 1972, the seditious flag itself was publicly displayed for the first time since it had been souvenired by one Constable King on the morning of the battle.[9]

The Royal Commission which inquired into the causes of the Eureka revolt felt that the diggers would have resorted to arms even if no foreigners had been among them. However this may be, there is general agreement among historians that the "white Australia" policy stemmed largely from passions aroused by the presence of foreigners on the goldfields. We have seen that most white Australians brutally ill-treated Aborigines almost from the moment of first contact, but there were few other non-white people to excite racial passions and even the most murderous "dispersers" of the Aborigines balked at the idea of deporting them from their own country. After the gold-rush decade, racist attitudes, and legislation aimed at excluding coloured people, continued to increase until they were given continent-wide force by the Commonwealth *Immigration Restriction Act* of 1901. Yet the influence of foreigners during the decade has often been exaggerated. The vast majority of immigrants continued to come from the British Isles, and a great many of them brought wives and children with them. In 1862, 92.5 per cent of the whole non-Aboriginal population had been born in the British Isles or in Australia. Most of the alien gold-seekers came without dependants, and many of them left after a few years on the diggings. Most of those who stayed were assimilated into the Australian society almost as readily and rapidly as the newcomers from Britain, but this was emphatically not the case with the Chinese, who comprised at once the largest group of foreign nationals and the only considerable non-European one. In 1857 in the colony of Victoria, about one in every seven males was a Chinese.

The Chinese seem on the whole to have been singularly law-abiding and inoffensive people. They were conspicuous by their absence at Eureka, and not even the most prejudiced colonist ever imagined the existence of a Chinese conspiracy to seize power. It was rather – as with the Australian Aborigines – that their very meekness was their undoing. Nearly all were of the coolie class, imported in the first instance by a few of their wealthy compatriots to dig till they had paid their debts for fares to "the great gold mountain". Generally they kept to themselves on the goldfields, only venturing to work "tailings" on claims that had been dug over and deserted by Europeans. Later many took up occupations such as market-gardening and laundering which were disdained by most colonists. Yet their low standard of living, their strange appearance and manners, and their completely alien culture aroused distrust which, by guilt reaction in the minds of the white majority, soon became hatred. People did not fear them, but feared that more and more would come to live in Australia until they became the majority when, naturally, they might do as they had been done by.

This nightmare vision of Australia being taken over piece-meal by gradual Chinese immigration was not as far-fetched to Australians in the second half of the nineteenth century as it seems today. At some places and times it seemed an imminent possibility – at the Palmer River Gold Rush for instance. This field, discovered in 1873 by James Mulligan from County Down, proved the richest alluvial gold-field ever found in Queensland. It was also the most disease-ridden and difficult in terms of access. Miners had to climb over the Great Dividing Range from Cooktown and run the gauntlet of unusually aggressive Aboriginal tribes before they could even stake their claims. Within a year or two about 5000 European miners were at work, but in 1876 there were no fewer than 17 000 Chinese on the Palmer, almost all of them adult males. The census of the same year showed that there were ony 17 042 white Australians in the whole of North Queensland, many of whom naturally were women and children. According to tradition, the old Australian defenders of their soil, the Aborigines, killed and ate Chinese invaders with more zest than they did the European ones.[10]

White Australian passions were further influenced at this time by the Kanaka trade, initiated in 1863 by Robert Towns, arguably the most hard-driving and acquisitive businessman of his day. He was the first person to import from the South Sea Islands indentured labourers, under one of the first acts passed by the newly established Queensland government. "Kanaka" is a Melanesian word for "man". Towns' men came to work on cotton plantations in the Logan River valley near Brisbane, but cotton-growing in Queensland failed with the end of the American Civil War in 1865. Sugar-growing along the Queensland coast began, however, at this time. By 1884 it had become one of the most important colonial industries, the profits of which were seen to depend on cheap Kanaka labour. How cheap was luridly demonstrated in that year when, of the thousands of Kanakas employed in Queensland, no fewer than one in every seven died.[11]

Legally and theoretically the Kanakas were free men who contracted to work on the sugar plantations for a fixed term, usually three years, in return for wages and "keep" as specified in the contract. In fact, many contemporaries thought Kanakas on the sugar plantations were little better off than slaves had been in the American South before the Civil War. The worst abuses occurred not in Queensland but on board the "recruiting" ships, which plied between Australian ports from Grafton northwards to Cooktown and Melanesian islands between Fiji and New Guinea. In June 1871, for example, the brig *Carl* set out to recruit labourers in the New Hebrides. At the subsequent trial for murder of the captain and one of the crew, Dr James Patrick Murray, part-owner of the vessel, turned Queen's evidence to save his own worthless hide.

Since the Kanakas were unwilling to volunteer for plantation work, Murray explained, they were kidnapped. The *Carl*'s men sank the Melanesians' canoes by dropping pig-iron through their bottoms, and then hit the swimming natives on the head "with clubs or slung shot" before dragging them aboard. In this way the *Carl*'s hold was soon filled with eighty Kanakas. On the night of 13 September, these men used the wooden beams from smashed bunks to try to batter their way out of the hold to freedom. The *Carl*'s crew subdued them by firing guns into the hold continuously for the eight hours of darkness. In the morning fifty men were dead, and only "about five" unwounded. About sixteen of the remainder were badly wounded but conscious. "There was," deposed the unspeakable Dr Murray, "a discussion as to what should be done with these men, and the general cry was — 'Over with them at once'." And so it was done, though the ship was out of sight of land and some of the wounded Kanakas were bound hand and foot.[12]

The drive into the Pacific was given a further push by Sir Thomas McIlwraith, like Towns an acquisitive and enterprising immigrant deeply imbued with the puritan work ethic. He reached Victoria in 1854 but soon invested his considerable capital in Queensland and became premier of that colony for the first time in 1879. The governor, Sir William MacGregor, thought him "an able bully with a face like a dugong and a temper like a buffalo". Others have seen him as the true founder of an Australian political tradition most evident in, but by no means peculiar to, Queensland — that a premier should put forward policies which *may* enrich the country, but which certainly *do* enrich himself or his relatives. McIlwraith's annexation of eastern New Guinea in 1883 was certainly not unconnected with the growing trade in Kanakas and other commodities between Queensland and that island, or with his family's growing shipping business. The British government disowned McIlwraith's action, but a year later partitioned the eastern part of the island with imperial Germany. More contacts with Papuans increased anxiety and compensatory delusions of superiority among white Queenslanders.[13]

Australian racist feelings were augmented too by the arrival at the diggings of many Americans, perhaps the largest group of foreign migrants after the Chinese. L.G. Churchward has calculated that about 20 000 persons from American ports landed in Melbourne and Sydney between 1852 and 1857. This compares with about 40 000 Chinese in Victoria alone in the latter year. Most stayed here for only two or three years, yet they exercised on Australian life an influence out of all proportion to their numbers. Many of them came from the Californian goldfields and their very similar frontier outlook, their more colourful "go-ahead" ways and their democratic republican background appealed strongly to colonists standing impatiently on the threshold of self-government. There is evidence to suggest that some American diggers, bringing with them their pre-Civil War racist attitudes, had an appreciable influence on the growth of colour-prejudice in Australia. The two major anti-Chinese riots on Victorian goldfields at Bendigo in 1854 and on the Buckland diggings in 1857 took place on the fourth of July, the anniversary of the American Declaration of Independence. At the Hanging Rock goldfield in northern New South Wales, another riot marked the "Glorious Fourth" in 1852, because a party of seven Americans "had a notion to Lynch [the Chinese]".

Americans also took a leading part in revolutionising land transport at this time. Before 1851, four-wheeled vehicles had been almost unknown in Australia outside the capital cities – and were not very common even there. In the bush people travelled on horseback, or else plodded along on foot beside the ponderous two-wheeled bullock-drays which carried all stores into, and wool out of, the interior of the country. There were practically no roads, and bush tracks were held to be impassable by four-wheeled vehicles. In 1851 and 1852, most of the newly arrived gold-seekers walked the hundred or two kilometres from Sydney or Melbourne to the diggings, but from 1853 onward most rode in the new, fast coaches. Freeman Cobb and James Rutherford, two newly arrived Americans, had most to do with the transformation. Despite the gloomy forebodings of the old colonial hands, the sturdily built four-wheeled Yankee-style coaches proved quite capable of negotiating bush tracks. With five stops to change horses, they carried passengers and mails up to 130 kilometres in a day, as against the bullock-dray's performance of as many kilometres in a week – under favourable conditions. Cobb and Co. began operating their coaching service between Melbourne and the main Victorian goldfield towns like Ballarat and Bendigo. By 1870, in the three eastern mainland colonies, the company was harnessing 6000 horses a day, its coaches were covering about 45 000 kilometres per week, and it was drawing about £100 000 a year in mail subsidies from the colonial governments. For more than half a century in Australia, the name Cobb and Co. was almost synonymous with "inland travel", although Cobb himself sold out early. He returned to America, became for a time state senator in the Massachussetts legislature, and then went to South Africa in 1870 to build another coaching empire; but he died there three years later.[14]

Inland transport was improved almost as much by navigation of the Murray–Darling river system, at least in the most populous southeast of the continent, as it was by the new-style coaches. In 1853, the same year that witnessed the first coach trips between Melbourne and Ballarat, two men sailed locally built paddle-steamers on the waters of the Murray. William Randell launched his *Mary Ann* at Mannum in South Australia, established a store at Hay on the Murrumbidgee and later sailed a boat up the Darling as far as Walgett, only about 100 kilometres from the Queensland border. Francis Cadell had his *Lady Augusta* built in Sydney, whence she paddled her way to Port Elliot in South Australia. There Cadell took command and successfully took her through the shifting and treacherous shoals of the Murray mouth – a feat of seamanship that has rarely been equalled. Soon hundreds of paddle-steamers, usually towing strings of barges, were carrying station stores into and wool out of the interior of four colonies, and carrying them more cheaply than the drivers of bullock and horse teams could do. The river trade did much to draw together the commercial and other interests of the four eastern mainland colonies. In rare wet seasons, river boats occasionally passed Walgett and reached stations on the Queensland border. Gundagai was the effective head of navigation on the Murrumbidgee and Albury on the Murray. The river traffic increased the prosperity of both towns, prosperity which had sprung initially from their being the best practicable crossing places on the main overland route, pioneered by Hume and Hovell, between Sydney and Melbourne. In the 1880s, when the river trade was at its peak, the busiest port was Echuca on the Murray, the first point on that river to be

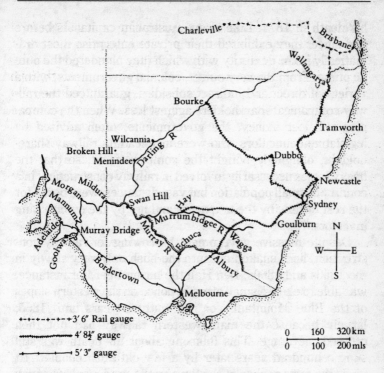

Figure 19 River traffic and main railways built by 1888

joined to Melbourne by rail. In the 1860s and 1870s, more than one-third of all New South Wales wool was sent to market by paddle-steamers.[15]

Railway building in Australia was much discussed in the late 1840s, but the first shovelful of earth on the first railway to be planned, from Sydney to Parramatta, was not actually dug until 1850. When it was finished five years later, Victoria's first line, from Melbourne to Port Melbourne, had been carrying goods over its 4 kilometres of track for a year. South Australia followed with a line from Adelaide to its Port a few years later. All these railways were instigated by private capitalists, men like Thomas Mort, whose statue in Macquarie Place looks across the street today, appropriately, at the Sydney Stock Exchange founded only two years before his death in 1874. Like many Australian capitalists before and since, they exhibited their private enterprise most dramatically in the dexterity with which they plundered the public purse. From the very outset, colonial governments, with a variety of direct and indirect subsidies, guaranteed the railway companies' shareholders against loss. When the companies still lost money, the governments, often advised by legislative councillors who were also leading railway shareholders, obligingly bought the companies out, so that the heavy losses necessarily involved in railway construction, in a country of small population but vast distances, were borne for the rest of time by the taxpayers and not by the enterprising investors.[16]

Despite massive government borrowing for railway construction, lines snaked out into the bush only very slowly in the 1850s and 1860s. Ben Hall the bushranger, for instance, was able to elude a small army of police on the western slopes of the Blue Mountains for nearly three years until 1865, largely because the main western railway had not then crossed the range. This folksong about his death was still sung a hundred years later by a few old bush people.* (It gives the facts as seen at the time by the dead man's friends):

Come all you Lachlan men and a sorrowful tale I'll tell,
Concerning of a hero bold who through misfortune fell.
His name it was Ben Hall, a man of good renown,
Who was hunted from his station and like a dog shot down.
Three years he roamed the road and he showed the traps some fun.
A thousand pound was on his head with Gilbert and John Dunne.
Ben parted from his comrades, the outlaws did agree
To give away bushranging and cross the briny sea.
Ben went to Goobang Creek and that was his downfall,
For riddled like a sieve was valiant Ben Hall.
T'was early in the morning upon the fifth of May
When the seven police surrounded him as fast asleep he lay.
Bill Dargin he was chosen to shoot the outlaw dead.
The troopers then fired madly and filled him full of lead.
They rolled him in a blanket and strapped him to his prad,
And led him through the streets of Forbes
            to show the prize they had.

They led him through the streets of Forbes
    to show the prize they had.
* *Source:* Sung by Mrs Sally Sloane, who learnt the song from her grandmother.
Note: traps — policeman; prad — horse

By 1880, when Ned Kelly was captured at Glenrowan by a
trainload of police despatched from Melbourne, railways had
crossed the Great Dividing Range in many places and were
beginning to annihilate time and distance in country travel.
By 1888 the four main railway systems of Queensland, South
Australia, Victoria and New South Wales had joined at the
colonial borders. In that year Lawson wrote nostalgically,
"The mighty Bush with iron rails is tethered to the world".[17]
Passengers could go by rail from Adelaide to Brisbane and
back again, though not without the annoying change of gauge
at the borders which plagued travellers for so long afterwards. As the railheads moved further out to more remote
townships, the coaches moved too, providing feeder-services
from outback mining camps and cattle-stations to the rail termini. By 1890, travellers from even the most distant parts of
a colony could reach the colonial capital or other coastal port
in a day or two where it had taken as many months only forty
years earlier.

Communication between Australia and the rest of the
world, particularly that part of it which most colonists continued to call "Home", speeded up just as dramatically. The
First Fleet took about eight months to reach Botany Bay.
Twenty-seven years later, British and Prussian soldiers defeated Napoleon's Old Guard at the Battle of Waterloo in
June 1815. Official news of this momentous victory, which
determined the shape of European and world politics for a
century afterwards, did not reach Sydney until March 1816
— again about nine months later — but by then the average
time for a voyage had been reduced to about five months. In
the last decade before gold, voyages of about four months
were not uncommon, but in that same decade occurred the
greatest revolution in shipbuilding since the European Renaissance. Spurred partly by competition from early steamships, shipping men in the Canadian maritime provinces of

Nova Scotia and New Brunswick and in the New England states of the United States designed and built hundreds of new streamlined sailing ships. These came to be known as "clippers" because, Americans said, they moved "at a fast clip" and they seemed constantly to be clipping days off the duration of a voyage. By running before the "roaring forties" from the Cape of Good Hope to Melbourne, the clipper ships in the golden decade reduced the time for an average voyage to about fourteen weeks. Great clippers whose names have become legendary – such as *Lightning, James Baines, Thermopylae, Cutty Sark* or *Flying Cloud* – sometimes made it in as little as nine weeks. Some crack ships of the Black Ball or White Star Lines claimed to have covered 400 sea-miles in a single day in the Roaring Forties. Legend holds that on such occasions skippers like the famous "Bully" Forbes would hold a lighted candle on the plunging deck – the ship was moving at almost the same speed as the wind.[18]

The first steamships – or rather, steam-assisted ships – also reached Australia before or during the golden decade. At first they were not much faster and a good deal less reliable than the clipper ships. Sydney citizens rejoiced exceedingly when the "first" mail steamer, the P&O Company's *Chusan*, arrived on 3 August 1852, but she had taken sixty-seven days of "actual running time", that is, time exclusive of days or weeks spent in ports en route. The opening of the Suez Canal in 1869 cut time for steamer-borne mails from London to Melbourne to about fifty days, but windjammers still carried most goods and passengers to Australia. In 1880 most overseas ships to visit Australian ports were still moved by the winds. By 1900 most were steamers capable of making the trip in about five weeks.[19]

Transmission of news by the electric telegraph represented the greatest leap forward in communications in world history, far greater in its immediate effects than the invention of aircraft or wireless telegraphy or television. Telegraph lines were first put to practical use in North America and Europe in the late 1840s and the 1850s. In Australia the four largest colonial capitals were connected with each other, and with a few large country towns, by 1861, but news still took at least five weeks to come from Britain even after the opening of the Suez Canal eight years later. Then, on New Year's Day 1870, Charles Todd became postmaster-general and superintendent of telegraphs for the province of South Australia, which had recently acquired from New South Wales responsibility for the Northern Territory. In a little more than two years he planned and supervised the building of the overland telegraph line to Palmerston (Port Darwin). There was no time for a proper survey. Todd and his men relied, perforce, on the rough maps made by the explorer John McDouall Stuart ten years earlier. Their job was not made any easier by the Aborigines who quickly learnt that the porcelain insulators made excellent spearheads. Yet the line was pushed through about 3250 kilometres of bush and desert in two years: no other public work in the history of Australia can have been carried out so expeditiously. The two ends of the line met north of Alice Springs, named after Todd's wife, on 22 August 1872, though messages could not be sent on through the submarine cable from Darwin for another two months. Thenceforth world news reached the solid citizens of the eastern cities with their breakfast newspaper instead of five weeks after it had happened.[20]

The gold rush of the 1850s exacerbated racist prejudice among white Australians and brought about, or at least accompanied, a revolution in transport and communications. What other important effects did it have on our history? Most obviously it caused a sudden increase in population and wealth and in the rate at which Sydney, Melbourne and other colonial capitals changed from administrative townships into great cities. In the sixty-odd years after the First Fleeters landed at Sydney Cove, the white population increased slowly to 405 000. In the decade of the Gold Rush, 1851–61, this figure grew to about 1 146 000. In these ten years the white population of the continent nearly trebled, while that of the infant colony of Victoria increased sixfold from 87 000 to 540 000. For the next forty years or so, Victoria, and not the mother colony of New South Wales, was the most prosperous and influential colony. National wealth and the gross value of exports increased proportionately during the decade.[21] Naturally contemporaries thought that it was scarcely possible to exaggerate the importance and the likely results of the discoveries. Most seem to have felt that W.C. Wentworth was uttering only a truism when in July 1851 he said that gold had opened a new era "which must in a very few years precipitate us from a colony into a nation", yet ten years later many people doubted whether the golden decade had made very much difference to Australian society. In 1861 the first principal of Sydney University, John Woolley, gave a public lecture in which he painted a somewhat idealised picture of the cultural and national unity of ancient Greece. He then asked:

> Can we hope that Australia in a hundred years will present a counterpart to this picture? Five years ago [i.e. at the time of the inauguration of responsible government] we should have answered with an indignant and enthusiastic affirmative. But experience has taught us humility; we have learned that no accidental impulse can precipitate an infant community into a nation . . . A corporate like a national body grows only from within.[22]

Historians have tended to echo these conflicting opinions but with a time lag of a century or so. Many were motivated by a conscious or unconscious desire to minimise the influence of Australia's convict origins. Until quite recently, most writers exaggerated the revolutionary effects of gold. Some even spoke at times of the "second" or "real" foundation of Australia in 1851. Now the wheel has come full circle, and most historians would probably endorse I.D. McNaughtan's words in Gordon Greenwood's *Australia* (1955):

> With the perspective of a century it can be seen that the digger's era left a fainter impression on Australian life than the first ten years of the squatting age [1832–1842] . . . Gold . . . gave a greater complexity to Australian society and a powerful impulse to existing trends . . . Certainly it did not create a nation. The Colonies had before them another generation of parochialism and hard pioneering before political, economic and social life began to set in the native and characteristic forms of modern Australia.[23]

There is something valid in both views. If the gold discov-

eries did no more than accelerate most existing trends, the
degree to which some of them were speeded up was immense. On the other hand, gold actually slowed down, or
masked for a generation, the development of other trends —
most notably of an indigenous national sentiment. Both
effects stemmed largely from the very marked growth of
middle-class influence brought about, especially in the cities,
by the gold rush.

We have seen that, with the cessation of transportation to
the eastern mainland in 1840, thousands of assisted migrants
were brought out to supply the labour market.[24] The pastoral
boom attracted also a much smaller number of aspiring squatters, many of whom were men of substance and culture. Yet
in an almost purely pastoral economy the number and influence of city-dwelling, middle-class, commercial and professional people remained relatively slight — certainly by
subsequent Australian standards. There was undoubtedly an
element of exaggeration in the 1851 *Remonstrance of the Legislative Council of New South Wales*, addressed to the home
government, which roundly declared that the majority of the
assisted immigrants were the spiritless "outpourings of the
poor-houses and the unions of the United Kingdom", but
until that year most observers endorsed James Dixon's opinion that Australia was "a country possessing two distinct
sorts of mankind [sic] . . . Perhaps in all societies it is in some
measure the same, but here it is more strongly felt."[25] Gold
rapidly changed this state of affairs. The major colonial governments suspended, or greatly reduced, their assisted immigration programs as it became clear that thousands of
migrants, able and anxious to pay for their own voyages,
were crowding Australia-bound ships. Most of those who arrived during the golden decade had at least enough money to
pay the high fares demanded, and there is certainly something in the view that they were usually much more self-reliant and enterprising people on landing than the earlier
immigrants had been. It seems too that they included a lower
proportion of unskilled labourers and a correspondingly

higher proportion of skilled and semi-skilled artisans, trades-men, white-collar workers and professional men.

The vast majority of all post-1851 immigrants were, in contemporary English terminology, lower middle-class or upper working-class people, almost all indeed middle class in terms of their aspirations. Most were deeply imbued with the Protestant work ethic and with Samuel Smiles' doctrine of self-help. Comparatively few of them had working-class backgrounds and fewer still thought of themselves as belonging to the working class. Nearly all yearned, more or less passionately, to "become independent": by which they meant to become their own masters, if not necessarily the employers of others. They were possessed by bourgeois ideology and many of them during the long boom up to about 1890 succeeded in joining the petty-bourgeoisie. Some of course, like J.M. Bruce, father of the future prime minister, Lord Bruce of Melbourne, became great commercial magnates. Most of them, like David Syme, founder of the *Age* newspaper, after a quite short sojourn on the diggings, moved to the city, for that was where money might be made and "independence" won.

Gold thus began the process of "urbanisation", a word some historians have treated with the reverential awe they reserve for abstract concepts which seem to explain everything: but urbanisation was a dramatic rather than an awesome process. When gold "broke out" in 1852, Melbourne – the second largest settlement in the content – numbered 23 000 people – by world standards a small town rather than a city. Nine years later the population had risen to 140 000 and by the census of 1891 to 491 000, nearly half a million. In the same forty-year period Sydney grew from 54 000 to 384 000 and the smaller colonial capitals grew proportionately: Adelaide, for instance, from 14 000 to 133 000. By the end of the century, both Sydney and Melbourne were great cities by any standard. David Syme's *Age*, Melbournians boasted, had the greatest circulation of any newspaper "in the southern hemisphere". In 1883 Melbourne installed a system of cable trams many years before trams of any sort were seen elsewhere in Australia. Visitors as well as residents spoke of "Marvellous Melbourne", which was seen as bustling, up-to-date and "yankeefied" in contrast with staid and old-fashioned Sydney, sometimes referred to by Melbournians as "Sleepy Hollow". Jealous Sydneysiders in turn sneered at "S'Marvellous s'Melbourne", in not very subtle allusion to the already polluted River Yarra, for at this period Melbourne was easily the greatest manufacturing city in the colonies as well as the greatest commercial and financial centre. Merchants, manufacturers and retired squatters like Sir William Clarke, Australia's first native-born baronet, built in the suburbs princely mansions on the profits of their varied enterprises. Very often the same person engaged in both rural and urban activities. Thomas Mort began as a Sydney auctioneer who later invested in country properties and the manufacture of refrigerating machinery. In Melbourne, Sir Frederick Sargood combined an extremely lucrative business career with service as politician and the proprietorship of sheep stations in New South Wales.[26] Perhaps the most successful man of the period was a Canadian immigrant named Simon Fraser, grandfather of Malcolm Fraser, prime minister of Australia from 1975 to 1983. Simon Fraser dug up a small fortune in the early gold rush to Bendigo, made a great one as a railway construction contractor, bought pastoral properties in three colonies, pioneered the search for artesian water and became a member of the Victorian, and then the Commonwealth, parliaments for nearly forty years. He was probably the only eminent Victorian in Australia to have his portrait painted by Millais.

Yet though the great cities spawned ever-growing numbers of factories, banks, import and export agencies, warehouses, shops, Italianate mansions for the wealthy and slums of terrace-houses for the poor, their growth depended largely on the country areas whence they drew so much of their wealth. Gold, of course, was found in the bush, not in the streets of Melbourne or Sydney, or even Adelaide or Perth. From 1852 to 1870 it was the most valuable export, bringing back more goods and money even than wool, but practically every ounce of gold was bought and sold through the head offices of banks in the colonial capital where, for the most part, brokerage fees and other profits remained. The pastoral industry continued to expand until about 1890 and wool remained Australia's staple commodity and major export until long after World War II, but the colonial cities profited more from it than did those who produced it on the stations. Roads and railways radiated out from the capital city in each colony, ensuring that wool, like minerals and every other primary product of the land, would be brought to, sold or processed in, and exported through, the cities.

We have seen that this was true even of gold, though paradoxically gold did more, before it was exported, to populate the countryside than did wool production. Gold, as it happened, was found here and there on the slopes, mainly the inland slopes, of the Great Dividing Range, just that part of the country best suited to support many more people than could be employed in the pastoral industry. In a great arc stretching from inland Victoria to beyond Charters Towers in North Queensland gold attracted people to found scores of towns like Bendigo, Ballarat, Beechworth, Young, Orange, Parkes, Gympie and Cloncurry, or to swell the population of older ones like Wangaratta, Bathurst, Toowoomba, Tamworth or Gundagai. Though most people came for gold, many remained after the lodes were worked out, to supply goods and services to farmers in the surrounding countryside. Thus gold helped to realise, to some degree, the great dream of nineteenth-century Australian liberals, that the better parts of the bush should support people instead of sheep.[27]

Historians who ascribe peculiar virtue to the shibboleth "urbanisation" count all these country towns, and indeed any hamlet of more than 500 people, as cities, and their history assumes that the dwellers in bush townships were generally sophisticated people of the same kind as the citizens of Melbourne or Brisbane or Perth. This is ridiculous. Apart from Ballarat and Bendigo, even the biggest country towns at this period numbered their population in thousands rather than in tens of thousands. By world standards they were large villages rather than small cities. They were and have remained purely local centres whose inhabitants generally regarded themselves as living "in the bush" rather than in the wicked city, and who generally articulated "bush" attitudes in politics and other spheres. The simple truth of the matter is summed up in the old folk saying "Sydney or the Bush" — where Sydney means any Australian capital city.

In both places, but especially in the cities, the gold-rush immigrants did much to raise the general standard of education, refinement and culture. The University of Sydney, for instance, was founded in 1852 and the Australian Museum in the same city in the following year. Melbourne opened its university in 1854 and its great public library in 1856. Universities opened their doors also in Adelaide and Hobart before 1891. In this same period following the gold discoveries, art galleries and libraries were begun in the colonial capitals. Lord-mayors and aldermen symbolised their faith in progress by building in stone ornate, Victorian–Gothic town halls — usually both more commodious and more inconvenient than anything of the kind erected since.

Most important of all these cultural developments, at least in its long-term effects, was the Churches' establishment of the great secondary schools in the cities, like Melbourne Grammar School and Presbyterian Ladies' College in Melbourne, or Prince Alfred College in Adelaide or Hutchins School in Hobart. There were no public or state secondary schools so that, inevitably, except for a handful of "scholarship girls and boys", the only Australian children to receive any secondary schooling at all were those whose parents were rich enough to pay the high fees demanded. Higher or secondary education was thus the preserve of the upper bourgeoisie. Many people scraped money together to send their children to these schools so that they might make friends with "nice people", who might be useful to them in later life. Though most schools gave as good an education as could be had anywhere in the world at the time, they also did much to accentuate class divisions and to produce snobs. Catholic secondary schools took religious education seriously. Protestant ones often tried to, but in practice boys and girls learnt to set more store by "good form" and "right thinking" than by the example of the Judean Carpenter. Even more divisive of the Australian community was the heavy emphasis these schools placed on loyalty to Britain and their deprecation of all things Australian. Their headmasters and headmistresses were almost always imported from Britain. Naturally they looked to their homeland, even more fervently than well-to-do Australians usually did, as the fountainhead of all learning, loveliness and culture. From the 1850s onwards, Church secondary schools did much to perpetuate the already strong tendency of middle-class Australians to look to Britain as their true homeland.

The success – and failure – of their efforts is exemplified by the life and work of Ethel Richardson ("Henry Handel Richardson"), arguably the most distinguished scholar of the Melbourne Presbyterian Ladies' College, or any other girls' Church school of the period. When she left school in 1886 she had received one of the very best educations available to the children of the bourgeoisie in either Australia or England. Like many other young Australians of the time, she thus acquired – and kept – an outlook on life very much more subtle, sensitive and sophisticated than had been available to earlier generations of colonial youth. Yet her teachers would have sighed over her when she first arrived in England at the age of 17, "a sturdy young radical, convinced that one man was as good as another" and detesting English snobbery and subservience to titled persons.[28] She nevertheless lived in England for most of her life and wrote there what many critics think the greatest of all Australian novels, before the advent of Patrick White, *The Fortunes of Richard Mahony*. This work shows, perhaps more than her life, how imperfectly successful her teachers had been. Mahony, the protagonist, spends his life wrestling with what sociologists, an unknown species in his day, would have called an identity crisis. Is he English or Australian? He loves and hates much in both countries and travels back and forth between them, but is really at home in neither. His inability to resolve the conflict finally helps to drive him mad.

No doubt most of Ethel Richardson's classmates, like most other middle-class girls, lived out their lives in Australia, thereby mitigating the severity of the identity crisis their education had prepared for them, but it had prepared them also for a life very much fuller, freer, even more equal – within the constraints of a still very male-dominated society – than their mothers had known. Many of the latter were no doubt some of Caroline Chisholm's immigrant girls who had fulfilled her fondest hopes. They had joined God's police force themselves and thereby assured their daughters of a place in the bourgeoisie.

For women in less exalted strata of society, especially those who lived in the still-barbarous bush, life had become on the whole harder because of the increasingly puritan, not to say wowserish, temper of society. How much harder is vividly suggested by the life story of Margaret McTavish, born in 1843 on Duntroon Station, now the site of the Royal Military College, Canberra. When she was 14, her father caught her in the act of riding a horse astride. For this disgracefully immodest act he thrashed her so brutally that she was confined to her bed for "several weeks". As soon as she could walk again she sought refuge with the other abused section of colonial society, "the local tribe of Blacks", who "were very kind to her and never insulted or abused her in any way". After a months's freedom her father caught her and "burnt the soles of her feet with a hot iron" to prevent her running away again. This time, on recovery, she disguised herself as a boy and got a job as a bullock-driver's offsider. She worked for the next six years as a bullocky and horse-breaker, her true sex being revealed only as a result of injuries she sustained when an outlaw horse fell on her. When she was well again she married a Monaro squatter and raised a family of seven children. Of course, Margaret McTavish was extremely unlucky. Few males can have been as tyrannical as her father, whom local opinion forced to leave Duntroon when her story became known, but there is no reason to think her experiences unique.[29]

The continuing exploitation of so many women may serve to remind us that the cultural aspirations of the period were considerably more impressive than its achievements. For the thirty or forty years following 1851, even in many ways until the end of World War II, Australia remained basically a remote, provincial British society. In some ways its British character was actually accentuated, at least temporarily, and especially in Victoria and in the cities, by the effects of the gold rush. This was so for two reasons. First, the sudden influx of British immigrants greatly increased the already high proportion which was in fact British by birth and nurture, as well as by sentiment. Second, the high proportion of middle-class people among the newcomers strongly reinforced that respectable section of Australian society which, as we have seen, always tended to look to the mother country – naturally the source of culture and civilisation – for its inspiration. Yet this does not mean that the new immigrants exercised a conservative political influence. Quite the contrary – unless we equate conservatism with stability rather than with preservation of the *status quo*. On the whole they seem to have had a stabilising effect on colonial life precisely because most of them were liberal or radical in outlook. There were, after all, very few immigrants of aristocratic or upper class (in a contemporary English sense) background among the newcomers. These few were often labelled by the colonists "remittance men" or "broken-down swells". Few of the artisans, white-collar people and tradesmen who made up the majority dreamed of entertaining socialist or revolutionary notions.

As Peter Lalor said in a well-known speech, "I would ask these gentlemen what they mean by the term 'Democracy'. Do they mean Chartism or Communism or Republicanism? If so, I never was, I am not now, nor do I ever intend to be, a Democrat." Lalor's speech was made after, not before, the Eureka affair and it certainly plays down the extent of Chartist influence among the diggers. Even so, most of them seem to have belonged to that middling, if rising, order of contemporary British society which made Mr Gladstone such a power at the time in England. As Sir Charles Dilke said of the period, Australian society was English "with the upper class left out". Thus, in the third quarter of the nineteenth-century, Australian political sentiment was overwhelmingly liberal, even radical, but at the same time strongly individualist and not markedly either collectivist or nationalist. John Stuart Mill was the philosophical mentor of most politicians literate enough to be aware of theoretical writings.

In 1850, even before the gold discoveries, the imperial Parliament had passed an *Act for the Better Government of Her Majesty's Australian Colonies*. This Act gave to the then four major colonies (New South Wales, Van Diemen's Land, Victoria and South Australia) Legislative Councils, two-thirds elective on the New South Wales model; but it also extended the franchise on which they were to be elected, and invited them to submit for imperial approval constitutions of their own devising, subject only to the proviso that final control of Crown lands and of the civil services were to remain in the hands of the imperial government. In New South Wales, W.C. Wentworth, who had grown steadily more conservative with the years, chaired the Council's committee of constitution-makers, which included also James Macarthur. As leader of the squatters, Wentworth's voice was loudest in demanding that the new colonial legislatures should control fully the disposal of Crown lands and all colonial revenue including the civil lists; but at the same time he sought to ensure that the new parliaments would themselves be controlled by the great propertied "interests" of the colony — primarily, that is, by the squatters. The demand for full responsible self-government was quickly conceded by the secretary of state for the colonies, in large part because, as he wrote in a dispatch in 1852, the gold discoveries had "imparted new and unforeseen features to [Australia's] political and social condition".[30] The lingering aroma of convictism was no longer deemed a sufficient reason for refusing to the Australian colonies what had already been granted, following the Durham Report of 1839, to the major North American colonies and was in the process of being granted to New Zealand.

The other constitutional recommendations of the Council's Select Committee provoked determined local opposition. Wentworth, Macarthur and their supporters sought conservative safeguards, including the creation of an Upper House consisting of an order of hereditary colonial baronets, electoral arrangements which would give the squatting districts grossly disproportionate representation in the Lower House, and a provision that the constitution could never be altered except by an "unusual majority" of two-thirds of the members of both houses. The first proposal for a hereditary aristocracy was, so to speak, laughed out of court, partly as the result of a speech by Daniel Deniehy, a 24-year-old Currency lad of convict stock who might have made a bigger mark in the world if he had not drunk himself to death a few years later. He suggested that in the proposed "bunyip aristocracy" James Macarthur would become at least an earl, and offered as the coat-of-arms for his family "a field vert, and emblazoned on this field . . . a rum keg of a New South Wales order of chivalry".[31] In the event, New South Wales acquired an Upper House whose members were nominated – for life terms – by the governor, but in the other three colonies Upper-House members were elected on a moderately restrictive property qualification. Ironically, these elected Upper Houses proved on the whole more effective in resisting change than the nominated houses in New South Wales and Queensland.

In Victoria, for instance, there were two major battles between the two houses in fourteen years. In 1865–66 the Legislative Council rejected Victoria's first, and very moderate, protectionist tariff, introduced by a ministry led in the Legislative Assembly by the liberal politician James McCulloch. In 1877–78 the Council rejected a bill renewing payment for members of parliament, sent up from the Lower House by Graham Berry's radical protectionist government. On both occasions passions were torn to tatters inside and outside the

Table 3
Progress of "Liberalism" in the various colonies, 1850–1908

COLONY	FIRST SELECTION ACT PASSED	CRUCIAL SECULAR EDUCATION ACT PASSED	RESPONSIBLE GOVT GRANTED	ADULT MALE SUFFRAGE FOR ENROLLED ELECTORS	SECRET BALLOT	ABOLITION OF PLURAL VOTING	FEMALE SUFFRAGE	PAYMENT OF MEMBERS	TRIENNIAL PARLIAMENTS
NSW	1861	1880	1855	1858	1858	1893	1902	1889	1874
TAS	1858	1885	1856	1900	1858	1900	1903	1890	1891
WA	1872	1893	1890	1893	1877	1907	1899	1900	1900
VIC	1860	1872	1856	1857	1856	1899	1908	1870	1859
SA	1872	1875	1856	1856	1856	1856	1894	1887	1856*
QLD	1860	1875	1859	1872	1859	1905	1905	1886	1890

*Five-year Parliaments 1933–1939

houses, partly because the desired measures had been
"tacked" on to supply bills. On "Black Wednesday", 8 January 1878; Berry dismissed hundreds of judges, magistrates
and other senior civil servants, because there was no money
left in the Treasury to pay them, and also, he said, in order to
be revenged on the recalcitrant Upper House by hurting
great numbers of its members' friends. During these and
comparable confrontations between the two houses in other
colonies, the governors supported the ministries of the day,
so long as they commanded majorities in the Lower House,
and in the end political compromises were reached – compromises which usually left intact the great powers of the
elected legislative councils. The other major safeguard of
propertied interests, the two-thirds majority clause, was defeated in Great Britain. When the New South Wales Constitution Bill came before the House of Commons, Lord John
Russell, the architect of the British Great Reform Bill of
1932, was serving as Colonial Secretary. His influence may
have been instrumental in having the bill altered so as to
allow for constitutional amendment by a simple majority.
Wentworth was dismayed at this opening of the flood-gates
to the influence of "mere population . . . selfishness, ignorance and democracy". The old patriot returned only briefly
to the scene of his triumphs, now saddled, as he saw it, with
"a Yankee constitution". He retired in 1862 to live in England and died there ten years later.

Thus in the years 1855 and 1856 the four major colonies
achieved – or were given – almost complete control of their
own destinies. Queensland was granted a similar constitution
upon its separation from New South Wales four years later,
but Western Australia, which was still receiving convicts,
had to wait until 1890, long after its convict period was over.
Some of Wentworth's forebodings were fulfilled with what
seemed, to many contemporaries, astonishing rapidity. By
the end of 1858 the three most populous colonies of Victoria,
New South Wales and South Australia had established constitutions which were among the most democratic then existing in the world, South Australia's particularly. Its first

responsible parliament was elected in 1857 on universal manhood suffrage and by secret ballot. The latter method of voting is still sometimes called, in Britain and North America, the "Australian ballot". Moreover, about two-thirds of the seats in the Lower House, the Legislative Assembly, were given to Adelaide and its immediate neighbourhood, and the whole colony voted as a single constituency, on a moderately restrictive property franchise, for the Legislative Council. Thus the influence of "mere population" was given much weight from the beginning. Herman Merivale, the liberal-minded under-secretary of state for the colonies, was intrigued to see how what he saw as perhaps "the only thoroughly Benthamite constitution" in the world would work.

Victoria also employed the secret ballot from the beginning. Within two or three years popular pressure on elected representatives had won the secret ballot and almost complete manhood suffrage in New South Wales also. Many contemporaries felt that the Australian colonies had "shot Niagara", and such people looked forward apprehensively with Wentworth to the results of giving political power to "mere numbers". But they were wrong. As Professor C.M.H. Clark has stressed, unobtrusive safeguards for propertied interests were still embedded in the colonial constitutions. Except in South Australia, plural voting – for those with property in more than one electorate and for some other presumptively respectable persons – continued until the late 1880s and sometimes longer. Nomadic pastoral workers, of whom there were many, and other men of no fixed address, were excluded from voting at least as long, as were all women. Payment of members was not introduced until 1870 in Victoria, and not until the late 1880s in the other colonies, and its absence effectively helped to deprive working-class voters of direct representation in parliaments by men drawn from their own ranks. There were other and deeper reasons, however, for the moderate tone of colonial politics from the granting of responsible government until the late 1880s.

Some of them have been mentioned already. Responsible government might not have been established when it was, if it had not been for the great strengthening of the middle class brought about by the gold discoveries. Moreover, without this middle order of liberal-minded but respectable townspeople, self-governing institutions would probably not have functioned as smoothly as they did. Second, gold mining caused a great diversification of the economy. For two decades, gold surpassed wool as the staple export. For the first time, retail trades of all kinds flourished, and many rudimentary manufacturing industries, such as food-processing, and the making of builders' supplies and of clothes for the local market, were established. Though there were brief periods of recession, until about 1890 there was no serious check to the prosperous and steadily expanding colonial economies. Under these conditions, skilled workmen, no less than their employers, could aspire to vastly better living standards than obtained in contemporary Britain. Artisans formed trade unions in the cities, and many skilled building workers won for themselves an eight-hour day from 1856 onward in Sydney and Melbourne. But most workers, including almost all rural employees, remained unorganised until the later 1880s, and most of the small craft unions in the towns spent almost as much time keeping unqualified men out of their ranks as they did agitating for better pay and conditions. Many, even of their leaders, held to the conservative belief that trade unions should "keep out of politics". Thus the colonial parliaments were filled during the period largely by middle-class townspeople. A radical-minded Victorian barrister, George Higinbotham, who was himself a member of parliament for many years, sardonically characterised contemporary politicians as men drawn for the most part from "the wealthy lower orders . . . lawyers, journalists, officials, publicans and traders of the metropolis". This was so in the first instance because working-class voters, insofar as they were politically conscious, agreed with middle-class businessmen in resenting the traditionally established dominance of affairs by the "pure merino" squatting interests. It continued to be so for thirty years because of the political, social and economic conditions sketched above. So true was Dilke's dictum that Australian society lacked an "upper class" that, until the 1880s, it is hard to see many signs of growth of political parties based on fixed principles, or on class, religious, regional or other interests. From as early as 1860 onwards, nearly all actual or aspiring politicians at least liked to let it be thought that they were "liberals". Men of unusual ability, like Henry Parkes or John Robertson in New South Wales, or Graham Berry in Victoria, or C.C. Kingston in South Australia, tended to attract a band of personal followers which could be held together for brief periods by the conferment of places or perquisites, or of public works in the right electorates: but as every member gloried in his "independence" and felt free to vote on each new issue as private principles, conscience or interest dictated, these alliances were usually brief and precarious. The promise of a new railway extension to the member for one constituency, or of a few places in the civil service to the clients of another might put a governing coalition into or out of office. The result was that governments rose and fell much more often than they have done since and that, for most of the period in most of the colonies, parties could be distinguished only as the (temporary) "ministerialists" or "opposition". Thus John Martineau wrote in 1869:

> It is a fact notorious in Victoria that a proportion of the Legislative Assembly, sufficient to sway its vote on almost any measure . . . is altogether corrupt and amenable to bribes! . . . In answer to a question as to the character and composition of the [New South Wales] Lower House . . . I was told that it was *now* no worse than that of Victoria.[32]

Yet we should notice that not even this hostile witness claimed that the *majority* of members were altogether corrupt. Some consistently held throughout long parliamentary careers to at least a few general principles, like support for free trade or protectionist fiscal policies, and some naturally proved in office more liberal than others. Though the level of political corruption was, understandably, higher than it became later after payment of members was introduced and fixed parties developed, many members undoubtedly worked conscientiously for the public weal, as they "independently" saw it. During the thirty years or so following 1856, they spent much time wrangling over local developmental questions — "roads and bridges" issues, as they were often called — but even these parish pump arguments usually resulted in added, if piecemeal, development of the country's resources. The politicians also debated and legislated upon three great questions which were agitating their constituents. These were the control and use of the land, the control of education, and the best kind of fiscal policy to be followed. We shall glance at each in turn.

By the time gold was discovered, much of the best and most accessible country had already been occupied by graziers. In the oldest colonies of New South Wales and Van Diemen's Land, quite large areas near Sydney, Hobart and Launceston had been granted as estates in freehold to wealthy settlers like the Macarthurs. Farther out, vast areas were leased by the squatters under easy terms which gave them a "pre-emptive right" to buy the best pockets of country outright. Yet much of this land was well-watered and fertile enough to support agriculture. As the gold fever subsided, people asked more and more loudly why so much land should be "locked up" in pastoral leases which supported only a very sparse, and relatively impoverished, human population of shepherds and bush-workers. If the vast sheepwalks were cut up into small blocks and sold to working agricultural proprietors, it was held that an "independent" class of yeoman farmers would, with their families, bring new population and prosperity to the bush. Thus, almost from the beginning of the gold-rush decade, there arose an increasing popular clamour to "unlock the lands", and contention over the land question was the main preoccupation of colonial parliaments for the first ten years or more of responsible government.

Historians used to believe that the *Free Selection Acts* of 1860 and following years were passed in response to this popular demand. However, research by D.W.A. Baker and others has shown that the matter was by no means as simple as this. There were in fact relatively few successful diggers and other small capitalists who yearned to become farmers on their own account. It now seems that the "lawyers, journal-

ists, officials, publicans and traders of the metropolis", and of
the country towns, who had no such ambition for themselves,
provided most of the movement's impetus. These people,
whose numbers had been so mightily augmented by the in-
rush of new immigrants, resented what they — in common
with the rest of the population — saw as the squatting
interest's near-monopoly of political and economic power.
Thus the cry to "unlock the lands" was not so much the result
of genuine land hunger as a popular slogan for uniting all who
wished to attack the "privileges" and pretensions of the
squatters. Moreover, there were also cogent economic reasons why middle-class townspeople wished to see the countryside populated with self-employed smallholders instead of
sheep. In the 1850s and for decades afterward, most squatters spent little money in the country towns near their stations. Generally their drays took the wool clip to the colonial
capital each year and carried back flour, tea, sugar, tar, tools
and other station supplies bought from wholesale importing
houses near the wharfside. Naturally retail traders, lawyers,
doctors and other professional men tended to believe that
their own prosperity would be enhanced by the creation of the
"numerous, industrious and virtuous agricultural population" advocated by the Rev. Lang and others.[33] Acts which
aimed, or which at least purported to aim, at placing "small
men" on the land were passed by the New South Wales Parliament in 1861. They were piloted through the House by the
Secretary of Lands, John (later Sir John) Robertson, who was
himself a squatter and also the owner of considerable freehold land. A folk song of the day celebrated, somewhat pre-
maturely as it turned out, the popular triumph.

> Come all you Cornstalks the victory's won,
> John Robertson's triumphed, the lean days are gone!
> No more through the bush we'll go humping the drum,
> For the Land Bill has passed and the good times have come.
>
> No more through the bush with our swags need we roam,
> For to ask of the squatters to give us a home:
> Now the land is unfettered and we may reside
> In a place of our own by some clear waterside.[34]

As the song suggests, Robertson was probably the most well-loved, if not exactly most revered, of all Australian politicians. Born in London, he was brought to Sydney by his parents in 1822 when he was only 5 years old. Thus, though technically an immigrant, he made friends with the native-born pupils at Reverend Dr J.D. Lang's primary school and, like the doctor himself, was regarded all his life as a kind of honorary Currency lad. As a young man he worked on stations in the Upper Hunter and Liverpool Plains districts, looked for new country out as far as the Darling River, and became an excellent bushman. His immense popularity with the electors sprang from the fact that he exhibited in his own person all that was best and worst in the native-born bush people. He was a hard-riding, hard-drinking, hard-swearing man, never acceptable to polite society and never, it seems, in the least anxious to be accepted among the refined people in the colony. He never by any chance called a spade a spade, but always a bloody shovel, and most electors loved him for it. He was one of only two politicians in whose honour Henry Lawson ever wrote verses. He was born with a cleft palate but, like the ancient Greek, Demosthenes, became an effective orator despite this handicap. There are innumerable stories about his language and character. One of the best relates that a delegation from an outback township came to ask him during one of his premierships to have the telegraph system extended to its district. Robertson explained that there was a shortage of copper wire so that nothing could be done until the next shipment reached Sydney. The delegation pressed its case. Robertson, whose temper had a very short fuse, exploded, "Gawd, yentlemen, d'you think I'm a bloo'y thpider tha' I can thpin the bloo'y thtuff out o' my arth![35]

The Robertson acts seemed to rest on the principle that he who would live on and cultivate the land had the first claim to it. Anyone — man, woman or child — could select a block of Crown land for their farm, before it had been surveyed and whether it was part of a pastoral lease or not. The block must be not less than 40 or more than 320 acres in extent. The selector had to pay a deposit of five shillings an acre to receive their right to occupancy, and the remaining fifteen shillings per acre were supposed to be paid within three years. They had also to live on the selection for at least one year and "improve" it to the value of at least £1 an acre to receive a freehold title to the land. At the same time, the acts sought to protect the squatters' equity in their leaseholds and to give them some protection from too many genuine selectors or from blackmailing speculators. The squatter was given, for instance, a pre-emptive right to one-twenty-fifth of his station and to particular areas on which he had built "improvements" such as shearing sheds, dams or fences. In practice, the acts failed to increase markedly the number of agricultural smallholders in New South Wales. Instead, they had the effect of vastly increasing the amount of freehold land in the hands of big graziers and pastoral companies. In the twenty-two years from 1861 to 1883, 29 million acres of Crown land were alienated, but the area under cultivation grew by only about half a million. E.G. Shann summed up in a well-known phrase the general effects of the *Free Selection Acts* in all colonies: "And it came to pass that demagogues dispersed the public estate and pastoralists gathered up the freehold thereof."[36]

The reasons for the failure of the land acts have been much canvassed. Historians have pointed to the vast amount of sharp practice engaged in by men of all classes, usually within the letter, thought not the spirit, of the law. The squatters acquired millions of acres in freehold by "dummying". The wife, children, friends or permanent employees of a squatter would select on his behalf the best parts of his run in order to keep out selectors. When the "dummy" had obtained full legal title to this selection, ownership was transferred to the squatter. An opposite manoeuvre was known as "peacocking", an expression apparently derived from the great number of beautiful "eyes" in the tail of a displaying peacock. Small speculators or large "land-sharks" would select the "eyes" or richest parts of a run – with or without the help of dummies – solely in order to force the squatter to buy, at an enhanced price, these well-watered blocks without which the rest of his run was useless. When taxed with the failure of his selection acts, Robertson replied, with characteristic spirit, that they were designed for honest men not for "bloody rogues"; but it is probable that, even if all men had been honest idealists, the land acts would have met with little more success. Except in South Australia, farming techniques were extraordinarily backward at this period. Capital, which most genuine selectors lacked, was just as necessary as a strong back and a stout heart. Most crippling of all was the primitive state of transport. In 1861, for instance, it was still much cheaper to transport a ton of wheat across the Pacific from Valparaiso to Sydney than to carry it about 250 kilometres by bullock-dray from the vicinity of Goulburn on one of the main bush "roads" of the period.[37] It was not until railways began to criss-cross the transmontane wheatlands in the last two decades of the nineteenth century that agriculture became a reasonably stable and expansive industry in New South Wales.

In Victoria, to the accompaniment of much agitation for legislation on the model of the American homesteading acts, three major bills were passed in 1860, 1862 and 1865. These resulted in putting rather more genuine farmers on the land. Between 1861 and 1881 the area under crop increased by about a million acres; but even more land than in New South Wales – relative to the total areas of the two colonies – found its way into the freehold possession of pastoralists. In Queensland, despite the passage of ten land acts between 1860 and 1884, the results were even less impressive, while in Tasmania, over an even longer period, the amount of cultivated land in the colony remained almost constant. The effort to settle farmers on the land was successful only in South Australia, but this achievement sprang from the peculiar character of the province's geography and population rather than from any peculiar genius in its politicians. South Australian wheatlands lay in a compact area near the capital, on a fertile coast plain blessed by a climate ideal for wheat-growing. The crop could be carted cheaply, over very short distances, to one of a dozen small ports or to Port Adelaide.

South Australia's pious farmers worked hard and intelligently. In the 1840s, when other Australian farmers were still reaping their crops by hand, John Ridley and John Wrathall Bull invented a mechanical stripper. Seed drills and stump-jump ploughs were invented in the same colony during the following decades. The latter implement, by a simple system of levers and weights, allowed the ploughshares to cultivate soil from which ground-level stumps and tree roots had not been completely removed. Between 1860 and 1880, South Australia's wheat crop was about equal to that of all the other colonies combined, and she was exporting her surplus to Britain as well as to Sydney and Brisbane.

The selection acts generally failed, then, to accomplish what was ostensibly their prime purpose. Yet we should notice that they — or the struggle around them — did much to achieve what was at least a secondary aim of many who participated in the drawn-out campaign — namely, to transfer the balance of political power to the urban population under the leadership of middle-class business and professional men. Economically, the wool industry soon regained its pre-eminence, although many new industries, both primary and secondary, were growing up in its shadow; and, paradoxically, even wool contributed to the dominance of city interests as banks and finance companies took over the ownership of more and more pastoral properties toward the end of the period. The social prestige of the great pastoral proprietors remained high, as it still does. Their economic power remained great, too, but became relatively less. Their domination of the political scene was broken in the first ten years of responsible government. Thereafter, their political influence was exercised more and more indirectly, and on more equal terms with that of other pressure groups in the community.

The history of education in Australia is very complex, but basically it may be said that most schools might still be under religious control if it had not been for the seemingly irreconcilable differences between different bodies of Christians and even, at times, between those within the same churches. In the early days, the Church of England was naturally the official church but, despite attempts to make it so, it never quite became the established church as in England. The fact that until Governor Darling's time Anglican chaplains were frequently also civil magistrates, who were wont to order floggings no less generously than their lay brethren, strengthened opposition to such a step — among the emancipists naturally, but also among many influential freemen such as the Reverend Dr Lang. Thus, in most colonies before the gold rush, the general procedure was for the governments to subsidise the major religious sects, usually the Anglicans, Roman Catholics, Presbyterians and Wesleyans, partly in order to assist these churches in their self-imposed task of providing schools. However, some dissenting sects and not a few members of all Protestant churches rejected, or at least gravely mistrusted, government aid because they feared the measure of state control which might accompany it. Naturally, rejection of state aid and support for the "voluntary principle" was strongest in South Australia. In 1851 the newly established provincial Legislative Council, inspired by Richard Davies Hanson who had helped draft the Durham Report, ended all subsidies to churches and set up a Central Board of Education on which no minister of religion might serve. The Board's task was to administer a secular "national" system of schools, in which teachers might read from the Bible but might not give any kind of denominational or dogmatic religious instruction. Education in South Australian "national" schools was not yet, however, either free or compulsory. Churches, naturally, remained free to maintain their own schools on the "voluntary" principle.[38]

Meanwhile, Victoria and New South Wales established a dual system, maintaining a number of "national", undenominational schools, while at the same time continuing state aid to churches. The dual system proved increasingly costly and inefficient. Some districts had more schools than they could support, while others had too few or none at all. Moreover, those dissenting groups which refused, on voluntarist principles, to accept government aid tended to resent its acceptance by others, and there were many voluntarists even in the Church of England. While leaders of religious opinion wrangled, an increasing number of liberal-minded people pressed ever more strongly for a single, national system (within each colony) of "free, compulsory and secular" education which, they hoped, would at least succeed in teaching the "three R's" to all children irrespective of the wealth or religious beliefs of their parents. Among these people was a relatively small but influential group of radical secularists, men like the great novelist Marcus Clarke, who, if not always convinced rationalists, were at least positive anti-clericals. Many sincerely religious people also opposed sectarian control of education because they felt it tended to perpetuate, or even create, class and "national" divisions in the Australian community.

The last argument was held by some to apply with special force to the Roman Catholic schools, for in Australia the great majority of the Catholic priesthood and laity were Irish by descent and so were suspected by traditionalists of disaffection. At the same time, the Catholic religious body as a whole was almost solidly united in opposition to the introduction of a "national" system. In June 1879 the Catholic Archbishop of Sydney denounced secular schools in a pastoral letter, declaring that they were "seed-plots of future immortality, infidelity, and lawlessness, being calculated to debase the standards of human excellence, and to corrupt the political, social and individual life of future citizens". While the controversy lasted, some secularist leaders at least matched the intemperance of this language. In reply, David Buchanan, a leading secularist and member of the New South Wales parliament, declaimed to a public meeting a letter he had received from the great Italian patriot, Giuseppe Garibaldi:

> I trust you will not suffer the presence of this human reptile in your beautiful and virgin country; and if anyone says there must be liberty to all, answer him that you will not give liberty to vipers, assassins and crocodiles – and the Jesuit priest is worse than any or all of these.[39]

The same resolution of the conflict was reached in all the colonies, though at different times. State aid to church schools was withdrawn and national (that is, colony-wide) systems of state-supported and controlled education were set up. If these state schools were not at first entirely free, they soon became so — as well as secular, and compulsory in the sense that children who did not attend voluntary church schools were obliged by law to attend the state schools. The decisive acts were passed in Victoria in 1872, in South Australia and Queensland in 1875, and in New South Wales in 1880.

Yet both religious and secular prophets of woe did not see their fears, or hopes, fulfilled. Thenceforth, the great majority of all Australian children attended the state schools — and became on the whole more law-abiding than their progenitors had been. On the other hand, Roman Catholics, by prodigious efforts, established their own religious school system. Nearly all Catholic children have attended these schools ever since, and few observers believe that their existence has had a seriously divisive effect on the Australian community. As we have seen, however, the expensive, élitist, Protestant church schools have done much to accentuate class divisions and to strengthen imperial loyalty while playing down Australian nationalist sentiment.

To contemporaries, fiscal policy seemed to be a most important, as well as a most divisive, issue: this is strange because the historian, even with the benefit of hindsight, cannot see that either free trade or protection conferred marked advantages on the colonies that adopted them. Yet insofar as politicians of the period divided on questions of fixed principle at all, they did so on fiscal policy. In the last two decades of the nineteenth century, organised Free Trade and Protectionist parties appeared in most of the legislatures. This development occurred even earlier in Victoria, which adopted increasingly high protective tariffs from 1866 onward. Tasmania and South Australia, though less enthusiastically, followed the Victorian lead — partly, perforce, as their economies were largely dependent on Victoria's. New South Wales remained throughout the period resolutely wedded to free trade, while Queensland maintained an uneasy position of compromise.

It may be that the greater proportion of Americans in Victoria, the premier gold-mining colony, had some influence on the early growth of protectionist sentiment there. More important, certainly, was the business recession, accompanied by mounting unemployment in the towns, which set in after 1857, when the most easily won gold had been worked out. It is hard also to overestimate the importance of David Syme, a young Scots radical who came looking for gold but stayed to become proprietor of the Melbourne *Age*, then and still one of the most influential newspapers in the continent. It has been suggested, not altogether jestingly, that New South Wales stuck to free trade for no better reason than that its younger but more populous rival became protectionist. It is also true that the wool industry, which in Australia never needed fiscal protection from any competitor, continued to occupy a more prominent position in the mother colony than in any of the others; Henry Parkes, the most influential Sydney politician throughout the period, remained an inflexible free trader. Customs houses were established along the colonial borders, though the population was so sparse that it was impossible to prevent smuggling. The opposed fiscal policies gave rise to much political rhetoric and to much jealousy, especially between New South Wales and Victoria, yet both prospered. Secondary industry increased in Victoria at a somewhat faster rate than it did in New South Wales, but the population of the latter colony grew more quickly. During the last decade of the century it resumed its place as the most populous of all the colonies. Yet after Federation in 1901 it was protection which became the fixed policy of the Commonwealth.

The most dramatic demonstration of colonial rivalry took place in the field of exploration. By 1860 Victoria was incomparably the richest and most populous colony, yet she had done nothing to explore the still unknown interior as South Australia had. Even Western Australia, which had been almost unaffected by the mid-century gold rush to the eastern

colonies, had explored much of the interior. For more than
twenty years from its foundation in 1829, the Swan River colony had barely survived. In 1850 the 5000 white colonists or,
rather, the superior gentlemen who took it upon themselves
to speak for all, begged the British government to set up a
convict establishment in Western Australia. Her Majesty's
ministers in London were graciously pleased to comply with
the humble petition of such a poor and remote colony. In the
following sixteen years about 10 000 convicts were sent to
Fremantle and the money sent to feed them and to pay their
gaolers did provide some stimulus to the colony's sluggish
economy. The convict establishment also produced a colourful incident which focused a measure of attention on Western
Australia for the only time before the western gold rush of the
1890s.

The last convict transport to sail for Fremantle, the
Huogomont, carried in 1866 six Fenian prisoners sentenced to
transportation for their patriotic efforts to free Ireland of its
British rulers. The Irish Catholic chaplain in Fremantle gaol,
Reverend John O'Reilly, proved to be sympathetic to Fenian-
ism if not a member of the brotherhood. A group of American
Fenians raised money and despatched a whale-ship, the *Catalpa*, to rescue the six Irish patriots from Western Australia.
With the covert assistance of Father O'Reilly, the seditious
plot succeeded. On Easter Monday, 17 April 1876, while
most Fremantle police and other officials were enjoying
themselves at the annual regatta in Perth, 18 kilometres up
the river, the six men were smuggled aboard the *Catalpa*
which had been standing on and off the coast for some weeks.
An ancient paddle-steamer, the *Georgette*, manned by old
British Army pensioners, gave chase but failed to fire on the
Catalpa when she hoisted the American flag a few miles outside British territorial waters. Most white Western Australians, though Protestant, were excited and delighted by these
stirring events. They felt that the Fenians should not have
been punished like common criminals for political "crimes"
motivated by patriotism. To commemorate the escape, unknown western citizens made up a ballad which was sung in

waterside pubs and elsewhere for a century afterwards. The chorus went:

> Now come all you screw warders and gaolers.
> Remember Perth's Regatta day.
> Take care of the rest of your Fenians,
> Or the Yankees will steal them away.[40]

The convict "establishment" thus provided early Western Australians with some relief from what many felt to be the tedium of existence on the banks of the Swan River, but it hardly ushered in a period of expansion and prosperity such as the eastern colonies enjoyed at this time. Yet Victorians were jealous of the achievements of Western Australian, to say nothing of South Australian, explorers.

In 1860 John McDouall Stuart, sparingly financed by two South Australian pastoralists, had reached Tennant's Creek before turning back. The Royal Society and the Government of Victoria hastened to organise an expedition which would snatch from South Australia the honour of first crossing the Australian continent. To lead it they chose Robert O'Hara Burke, a well-bred, Protestant, Anglo-Irish gentleman working as a police superintendent at Castlemaine but thirsting desperately for glory. He was given every opportunity to achieve it. The expedition, which left Melbourne on 20 August 1860, was easily the largest and most lavishly equipped in Australian history. There were fifteen men and the drivers for twenty-five camels, dozens of horses and wagons and enough food and provisions for two years. Perhaps the most grotesque item in the immense baggage train was six tons of firewood! Even Leichhardt would probably have drawn the line at that, but Burke was certainly the worst bushman ever placed in charge of an exploring party and probably the worst in the world.

He dumped most of the stores at Balranald and Menindee and hastened on with a few companions to establish a depot at Cooper's Creek. It was a wonderful season. Sturt's Stony Desert was sprinkled with lily ponds and Burke and his three companions who made the dash for the Gulf of Carpentaria never had a moment's anxiety about drinking water. Nor did

they take with them any drivers for the camels. These un-
gainly beasts are fashioned for walking on dry sand, not wet
mud. They floundered and got bogged in it and died of ex-
haustion. Burke, mad enough to choose to walk when the
party left Cooper's Creek, had no choice on the return journey. He, his second-in-command Wills, and a young man
named King staggered back into the depot half-starved and
scurvy-stricken, only to find that the base-party had left for
the south a few hours before. Even so the two leaders might
have survived if they had been sane enough to accept the help
of the local Aboriginal tribe, as did young King. Instead,
when the black men came into his camp bearing gifts of fish,
Burke "dispersed" them with revolver fire.[41]

Meanwhile, a tough, nuggety little bushman, no less fond
of a spree in town than others of his kind, was discovering
central Australia. With only two or three companions, half a
dozen horses, no camels and not very much more in the way
of supplies than he could shoot for the pot, Stuart continued
his careful probing northward. In July 1862, about eighteen
months after Burke's party had reached the Gulf, he reached
the Arafura Sea not very far from the present site of Darwin.
He had lost the "race" across the continent but, unlike
Burke, had discovered a route furnished all the way from
Port Augusta to Darwin with permanent water-holes. Ten
years later his path was followed by the Overland Telegraph
line and virtually all inland traffic between north and south
has moved along it since.[42]

Ernest Giles was an even better bushman and probably an
even deeper drinker than Stuart. Blessed with the constitution of a camel and the toughness of an old mallee-root, he yet
had a genuine appreciation of poetry and an imaginative, if
somewhat florid, literary style of his own. He must be considered the greatest of our inland explorers. After McDouall
Stuart's journey, the great object of exploration became to
cross the still unknown part of the continent between the Indian Ocean and Stuart's north–south line of water-holes piv-
oted on Alice Springs. P. Egerton Warburton led the first
successful east–west crossing in 1874 and a few months later

that year, John Forrest, later premier of Western Australia and Minister for Defence in the Commonwealth government, successfully led an expedition from west to east. Within the next two years, leading small and very economically equipped parties, Giles crossed the central deserts in both directions, each traverse being through even worse country than Warburton and Forrest had passed through. In the 1890s he joined in the gold rushes to the Kimberleys and to Coolgardie, where he died as a clerk in the mining warden's office in 1897. His fellow townsmen waited a few days for Sir John Forrest, then premier of the colony, to arrange a state funeral for his fellow explorer. When no sign of interest came from Perth, they buried him in the town's graveyard like any other bushman.[43]

Giles, like most of the later explorers, avoided the Aborigines as far as possible but, unlike Sir Thomas Mitchell, sought good relations with those he had to meet. In settled and frontier areas degradation and "dispersion" of the tribespeople proceeded as before. In the County of Cumberland surrounding Sydney in 1857, there was only *one* survivor of the 2000-odd tribespeople who had seen the coming of the white men seventy years before. With an apt symbolism, utterly lost on himself and the whites, this old man was always to be found begging in the gutter in South Head Road, outside the front gate of the residence of the speaker of the newly created Legislative Assembly.[44]

On the pastoral frontier in Queensland and elsewhere, clashes between blacks and whites were more frequent and bloodier than they had been earlier, partly because of the activities of the Native Police. It is hideously ironic that one of the most humane men of the time, Alexander Maconochie, should have recommended to Governor Bourke in the 1830s that Aborigines be recruited as constables. In Queensland throughout the second half of the nineteenth century, always directed by white officers, they butchered many thousands of tribespeople, without respect to age or sex, always of course strangers to the police troopers. "A University Man" who worked in north Queensland during the 1860s gave the following account of the work of the Native Police:

> On occasion, when their prey takes to the scrubs, they are willing enough to strip off their uniforms, all but their belts and cartridge boxes, and go in after them, when they seldom fail to give a good account of their errand. I have seen two large pits, covered with branches and brush, secured by a few stones, and the pits themselves were full of dead blackfellows, of all ages and of both sexes.
>
> On another occasion, I was travelling along a road where for more than a quarter of a mile the air was tainted with the putrefication of corpses, which lay all along the ridges, just as they had fallen.[45]

It is only fair to the Native Police and their officers to remember that the squatters and their men very often murdered the blacks without any professional assistance. It is only fair to the Aborigines to record that they retaliated more effectively in Queensland than they had often done earlier. At Cullin-la-ringo Station, for instance, on the afternoon of 17 October 1861, Aborigines surprised and killed nineteen white people led by an experienced grazier, Horatio Spencer Wills, father of Thomas Wills, the early cricketer and "inventor" of "Australian Rules" football. On this occasion, made wise by experience of the ways of the white men, the Aborigines slaughtered women and children along with the men. The indignation of the colonial press knew no bounds, nor did the vengeance exacted by a punitive force.[46]

In white Australia throughout this period of steady, if unspectacular, growth, the leading role was played in the capital cities by liberal, middle-class people, most of whom were immigrants. The wage-earning majority of citizens took little active part, and relatively little interest, in politics, while the Australian-born minority of mature voters had little scope for giving political or other overt expression to the nationalist (as distinct from democratic) aspirations of which we saw inchoate signs before the gold rush. It seems that, to a significant extent, bushranging gave symbolic form to these half-formed nationalist sentiments.

Visiting writers during the 1860s and 1870s were much

impressed by the prevalence of bushranging. John Martineau called it "the peculiar institution" of the country, thereby consciously comparing it with slavery in the southern United States as an institution discreditable in itself, but one to which most of the citizens were strongly attached. Martineau was right, for bushranging was distinguished from similar lawlessness in the United States and elsewhere mainly by the extraordinarily widespread sympathy felt for the criminals. He was right too in remarking that the institution flourished principally in the mother colony which (with Tasmania) had the highest proportion of native-born citizens. Without at least the tacit support of the majority of bush-workers and free-selectors, the most accomplished scoundrels would have been captured in days or weeks. As it was, they commonly ranged at will for months or years, robbing for the most part from the rich who were most worth the trouble, and giving to the poor considerable quantities — at least of other people's rum. When arrested and taken for trial to the capital cities, they were often given heroes' welcomes by large crowds.

This widespread sympathy stemmed from convict days when emancipist–exclusionist enmity had run high, but there is evidence that it was also in part a symbolic and only half-conscious expression of lower class and nationalist resentment at the *de facto* exclusion of these elements from any considerable political and social influence on events during the period.[47] The name of Ned Kelly, native-born and bush-bred son of an emancipist free-selector, and most colourful of the outlaws, is firmly entrenched in Australian language, literature and art. "As game as Ned Kelly" is a household expression throughout the continent. In 1964 a huge traffic "snarl" in the centre of Sydney was caused by a car bearing a Victorian number plate. Good temper all round was restored when a Sydney driver shouted at the embarrassed Victorian, "Where do you come from, mate — Glenrowan?" No frustrated motorist had to be told the name of the Victorian township where Kelly was finally cornered and caught. As an opposing symbol we may take Sir Redmond Barry, free immigrant of respectable middle-class background and liberal views. Barry was the first chancellor of the University of Melbourne, where stonemasons had been working in 1856 when they struck for the eight-hour day. He was first president of the trustees of the Public Library of Victoria and of the Melbourne Mechanics' Institute, and from 1852 a judge of the Victorian Supreme Court. He was one of the worthiest citizens of his day and his statue stands before the main entrance to Melbourne's Public Library, yet few people even in Victoria notice it and fewer now remember his name, though many pilgrims visited the nearby Exhibition Building where Ned Kelly's armour was kept until a few years ago.

In November 1880, Barry closed the bushranger's trial by pronouncing the words, "Edward Kelly, I hereby sentence you to death by hanging. May the Lord have mercy on your soul." In a clear, level voice the outlaw replied, "Yes, I will meet you there!" As it happened, Barry died about a fortnight later, but the most celebrated trial in Australian history may have had some more general historic significance, at least of an allegorical sort. During the following thirty years or so, the two opposing, yet interpenetrating streams of influence symbolised by the two men did meet, and they coalesced to a remarkable degree, though in ways which would on the whole have pleased Sir Redmond more than Ned.[48] We shall outline this process in the following chapter.

5 Radicals and nationalists
c. 1886–1913

In 1888 the citizens of New South Wales celebrated the centenary of the beginning of the white conquest of Australia. Surviving black Australians were ignored by the merry-makers just as they had been for the whole period in those parts of the continent where they had already been "dispersed", if not wholly destroyed. For their part, the Aborigines ignored the corroboree in Sydney as did, for the most part, white settlers in the other five colonies and in New Zealand, still then thought of as one of the Australian, or Australasian, colonies. Apparently most white Australians still thought of themselves as settlers in separate colonies. Yet within thirty years they had set up the political apparatus of nationhood and most had come to think quite clearly of themselves as Australians first and Victorians, Tasmanians or Queenslanders second. Vance Palmer wrote in 1954 of this great historical change:

> There has grown up a legend of the Australian nineties as a period of intense artistic and political activity, in which the genius of this young country had a brief and brilliant first flowering. Something new, it is claimed, emerged into the light. A scattered people, with origins in all corners of the British Islands and in Europe, had a sudden vision of themselves as a nation, with a character of their own and a historic role to play, and this vision set fruitful creative forces in motion.[1]

The main "creative forces" were those symbolised respectively by Sir Redmond Barry of the Supreme Court of Victoria and Edward Kelly, outlaw from Nine Mile Creek in the same colony. For a hundred years most well-to-do, middle-class Australians, whether immigrants or native-born, had seen themselves primarily as colonists whose first and "natural" loyalty was to the "Old Country". For the same period, most poor "working-class" Australians, particularly if they were native-born, had thought of themselves primarily as Australians whose first loyalty was naturally to their own country. Yet up until the turn of the century, the first group had enjoyed a practical monopoly of political and social power. Bushranging was in part a protest – symbolic if you will – against the exclusion of the second group from virtually all positions of influence or prestige. The archetypal exemplar of local Australian nationalism, the "Man from Snowy River", was created by "Banjo" Paterson in the centennial year. In the following thirty years Ned Kelly's troops, the previously poor and excluded majority of the population, joined with a vengeance the political and social nation, on terms formally at least equal to those enjoyed by Barry's "bourgeois" forces. During the same period, many "middle-class" Australians, like Paterson, Lawson, Joseph Furphy, Barbara Baynton, Tom Roberts and other writers and artists of the time, joined the newly active popular forces – at least to the extent of becoming Australian patriots first and imperial patriots second.

The newly created Labor Party was one means, though certainly not the only one, through which the masses exercised their influence on national life, but it is important to realise that, from its very inception, Labor in Australia was never a revolutionary or Marxist party. A handful of activists undoubtedly held Marxist views, but the great majority of all Labor members and supporters did not. Many historians have suggested that at this time Australian working people became a class, in the Marxist sense of becoming conscious of themselves as such. The wealth of supporting evidence assembled is persuasive but not convincing.[2] Certainly leading trade union and political figures like Randolph Bedford, W.G. Spence, J.C. Watson and most of their followers were socialists only in the sense that they gradually sought to institute

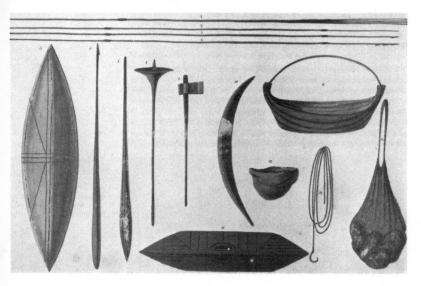

A representative collection of Aboriginal tools and weapons in use from about 6000 B.C.
(Source: Mitchell Library, State Library of New South Wales)

From the very first European contact with Australia, blacks and whites fought each other.
It was a battle in which, as S.T. Gill pointed out in this mid-nineteenth-century impression,
both sides took ruthless reprisals on their enemies. (Source: *The Avengers* by S.T. Gill,
Mitchell Library, State Library of New South Wales)

This painting of the death of Cook was done by John Webber, who sailed with Cook on his last voyage (Source: *The Death of Cook* by J. Webber, Dixson Library, Sydney)

These convicts were drawn by Juan Revenet, a member of a Spanish scientific expedition which called at Port Jackson in 1793 (Source: *Convicts in New Holland* 1793, by J. Revenet, Dixson Gallery, Sydney)

Even in the 1860s, when Henry Mayhew compiled his survey of *London Labour and the London Poor*, there were parts of London where the arm of the law did not reach. This illustration from Mayhew's classic work shows a thieves' kitchen in Fox Court, Gray's Inn Lane. (Source: The Kitchen, Fox Court, Gray's Inn Lane in *London Labour and London Poor*, London 1851, State Library of New South Wales)

A sketch by Lieutenant William Bradley showing part of the First Fleet entering Botany Bay (Source: Botany Bay – Sirius and Convoy Going in: Supply and Agent's Division in the Bay 21 January 1788 by W. Bradley in *The Journal of William Bradley*, Mitchell Library, State Library of New South Wales)

An engraving from the series "Industry and Idleness" by William Hogarth (1697–1764) shows a London prostitute robbing her client. At least one convict woman in every five was a prostitute at the time of her arrest.

Based on a sketch by John Hunter, this engraving shows officers of the First Fleet trying to establish friendly relations with an Aboriginal mother and her child (Source: *HMS Beagle*, 1834 by C. Martens from *An Account of the Historical Transactions at Port Jackson and Norfolk Island*, London, 1835, Mitchell Library, State Library of New South Wales)

William Hogarth's bitterly satirical engraving, "Gin Lane", dates from a time when Londoners could get drunk for a penny and dead drunk for twopence. In the early days of New South Wales, imported rum, marketed by the "Rum Corps", had a similarly debauching effect. (Source: *The Works of William Hogarth,* London 1793, Mitchell Library, State Library of New South Wales)

This contemporary print showing soldiers dragging Governor Bligh ignominiously from under a bed in Government House was probably a piece of rebel propaganda, as his courage had been well proven in the past (Source: Mitchell Library, State Library of New South Wales)

A view of Sydney Cove from The Rocks, showing the bridge over the Tank Stream (Source:
View of Sydney, Port Jackson, New South Wales by J.W. Lancashire, Dixson Gallery, Sydney)

A contemporary print showing Major George Johnston and his troops routing the Irish con-
vict-rebels at the Battle of Vinegar Hill, now known as Rouse Hill, near Windsor, New
South Wales (Source: *Major Johnston with Quarter Master Laycock, one Sargeant . . . 5th
March, 1804*, Rex Nan Kivell Collection (RNK), National Library of Australia)

A contemporary view of Hyde Park Barracks, which so pleased Governor Macquarie that he gave Francis Greenway, the convict builder, an unconditional pardon (Source: *Convict Barracks* by J. Lycett, Mitchell Library, State Library of New South Wales)

A contemporary print of Hobart in the 1820s by Augustus Earle, at the time when it was a centre for the local whaling and sealing fleets (Source: *Hobart Town*, 1826 by A. Earle, Dixson Gallery, Sydney)

By the 1820s Aborigines living near Sydney had either been "dispersed" or debauched, and their wretched state was nowhere better depicted than in this drawing by Augustus Earle (Source: "Natives of New South Wales" by A. Earle in *Views of New South Wales and Van Diemen's Land*, vol. 2, London 1830, Mitchell Library, State Library of New South Wales)

Free farmers and pastoralists were assigned convict labourers whom they were free to treat well or badly. This fanciful old sketch shows convicts carrying loads of shingles for roofing. (Source: "Our Convicts What We Do and What Becomes Them" in *Sketches of Australian Life and Scenery,* London 1876, Mitchell Library, State Library of New South Wales)

A London cartoonist's view of the Founding of Western Australia in 1829 (Source: British Museum)

King George's Sound settlement, Western Australia, founded in 1826, was some 3000 km by sea from the nearest white settlement at Hobart (Source: *Panoramic View of King George's Sound, Swan River* 1834, by R. Dale, Mitchell Library, State Library of New South Wales)

A water-colour by S.T. Gill in 1845 shows Adelaide's King William Street, named after the "sailor-King" (Source: *King William Street, Adelaide, Looking North* 1845, by S.T. Gill, Art Gallery of South Australia)

Melbourne in 1841, from the eastern end of Collins Street (Source: *Melbourne from the Eastern End of Collins Street* 1841, by R. Russell, Mitchell Library, State Library of New South Wales)

"Homeward Bound", a water-colour by S.T. Gill, shows weary stockmen and their horses droving a herd of cattle. The inland's aridity, distance from markets, and poor communications encouraged the growth of large-scale sheep and cattle stations. (Source: *Homeward Bound 1854-63*, by S.T. Gill, Mitchell Library, State Library of New South Wales)

The squatting rush to the interior signalled the expropriation of Aboriginal land rights. S.T. Gill's pithily captioned paintings sum up the situation. (Source: Top: *Squatter of New South Wales. Monarch of all he Surveys 1788* by S.T. Gill; Bottom: *Squatter of New South Wales. Monarch of more than all he Surveys 1863*, by S.T. Gill, Mitchell Library, State Library of New South Wales)

To some white pioneers, Aborigines were curiosities to pose among. To others they were pests to be exterminated. Some white men took Aboriginal "wives", but rarely endowed them with that legal status. (Source: Mitchell Library, State Library of New South Wales)

Caroline Chisholm, the champion of female immigration and of women's rights in New South Wales and Victoria. Her efforts helped to redress the imbalance of the sexes in the bush.

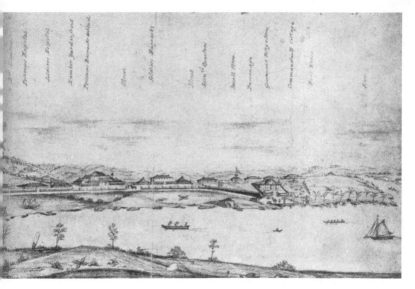

A pencil sketch of the early Moreton Bay settlement on the Brisbane River (Source: *View of Moreton Bay* 1831, Mitchell Library, State Library of New South Wales)

In contrast to the Californian discoveries, the early Australian goldfields were in areas adjacent to seats of firmly established government — which resulted in a relatively ordered life on the diggings. This painting by E. Roper shows the Ararat diggings in 1855. (Source: *Gold Diggings, Ararat* 1855, by E. Roper, Mitchell Library, State Library of New South Wales)

This scene at the Ballarat diggings, by S.T. Gill, shows new arrivals queuing for their mining licences

The mateship of the diggings did not extend to the Chinese, the largest group of foreign nationals. Hard-working and self-sufficient, they were often the target for abuse and violence from white diggers. S.T. Gill captioned this picture "Might versus Right". (Source: *Might Versus Right 1854-63*, by S.T. Gill, Mitchell Library, State Library of New South Wales)

A contemporary illustration of the appalling massacre of kidnapped Kanakas by the crew of the *Carl* in 1871, after the Kanakas had tried to escape. The wounded survivors were thrown overboard.

By 1870 Cobb & Co.'s coaches were covering about 45 000 kilometres per week and for more than half a century their name was almost synonymous with inland travel (Source: *Cobb and Co. Coach* by N. Bayley, Mitchell Library, State Library of New South Wales)

Slum dwellers photographed about 1875 in Clarence Street, Sydney. The growth of Sydney and Melbourne into large cities increased the numbers of urban poor. (Source: Mitchell Library, State Library of New South Wales)

A selector's ramshackle hut. From the 1850s there was popular agitation to "unlock the land" from the grip of the squatters and to redistribute it among "independent" yeomen farmers. (Source: Mitchell Library, State Library of New South Wales)

Throughout the second half of the nineteenth century, Queensland native police, directed by white officers, helped to butcher thousands of tribespeople (Source: Australian Information Service, Canberra)

A Melbourne Building Society on pay night. This contemporary illustration shows men and women crowding to deposit savings. Chief among them is a carpenter with his wife and baby. Wage-earners may have taken little part in political life in the latter years of the nineteenth century, but they were regarded as intelligent, stable and responsible – thanks to universal primary education. (Source: *The Australian Sketcher,* 14 June 1873, State Library of Victoria)

Sympathy for bushrangers was extraordinarily widespread among nineteenth-century Australians. (Source: *Bushrangers Robbing the Mail 1866*, by G. Lacey, RNK, National Library of Australia)

In the hands of popular writers and illustrators, the Ned Kelly legend was amplified to mythical proportions. (Source: Mitchell Library, State Library of New South Wales)

A bushranger pursued by mounted police, depicted by S. T. Gill. Bushranging was in part a protest against the exclusion of working-class Australians from virtually all positions of influence or prestige.

Sir Lionel Lindsay's sketch of Ben Hall's Homestead, 1926 (Source: National Library of Australia)

Ben Hall's grave, Forbes cemetery (Source: *Forbes Advocate*)

Newly landed immigrants at Queen's Wharf, Melbourne. From 1860 onward, immigration could be likened more to a steady trickle than to the flood of the gold rush. (Source: *Illustrated Sydney News*, National Library of Australia)

During the lockout at the Broken Hill mine in 1909, strikers built mock graves for scabs such as the one pictured here beneath the "Death or Victory" sign (Source: Mitchell Library, State Library of New South Wales)

Food is distributed to the unemployed at a South Melbourne depot during the depression of the 1890s (Source: *Illustrated Australian News*, 1 May 1894, State Library of Victoria)

Colonel Tom Price mobilising his volunteer Mounted Rifle Corps during the great maritime strike. He became notorious for advising his men to "fire low and lay them out". (Source: *Illustrated Australian News*, 17 September 1887, State Library of Victoria)

The *Sydney Mail*, 22 September 1894, printed this photograph of striking shearers camped near the Darling River during the strike of 1894 (Source: *Sydney Mail*, 22 September 1894, State Library of New South Wales)

The Earl of Hopetoun taking the oath of office of Governor-General and thereby inaugurating the Commonwealth of Australia, on 1 January 1901 (Source: Mitchell Library, State Library of New South Wales)

The Sudan Contingent marches toward Circular Quay, Sydney, for embarkation on Tuesday, 3 March 1885, proclaimed a public holiday (Source: Mitchell Library, State Library of New South Wales)

"Breaker" Morant (second from left) and Lieutenant Handcock (first on left) were court-martialled in February 1902 for having murdered Boer prisoners (Source: Mitchell Library, State Library of New South Wales)

Gallipoli, 1915, where 10 000 Australian and New Zealand soldiers, as many French soldiers, and nearly three times as many British troops died for no appreciable military gain (Source: Mitchell Library, State Library of New South Wales)

Police break up a demonstration of unemployed in Sydney's Railway Square during the Depression. For a time nearly 30 per cent of breadwinners were unemployed. (Source: *Sydney Morning Herald*)

The Depression intensified the traditional belief that the state's first duty is to look after the welfare of all its citizens, especially the less fortunate among them. A workless family photographed outside its humpy. (Source: *Sydney Morning Herald*)

Camps of the unemployed in the Domain, Sydney, during the Depression (Source: *Sydney Morning Herald*)

Censorship was not confined to imported books, and Norman Lindsay was forced to redraw the cover of his 1921 edition of *A Curate in Bohemia* to comply with ''wowser'' policy (Source: *A Curate in Bohemia* by N. Lindsay, Sydney 1913 and 1921, Mitchell Library, State Library of New South Wales)

A soldier tends a wounded comrade during the battle at Milne Bay, New Guinea, where Australian troops inflicted on Japanese land forces their first real defeat of the war (Source: Australian War Memorial)

After the war the severe housing shortage reduced some ex-servicemen and their families to makeshift homes like this, built out of corrugated iron and a dilapidated water tank (Source: *Sydney Morning Herald*)

Aboriginal shanty dwellers about to move from a reserve in January 1969. "Fringe-dwelling" Aborigines continued to live in ghettos on the outskirts of most country towns and were forbidden by custom and terror from using public facilities on the same terms as white citizens. (Source: *Sydney Morning Herald*)

Menzies believed that aiding America in Korea would ensure American protection of Australian interests. To this end, these Australian volunteer troops were sent to serve in Korea. (Source: Australian Information Service, Canberra)

Mrs Petrov, flanked by Russian couriers, was escorted dazed and weeping to an airliner at Mascot after her diplomat husband made apparently startling disclosures about espionage in Australia (Source: *Sydney Morning Herald*)

Moonie was Australia's first commercial oil field. Commercial production was begun in March 1964. (Source: Australian Information Service, Canberra)

The new affluence and technological changes of the 1950s and 1960s made life somewhat easier for Australian women. The stigma of being "single" lessened, divorce increased, and married women sought jobs outside the home. Women's fashions reflected their more relaxed way of life, as this Melbourne street scene from the late 1960s shows. (Source: Australian Information Service, Canberra)

In the early 1960s Joern Utzon was imported by the Labor government of New South Wales to create the Sydney Opera House, one of the architectural masterpieces of the modern world. Many people dubbed it the "Cahill Mahal". (Source: Australian Information Service, Canberra)

The Christmas week crush on Bondi Beach in December 1967. Many prosperous citizens had long agreed with the multitude of visitors who declared that average Australians were far too leisure- and pleasure-loving for either their own or the national good. (Source: *Sydney Morning Herald*)

In 1972 black Australians, no longer content to be segregated and ignored, set up an "Aboriginal Embassy" in the grounds of Parliament House, Canberra (Source: *Sydney Morning Herald*)

Prime Minister Holt arranged for President Johnson to visit Australia a month before the general election of November 1966. Johnson's train included 400 American press representatives plus a great number of secret police, spies and security guards. (Source: *Sydney Morning Herald*)

Young radicals, often sceptical of political action, believed passionately in "confrontation politics". They organised massive demonstrations against conscription, US imperialism, Australia's involvement in the Vietnam war and racist practices at home and abroad. (Source: *Sydney Morning Herald*)

Demonstrations against Australia's involvement in Vietnam continued until 1972 when the Labor government, under the leadership of Gough Whitlam, withdrew Australian troops (Source: *Sydney Morning Herald*)

In the winter of 1971 a racially selected South African rugby football team, the Springboks, visited Australia. Almost everywhere the tour provoked massive hostile demonstrations. In this one, at the Sydney Cricket Ground, policemen crouch over a prone demonstrator. (Source: *Sydney Morning Herald*)

Through the 1970s many Australian women campaigned for equal rights for women and took part in demonstrations such as this one (Source: *Sydney Morning Herald*)

A Vietnamese ceremony in Hyde Park, Sydney, 1979, to mark the fourth anniversary of the fall of South Vietnam (Source: *Sydney Morning Herald*)

On 24 November 1973, 40 000 Aborigines enrolled and voted to elect a forty-one-member National Aboriginal Consultative Council to advise the Minister for Aboriginal Affairs on policies and decisions affecting Aboriginal people (Source: Australian Information Service, Canberra)

R.J. Hawke, eighth Labor Prime Minister, addresses the National Economic Summit in the House of Representatives (Source: News Ltd)

reforms within capitalist society and to obtain for the majority of people a somewhat greater share of the good things that society had to offer: from the beginning, Labor was just as interested in promoting local Australian nationalist sentiment, including racist "white Australia" sentiment, as it was in social reforms. Thus at its first meeting on 1 August 1890, the Council of the Australian Labor Federation wrote the first plank in its parliamentary platform as "Universal White Adult Suffrage for all parliamentary and local elections"; and in 1905 the federal parliamentary platform began:

> Objective, – (1) The cultivation of an Australian sentiment based upon the maintenance of racial purity, and the development in Australia of an enlightened and self-reliant community.
>
> (2) The securing of the full results of their industry to all producers by the collective ownership of monopolies and the extension of the industrial and economic functions of the State and Municipality.[3]

In the thirty years or so following 1888, Australians became conscious, not to say self-conscious, of their nationhood, gave this sentiment formal political expression by establishing the federal government, and hammered out broadly accepted national policies which have largely determined the course of later developments. After a hundred years much of what the currency lads had felt, and the bushrangers had symbolised, was accepted by most middle-class Australians – though largely in their own terms – as part of the image of the new nation. Yet since many people also felt that there was, in the brief national past, insufficient on which to build a proud tradition, the awakening patriotic sentiment was strongly coloured by a strand of utopian idealism which looked to the future. Unhampered by the inherited quarrels and entrenched injustices of older countries, Australia should become the exemplar of the just society of the common man – the white Australian common man, of course! A contemporary poet, Bernard O'Dowd, native-born son of a trooper in the Victorian Gold Escort, captured this mood exactly in a sonnet beginning:

Last sea-thing dredged by sailor Time from Space,
Are you a drift Sargasso, where the West
In halcyon calm rebuilds her fatal nest?
Or Delos of a coming Sun-God's race?
Are you for Light, and trimmed, with oil in place,
Or but a Will o' Wisp on marshy quest?
A new demesne for Mammon to infest?
Or lurks millennial Eden 'neath your face?

The importance of this utopian theme has often been exaggerated by later writers. So has the extent of the influence on events exercised by Marxists and other visionaries in the working-class or "Labor" movement. Self-interest, and economic and political horse-trading, played as big a part in the Australia of the 1890s as they customarily do in human affairs. Yet historians generally agree that this is the crucial period for an understanding of modern Australia, especially for an understanding of whatever is distinctive about the tone and texture of Australian life.

In the last chapter we saw that the great influx of mid-century gold-rush immigrants accelerated the growth of democratic institutions, while at the same time it delayed the growth of Australian nationalism – at any rate, among the more cultivated and articulate sections of society. We must now notice that, from about 1860 onward, immigration could be more properly likened to a steady if substantial trickle than to a flood. The result was that while the gold-rush immigrants were being gradually but thoroughly acclimatised, the proportion of native-born people in the country as a whole rose far above the 43 per cent it had reached in New South Wales in 1851. Natives comprised 60 per cent of the continent's total white population in 1871, 75 per cent in 1891, and 82 per cent in 1901. This growing preponderance of the native-born was probably the greatest single underlying cause of the growth of national sentiment toward the end of the century, for while immigrants ("Jimmy Grants" – "Pomegranates" – "Pommies") naturally tended to feel more British than Australian patriotic sentiment, the natives had from the earliest days tended to regard themselves – intercolonial rivalries notwithstanding – as Australians first,

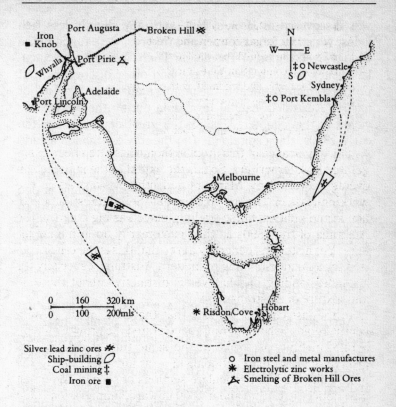

Figure 20   Twentieth-century operations developed by the BHP Company

and only in certain contexts as Victorians, Queenslanders and so forth. At no time did regional differences develop to anything like the extent that they did in the United States and Canada. This was partly because of the national and cultural homogeneity of practically all the colonists, and partly because the predominantly pastoral and mining economy of nineteenth-century Australia promoted much more movement and mixing of the colonial populations than did the predominantly agricultural North American economy.

It should be noted too that mining, though for base metals rather than gold, continued to be of fundamental importance. In 1883 one of the richest silver–lead–zinc fields in the world was discovered at Broken Hill, and only slightly less rich lodes, which included copper and tin ores, were found in the Mount Lyell region of Tasmania. There were few spectacular rushes connected with these and other discoveries, but profits from investment in the mining industry played a major part in Australian capital formation during the period surveyed in this chapter. Despite the great depression of the early 1890s, this capital aided in the modest though steady growth of secondary industry which had begun in the golden decade. Especially important was the Broken Hill Proprietary Company itself. From silver–lead–zinc mining in one colony, it expanded into other fields of enterprise and into other colonies. Rich iron ores were mined in South Australia and carried to the Newcastle coalfields, north of Sydney, there to lay the foundations of Australian heavy industry, while coal was carried back to South Australia to process some of the Broken Hill ores.[4]

Perhaps the next most importance force in the foundation of Australian secondary industry was the Colonial Sugar Refining Company, formed in 1855. Beginning with processing the sugar crop in Queensland and northern New South Wales coastal districts, CSR, like BHP, later moved into shipping – and acquired extensive interests in Fiji and New Zealand. With other new companies, these two colonial giants laid in this period secure foundations on which Australian heavy industry and commerce built rapidly later, especially after World War II.

By the end of the century, most middle-class Australians had begun to feel as much at home in the no-longer strange continent as working people had long felt, though often not in quite the same way. Well-to-do people, educated still almost exclusively in English literature, history and culture, tended to think, in the spirit of W.C. Wentworth's 1817 poem,[5] of "a new Britannia in another world" rather than to accept, as the masses did without much conscious thought, the fact of Australia's own developing identity. Still, most Australians no longer thought of themselves as Britons living in temporary exile. It was time therefore to think about what they *were*. Moreover, at the practical tasks of pioneering, native-born people and experienced old colonists had long been preferred by employers. In white-collar and professional occupations this was by no means the case. It was still assumed that the most important and well-paid positions in education, the church and the professions — and even to some extent in business — could usually be filled adequately only by British immigrants. Many in high places were irked by this attitude. Sir Samuel Griffith, scholarly premier of Queensland and one of the chief advocates of federal union, had come to Australia as a boy of 9. He spoke for almost all his countrymen, irrespective of wealth, education, politics or religion, when he said at the Federal Convention of 1891:

> I am tired of being called a Colonist. The term is used no doubt at the other end of the world without the slighest intention of using a disparaging expression, but unconsciously as a term of disparagement. The colonist is really regarded by the usage of the term as a person who does not enjoy the same advantages and is not quite entitled to the same privileges as other members of the Empire.[6]

The patronising attitude to which Griffith referred continued for a long time afterwards to be voiced by eminent British sojourners in Australia and, by reaction, to accentuate the growing national sentiment. That it was often only unconsciously disparaging naturally rendered it more obnoxious, or ridiculous, to the "colonists". In 1899, for instance, Earl Beauchamp came out to govern, briefly, New South Wales. In a telegram from Albany he quoted a poem in which Rudyard Kipling spoke of Australia's having turned her "birth-stains" to good. For years afterward the popular Sydney *Bulletin* filled occasional spaces at the foot of a column with a pseudo-advertisement: "For birth-stains, try Beauchamp's Pills!" — Beecham's Pills being one of the most widely advertised patent medicines of the period.

None, naturally, reacted more strongly to English condescension than the Irish-Australians, who comprised about 20 per cent of the population. In convict times Irishmen and women, and people of Irish descent, had numbered 30 per cent. From the beginning they had tended to acclimatise themselves more readily and completely than other immigrants: first because they were Irish, and second because a grossly disproportionate number of them were to be found among the unskilled, wage-earning section of the community. If, as many English and Scottish immigrants felt in the last century, Australian national sentiment savoured rather of "disloyalty" to the old country, Irish immigrants naturally embraced it more readily for that very reason. And working people generally, because they were on the average less well educated and less able to keep up cultural or other connections with Great Britain, inevitably took on the colour of their surroundings more rapidly than was usual among the well-to-do. Possibly the Vatican was not unmindful of these factors when it chose bishops for the Australian colonies. At any rate, until the 1870s, relatively few Catholic prelates came from Ireland whence had sprung the vast majority of their flocks. Much more typical in the early period was R.W.B. Vaughan, Archbishop of Sydney from 1877 to 1883, an aristocratic Englishman one of whose ancestors had distinguished himself at the Battle of Agincourt. Among the mid-century immigrants was a higher proportion of educated middle-class Irishmen, both Protestant and Catholic, like Peter Lalor of Eureka fame or Charles Gavan Duffy, already well known for his leadership in the Irish home rule movement when he emigrated. It was no accident that Gavan Duffy, for a time premier of Victoria, also took a leading part in the early (and premature) Federation movement.[7]

In 1884, another and very remarkable Irishman came to Australia. Francis Patrick Moran, the new Catholic Archbishop of Sydney, announced on landing at Port Jackson, "On this day I became an Australian, and I am determined to live as an Australian for Australia." The contrast between this and the customary Earl Beauchamp type of pronunciamento made by newly arrived dignitaries was not lost on the inhabitants. Moran became the first Australian cardinal and worked prodigiously until his death in 1911. In addition to performing his purely pastoral duties and building the Catholic school system, he gave great encouragement to the emerging Labor Party and played an active, possibly a decisive, part in nurturing pro-Federation sentiment in New South Wales — the colony which was most reluctant to join in creating the new nation. His speeches and actions alike suggest that he foresaw, before many of its own members did, the rise of the Labor Party to a position of decisive political importance; that he realised that most Australian Catholics would, for economic reasons in any case, be attracted to it; and that, influenced by the ideals of social justice propounded in the 1891 Papal Encyclical *Rerum Novarum*, he sought to strengthen the Labor movement no less than to ensure that it would be moderate, reformist and non-revolutionary in both its methods and aims. At the same time, he campaigned actively (far too actively, some thought) for federation, even though Labor was for the most part officially opposed to it.[8] Sir Henry Parkes, until his death the most prominent New South Wales federalist, had also been the father in that colony of free, compulsory and secular education. As such, he tended to be regarded by Catholics as their chief political enemy. Yet, just before his death in 1895, Parkes said of Moran:

> There is another person, who is an entire stranger to me, and, I should think, a gentleman who has no very high opinion of me, whose services I should acknowledge. Of all the voices on this question, no voice has been more distinct, more full of a worthy foreshadowing of the question's greatness and more fraught with a clear prescience of what is likely to come as a result of Federalism, than the voice of this eminent prelate.[9]

Thus for the first time the mass of the Australian people, including those of Irish descent, came to play an active role in shaping political and national life. Since they had long taken their basic Australianness for granted, it is not surprising that the period should have seen such an upsurge of nationalist sentiment — of which political federation was only one, and perhaps not the most fundamental, aspect.

The new mood was manifested most dramatically in the arts. By the 1890s public education systems had made people literate. A racy folk literature which clothed the once-strange environment with indigenous songs, tales and figures of speech had long circulated orally among working people, particularly in the bush. Now a man who might once have helped improvise a new ballad was more likely to write it down and send it to a magazine for publication. More importantly journalists, poets and other "accredited" literary people began to see Australian life directly with their own eyes rather than through the inherited spectacles of English literary and social conventions. Previously most Australian writing aspiring to the status of literature had been done primarily with a cultivated English audience in mind — even when the writer happened to be an Australian by birth; and of course some creative writers like Christopher Brennan continued at this period, and have continued since, to be little affected by the nationalist temper. There is nothing either odd or unhealthy about this. After all, English is the leading world language, and Henry James and T.S. Eliot remind us that even some American literary men of the first rank have continued to feel more at home in England than in their own country. But during and since the last decade of the last century, most Australian literature has been written primarily about Australian life and for an Australian audience. Less emphatically, the same can be said of the visual arts. In the same period men like Tom Roberts, Arthur Streeton, Frederick McCubbin and Charles Conder established a distinctively Australian tradition of painting which, like the new literature, tended to emphasise outback life because it was felt to be more characteristically Australian than life in the cities. These painters are often spoken of as belonging to the Heidelberg School. The name comes from a village on the outskirts of Melbourne where some of them established a camp and worked together.[10]

In literature the great names were A.B. ("Banjo") Paterson (1864–1941), Henry Lawson (1867–1922) and Joseph Furphy ("Tom Collins") (1843–1912), but many lesser people like Barbara Baynton, Victor Daley, Bernard O'Dowd, Francis Adams, Roderick Quinn and C.J. Dennis produced significant work in the same genre. At its worst their writing was slipshod and "near enough" in execution, and brash and bumptious in manner, being far too self-consciously concerned with "Australianism". Established and tradition-minded critics were quick to emphasis these weaknesses. In a letter about his great novel first published in 1903, Furphy unrepentantly rejoined that his work was "in temper democratic, bias offensively Australian", and his title *Such Is Life* is held to have been Ned Kelly's last utterance from the gallows. At its best the new writing was original, idomatic, vigorous and absolutely true to the Australian experience. As suggested by Furphy's remark, it was concerned equally with nationalism and with democratic egalitarianism. Indeed, to many if not most contemporaries, nationalism and levelling, democratic ideas seemed merely different aspects of a single ideal, summed up in its most romantically exaggerated form by the *Bulletin* in an editorial of 2 July 1887:

> By the term Australian we mean not those who have been merely born in Australia. All white men who come to these shores — with a clean record — and who leave behind them the memory of the class-distinctions and the religious differences of the old world; all men who place the happiness, prosperity, the advancement of their adopted country before the interests of Imperialism, are Australian . . . In this regard all men . . . who leave their fatherland because they cannot swallow the worm-eaten lie of the divine right of kings to murder peasants, are Australian by instinct — Australian and Republican are synonymous.

The *Bulletin* was a weekly journal first published in Sydney in 1880. Under the editorial guidance of J.F. Archibald, its policy was strongly nationalist, radical and republican. After the achievement of federation in 1901, republicanism was quietly dropped from its program, and it became less radical and less "anti-imperialist" or anti-British with the years, but it did not take on its later conservative colouring until about the time of World War I. The early *Bulletin* was immensely popular and far more influential than any Australian journal before or since. After its first few years it circulated widely in all colonies, not just in New South Wales. In keeping with the widespread feeling that truly or "typically" Australian values were to be found in bush life, the paper gave disproportionate space to outback news, views and themes. It came to be known as the bushman's Bible. It is said that the diggers on the Western Australian goldfields declared a holiday when copies reached them, but in fact it was read in almost every barber shop in the cities as well as in those of the country towns. Its success sprang partly from Archibald's policy of encouraging reader participation. Every issue contained many short, pungent paragraphs sent in by readers, and in one of these readers, A.G. Stephens, whom Archibald made the paper's literary editor, the *Bulletin* found the first Australian literary critic of stature. Almost every Australian writer of the period found a congenial forum in its columns. Yet literature, after all, reflected the national mood quite as much as it created it. The same may be said of politics. What were the significant changes in this sphere?

Most important and far-reaching in its effects was the movement of working people into active participation in political life. We have seen that wage-earners took little direct part in politics before this time; but by about 1890 the *Education Acts*, together with liberal measures such as payment of members of Parliament, had done much to make the direct representation of wage earners in the legislatures at least possible. At the same time a new kind of industrial trade unionism sprang up, not only in Australia of course, but in Europe and North America too. Stonemasons in small, exclusive craft-unions had won the eight-hour day for some skilled tradesmen in the large Australian cities as early as 1856; but the new industrial unions sought to embrace all workers, including semi-skilled people and even unskilled labourers. They were more or less strongly influenced by European and American radical ideas. In fact the two "socialist" tracts most influential in Australia at the period were both American works – Henry George's *Progress and Poverty*, and Edward Bellamy's *Looking Backward*. William Lane, the most influential Labor journalist in Australia, reprinted *Looking Backward* in serial form in the Brisbane *Worker*. However, this is to anticipate a little. In the United States, Canada, Great Britain and elsewhere, the new unionism was based primarily on organisations of miners and transport workers. In Australia, also, these groups were important, but perhaps less so on balance than the pastoral workers. Rural labourers are traditionally conservative and slow to join trade unions, but in Australia most bushmen worked on large pastoral holdings where the impersonal relation between employer and employee was more like that in a large urban factory than in a small farm or business. William Guthrie Spence, leading union organiser of the period and later a Labor member of the federal parliament, described the appeal of the new unionism to the bush-workers thus:

> Unionism came to the Australian bushman as a religion . . . It had in it that feeling of mateship which he understood already, and which always characterised the action of one "white man" to another. Unionism extended the idea, so a man's character was gauged by whether he stood true to union rules or "scabbed" it on his fellows . . . The lowest form of reproach is to call a man a "scab" . . . At many a country ball the girls have refused to dance with them, the barmaids have refused them a drink, and the waitresses a meal.[11]

The Amalgamated Shearers' Union, founded in 1886, organised bush-workers in New South Wales, Victoria and South Australia. The Queensland Shearers' Union, begun in the same year, worked smoothly with the ASU until both organisations merged under Spence's leadership in the Australian Workers' Union, still perhaps the most powerful, though no longer the most militant, trade union in Australia. The new unions did not condone violence, and they preferred negotiation to strikes. Nevertheless, it was a time of falling wool prices, and there were more strikes in the pastoral industry between 1886 and 1889 than in all other Australian industries put together. At first the unions were generally successful in maintaining working conditions at the existing level, and they even won some concessions from employers. Trade unionism in Australia was stronger than in any other country at the time. The high degree of optimism and idealism among union members was dramatically shown when the London dock-workers were on strike in 1889. Not without some feeling of condescension to the "backward" English workers, Australian sympathisers contributed £30 000 − say $3 million in terms of purchasing power in 1990 − to the London strike fund. The gift had a decisive effect on the strike's success. In the following year of crisis when Australian strikers needed help, British sympathisers contributed £4060.[12] The onset of the great depression of 1890–94 had a strong catalytic effect on the developing Labor movement. It also stimulated nationalist sentiment and − not always quite the same thing − sentiment in favour of a federal union of the colonies.

The long-continued expansion of the 1870s and 1880s had been based mainly on over-optimistic borrowing, both governmental and private, from British investors. In "Marvellous Melbourne", speculation was such that real estate prices of some central city blocks soared to levels higher than any reached again for about fifty years. As wool, wheat and base metal prices continued to fall, foreclosures and bankruptcies snowballed into a financial panic. In 1893 most banks in Australia suspended payment and were laboriously reconstructed, while many failed completely. Tens of thousands of people lost their life's savings and their jobs too, though very few of the great capitalists and financiers at the peak of the economic dunghill lost their money and their power over the lives of lesser mortals. That the depression was more severe in Victoria than in New South Wales was partly due to the cool and astute handling of the banking crisis in the latter colony by its premier, Sir George Dibbs, who was moved to write in 1894: "It is not indeed, too much to say that the Banking panic here largely arose through British withdrawals, and was intensified by fears that British depositors would secure their money first."[13] Few citizens had Dibbs' knowledge of the money market, but many found their nationalist aspirations strengthened by his belief that the machinations of British financiers had significantly helped to cause all the unemployment and distress.

All the eastern colonies were hard hit, especially Victoria and South Australia, which actually decreased in population during the 1890s. Tens of thousands of people left the eastern colonies for Western Australia, attracted thither by the dis-

Scene in Collins Street, Melbourne, during a panic run on the City of Melbourne Bank (Source: *Australasian Sketcher* 5 July 1879, State Library of Victoria)

covery of rich goldfields. In 1881 the white population of the whole million square miles of the western colony was still only 30 000. The Aboriginal population, perhaps twice as numerous, had no interest in the state of the economy and in any case was not counted as citizens in the census. Then in 1886 gold was discovered in the Kimberley district in the far north, about 2000 kilometres as the crow flies from Perth. Many tough old bushmen, including Ernest Giles the explorer, joined in the rush. They were soon joined by graziers like John Costello and Patsy Durack, who "overlanded" horses, cattle and families from their stations in the "channel country" of south-western Queensland.[14] The Kimberley goldfields proved disappointing, but in 1892 Arthur Bayley and William Ford discovered a fabulously rich lode at Coolgardie, on the edge of desert country only about 500 kilometres east of Perth. In the following year an Irish prospector discovered a richer field at Kalgoorlie, richer even than the original Victorian find at Ballarat forty-one years earlier. Today, a hundred years later, a bronze statue of "Paddy" Hannan adorns Kalgoorlie's main street, which is named after him, and Kalgoorlie's mines are still producing millions of dollars worth of gold annually.

The Western Australian gold rush had dramatic effects on the history of the whole continent. At least temporarily it transformed the most backward and poverty-stricken of the colonies into the most prosperous and progressive. In the twenty years to 1901, the white population of "Australia's western third" rose from 30 000 to 184 000. In popular opinion, "the land of sand, sin, sorrow and sore eyes" became "the golden west". People in the eastern colonies were delighted, instead of being made jealous, by the good fortune of the "sandgropers". Scores of thousands of unemployed and desperate men from Victoria, South Australia and the other colonies sailed to the west to try their luck. Some pushed all their remaining possessions on wheelbarrows from Perth to the goldfields. Few "struck it rich", but most, like the aging Ernest Giles, found other work and stayed in Western Australia, whose inhabitants thus became more attuned to the outlook of people in the eastern colonies.[15]

Relatively few diggers from overseas joined the gold rush to Western Australia. One who did, Herbert Hoover, became the manager of the Sons of Gwalia mine 160 kilometres north of Kalgoorlie and left to posterity as a memento of his visit an outstandingly bathetic poem to the seductive charms of a Western Australian barmaid. He is better remembered, perhaps unfairly, as the worst president the United States of

America ever had up until the election in 1968 of Richard Nixon. Better known in Australia at the time was another young overseas visitor, no remittance man but a genuine British aristocrat, the Honourable David Carnegie. Youngest son of the Earl of Southesk, he was not too proud to learn mining and bush skills from rude colonial diggers. In four years' work he won enough gold to buy some camels and organise his own modest but successful exploring expedition. Striking north from Coolgardie in July 1896, he became the first white man since J. McDouall Stuart to cross the central desert area from south to north and back again instead of from east to west as Giles, a fellow citizen of Coolgardie, and Forrest, the ruling premier of Western Australia, had done some years earlier. When he emerged at Hall's Creek in the Kimberley district near the Duracks' station, he had pioneered a track across drier and more difficult country than either Burke and Wills or McDouall Stuart had faced. Carnegie succeeded because he consistently treated the Aborigines more ruthlessly, in one important respect, than most earlier explorers had done. His practice shows that by the 1890s even the best educated and most humane white Australians, instructed by the "scientific" ideas of social Darwinism, felt justified in treating black people with the brutal contempt that the majority had always used towards them. To find water, Carnegie simply kidnapped a member of a desert tribe, young or old, male or female, and kept him or her prisoner without water until his party was led to the nearest well. Of one such guide, he wrote: "The gin, on showing us the well had been at once liberated a step which I now rather regretted — but one cannot be unkind to ladies, even though they are black, naked savages, little better than beasts." [16]

The Western Australian gold rush enriched many capitalists both in the eastern cities and overseas. It set "the golden west" on the path to prosperity and it relieved the distress caused by the "great depression", but it did not end the depression in the eastern colonies. Before the financial collapse reached its nadir, what Australians still often call "the great strikes" of the 1890s had begun.

The *Bulletin*'s view of the real issues underlying the maritime strike of 1890 (Source: *Bulletin*, 16 August 1890, Mitchell Library, State Library of New South Wales)

The first Inter-colonial Trade Union Congress was held in 1879, and the second in 1884. Thereafter, congresses met annually or biennially and carried resolutions which became more militant in tone and more implicitly "political" in nature as the new industrial unions gathered strength. The Congress of 1888, which met in Brisbane, planned a nationwide trade-union organisation with a central leadership to co-ordinate both industrial and political policies. At the same time, as we have seen, the shearers were remarkably successful at resisting the understandable attempts of pastoralists to pass on the effect of falling wool prices by cutting the standard wage of £1 per hundred sheep shorn. Naturally trade-union militancy and combination were met by a reaction among employers, who also began to combine in such organisations as the Pastoralists' Union with its own Federal Council. In such ways federation was becoming a fact of Australian life long before it became a fact of Australian politics. Some trade-union leaders even urged the formation of employers' associations so as to facilitate bargaining for minimum wages, as they hoped, by workers in every industry in the country; and in 1890 a Queensland wharf-labourers' strike helped force on the squatters an agreement to employ none but union labour in their shearing sheds.

Such successes invited emulation, and the radical movement's force was shown by the extraordinary fact that the maritime strike, which precipitated the trial of strength between Capital and Labor, was triggered not by the demands of manual workers but by the action of ships' *officers*. Having formed a trade union of their own, the marine officers affiliated with the Melbourne Trades Hall Council. It was too much for the shipowners. They refused even to discuss the officers' other claims until they withdrew their affiliation and stopped behaving like common workmen. In August 1890 the officers walked off the ships in defence, as they saw it, of their right to form a trade union and associate with others for the common good, or to refuse, in pursuit of the same ends, to associate with non-unionists. The employers, of course, saw the great principle involved equally clearly, but from an opposite point of view. They fought, as they saw it, for freedom of contract — for their right to employ whomsoever they chose at mutually agreed rates of payment and without union interference. Within hours of the officers' action, the employers had advertised for non-union wharf labourers, and within a month tens of thousands of unionists — seamen, waterside

workers, miners, pastoral workers, and others — were on
strike. The marine officers' dispute was almost lost to sight in
this head-on clash of principle.

The "great maritime strike" was defeated over the course
of the next month or so, but the struggle was renewed again
and again, especially by the shearers in 1891 and 1894. The
"rebel" Southern Cross flag of Eureka Stockade was raised
over some of the strikers' camps in Queensland, and hot-
heads on both sides talked at times of civil war, but though
brawls and bad words were common enough and arson occurred, there seems to have been no loss of life.[17]

An episode which shocked respectable citizens and correspondingly elated the wicked strikers and their friends, was
the burning in 1894 of the river paddle-steamer *Rodney*. Since
"free labourers" or "scabs" could not be found in the outback, some western New South Wales pastoralists hired in
Melbourne forty-five unemployed men who claimed to be
shearers and embarked them on the *Rodney* for Tolarno Station on the Darling. The steamer was also towing a barge
loaded with merchandise for Wilcannia. At Pooncarie the
captain was warned one Saturday morning that strikers at
Polia woolshed were determined to prevent the free
"shearers" from disembarking at Tolarno. He moored his
vessel in a lonely part of the river that night, but at four
o'clock on the Sunday morning masked unionists swarmed
aboard, turned the crew adrift, threw the "scabs" and their
swags into the swamp and burnt the *Rodney* to the water's
edge. None of the assailants was ever punished because no
reward was great enough to tempt any of the scores of
witnesses to give evidence against the shearers.[18]

In preserving "law and order", the colonial governments
collaborated with employers' organisations, while the press
almost unanimously denounced those of the employees.
Twelve trade-union leaders were arrested and charged under
an act of George IV, which had been repealed in Great Britain
but not in the colony of Queensland. Acquitted by a jury, they
were re-arrested, charged with conspiracy, and sentenced to
three years' imprisonment. By the end of 1894, "freedom of

contract" had been temporarily established, and the trade-union movement, employers felt, had been taught a lesson — not so devastatingly, however, as to prevent its regaining by the end of the century its former numerical and organisational strength, if not quite its former militancy. Under the leadership of William Lane, a few hundred idealists sailed away to South America to found, in the wilds of Paraguay, a socialist community to be known as New Australia, but the defeat of the strikes caused more practical Labor leaders to turn more decidedly towards parliamentary action. In their view all the colonial governments, whether Free Trade or Protectionist, had taken sides with the employers against the employees, while the clergy, with a handful of exceptions, had left the people of Australia to "grope amidst the gloom of sacerdotal clap-trap". Easily the most notable exception had been Cardinal Moran, for whom a strike procession had given three cheers as the men marched past St Mary's Cathedral in Sydney.[19]

Yet the defeat of the strikes did little more than accelerate the Labor movement's entry into the political field. In New South Wales, for instance, thirty-six Labor Party members who held the balance of power in the Legislative Assembly had been elected to parliament in 1891, and by 1893 a similar situation existed in Queensland. In the southern colonies, partly because more liberal legislation had already been enacted there by radical middle-class politicians, Labor parties gained influence — and internal cohesion — more slowly, but essentially the same changes took place. Oddly enough, in view of the stress Labor from the first placed on party organisation and discipline, the six colonial (after 1901, state) Labor parties did not formally set up a nationwide organisation until 1915 — years after the party had grown quite accustomed to occupying the treasury benches in the national parliament. From the time when Labor members were first elected, the party programs stressed the importance of Australian nationalism, "racial purity" and practical reformist measures, rather than any kind of general, doctrinaire socialist plans for reconstructing society.

Until 1909, Labor usually held the balance of power in the various parliaments and openly offered "support in return for concessions" to rival parties which wished to form governments. Thus, even before federation, most colonial governments with Labor support – perhaps pressure would be a more appropriate word – enacted a good deal of social legislation which sought both to make the economy work more effectively and to protect less fortunate citizens from its untrammelled operations. Much of this legislation was accepted by conservatives as well as liberals – at least partly because of the great strikes. Most people, wishing to avoid any further such experience, were readier than they had earlier been to accept, and even to applaud, some forms of state inteference in industry. Thus most colonies during the 1890s set up some kind of legal machinery for arbitrating disputes between employers and employees. Minimum working conditions and maximum hours of labour were laid down in a number of factory and mining acts, while early closing acts shortened the long hours for which shop-assistants worked. Under closer settlement acts, governments repurchased land from pastoralists or land companies, subdivided it, and sold it back on easy terms to small farmers to whom they lent money until they were able to stand on their own feet. Such legislation was considerably more successful in establishing small farmers on the land than the *Selection Acts* of the previous thirty years had been. Most colonies, largely under Henry George's influence, introduced land taxes – both to raise revenue and, some hoped, to help break up the large pastoral estates. Old-age pension schemes were also established in the two largest colonies by the end of the century.

It must not be thought that all these reforms were simply and solely the result of Labor pressure. Some middle-class politicians of the traditionally established Free Trade and Protectionist parties held genuinely "progressive" views and, in certain fields, needed no pushing from their allies. Moreover, on the matter of setting up arbitration courts, for example, Labor was by no means solidly enthusiastic. Its view of the state's role in the great strike struggles suggested to some, rather, that state arbitration might prove another employers' device for coercing the wage earners. Still, Labor's influence in bringing about this plethora of social legislation was generally considerable.[20]

It was probably least so in the emancipation of women from age-old customary disabilities, although many changes in the lot of women did occur at this time. The invention of pneumatic tyres made cycling a relatively cheap and popular sport in which women participated freely — despite the dire fulminations of the Pope and other moralists. For the first time tennis was played by large numbers of both sexes. Rubber introduced also the use of condoms, pessaries and other contraceptive devices which, ineffecient though they were, made possible some measure of family planning and spelt the beginning of the end of the typical Victorian family of a dozen or twenty children. Those who were beginning to be called wowsers tried to ban discussion of the subject. In 1888 a Sydney bookseller named Collins was convicted by a magistrate for selling an obscene publication, Mrs Annie Besant's *The Law of Population*, a pamphlet which explained, among other things, how to use the new devices. Collins appealed to the Supreme Court of New South Wales which, in a remarkably enlightened judgment written by the Senior Puisne Judge, W.C. Windeyer, found nothing obscene in a discussion of the new birth control methods.

Australian feminists agitated tirelessly for the extension of female rights and opportunities and for, as they saw it, the shielding of women from some of the grosser forms of male exploitation. As in comparable countries at the time, the leading feminists were nearly all thoroughly white, respectable, middle-class, Protestant, bourgeois people. Perhaps that is why they put rather more effort into the protection of women than into their liberation. In organisations such as the Women's Christian Temperance Union they worked for the control and, if possible, the prohibition, of "the drink traffic". They sought not to extend the freedom of rich women — to drink in public bars for instance — but to protect poor women and children from the onslaughts of drunken husbands and

THE NEW WOMAN—HER LATEST SNAG.
" The Pope has pronounced against women cycling in 'rational' dress."—CASTA.

The early *Bulletin* was immensely popular and far more influential than any other Australian journal before or since. It became famous for its satirical cartoons, such as this comment on the Pope's attempt to forbid female cycling and dress reform. (Source: *Bulletin*, 7 December 1895, Mitchell Library, State Library of New South Wales)

fathers returning from the pubs late at night. In 1915 they succeeded in having most Australian bars shut at six o'clock and thereby, some argued, in merely bringing forward the hour at which many women and children had to suffer abuse from brutal breadwinners.

It might even be held that organisations like the Women's Christian Temperance Union were concerned not with the protection of women but rather with the protection of the idea of the Christian bourgeois family. Neither the trade unions nor any other organisations or persons at this time seem to have worried about equal *social* rights for women. No one, not even people in the labor movement, dreamed of "equal pay for equal work". Many trade-union leaders led all the rest in insisting that female wages must be kept down in order to protect the male breadwinners, seen in this context not as drunken thugs but as virtuous and industrious "heads of families". There was, however, a significant move by women out of domestic work into factory and business jobs. Between 1890 and 1910 the female percentage of workers in manufacturing industry in the two main states, New South Wales and Victoria, rose from about 12.5 per cent to about 29 per cent.[21]

Equality of opportunity was achieved in some spheres, however. By the 1890s, tertiary education was made available to women on the same terms as to men, namely, that their parents were rich enough to pay for it. On 6 April 1881 the University of Sydney decided to admit women students for the first time. Its governing body was confident that male and female students could attend the same classes provided that the lecturers said "nothing of a nature to shock female delicacy".[22] Australian women also won for themselves at this time political equality, or at least the appearance of it, many years before most of their sisters in other countries did so. In the 18780s and 1880s the vote was given to women in a few western territories of the United States, including Wyoming, Utah, Washington and Colorado. Apart from these cases, complete women's franchise was introduced first in New Zealand in 1893 and in South Australia in 1894.

Agitation and lobbying by people like Rosa Scott in New South Wales, Vida Goldstein in Victoria and Catherine Spence in South Australia had brought about a situation in which women's suffrage was seen as a natural extension of the process of liberal reform, which had over the previous forty years brought manhood suffrage, secret ballots, payment of members and other democratic reforms to most Australian colonies. Female franchise was seen, very wrongly, as the key to complete equality in all spheres with man, but the spirit of colonial liberalism and empiricism was so strong that women felt no need to fight for the vote, nor conservative males to fight against it, with any of the fury generated later in Britain and the United States. "King Dick" Seddon in New Zealand and Charles Cameron Kingston in South Australia both led populist radical governments, Kingston's being supported by half a dozen newly elected Labor members. Kingston enfranchised South Australian women in 1894 purely because he thought it would advantange him politically. The ratio of women to men was markedly higher in city electorates, which generally supported him, than it was in country electorates which usually supported his opponents.[23] The radical premiers probably thought too that most women would vote for them, from principle or gratitude. If so, they were quickly disillusioned. Ever since their enfranchisement, Australian women have consistently voted more conservatively than men.

That likelihood was certainly clear to the arch-conservative premier of Western Australia, Sir John Forrest, when he enfranchised women in 1898. He and his family had ruled Western Australia for many years and he guessed correctly that giving votes to women would keep him in power for some years more. In 1898, male, and generally radical, goldseekers from the eastern colonies dominated the Western Australian goldfields. In spite of a massive electoral, gerrymander against them, they seemed about to dominate the politics of the whole colony, but there were very few white women among the recently arrived "t'other-siders". The vast majority of all white females in the colony lived in the "old" Western Australian electorates of Perth and the "South West". Thus, by giving all women the vote, Forrest considerably strengthened the conservative political position for the next ten years.

Enfranchisement of women in the other colonies was an incidental result of federation. The federal constitution specifically ruled that Commonwealth politicians should be elected only by citizens who already had the vote in each state. Thus South and Western Australian women voted for members of the first national parliament while women in other states did not. A majority of even the all-male parliament thought this situation ridiculous and voted in 1902 for the enfranchisement in federal elections of all Australian women. This act in turn produced a ridiculous situation in the four eastern states where women could vote in federal elections but not in state ones. The male-dominated state legislatures fell into line fairly rapidly, because not to do so was seen by most voters as both illogical and illiberal. Even so, in one of the first indications that what had been the most "progressive" and liberal colony in the nineteenth century was fast becoming the most conservative one, Victorian politicians kept the threatened invasion out of their citadel till 1908.

Labor's influence on the organisational forms of Australian politics was probably even greater than its influence on social change. We have seen that during the first thirty years or so of responsible government in the various colonies organised parties hardly existed, and that consequently politicians were even freer than they are today in the United States to vote as conscience, or interest, directed them. On the whole, politicians had been much more impressed with the merits of this situation than had the electors. So the founders of the Labor Party in the various colonies sought for some way of binding their parliamentary representatives to the policies of those whose votes were to send them to the seats of the mighty. Thus was evolved the "pledge" and the "caucus". Every Labor member pledged to carry out the party program, as determined primarily by the extra-parliamentary organisations of the party, and to this end promised to cast his vote on every question as decided beforehand by a caucus, or private meeting, of Labor members of parliament.

Newspaper editors and traditionalists of all hues thundered at what they saw as the wickedness of these arrangements. Their most plausible argument was that Labor procedures, by predetermining outside parliament the party's vote, made a mere mockery of the parliamentary process of debate and decision. Labor members were denounced as "mere delegates", or mechanical puppets who had sold their own souls, it was implied, to the Devils in charge of the Trades and Labor Councils. Nevertheless, the Free Trade and Protectionist parties or groupings, if only in self-defence, were compelled by Labor's example to tighten party discipline and strengthen their own organisations in other ways. An important side-effect of this process was to help make Australian political life cleaner on the whole in the twentieth century than it had been in the nineteenth — and this despite the corrupting efforts of larrikin gangers like John Wren who rose to wealth and infamy from about the turn of the century onwards.[24] Stricter party discipline both reduced the area for devious manoeuvre available to individual members and made them more responsible to their electors — or at least more responsible to the fixed principles for which the electors now knew the fixed parties claimed to stand. Yet this alignment of parties with principles took place only gradually. Throughout the 1890s in most colonies, Labor avoided commitment in principle to either free trade or protection, while no party as such stood unequivocally for federation.

It is clear that nationalist sentiment was increasing in all sections of the community, but the keenest nationalists did not always see federal union as the necessary, or even desirable, way of giving effect to their aspirations. The *Bulletin*, for instance, preached nationalism more fervently than any other journal, but was anti-federalist until the last three or four years of the century. Because some conservative opinion supported Australian federation, the *Bulletin* for long suspected it as a stalking-horse for the bringing about of imperial federation. This was a *fin-de-siècle* scheme, agitated for, but never very clearly defined by, some British politicians and publicists, for forming some sort of federal imperial government to which the self-governing colonies at least should send representatives.[25] The plan roused little enthusiasm in Australia, even among conservatives, certainly no more and perhaps less than did the republican visions of some radicals and

Some of the corruption endemic in nineteenth-century colonial politics — grossly satirised in this cartoon — was cleaned up with the development of party organisaton and discipline (Source: State Library of New South Wales)

liberals; but its effect on the federal movement exemplifies the complex manner in which the federation issue was enmeshed with so many others. Yet it is clear that the rising tide of nationalist sentiment did increasingly spill over into the federal movement, and that to a considerable extent it forced the hands of some important politicians like George Houston ("Yes–No") Reid, Free Trade premier of New South Wales from 1894 to 1898. It is less clear, but equally true, that federation sentiment was strongest among working-class and middle-of-the-road citizens and weakest among conservatives.

Yet this could not be easily deduced from the behaviour of politicians. As we have seen, Labor's political leaders actively opposed, or at best were lurkewarm towards, federation. Some thought it a conservative device for distracting atten-

While the *Bulletin* preached nationalism more fervently than any other journal in the last years of the nineteenth century, it often took a cynical view of the movement towards federation, as this map showing "the progress of federation" demonstrates (Source: *Bulletin*, 4 February 1899, National Library of Australia)

tion from the need for social reforms. Others thought the proposed constitution gave far too much ill-defined power to the Governor-General, a view that was to be proved disastrously true seventy-five years later.[26] Conservatives, whether Free Trade or Protectionist in complexion, were divided over federation. Overwhelmingly the lead came from liberal, middle-class politicians like Alfred Deakin of Victoria, Sir Henry Parkes of New South Wales, and Charles Cameron Kingston of South Australia.

Such men and their supporters were inspired by a sincere

and often deeply felt Australian patriotism, but they were also highly practical politicians who seldom lost sight of more mundane matters. They thought, rightly, that federation would pay. Tasmania, for instance, with its small area and largely rural population, depended heavily upon its exports of agricultural produce to the mainland colonies. One federal propagandist in the "Apple Isle" found the following speech enormously effective:

> Gentlemen, if you vote for the Bill you will found a great and glorious nation under the bright Southern Cross, and meat will be cheaper; and you will live to see the Australian race dominate the Southern seas, and you will have a market for both potatoes and apples; and your sons shall reap the grand heritage of nationhood, and if Sir William Lyne does come back to power in Sydney he can never do you one penny worth of harm.[27]

(Lyne was the Protectionist leader in New South Wales who, it was feared, might ruin Tasmania by introducing tariffs to protect the mother colony's agriculture against Tasmanian competition.)

There is barely space in this book to mention some of the major arguments of the federationists and the series of convocations and referenda by which union was brought about. As the last British soldier had left Australia in 1870, the need for a unified system of national defence was much canvassed. Many men, especially in border districts like the Riverina, were increasingly irked by intercolonial customs barriers, and many merchants, especially in Victoria where manufacturing industry was strongest, looked to the advantages of a continent-wide market. Almost everyone agreed that a national government could best deal with questions of immigration and relations with foreign powers, especially with those like Germany and France which had interests in the Pacific. Everyone, except the despised Aborigines, agreed that the British, or Anglo-Saxon, or even Anglo-Celtic "race" was the salt of the earth, appointed equally by God and godless scientists, to rule forever over inferior, especially "coloured" peoples. Practically everyone except some Queensland sugar-plantation proprietors agreed that the new national

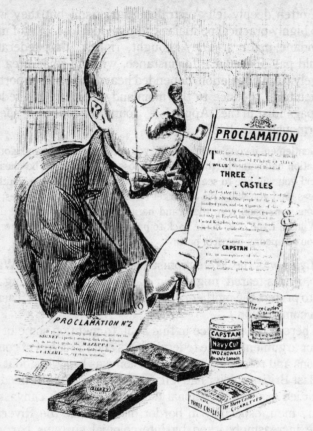

George Houston Reid, Free Trade premier of New South Wales, was not too proud to appear in this advertisement for tobacco in the *Bulletin* in 1896 (Source: *Bulletin*, 12 December 1896, Mitchell Library, State Library of New South Wales)

government's most important task would be to enact the "white Australia policy", reserving the world's sixth continent forever to the white Australian people and their heirs.

There was one underlying factor of prime importance that has not always been given the attention it merits: namely, the newly acquired geographical propinquity of the separate colonies. Founded separately, and to a considerable extent settled separately from distant Britain, each colony had for long been a distinct community, centred on its coastal capital and separated from each of its neighbours by hundreds of kilometres of virgin wilderness. But the gold discoveries of the 1850s and the slow but steady spread of agricultural settlement thereafter, brought people, townships, roads, and finally telegraphs and railways, to the bush. Except for Western Australia, the separate colonies had already become one in a geographical sense, and Western Australia tried hard but unsuccessfully to secure the promise of a railway link from the federal government-to-be as a condition of its joining. Even so, the west's adherence was made certain by the overwhelming pro-federation vote on her goldfields of the "t'other-siders" from the eastern colonies.

There had never been any really significant racial, linguistic, cultural or even economic differences between the people of the various Australian colonies, as there had been in the United States and Canada. Now that settlement had spread through the bush until the colonies fused geographically, it was natural, if not quite inevitable, that they should join to make one nation in the broadest cultural sense. Indeed, it is not too much to suggest that, just because of this implicitly existing natural unity, the Commonwealth's founding fathers felt they could afford to follow the American precedent of leaving all residual powers to the states, while Canada's confederationists, in 1867 at the end of the American Civil War, were so conscious of French-speaking Quebec and other divisive regional differences that they felt constrained to reserve all residual powers to the central government.

Ever since 1847 some politicians in Britain and Australia had made sporadic federation proposals. All were abortive, because they were made before the colonies had merged geographically. The beginning of the final successful movement dates from a speech made in 1889 by Sir Henry Parkes in which, as an eyewitness reported: "for the first time the voice of an authoritative statesman gave soul and utterance to the aspirations of a people. It was truly remarkable and not without a touch of sublimity".[28] Nor was it accidental that the ancient political warrior, more sensitive than any of his competitors to the ground-swell of public opinion, gave tongue to his "clarion call" at Tenterfield, a New South Wales country town on the newly completed railway joining the Queensland system at the border only about 30 kilometres to the north. From this time onward, federation became an increasingly real issue. Yet the first round of conferences and conventions ended abortively in 1891, largely because the whole question was still being dealt with at an inter-government level. After this check, bands of devoted federalists, many of them young, liberal-minded middle-class people like Dr John Quick, set about rousing and articulating public opinion so that politicians would be compelled to respond effectively to it. Voluntary, non-party political bodies, such as the Australian Natives' Association and the Federal League, played a leading part. The success of this second round of convention meetings was due largely to this strong popular movement, which inspired the delegates to hammer out a workable constitution in the face of very real difficulties.[29]

Perhaps the most intractable problem was that of somehow reconciling responsible government in the British sense, that is, responsibility of the prime minister and cabinet to the popularly elected lower house, with the necessary federal principle of equality of rights for the constituent states. If the States' House or Senate were given equal powers with the House of Representatives elected on a population basis, how could the majority be said to rule, since more than two-thirds of the Australian people lived in the two prospective states of New South Wales and Victoria? On the other hand, if the two houses were not given equal powers, how could it be claimed that the six states, which were, of course, to be equally represented only in the Senate, would be upon a footing of equality? Naturally, the constitutions of the United States and Canada were closely studied by some convention delegates, and freely argued about by all. The above difficulty was solved by a series of compromises, and the constitution finally recommended to the people owed a great deal to that of the United States. Indeed, in many respects the Australian constitution is modelled directly upon that of America. The

Commonwealth's High Court, for example, like the American Supreme Court, is not only a tribunal to which litigants may appeal from the state supreme courts, but it also plays a very important and independent role in government through its power of interpreting the federal constitution.

The draft constitution was confirmed by popular referendum and then enacted as a statute by the British Parliament in London. The birth of the new nation was formally proclaimed on the first day of the new century, 1 January 1901. Its flag appropriately symbolised the marriage which had been consummated between traditional British values and the new indigenous values springing from a century's struggle with the harsh, but no longer strange, environment. The Union Jack was balanced by a large star symbolising the unity of the six states and by the stars of the Southern Cross which had waved over the Eureka Stockade.

The growth of local nationalist sentiment and the related move towards federation at the end of the century were reflected in changing attitudes to Australian participation in her first two wars. In 1885 loyal colonists were at least as stirred to patriotic frenzy as were most people "at Home" by General Gordon's death in Khartoum. The acting premier of New South Wales, William Bede Dalley, native-born son of an Irish convict, sent 750 men to help Britain in the Sudan. The great majority of Australians, including the volunteer soldiers themselves, felt that they were British colonists, fighting in a quarrel of their own country, of which Australia was merely a sort of extension where they happened to live. Yet even in 1885 there were some Australian nationalists who, along with the *Bulletin*'s editors, condemned British imperial and colonial wars, and felt that Australians should have no part or interest in them.[30]

When the Boer War broke out in 1899, all the separate mainland Australian colonies sent contingents in much the same spirit as the men from New South Wales had been despatched to the Sudan fourteen years earlier. There were differences in attitude however. The 15 000 volunteers were seen, and saw themselves, much more as Australian soldiers with something of their own to contribute to the mother country, as indeed they had. The mounted Boer farmers might have carried on their guerilla resistance for years longer than they did, if they had not been matched by equally good horsemen, mostly bushmen from the Australian countryside. One of these was "Breaker Morant", an English confidence man who became in the sixteen years before 1899 a legendary figure in outback Queensland and New South Wales. He was a magnificent horseman, pugilist and all-round bushman, a tolerable musician and balladist, an inveterate gambler, a deep drinker, recklessly generous with other people's property, impeccably loyal to his mates while being callously brutal to those outside the charmed circle, a vicious racist, one who in a later day would have been termed a "male chauvinist pig" of the worst sort and, like nearly all bushrangers, a man always "brimming over with flashness" – as he was described by "Banjo" Paterson's uncle, Andrew Barton. In short, this engaging, but not very admirable, Englishman was seen as the very epitome of characteristically national Australian virtues and vices. In February 1902 he was court-martialled and shot with another Australian officer, Lieutenant Handcock, for having murdered Boer prisoners.[31]

Their defence was that the British high command had ordered the execution of Boers captured wearing British uniforms, and that most officers in the British forces during the last months of the war had obeyed the order as they had. They were shot nevertheless and thus became folk-heroes of Australian nationalism. In popular Australian opinion, Morant was held to have been *selected* as the scapegoat for the sins of the whole British Army and its Commander-in-Chief, Lord Kitchener, *because* he was an Australian and an outstandingly "typical" Australian at that. Australian officialdom disowned Morant and Handcock with indecent haste – as Austral-British patriots have always been wont to do in such cases – but popular opinion had the truth of the matter, though very far from the whole truth. The execution of these two murderers, a year after national federation, possibly did more than any other single event before or since to strengthen local Australian nationalism and weaken a little the older imperial loyalty.[32]

That is not to say that most Australians thenceforce were in any sense anti-British. Indeed, most politicians and other leading people continued to feel more imperial than local loyalty. But after 1902 most people identified naturally with Australia, their own land, which they saw as the most socially "advanced" and "progressive" part of the British Empire – and to which they also "belonged".

The breadth of the existing consensus is indicated by the impressive legislative achievements of the first Commonwealth parliaments. It is hardly too much to say that they fixed the broad lines of development along which Australian society has moved ever since, and this despite the fact that until 1909 three parties, none of which ever had a clear majority by itself, contended for power. For these nine years each of the Free Trade, Protectionist and Labor parties continued to win roughly a third of the seats – give or take a few – in the federal parliament, though Labor's share continued to increase at the expense of the two middle-class groups. Though there were liberal Free Traders and conservative Protectionists, the Free Trade Party was, generally speaking, farthest to the right. It drew much support from chambers of commerce, importing agencies and the strong pastoral interest. The Protectionists naturally enjoyed the support of manufacturers and other business interests struggling to build up local secondary industries against overseas competitors, and partly for this reason they attracted the votes of many keen nationalists. The party had a strong liberal wing and properly enough came to be known as the Liberal-Protectionist, or often simply the Liberal Party.[33] The Labor Party, of course, claimed to stand for the interests of trade unionists and wage earners in general, and it retained an even better claim than the Protectionists to be the party of Australian nationalism, but the faint note of doctrinaire socialism became even fainter as its parliamentary members began to savour the delights of place and to be chastened by the responsibilities of power.

General Election Held	Seats won in House of Representatives			Labour % of votes cast	Prime Minister
	Free Trade	Protectionist	Labor		
March 1901	27	32	16	13.5	Barton (Protectionist)
December 1903	24	25	25	30	Deakin (Protectionist)
					J C Watson (Labor)
					Reid (Free Trade)
					Deakin (Protectionist)
December 1906	32	17	26	39	
		FUSION			Deakin (Protectionist)
April 1910		31	41+3	50	Fisher (Labor)
May 1913		38	37	48.5	Cook (Liberal Fusionist)
August 1914		32+1	42	50.9	Fisher (Labor)

Figure 21   Development of party politics in the early federal parliaments

Still, Labor usually sought to carry liberal reforms farther and faster than even the most radical of the Protectionists.

Under these circumstances, during its first decade the Commonwealth was governed for the most part by the Liberal-Protectionists with Labor support. On many of the great issues parliament dealt with, the Free Trade oppositionists fought the government over matters of detail, timing and emphasis rather than of principle. The Protectionist leader, and prime minister for most of the period, was Alfred Deakin. Native-born son of a Cobb and Co. book-keeper, Deakin studied law at the University of Melbourne and then became a journalist and a protégé of "King David" Syme, proprietor of the Melbourne *Age*. He was elected to the Victorian parliament in 1880 when he was only 24, and became a cabinet minister three years later. In 1884 he visited the United States to study American irrigation laws and practices. He was the author of much pioneer factory legislation in Victoria and a leading federalist who became the attorney-general in Barton's first (Liberal-Protectionist) Commonwealth government from 1901 to 1903. On Barton's retirement to the High Court Bench, Deakin became prime minister of the Commonwealth for three periods, 1903–1904, 1905–1908 and 1909–1910.

If Australians were half as interested in statesmen as they have been in bushrangers, boxers and racehorses, Deakin's name would be a legend in the land he served so well. As it is, he is remembered, if at all, by the slightingly sardonic nickname of "Affable Alfred", fixed on him by his political enemies. His fervent nationalism was directed by his strong common sense and by a wide knowledge of people and of other lands in addition to his own. He was a gifted and persuasive orator, though enthusiasm sometimes made him speak too rapidly for his audience. Deeply practical, yet scholarly, sensitive and astute, he was in his own person a compelling refutation of the ancient myth that "colonials", especially radically inclined ones, were certain to be either bumptious bounders or subservient spiritual adolescents. At imperial conferences he more than held his own with British prime ministers, and he returned home with his accent and opinions not perceptibly affected by the offer of a knighthood (which he declined), and by much flattery and exposure to aristocratic wealth. The worst that can be said of him is that for many years, in the capacity of anonymous Australian correspondent of the London *Morning Post*, he made not unfavourable reports on his own conduct as Australian prime minister. It was chiefly under his guidance that the first parliaments gave legislative form to the new nation's course.[34]

The most important enactments were concerned with fostering national sentiment and security or with raising living standards for the masses, but, as we have seen, these two policies appeared to many, if not most, people of the time to be two complementary aspects of the one broad national policy. The embarrassing "white Australia" policy, for instance, was established by the first parliament's *Immigration Restriction Act* and *Pacific Islands Labourers' Act*.

Was the policy inspired mainly by racist or by economic motives? Careful examination of all the speeches made in the House of Representatives and the Senate shows that both considerations were present in the minds of almost all members. On balance, arguments based on notions of "racial purity" and the supposedly innate inferiority of coloured people predominated over arguments for excluding Africans, Asians and Polynesians in order to preserve good wages and working conditions for whites, but practically all members who spoke showed that they wanted the legislation for both reasons. It is only fair to remember that the myth of innate white superiority, springing partly from Social Darwinist ideas, was almost universally accepted throughout the Western world at the time, especially in English-speaking countries. Australians were by no means uniquely wicked — or ignorant. Rather, they seemed to most literate contemporaries both wise and fortunately placed, when they deported indentured Melanesian labourers from the Queensland sugar plantations and sought to forbid for all time the immigration of any other coloured person. If the climate of contemporary opinion is taken into account, the racist arguments were expressed with rather surprising decency and restraint by some members, notably by Deakin. In a much-quoted speech, he held that the Japanese, for instance, were not inferior but simply different, indeed that they might well be superior in some respects. Other acts forbade the Commonwealth government to give mail contracts to coastal shipping firms employing any coloured labour, and specifically excluded Australia's first inhabitants, the Aborigines, from the benefits of much welfare legislation. Were they not also black and inferior?[35]

A series of Commonwealth defence acts established the principle that all male citizens were liable to compulsory service and training in the armed forces inside Australia, and in 1907 Deakin's government planned the creation of an Australian Navy which should co-operate with the British Navy in time of war. The Commonwealth took over responsibility for British New Guinea in 1902 and for South Australia's neglected Northern Territory in 1911.

In 1908 Deakin's administration passed a bill providing old age and invalid pensions, but farther reaching in its effects was the establishment in 1904 of a Commonwealth Court of Conciliation and Arbitration for settling industrial disputes. Its jurisdiction was limited to industries which operated in more than one state, but all the state governments increasingly tended to follow the federal lead in their own industrial court procedures. The Commonwealth Arbitration Court's second president was Henry Bournes Higgins, a capable and profoundly humanitarian lawyer who had been an independent radical member of the Victorian Parliament until 1900, when he lost his seat because, many thought, of his public condemnation of Britain's moral position in the Boer War. To understand the importance of the court's first major decision, we must place it in context.

In 1906 Deakin brought forward his policy of "New Protection". In that it consciously aimed equally at national aggrandisement and social welfare, it was perhaps the most characteristic and important legislation of the period. In the following year, by steeply increasing the tariffs on a whole range of manufactured imports, parliament went far towards making protection the settled fiscal policy of the country. But in accordance with Deakin's humanitarian aims — and of course with Labor's policy — the "New Protection" decreed that Australian manufacturers themselves would be exempt from the new duties only if each firm could show that its employees were enjoying good wages and conditions as their share of the prosperity fostered by the new tariffs. In the event, though the duties on imported goods remained, the High Court declared that the rest of the legislation was unconstitutional. Yet much the same result was brought about by the action of the Commonwealth Arbitration Court.

In 1907 H.V. McKay Ltd, a large firm of agricultural implement makers, sought exemption from the excise duties imposed by Deakin's still-untested legislation. As president of the court, Higgins heard a great deal of evidence and refused the exemption, holding that the wages paid by the company were not "fair and reasonable". They were insufficient, he held, to meet "the normal needs of the average employee regarded as a human being living in a civilised community". From an examination of current living costs, Higgins went on to fix the minimum wage which any firm operating in more than one state would have to pay, even to its most unskilled and unenthusiastic male employee — as long as he continued on the payroll. Many alterations and modifications to the method of minimum wage fixing have been made since 1907, but the concept of the basic wage itself remained a fundamental pillar of the Australian way of life. Strong trade unions for long helped to ensure that the minimum wage was not merely a figure on paper but a reality.

By 1908 both Liberals and Laborites began to feel that their partnership — which had not endured until then without strains and ruptures — had outlived its usefulness. In 1909 Labor formed a short-lived minority administration which was ousted by what seemed to many contemporaries an unnatural fusion between the two middle-class parties. Liberal-Protectionists and conservative Free Traders joined to form the Liberal Party, united at first mainly in its opposition to Labor. Thus by 1910 the continuing political pattern of the Australian two-party system was established. When the new "Fusionist" government met the House, Deakin was flayed by William Morris Hughes, not then the leader of the Labor Party but easily its most able and vituperative member. It was not fair to Judas Iscariot, Hughes said, to compare him with Deakin, for Judas "did not gag the man whom he betrayed, nor did he fail to hang himself afterwards". At the general election of 1910, the electorate showed that it felt there was some substance in Hughes's view of the manoeuvres which had led to fusion. Under the leadership of Andrew Fisher, Labor was returned with an absolute and resounding majority in both houses. The new prime minister was a Scottish coal miner who had immigrated at the age of 23. Steady, some said stodgy, he was yet unswervingly loyal to Labor's moderate ideals. Between 1910 and 1913 his government continued the old Deakinite or "Lib–Lab" policy of welfare-state nationalism, adding here and there a few bravura touches which the opposition denounced as rabid socialism, but which did not impress most electors as such.

The scope of old-age and invalid pensons was extended somewhat and maternity allowances were introduced. Government employees were enabled, as those in private industry had already been, to approach the Arbitration Court with grievances. Labor's views on this point had been a source of

bitter friction in the defunct Lib–Lab alliance. The government also imposed a Commonwealth land tax aimed partly,
like so much legislation since 1860, at "breaking up the big
estates", and thus helping to put small farmers on the land.
The land tax accomplished little in these directions, but
proved an acceptable and permanent source of revenue. Easily the most controversial legislation was the creation of the
Commonwealth Bank, sponsored most vociferously, if not always most effectively, by King O'Malley, a colourful Tasmanian Labor representative in the federal Parliament from
1901 to 1917. According to circumstances, O'Malley sometimes gave the impression that he had been born in Canada
and sometimes in the United States.[36] Similarly, the Commonwealth Bank was to be a "people's bank which would
drive "capitalist banks" out of existence and usher in the millennium, and it was to help and comfort private enterprise
too. In fact, from its inception the Commonwealth Bank controlled the note issue and increasingly exercised central banking functions. At the same time, it competed successfully
with private banks for all ordinary business and soon became
the dominant financial institution of the country.[37]

Fisher's government did much to confirm Labor's claim to
be the party of Australian – as opposed to generalised British
– nationalism. It pushed forward across the treeless desert
the railway line to Western Australia, which was completed
in 1917. It chose on the Monaro Tableland the beautiful site
of the future federal capital, and it conducted a world-wide
competition, won by an American architect, Walter Burley
Griffin, for the best city plan. The federal parliament continued to sit in Melbourne until 1927, when the new Parliament
House was opened in Canberra by the Duke of York, the
future King George VI. The Fisher government also built up
the Australian Army and Navy. The latter, consisting by
1913 of a battle cruiser, three cruisers, three destroyers, two
submarines and a number of smaller craft, comprised a large
and efficient striking force for a country of little more than
four million people, many of whom were inordinately proud
of their new fleet. But the Navy was staffed by volunteers.

The morale of the peace-time land forces was less good, for they were organised on a compulsory basis. Following a report from the distinguished British soldier, Lord Kitchener, called for earlier by the Fusionist government, Labor made all males between the age of 12 and 26 eligible for military training. Apart from the necessity of school attendance, Australians had never known such regimentation since convict times – and then they had shown marked aversion for peace-time military and police duties. No serious attempt was made to train the younger children, but from the beginning of 1912 onward the Commonwealth prosecuted upwards of 27 000 boys and young men for refusing or evading service. Most of these delinquents were fined, but nearly a quarter of the total were imprisoned. Two brothers called Size, aged 18 and 19, were kept on a diet of bread and water for days on end in a South Australian military gaol. When released, they still refused to drill and were again imprisoned. When World I broke out a few months later, the Size brothers emphasised the nature of their protest by volunteering for overseas fighting service with the first Australian Imperial Force.[38]

6　War and depression
c. 1914–38

During the whole course of World War I, more Australians than Americans died on the battlefields, and every one of them had volunteered to fight overseas. The total Australian population was less than five million – about equal to that of greater New York City at that time, or to one-twentieth of the population of the United States. It is not surprising then that the 1914–18 experience was a traumatic one for Australians. After a century of peaceful and surprisingly orderly development during which rumours of distant wars had hardly troubled people, events on the other side of the earth suddenly brought death near to practically every Australian home. The utopian dreaming of the past two or three decades was fractured, and with it the illusion that the young nation might forever escape involvement in Old World sins and quarrels. Worse – especially after the broad measure of agreement which had characterised the previous decade or more – the community was divided against itself more bitterly than at any time before or since. After the war Australian life never quite regained its provincial innocence, and even the tempo of material development did not really recover its former momentum for the next twenty years and more. None of this was foreseen, however, when the Great War began on 4 August 1914.

In the federal election campaign being waged at the time, the party leaders vied with each other in promising all-out support for the British war effort. Fisher, the Labor leader,

Tom Barker, the editor of *Direct Action*, was imprisoned during the war for publishing this cartoon by Syd Nicholls (Source: *Direct Action*, 4 December 1915, Mitchell Library, State Library of New South Wales)

Frank Anstey, a radical federal
politician, and seven Labor colleagues
made no secret of their opposition to the
European War (Source: Mitchell Library,
State Library of New South Wales)

undoubtedly spoke for the consensus of opinion, though not
for all members of his own
party, when he promised to help
defend the mother country "to
our last man and shilling".
Fourteen years of national independence and advancement
within the Empire seemed to
have liquidated the small but
vociferous republican minority
of the 1890s. Almost everyone
seemed to feel their Britishness
as the extension and guarantee
of their Australianness rather
than as any kind of limitation on
it. And yet there was from the
beginning a small band of Australian nationalists who opposed the war itself, or at least
dismissed it as a far-off imperial
struggle of no concern to young
Australia. The radical federal politician, Frank Anstey, and
seven of his ALP colleagues, made no secret of these views,[1]
though Fisher and the right wing of the party made, if anything, more bellicosely pro-British speeches than the most
conservative spokesperson. Within two years the tiny minority was to become a bare majority — at least to the extent of
opposing conscription of men for overseas service.

On 5 September Labor was returned to power with a comfortable majority in both federal houses. With no precedents
to guide it, the new government set about the difficult task of
organising the war effort. The Royal Australian Navy, al-

ready a going concern, immediately took over the almost defenceless German portion of New Guinea and then turned to home waters. The first considerable engagement with the enemy took place on 9 November 1914 in the Indian Ocean off the Cocos Islands. The German light cruiser, *Emden*, was caught and sunk in a duel with the slightly better armed Australian light cruiser, *Sydney*. Unrestrained jubilation marked the reception of the news. It was a small battle no doubt, but after all it was the first purely Australian one. In the Boer War Australian and other "colonial" soldiers had been distributed among British units in order, it was held, to "stiffen" their morale and provide them with reliable leadership.

That this practice was not followed in 1914 was largely due to the opposition of the first commander of the Australian Imperial Force, the volunteer army which was recruited to fight overseas. A grandson of Betsy Broughton, the survivor of the *Boyd* massacre,[2] Major-General W.T. Bridges pressed successfully for the principle that Australian soldiers should not be distributed among British units but should retain their own identity throughout the conflict. It was also established, perhaps partly in reaction to the execution of Morant and Handcock in South Africa, that Australian soldiers were not to be subject to the death penalty. Bridges planned to recruit a force of about 20 000 men, but the rush of volunteers at first almost overwhelmed the ability of the skeleton military organisation to cope with them. By the end of the war, over 330 000 soldiers had actually sailed to Europe or the Middle East as members of the AIF.

By the beginning of 1915 they were quartered at training camps in Egypt because there were not enough barracks and camp facilities ready for them in England. Thus, accidentally, they took a leading part in the ill-starred Gallipoli campaign. The plan, strongly supported by Winston Churchill, First Lord of the Admiralty, was to seize control of the Dardanelles and thereby open the Black Sea to Allied shipping, bring help to Russia, and perhaps knock the Turkish enemy completely out of the war. It was a good idea, but one doomed to failure by botched tactical planning and insufficient allocation of resources. In the half-light of early dawn on 25 April, thousands of Australia's bravest and best young men stormed ashore on a narrow beach at Gallipoli and clawed their way up an almost perpendicular hillside, in the face of murderous Turkish fire from prepared positions along the crest at the top of the ridge. Among those killed was Captain Peter Lalor, wearing the sword his grandfather had brandished at the Eureka Stockade. Those who survived dug in and, with reinforcements, retained their positions for eight months until the order for withdrawal was given. More than 10 000 Australian and New Zealand soldiers, including Bridges, as many French soldiers, and nearly three times as many British troops, were killed for no appreciable military gain. But to have been an "original Anzac" – a member of the Australian and New Zealand Army Corps at Gallipoli – is still a proud boast for a man and his descendants. The first response to the casualty lists was an increase in voluntary enlistments, and 25 April, Anzac Day, has become *the* Australian national day above all others. After the evacuation, some of the AIF stayed to fight on in Palestine until the final Turkish defeat. At their training camp in Egypt they were provided with horses from the Remount Depot commanded by the great poet and horseman, "Banjo" Paterson.[3] As the Australian Light Horse under Sir Harry Chauvel, these men created their own legend, but most of the Australians were shipped to England for regrouping before joining the Allied armies in France.

There Australian troops soon came to be known as "diggers" – probably from memories of the Gold Rush and Eureka as well as from the vast amount of trench-digging done by the men of all armies. In the long horror of trench warfare on the western front, the five Australian divisions fought valorously. Because they were volunteers, and perhaps also because they were less dependent on, and yet closer to, their officers than the men of European armies, they early came to be regarded as the best shock troops in the Allied ranks, and were employed accordingly. They suffered more casualties in proportion to the total number of enlistments –

nearly 65 per cent – than the soldiers of any other belligerent nation, including France and Germany. In the initial stages of the final attack on the Hindenburg Line, the Australian contribution was of decisive importance. By then the diggers were commanded by General Sir John Monash, a Jewish Australian born and educated in Victoria where he took degrees in Arts, Law and Engineering at the University of Melbourne. Such was his military genius that B.H. Liddell Hart, leading historian of World War I, thought this "unprofessional" soldier might well have become commander-in-chief of the British armies had the war lasted longer. He played a vital part in planning the attack that led to the final breakthrough and the defeat of Germany, but his civilian service to his country, both before and after the war, was hardly less distinguished. Australians are perhaps more apt than most people to expect little good from high-ranking military officers, but Monash understood and loved his men and was loved in return. His life helps to explain why there is probably less anti-Semitism in Australia than in most other English-speaking countries.[4]

At home, affairs were in charge of a very different type of man – William Morris Hughes, attorney-general in the Labor government until Fisher retired to become High Commissioner in London from October 1915, and thereafter prime minister. Born in Wales in 1864, Hughes emigrated to Australia at the age of 20 and become the most fantastic character – in both senses of that term – so far to distinguish Australian political life. Diminutive, skinny and gnome-like in appearance, he worked in his youth at a multitude of jobs. He claimed to have been at one time or another, among other things, a fruit-picker, student-teacher, shearer, cattle-station rouseabout, seaman, cook, tally-clerk, steward, actor, second-hand bookseller and umbrella-mender; but as early as the 1890s he was seeking better fortune in the trade-union and Labor movements. He sat in the New South Wales Parliament from 1894 to 1901 and was thereafter continuously a member of the Commonwealth Parliament until his death in 1952 – not, however, after 1917 as a Labor representative.

His early experiences may have helped to make him as cunning and as faintly scrupulous as he was able and energetic. Restless, irascible and ambitious, he drove those near him as hard as he drove himself. It is said that none of the hundreds of male secretaries who worked for him held the position for more than a few months. It is possible to discern throughout the turns and twists of his political career an underlying bias toward nationalist and reformist principles, but much easier to see him manipulating men and ideas toward his own ends. Yet his reputation as a great war leader is largely deserved, and in spite of everything he is more widely known and remembered – if not exactly revered – than any other Australian except the legendary Ned Kelly. Even his political opponents were sometimes half-charmed by his murderous wit, the effrontery of his opportunism, and what seemed for so long his sheer indestructibility.[5]

As the war dragged on into its second year, the first flush of adventurous enthusiasm gave way to a mood of dour endurance mixed, as in other countries at war, with some complaining at the irksomeness of censorship, price-fixing and other necessary but burdensome measures. Government and people alike realised, as casualty lists mounted, that a long and hard trial lay ahead. It was at this juncture early in 1916 that Hughes went to England to see for himself what was happening. His fiery speeches, and his apparent scorn for diplomatic finesse in dealing with dignified and conventional British politicians, appealed to many as typical of the younger fighting nation "down under", and Hughes was made much of by the British popular press. This adulation was echoed in Australian newspaper reports. His fellow-Welshman, David Lloyd George, Britain's wartime prime minister, had nothing to teach Hughes in the art of playing to the gallery. While abroad he also fought hard to persuade the British government that more ships must be diverted to the Australian run to bring badly needed supplies of wheat, wool and other essentials to the United Kingdom. Finally he bought for the Commonwealth a number of vessels, which as a government-owned line went some way toward solving the problem. He

War-time Prime Minister "Billy" Hughes, seen here as a monkey-puppet for the forces of conscription, is more widely known and remembered than any other Australian except the legendary Ned Kelly (Source: *Daily Herald*, 15 November 1917, Mitchell Library, State Library of New South Wales)

also became convinced that Australia must speedily introduce conscription for overseas service as Britain had already done.

At home universal service leagues had been urging compulsion even before Hughes' departure. The sweeping powers taken to itself by the government in 1914 under the *War Precautions Act* were probably wide enough to have enabled it to introduce conscription for overseas service by regulation, had it wished to do so. Alternatively the Liberal opposition, conscriptionists almost to a man, would certainly have joined with Hughes in passing a new law for the purpose, though the massive Labor majority in the Senate would probably have rejected such a bill and either course would obviously have split the Labor Party and brought down Hughes' government. While most Australians could support the voluntary system, a great many Labor voters, and certainly also some Liberals, balked at forcing men to fight and perhaps die on the other side of the world. Some Labor left-wingers were influenced by the internationalist ideals of doctrinaire socialism and others by the lingering isolationist–utopian aspirations of the previous period. Probably more important was the influence of Irish-Australians. Although Catholic enlistments in the AIF were slightly higher, proportionately, than those of men from other denominations, and although some prominent Catholics like Dr Kelly, Archbishop of Sydney, advocated conscription, the ancient Irish hatred of Britain was fanned into new life by the suppression of the 1916 Easter Rebellion in Dublin. Most important of all, perhaps, was the growing suspicion on the part of trade-union organisations that social advance had not merely been halted, but was being undermined by the government under cover of war emergency measures.

Hughes sought to circumvent the problem by putting the issue to a popular referendum. He was probably right in calculating that, if the people declared for conscription, many of the anti-conscriptionists in Labor's parliamentary ranks would be converted or at least neutralised. The chances seemed good. Most prominent and respectable citizens, the entire daily press of the country, and the still very influential Sydney *Bulletin* passionately advocated compulsion. And most church leaders concurred. The Anglican Synod in Melbourne passed unanimously a resolution certifying that the war was a religious one, that God was on the side of the Allies, and that conscription was morally necessary. If this were true the Devil found a powerful voice in the newly arrived Catholic Coadjutor Archbishop of Melbourne, Dr Daniel Mannix. At a great public meeting in that city he held that, though he wished for an Allied victory, Australia could continue to do its duty nobly under the voluntary system and that in some respects the conflict was "a sordid trade war". At the end of the meeting a large section of the crowd rose and sang *God Save Ireland*.

Hughes threw everything he had into the campaign while his party was crumbling round him. He was expelled from the Labor Party by the extra-parliamentary New

South Wales Executive and on the eve of the referendum several of his cabinet ministers resigned. Then the people decided, by 1 100 033 to 1 087 557 votes, against conscription. Anticipating a vote of no confidence in his leadership, Hughes walked out of a Labor parliamentary caucus meeting, followed by twenty-four others. Some said that the Labor Party had "blown out its brains", while others talked of rats and sinking ships. No one seems to have reminded Hughes of his remarks about Deakin at the time of the fusion. The bitterness was greatest of course in Labor's own ranks, but the whole community was divided more deeply than it had been even at the time of the great strikes. Hughes and his rump of the Labor Party formed a new minority "National Labor" government with the support of the Liberals, but before long the two groups fused to form the Nationalist Party with Hughes as its leader and prime minister.

In the 1917 general election, the Nationalists, on a platform of all-out support for the war effort, were returned to power with a resounding majority — partly because Hughes had promised in the most explicit terms that conscription would not be introduced unless it were approved at another referendum. The second referendum campaign in 1917 was even more envenomed than the first, not least because of the example set by the prime minister. His misuse of the wartime censorship powers went so far as, on one occasion, to make the anti-conscriptionist Labor premier of Queensland appear to have said the opposite of what he in fact had said in a public speech. In November 1917, when he attempted to address a small crowd in the Queensland town of Warwick, Mr Hughes' hat was knocked from his head by a rotten egg aimed by one Patrick Brosnan — who was duly fined ten shillings and costs three days later. This incident so inflamed the prime minister that he at once gave orders for the creation of a Commonwealth Police Force. This body has since proliferated to include secret security organisations of the kind deemed essential by all civilised countries, which, while guarding against foreign spies and domestic traitors, also tend to inhibit the expression by thoughtful citizens of new, unpopular or unconventional ideas. The addled Warwick egg marked, in a sense, the beginning of the end of Australia's age of innocence.

The bitterness of the referendum campaign was increased by the greatest wave of strikes in Australian history. In fact the strikers were motivated by the sharp fall in real living standards since the outbreak of war, but conservatives and Austral-British patriots shouted that they were being led by the nose by devilishly cunning, anti-conscriptionist enemy agents and in particular by members of the Industrial Workers of the World (the IWW), a revolutionary socialist sect which undoubtedly did exercise some influence on Australian trade unions at this time: much less, however, than during the first referendum campaign. Then twelve alleged IWW leaders had been arrested, charged with no less than conspiring to burn Sydney to the ground, and imprisoned. Most were set free after the war when a Royal Commission found that they had been "framed" by the arresting police. Some real leaders, including Tom Barker, the editor of the IWW newspaper, *Direct Action*, were imprisoned at the same time. Barker was found guilty under the *War Precautions Act* of prejudicing recruiting. His specific crime was to publish in *Direct Action* an anti-war cartoon drawn by a gifted young artist who had not long left school. It depicted an Australian soldier being crucified on an immense piece of artillery with a large, bloated gentleman collecting his blood in a bowl.[6]

The second referendum was even more decisively negatived than the first. Surprisingly, some thought, even the AIF men in France voted for conscription by only a very slender majority. Perhaps some diggers, knowing the hell of the trenches, could not wish anyone else to be forced into it, but more seem to have been motivated by the *esprit de corps* of a proud force which disdained to beg for unwilling recruits. It is difficult to say certainly why the referenda were defeated, but one motive by no means confined to Labor voters, was the wish of many people to preserve their own freedom of conscience. There were certainly many families like that of the future Liberal prime minister, Robert Gordon Menzies, which felt they had the right to keep one brother at home when the others had all enlisted. The fact that there was at no time any clear and present threat of invasion to Australia itself was probably decisive. Under such circumstances, and with the war being fought on the other side of the earth, one may doubt whether any people ever had, or ever would have, imposed conscription on itself by popular secret ballot.[7]

During the second campaign Hughes had repeatedly promised that he would resign if the referendum were defeated. He did so, but those on both sides of the House who had ingenuously assumed this would mean his stepping down from the prime ministership did not allow for his infinite resourcefulness. Since he was still leader of the majority party, he and his entire cabinet were solemnly sworn in again by the Governor-General two days later. Yet, when all is said, the incredible Welshman served Australia well. It was largely owing to his energy and persistence that the foundations of an efficient metallurgical industry were laid during the conflict. Pig-iron production, for instance, increased from 47 000 to 332 000 tonnes between 1913 and 1919. By governmental intervention he did more than any other man to ensure that the basic wool and wheat industries remained stable and productive, and that most of their output was shipped to Britain where it was needed so desperately. And at the Versailles Peace Conference he defended ably, if with characteristic truculence and showmanship, what almost all Australians then considered to be vital national interests.[8]

First he ensured that Australia was represented (by W.M. Hughes of course) as a separate nation, not merely as a part of the British Empire. When the dominating figure at the conference, President Woodrow Wilson of the United States, objected to the noise and delays emanating from the "little digger", Hughes replied crushingly, "Mr President, I speak for 60 000 dead. How many do you speak for?" Lest there should be any possible threat to the sacrosanct "white Australia" policy, he fought successfully, though by no means alone, to prevent having a declaration of racial equality incorporated in the League of Nations Covenant; and lest the Japanese or any other foreigners should benefit from the Australian conquest of German New Guinea, he bullied the League into creating C-Class mandates which gave Australia the substance, if not the legal form, of sovereignty over the area. This coup enriched white Australian planters, business-people, gold miners and others for the following thirty years or more, but did little for the black inhabitants of Papua New Guinea and the adjacent islands. Between the two World Wars, two large Australian shipping firms, Burns Philp and W.R. Carpenter, enjoyed a virtual monopoly of trade with the islands. That they made the most of it is suggested by the nicknames they earned among their customers — "Bloody Pirates" and "Would Rob Christ". The Melanesian inhabitants were protected from some of the grosser forms of exploitation by Sir Hubert Murray, whom Deakin had appointed Lieutenant-Governor of Papua in 1908, but when he died in 1940, just before the arrival of Japanese invaders, hardly one of the estimated two million natives of the country had received any kind of tertiary education.[9]

The surviving diggers returned to a country which had changed in many ways during their absence, most notably perhaps in the role accorded to, or claimed by, women. A much higher proportion of women, both single and married, had taken jobs outside their homes, particularly as clerks, typists and secretaries in business houses. Many returned men found the positions they had held on enlistment occupied by women. Since the female workers usually did the job just as efficiently as any male, and since they did it perforce for only a fraction of the male wage, even the most be-medalled returned hero frequently had Buckley's chance of getting his old job back again. Women also took to themselves a freedom of dress unknown to their ancestors during the 1900 years of Christian civilisation. Young women, nicknamed "flappers", wore skirts of knee length and cut short the long hair which St Paul had declared a shame to them, in several styles of which the Eton crop was felt to be the most daring. In Britain, the "flapper vote" was given in 1928 by a Conservative government to women between the ages of 21 and 30, but all

Australian women had then been enfranchised for twenty years. In both countries women began to drink alcohol and smoke cigarettes in public, but the liberation of the new woman was more apparent than real. Those who cropped, or bobbed or shingled, their hair also bound their breasts tightly so as to look as much like boys as possible. Half a century later it seems clear that the flappers of the 1920s felt that they approached liberation and equality in proportion as they imitated the god-like male who still dominated Australian life and ideology.

Efforts to help the returned soldiers adjust to peaceful living took two main forms – legislation guaranteeing "preference to returned soldiers", especially in government services; and schemes for settling them on the land. The latter proved, on the whole, costly failures. Preference to returned men was made a reality, at least in the Commonwealth government services, though it often made for lowered efficiency. The Returned Soldiers' League became, however, a very powerful political pressure group as well as a ubiquitous social club which did much for its members and their dependants.[10] Idolised as the "little digger" by many returned men, Hughes continued as prime minister, but was not so well trusted by many who had worked with him at closer quarters. His position was threatened particularly by the Country Party, a third grouping in politics which sprang up at this time.

As in the United States at the same period, most people wanted to forget about the war and get back to normal living as quickly as possible. And, in spite of the comparatively great development of secondary industries that had taken place, people and governments alike continued to act on the traditionally hallowed belief that Australian development must continue to be primarily rural development. Yet tariff protection of infant manufacturing industries, which inevitably raised farmers' costs, had become the settled policy of both the established political parties. For fifty years or more before the Fusion of 1909, Free Trade politicians had served the interests of graziers, farmers, importers and retail traders by keeping down the cost of imported articles. After the Fusion, most Free Trade legislators were forced to adopt the high tariff policy of their new bedfellows, the erstwhile Protectionists, representing primarily the interests of manufacturers and the new industrial bourgeoisie. At the same time, more and more Labor people adopted Protection because they saw it, from the time of Deakin's New Protection policy onwards, as providing well-paid jobs for armies of white Australian workers. The old, low-tariff alliance between the commercial bourgeoisie and the primary producers was left with no effective group to press for its interests. Revolt came first in Western Autralia, the state in which manufacturing industries had been hardest hit after federation by the powerful factories in the eastern states. In 1914 eight Western Australian rural seats returned Country Party members to the state parliament.[11]

After the war, Dr Earle Page[12] and others launched the Country Party in the eastern states. At the federal election of December 1922, the new party won fourteen seats, giving it the balance of power between the Nationalists and the Laborites, who had won thirty seats each. Page swore that he was ready to co-operate with anybody who would work for rural interests, but in fact the forces behind the Country Party were probably on balance more conservative than those which supported the Nationalists. Working with many members of the Nationalist Party who disliked or distrusted Hughes, Page succeeded in having him ousted from the leadership as the price of Country Party support.[13] The new government was a coalition of the Nationalist and Country parties led by Stanley Melbourne Bruce, a capable Victorian businessman and lawyer who had been educated largely in Britain and was more English in manner than many Englishmen.[14] Frank Anstey, the English-born radical Labor MP, said of the new conservative leader, "Stanley Bruce, an English gentleman [was] born in Australia – as other Englishmen are born in China, India or Timbuctoo". The Bruce–Page coalition set the pattern of co-operation between the two anti-Labor parties which has lasted ever since in the federal sphere and in most, though not all, of the states. Though tensions between the two groups boil over at times, on the whole they have been at least as successful in maintaining unity in face of their common enemy as Labor has been in containing its own internecine feuds.

These latter were at least as divisive as usual in the period between the two World Wars. Battered by the conscription campaigns and the desertion of some of its most capable leaders, the Labor movement was further weakened by a deepening distrust between its political and industrial wings. As political action seemed to have failed them, many trade unionists returned to the idea of militant industrial activity. They were also strongly influenced by the "One Big Union" ideal of the IWW. One popular IWW song deriding parliamentary and Arbitration Court procedures did not spare even that incorruptible radical, Henry Bournes Higgins. A Labor candidate for parliamentary honours sings:

I know the Arbitration Act
    As a sailor knows his "riggins"
So if you want a small advance,
    I'll talk to Justice Higgins.

So bump me into parliament,
    Bounce me any way;
Bang me into parliament
    On next election day.

From its foundation in 1920, the Australian Communist Party rapidly came to displace the IWW as the ideological focus of left-wing agitation, but majority Labor opinion continued overwhelmingly committed to gradualist reform through the parliamentary system.[15] Under these conditions it seemed almost as though the country as a whole distrusted Labor in the vital federal sphere where foreign policy was an issue, while welcoming piecemeal welfare legislation introduced by moderate Labor governments in most of the states. In the twenty-four years from 1917 to 1941, anti-Labor governments ruled the Commonwealth except for the two years

1930–31; yet the same electors returned Labor governments for much of the time in most of the states.

Under the slogan of "men, money and markets", the Bruce–Page coalition pursued a policy of developing national resources, primarily by tariff and other devices aimed at encouraging secondary industry. Protective duties on a wide range of manufactured goods were increased and the uneasiness of the government's Country Party supporters was appeased by the device of extending the protective umbrella to cover also many primary products such as sugar, canned and dried fruits, hops, butter and grapes. It seemed that there was to be protection for all — except of course for the basic wool and wheat-growing industries and, as it seemed to many trade-union members, for wage-earners. In its concern to keep down costs so that markets abroad could be found for Australian products, the government seemed to its critics to spend more energy in keeping down wages than in demanding greater efficiency from management. To many it seemed that the prewar effort to spread the benefits of protection evenly through the community was being abandoned. But the Commonwealth also spent considerable sums in assisting immigration from the United Kingdom, mainly to promote development but partly also with the "white Australia" policy in mind. If Australia was to be kept forever a "white" continent, more of its empty spaces would have to be occupied quickly by white people, and preferably by Britons. Thus schemes like the group settlements plan in Western Australia, which sought to transform at a stroke underprivileged British workmen into self-reliant Australian bush-dwellers, were encouraged. Generally speaking, the results were even less impressive than those of kindred plans which had been sponsored in the eighteenth century by J.D. Lang and others, but these schemes did bring over 200 000 new citizens to Australia, even if few of them became successful farmers.

While Labor was, if possible, even more firmly wedded than its opponents to white Australia, it was at best indifferent, and sometimes strongly hostile, to immigration. While unemployment figures remained high, as they did throughout the 1920s, Labor maintained that the government's first duty should be to look after its own citizens by promoting public works instead of bringing in more people to compete for the few jobs available. The government responded by introducing a public works program which included the building of better main roads in country districts – a project which naturally appealed strongly to its Country Party members; and also by pushing ahead with the building of Canberra whither the federal parliament repaired in 1927. Posterity may hold that the Bruce–Page government's greatest single achievement was the creation in 1926 of the Council for Scientific and Industrial Research, later to be known as the Commonwealth Scientific and Industrial Research Organisation, or CSIRO. This body of first-rate scientists, pure and applied, has wide freedom to carry out all kinds of research which may benefit Australian industry. Its findings are made known freely to all, and it has been of enormous importance to Australian development. Its best-known achievement is probably the "invention" of myxomatosis, a disease which brought the continent-wide rabbit plague under control after World War II.

Neither the CSIRO nor the federal and state governments had much to do with the great improvement in communications which took place at this time. The internal combustion engine and wireless telegraphy had both been invented before the war but had both improved greatly during it. Before the war most people and goods in Australia moved about by horse-drawn vehicles and rail; after the war, more and more quickly, motor transport replaced horse-drawn vehicles, even in the "feeder services" from railway termini. In 1924, for instance, the last Cobb and Co. coach was replaced by a motor bus in North Queensland. The last coach-driver was said to have been the father of Bill Harney, later warden of Uluru (Ayers' Rock).[16] During the 1920s, tractors gradually replaced horses in the pulling of ploughs, seed-drills and harvesters on farms. Motor transport did not displace that of animals completely or suddenly. In northern South Australia in the 1930s, one could still see huge wagons, loaded high with bales of wool, being pulled into Maree near Lake Eyre by teams of twenty or more camels. Nor had the last sailing ships been banished from the seas by steam- and oil-driven vessels. At Port Victoria in Spencer's Gulf, half a dozen four-masted barques from Finland loaded wheat for the European market each year until 1939. Oddly enough, horses were used longest, even in the cities, to pull the delivery carts of butchers, bakers, milkmen and other tradesmen. A few were still so employed at the outbreak of World War II. While motor vehicles multiplied, thousands of miles of "dirt" roads were paved with bitumen or cement to carry them. In November 1914 the *Sydney* had been able to intercept the *Emden* because of a timely wireless message, but wireless had no place at all in civil life. Twenty years later the Australian Broadcasting Commission and dozens of commercial stations were operating and very few Australian homes were without a wireless set.

When the war ended, most Australians had never seen an aeroplane. Within ten years aviation had developed further and faster here, relative to population, than in any other country in the world. Ross and Keith Smith, Charles Kingsford-Smith, Bert Hinkler and others had established – and broken – more record times for inter-continental and trans-ocean flights than the aviators of half a dozen other countries put together. More importantly, the "tyranny of distance",[17] which had so hampered Australian development for 150 years, was well on the way to being broken – at least insofar as transport of passengers and mails was concerned. An east–west air service between Perth and the eastern states was established in 1927, but very few Australians ventured into an aeroplane until after World War II, when air travel rapidly became commonplace. When the Labor Prime Minister, James Scullin, attended the Imperial Conference in London in 1931, the return journey, by the fastest means available, took about nine weeks. Twenty years later his successors flew frequently to London and back in a few days.

By 1929 signs of coming world depression had not been much marked by the Nationalist government. All through the

decade it had wooed prosperity but at the cost, in the view of
most unionists, of the traditional Australian regard for the
welfare of working people. There had been many strikes and
lockouts, particularly in the transport industries, and the government had passed several measures aimed at disciplining
the unions. Now unemployment was growing and yet there
seemed no way of increasing the productivity of labour.
Rather hastily, and without taking into his confidence all of
his own backbenchers, Bruce introduced a bill which would
have had the effect of virtually abolishing the whole Commonwealth system of arbitration with its built-in provisions
for safeguarding the basic wage. He argued that the state arbitration courts would take over, but the whole Labor movement and some of his own supporters suspected an all-out
attack on the national standard of living. Among the back-
benchers who had been kept in the dark was Hughes. Scent-
ing revenge for his deposition by Bruce in 1923, he organised
the Nationalist and Country Party malcontents and the government was defeated on his no-confidence motion. In the following election there was a landslide to Labor, which,
however, was left with a minority in the Senate. Hughes'
hopes of returning to high office were frustrated by the un-
diminished hostility of the Labor Party, which did not forget
or forgive what it regarded as his betrayal of his trust over the
conscription issue.

Owing to its heavy dependence on the export of primary
products, Australia suffered from the Great Depression
rather earlier and rather more severely than did most countries. For a time, nearly 30 per cent of breadwinners were unemployed.[18] Thousands tramped the bush roads again with
swag and billy-can, often ready to work for their keep if only
work of any kind could be found. In their bewilderment people did the only thing that offered even the satisfaction of
making an angry gesture – and blamed the politicians. The
federal government was only the first to be affected. Between
1929 and 1933 every government in the country was thrown
out of office by electors reduced to the expedient of "giving
the other mob a go – they couldn't be worse". South Aus-

tralia and the Commonwealth elected their only inter-war Labor governments at this time, and Queensland its only anti-Labor one, but politicians understood no more than electors how to cure the great slump. The main battles were fought in the federal and New South Wales parliaments.

James Scullin, the new prime minister, was a devout Irish-Australian who stood near the middle of Labor opinion. After a lifetime of working for party unity, he could act decisively enough when sure that all sections of the movement were behind him. When a new Governor-General had to be appointed, for instance, he virtually forced a most unwilling King George V to name Sir Isaac Isaacs, the first native-born Australian to hold the office.[19] The son of poor immigrant Polish Jews, Isaacs had been a Deakinite Liberal, prominent in the federation movement and later a distinguished High Court judge, and in appointing him Scullin was only implementing long-standing Labor policy, but his action caused hysterical outbursts in the daily press and among many Nationalist supporters. Unfortunately, the worsening economic problem was susceptible of no such simple solution, and Labor opinion on what should be done varied all the way from the abolition of the capitalist economic system by act of parliament to obeying exactly the advice of Sir Otto Niemeyer, Bank of England expert on that system, who was invited to Australia by the government to give his views. The only man in parliament who seemed to have any real understanding of high finance was Scullin's treasurer, the forceful and extremely able E.G. Theodore, known as "Red Ted" both for his views and the colour of his hair; but soon after the election he was heavily discredited by the Mungana Mines scandal which cast at least some doubt on his integrity.[20] So the government floundered indecisively while dole-queues lengthened and John Thomas Lang, in October 1930, was elected premier of New South Wales with an enormous Labor majority. Lang, or "the big Fella", as he was called by many admirers, was a forceful demagogue, somewhat on the left of parliamentary Labor opinion, though strongly anti-communist. He had already served as premier of his state from 1925 to 1927, and over the years he had built up a personal "machine" — of the type more familiar in American politics — for controlling the New South Wales Labor Party.

Before Lang's return to power, Sir Otto Niemeyer had addressed a premiers' conference called by Scullin in August 1930. At this Melbourne meeting, Niemeyer, reflecting the orthodox economic thinking of the time, strongly urged the adoption of deflationary policies. As he saw it, Australia had no alternative but to reduce its artificially high standard of living, not least by cutting salaries and wages. The premiers, however painfully, all agreed to this plan, but most of them did little to carry it out while argument proceeded over ways and means. Lang won power in New South Wales partly by denouncing the "Niemeyer Plan" as a sinister plot of overseas bondholders, and by promising to restore the forty-four-hour week and the state's civil service salaries, which had been cut by his Nationalist predecessor in office. He also proposed to end unemployment by an extensive program of public works. If money could not be found for these things, then the state should find it by postponing, or if necessary repudiating, interest payments on past overseas borrowings. Many hundreds of thousands of suffering people, not all in his own state, swore by Lang's supposed genius. Slogans such as "Lang is Right", "The Lang Plan" and "Lang is greater than Lenin" were repeated by many and heard by all. Conservatives naturally regarded him as a monster of wickedness, hell-bent on the destruction of all private property and public honour.[21] Feeling grew so intense that for a short time there came into existence an organisation of a type unknown, though not necessarily nonexistent, in Australia before or since. The self-styled "New Guard" was a quasi-military, quasi-secret band of "right-thinking" young men from the wealthier suburbs, sworn to preserve the country from Langism. They forcibly broke up some meetings of unemployed and radicals but, as so often in Australian history, there was no loss of life. In March 1932, when Lang was to open the new Sydney Harbour Bridge by cutting a ribbon, a New Guardsman named De Groot spurred forward on horseback and slashed at the ribbon with a sword, crying that he opened the bridge "in the name of His Majesty the King and all decent people". Excitement was intense, but the police, under the direct control of Lang's government, merely took De Groot to the reception house to be psychiatrically examined.[22]

Meanwhile, at a federal election in December 1931 there had been a landslide against Labor, already undermined by another internal split. Joseph Aloysius Lyons, a right-wing Tasmanian Labor member, had resigned from the cabinet over the Mungana scandal and also because he felt the government's vacillating policies were too dangerously radical. With a number of other right-wing Labor members he negotiated with the Nationalists to reorganise yet again the anti-Labor forces under the style of the United Australia Party, pledged like its predecessors to anti-communism, praise of private enterprise, and the support of respectability. Like Hughes before him, Lyons became leader of the new, or renamed, party and prime minister of Australia from 1932 until his death some months before the Second World War broke out in 1939. Cartoonists and comedians made much of the fact that he looked very much like a koala, for he had not Hughes' capacity to inspire admiration or hatred.[23]

The Lyons government set about the task of implementing what J.K. Galbraith has since called the "conventional wisdom" of the time.[24] Some months before the election, the distracted Scullin government had already been forced to begin carrying out what was essentially the policy of its opponents: a reduction of 20 per cent in all salaries, pensions, etc., a roughly commensurate reduction in interest rates, and steep tax increases. The UAP government continued these generally deflationary policies. It also helped to force Lang from office. He went quietly, and the succeeding UAP state government, led by B.S.B. (later Sir Bertram) Stevens, brought New South Wales back into line with the rest of the country. In doing so, Stevens achieved a nickname more colourful than most in the profane world of Australian politics. Denounced in the Sydney Domain by Stan Moran, a popular communist orator, as "that barnacle on the backside of the ship of state", Stevens was known by many thereafter as "Barnacle Bert".[25]

Very gradually, the depression eased, but there was still widespread unemployment when World War II broke out in 1939. Given the prevailing conditions, the deflationary policies adopted in Australia as elsewhere were no doubt inevitable, largely because the conventional economic wisdom of the period backed them vigorously and unanimously. Since then, however, the quite different economic theories of John Maynard Keynes, themselves born of the experience of the great world slump, have become conventional wisdom. It would be implausible to suggest that "the Big Fella" had any deep knowledge of economic theory. Indeed he was once heard to admonish a keen young Labor member discovered reading in the Parliament Library — "Reading eh? You'll soon get over that nonsense, son. No time for it here." But ignorance of economic theory in no way distinguished him from all the other political leaders of the day, state and federal, with the possible exception of Theodore, who had read Keynes' early works. What did distinguish him from them was his passionate advocacy of increased expenditure on public works and other "pump-priming" policies, more inflationary than deflationary in their tendencies. According to today's conventional economic wisdom, such policies would have been considerably more helpful in combating the depression than the ones which were generally adopted. We may freely agree that Lang's formulation of his policies was incoherent and emotional rather than logical, and that he would certainly not have been able, even if he had been given the opportunity, to carry them out effectively. Nevertheless, it now seems that, in the broadest sense — that of the direction economic policies should ideally have taken — Lang *was* right after all.

However that may be, the depression experience left a deep impression on Australian attitudes. The spectacle of such widespread involuntary unemployment, and even of actual undernourishment, in Australia, while at the same time wheat stacks at the railway sidings were overflowing with unsaleable grain, was not forgotten. The traditional belief that the state's first duty is to look after the welfare of all its citizens, more especially the less fortunate among them, was deepened in intensity. After the Great Depression and World War II, maintenance of full – not just high – employment became perhaps the greatest single preoccupation of all Australian governments whatever their political complexion. Between 1944 and 1974 in the Commonwealth as a whole, the number of registered unemployed only very rarely and briefly rose much above 2 per cent of the workforce. One important reason seems to have been that the electorate would not then readily tolerate a higher rate.[26]

The United Australia Party, with the accustomed support of the Country Party, continued to govern until 1940. Though trade recovered slowly, it was hardly a prosperous time. After all the government's declared policy, even on the hustings, was one of severe retrenchment and of caution. The UAP's most positive achievement was probably its courageous trade policy. As we have seen, protection had been the policy of the country ever since federation. Tariffs had risen steadily, right up to and including such emergency depression measures, introduced by the Scullin government, as total prohibition of some imports. There was considerable substance in the Niemeyer view that the national protection policy, with its inevitable tendency to raise internal costs, had placed Australia in an untenable position. The policy could not be simply reversed. Not even the Country Party any longer contained many outright free traders but, despite opposition from within its own ranks as well as from Labor, the government did lower tariffs here and there throughout the 1930s, while it sought reciprocal trade agreements with other nations and particularly with other British Empire countries. Under the Ottawa Arrangements of 1932, lower, preferential tariffs were extended to a wide range of British, Canadian and other Empire goods. These policies, despite the passionate objections of many Australian manufacturers, were certainly beneficial in the long run if only because they forced Australian secondary industry to become somewhat more efficient and competitive.

Under its general anti-communist mandate, the government sought to encourage what it regarded as right thinking at home and to protect citizens from impure or dangerous thoughts from abroad. On the whole, these efforts brought more discredit on the government than on its opponents. A censorship of imported books, administered largely by only modestly literate customs officials, sought to keep out of the country Marxist works and also such purely literary masterpieces as James Joyce's *Ulysses*. In 1934 Egon Kisch, a learned Czech author, came to Australia to attend a Melbourne anti-war conference. The government declared that he had affiliations with communist organisations and forbade him to land. Kisch jumped on to the wharf, broke his leg, and was taken to a hospital in Melbourne. The government decided to deport him under a clause of the *Immigration Restriction Act* which had been designed to safeguard the "white Australia" policy. Instead of saying openly that a man could not land because of the colour of his skin, this clause empowered officials to give a prospective visitor or migrant a dictation test in any European language. Its obvious intention was to enable officials to use a language unknown to the testee who could then be barred technically on some vague suggestion of illiteracy. Such was Kisch's reputation for scholarship, however, that the government thought it wise to give him a dictation test in Gaelic, the almost extinct language of the Highland Scots. Kisch duly failed. "Australia is disgraced," wrote the nationally respected scholar and essayist, Walter Murdoch. Later the High Court found that Gaelic was not a European language within the meaning of the act.[27] Possibly even more damaging to the government's reputation was the case of Mrs M.M. Freer. This respectable Englishwoman was given a dictation test in Italian and kept out of the country for nearly a year — for no other reason than that a minister of the Crown had listened to a personal friend, who told him he believed that Mrs Freer might "break up an Australian home". Such events demonstrated that the broad streak of petty provincialism, which has so often been associated with

Australian nationalism, was by no means confined to one side in Australian politics.

But even this strong tendency toward isolationism was not completely proof against Hitler's preparations for another war. Compulsory training had been abandoned by the Labor government at the beginning of the depression, ostensibly as an economy measure but possibly more in fact because of Labor's deep-seated distrust of any kind of militarism. As the international situation darkened the UAP government did little to strengthen the land forces but began to spend a little more money on naval rejuvenation. Labor, at the official parliamentary level, advocated instead the creation of a strong air force, partly because its leaders felt that an air arm, in view of Australia's remoteness from Europe, was in its nature a more defensive weapon than a navy. But in fact both parties, though for different reasons, found it almost impossible to formulate a coherent foreign policy. The electorate, as always in the past except during the actual fighting of World War I, continued to be vastly more concerned with bread-and-butter domestic issues. Almost everyone was horrified at the Nazis' bestial treatment of the Jews, and there was widespread support for Lyons' decision in 1938 to welcome 5000 refugees a year from Nazi tyranny; but what should be done to meet the military threat of Nazism seemed a more difficult but less urgent question.

Like conservative parties everywhere, the UAP was divided between its fear of the revisionist aims and violent, larrikin methods of the Fascist powers, and its hope that all this explosive force might in the end be spent on weakening or destroying Russian communism. Like "socialist" parties everywhere, Labor was divided between its hatred of all that Fascism stood for, and its strong traditional attachment to ways of peace, which inhibited it from preparing effectively for war. Thus, the UAP prepared half-heartedly for war, while at the same time making conciliatory and appeasing gestures toward Fascism; and Labor for the most part denounced Fascism in unmeasured terms, while at the same time it was even less willing than its opponents to underwrite really effective war preparations.

The paradox was vividly illustrated in 1938 when the UAP attorney-general Robert Gordon Menzies, acquired his sobriquet of "Pig-Iron Bob". In June, to scotch a Japanese scheme for importing large quantities of iron ore from Western Australia, the government imposed an embargo on its export from the whole country. Yet considerable quantities of pig and scrap iron continued to be shipped to Japan from eastern ports. The militant Waterside Workers' Union at Port Kembla refused to load such cargoes on the grounds that they would help Fascism and might be returned to Australia later in the form of Japanese bombs. Menzies threatened to coerce the union under some provisions of the *Crimes Act*, and he had the courage to face the men on the wharves personally to explain his government's point of view. Nevertheless, the whole incident was a great embarrassment to the UAP for many years, particularly after Pearl Harbor. At bottom the whole foreign policy debate had a faint air of unreality about it because everyone knew that in fact Australia, as in the past, would simply follow Britain's lead and go to war with her if things became really serious. And nearly everyone who thought at all of such matters agreed that this would be both natural and right.

In the arts there was a reaction between the wars against "out-backery" and "aggressive Australianism", healthy in itself but leading nowhere very much else at the time. On the whole the cultural achievement compares poorly with that of the thirty years before World War I. Compared with that of the Heidelberg school, most painting was derivative and pleasant rather than new and robust. In literature, "Henry Handel Richardson" and Christopher Brennan reached the first rank, but their work belongs as much to the earlier period as to the interwar one. In their anxiety to break away from the horse-and-stockwhip tradition of the 1890s many of the poets emphasised a neo-paganist, art-for-art's-sake approach which was a natural reaction to the prevailing shallow materialism, but which was also curiously reminiscent of the

literary attitude popular thirty years earlier in the England of
the "naughty Nineties". And the best works of Kenneth
Slessor, perhaps the most considerable poet of this *Vision*
group, owe little to its declared theories. Indeed, a poem like
his "Country Towns" does not so much repudiate the earlier
tradition as use it in a new, wry way to say something more
permanently worthwhile about Australia than was implied by
the contemporary cry for "men, money and markets".

> Country towns, with your willows and squares,
> And farmers bouncing on barrel mares
> To public-houses of yellow wood
> With '1860' over their doors,
> And that mysterious race of Hogans
> Which always keeps the General Stores . . .
>
> At the School of Arts, a broadsheet lies
> Sprayed with the sarcasm of flies:
> 'The Great Golightly Family
> Of Entertainers Here To-Night'
> Dated a year and a half ago,
> But left there, less from carelessness
> Than from a wish to seem polite.

In the 1920s Katharine Susannah Prichard wrote two good
novels, *Coonardoo* and *Working Bullocks*, and the following
depression decade inspired some worthwhile "realist" writing by Vance Palmer and others. Xavier Herbert's
Capricornia will probably always find readers and Kylie
Tennant's *The Battlers* deserves to. But for the most part the
writers themselves were among the first to contrast their own
barren time with what had gone before.

In what most Australians regarded as a far more important
sphere, there was less to be despondent about. They liked to
believe that they led the world in cricket, tennis and swimming. It was in this period that the swimming stroke known
elsewhere as the "Australian crawl" was adopted by most
other nations, as the "Australian ballot" had been earlier.
Surf and life-saving clubs, manned entirely by volunteers,
multiplied enormously, and an Australian who could not
swim came to be regarded as something of a cripple. On 6

February 1938, when three freak waves in succession swept thousands of surfers out to sea off Sydney's Bondi Beach, the local lifesavers rescued from drowning over 200 people in half an hour or so and only five lives were lost. More often than not Australia beat England in Test cricket and the whole world in tennis matches for the Davis Cup; and neither the Great War nor the Great Depression was allowed to interfere with the most important national ritual apart from Anzac Day, the running of the Melbourne Cup on the first Tuesday of November. Indeed, Australia's greatest horse, Phar Lap (actually raised in New Zealand), won the race in 1930 and competed in the following year only to die shortly afterwards – darkly, some insisted on believing – in America; but his body was brought home, stuffed and reverently mounted in the Melbourne Museum, while his heart was enshrined at Canberra.

In more conventionally important areas there was some advance in the mid-1920s, but before and afterwards the economy was hardly more than static even in "good" years. In fact, at the height of the modest postwar "boom" in 1926, 7 per cent of trade-union members were unemployed. During the depression that followed the total Australian population actually declined by more than 10 000 between 1931 and 1935. In 1937 the CSIRO's charter was broadened to include research in fields relevant to secondary industry. The Australian Broadcasting Commission was founded in 1932. Almost at once it began to raise the standard of public taste in music and the arts generally by its competition with privately owned radio corporations. And in the late 1930s, by admitting a number of graduate cadets into the Commonwealth government departments, the UAP did something toward raising the generally low standard of efficiency in the civil service. But this above all others was the time when Mechanics' Institutes and School of Arts, founded so hopefully in the previous century, fell into hopeless decay; and it was hard to see what, if anything, was to take their place. The number of universities, university teachers and students remained almost at the low pre-war levels, except in Western

Australia and Queensland where unusually beautiful university buildings were begun. The Western Australian wheat industry, too, really became important in the 1920s.

Not the Great War, the mini-boom of the 1920s or the great depression of the 1930s had any perceptible effect on race relations on the moving frontier of pastoral settlement, the place where murder and massacre had reigned for 150 years. Indeed, two particularly brutal massacres showed that British justice for the Aborigine had become a mockery, more callous by far than in the days of the butchery at Myall Creek a century earlier. Then a white policeman, Denny Day, had swiftly and honourably brought to their account the white murderers. In the 1920s white policemen led them.

In 1926 Aborigines killed a man called Hay in the Kimberley district of Western Australia. Two police constables, two "special" constables, Hay's partner, a person called Overheu, and seven Aborigines set out, ostensibly to arrest the murderers and bring them to trial. The party arrested some thirty Aborigines, yoked them together with neck-chains and then, either to "teach the blacks a lesson" or to save themselves trouble, murdered their captives and burnt their bodies in a number of campfires. Overheu subsequently murdered an Aboriginal employee who had witnessed the killings. This sickening story was pieced together by a Royal Commissioner, G.T. Wood SM, appointed by the Western Australian government to inquire into the affair; but though every bushman and beachcomber in the Wyndham district knew the facts, the bonds of mateship were so strong that no white man could be found to give effective evidence against the police party. None of the murderers was punished in any way.[28]

At this period white graziers were moving west from the Overland Telegraph Line at Barrow Creek and Ti-tree Well into poor pastoral country occupied by the Walpari tribe. In August 1928, on Coniston Station, tribesmen murdered Frederick Brooks for having, according to Walpari tradition, forcibly abducted some of the tribal women. A few weeks later the blacks attacked another white man, "Nugget" Morton, who escaped with his life. The Commonwealth government resident at Alice Springs, J.C. Cawood, despatched Mounted Constable W.B. Murray with orders to arrest the murderers and any other Aborigines who had been spearing the new settlers' cattle. With six or seven aggrieved pastoralists to help him, Murray scoured the district for Aborigines. He arrested two, who were later acquitted of Brooks' murder, but seems to have exceeded his orders by engaging in a *de facto* punitive expedition. He and members of his party seem to have shot down about seventy Walpari tribespeople, including a few women and children.

As with the Kimberley massacre, public uproar from missionaries and other concerned whites forced the holding of an inquiry – though mime would be a more accurate description of what took place. The Prime Minister, S.M. Bruce, appointed three government officials, the police magistrate from Cairns, the police inspector from Oodnadatta and Cawood himself, to inquire into Cawood's own orders to Murray and how well or badly Murray and his party had carried them out. Murray was allowed to be present and give advice throughout the hearings, but no one was allowed to represent the interests of missionaries, other critical whites or the Aborigines themselves. The board's finding did very little to clarify what had happened and nothing at all towards trying, or even reprimanding, the white killers. Nevertheless outback settlers and policemen, the latter also charged with "protection" of the Aborigines, were given a bad fright. The Kimberley and the Coniston killings had roused, however tardily, the conscience of most decent people "in the south" and in the cities. The prime minister's hand-picked board had shielded the guilty on this occasion, but the publicity given to this massacre gave some hope that it could be the last.[29]

R.M. Crawford characterised the 1920s as Australia's "mean decade", and few will disagree with his belief that the meanness derived in an important measure from the effects of World War I. Over 60 thousand of this small nation's most generous and gifted men, those who might have led the way, fought and died far from home in that war. But few will agree with Crawford's further suggestion that things began to look

UNRECORDED HISTORY

FAIR ADMIRER: "How splendidly you Australians have fought! What a hard time you must have given the English when they took your country from you."

Cartoonist Low's comment on the ambivalence of Australian national sentiment (Source: *Unrecorded History in Drawings* by D. Low, Mitchell Library, State Library of New South Wales)

up quite remarkably in the late 1930s. In fact, the whole interwar period, compared with those which preceded and followed it, was an uncertain, cautious, and shabby era. Honourable exceptions notwithstanding, most political and other leaders, made timid by their memories of the bitter conscription troubles and by the vivid if distant spectre of Bolshevism, sought to survive rather than to create. War had shattered the possibly naive, but nonetheless constructive, idealist national mood of the previous decades without substituting anything very positive in its place. Australians honoured the fallen and would continue to do so, but were not at all clear about what — other than the continued existence of Australia as a sovereign state — they had died for. So the fire went out of the vision which had inspired so many men of the previous generation, while contemporary experience suggested little more than a disillusioned continuance of the habitual attitudes from which the vision had sprung. Recovery and advance to a more mature national stance was to be the work of the diggers' children rather than of the survivors of the "war to end all wars".

7 War and affluence
c. 1939–66

When war began on 3 September 1939 the national mood was strikingly different from that of August 1914. There was no wild enthusiasm or false optimism – nor, for that matter, much sign of panic or profound fear. People knew now what war was like. They knew too that, since Japan was a member of the tripartite Axis bloc, this war might well be fought in part on Australian soil. At best a long and bitter trial lay ahead. On the evening of that day the new prime minister, R.G. Menzies, who had succeeded to the leadership of the UAP on Lyons' death only five months earlier, spoke to the nation on the radio. He said that, since the Nazi invasion of Poland had forced Great Britain to declare war on Germany, Australia was also at war. He spoke calmly and sadly but resolutely, thereby matching exactly the feeling of most citizens – though he was not fated to lead them through most of the conflict.

Born in a small country town in the Victorian wheat belt, Menzies was educated at Wesley College in Melbourne and later at the university there. He studied law and practised it very successfully for ten years before being elected to the Victorian parliament in 1928. He rapidly became deputy premier of the state, but in 1934 decided to transfer his ambitions to the larger sphere of federal politics. As the UAP candidate he was elected by the voters of Kooyong, a rather fashionable Melbourne suburban area, and they returned him continuously to the House of Representatives for thirty years. Menzies was endowed with a brilliant mind and a dominating personality, and his career makes an almost unbroken success story from his first days at school until he became prime minister at the age of only 45. His fall from power during the war years was so humiliating that few then imagined a recovery was possible. Yet such was his stamina that he brought his party, under yet another name, back to power in 1949 and ruled continuously as prime minister until 1966. He was a superb orator and parliamentary debater, and a platform speaker who thrived on interjections. His colleagues were forced to realise that his leadership was indispensable to the success of the party, yet few of them felt for him much personal warmth. His deputy prime minister for many years, Arthur Fadden, leader of the Country Party, privately called him "the *Big* Bastard" – with the accent on *Big*. For conservative voters he came in the end to possess almost the *mana* of a tribal god: he was powerful, wise, well bred, witty and above all, sound. Few Labor supporters denied his tremendous ability, but to them he appeared also as unscrupulous, opportunistic, condescending and insufferably arrogant.[1]

The government at once set about enrolling volunteers for the Second AIF. As Japan remained at peace, the decision was made, though with some misgivings, to send the soldiers first to the Middle East where their fathers had fought. In January 1940 the first contingent sailed from Sydney Harbour, some of the men travelling in giant liners from the North Atlantic run such as the *Queen Mary*, the like of which had never been seen previously in Australian waters. With the fall of France in June 1940 and Italy's entry into the war, the decision seemed to have been the right one. Australia's airmen shared in the epic defence of Britain while her soldiers and sailors fought in the Mediterranean and in North Africa, Syria, Greece and Crete. The AIF shared the task of driving Mussolini's legions out of Egypt and well back into the Italian colony of Libya, but when the Germans entered the Mediterranean war the diggers were in turn driven back to Egypt, leaving the heroic garrison of "desert rats" as a strong point behind the enemy lines at Tobruk. Australians formed the rear guard in Greece and Crete where many men were killed, wounded or taken prisoner. Syria, however, was cleared of Hitler's Vichy-French allies. Australian naval ships took part in the decisive Battle of Cape Matapan, which gave Britain precarious control of the Mediterranean Sea. Nearer home, ominously, Japan began to move south, first into French Indo-China, and other Australian forces were sent to Malaya, to points in the Dutch East Indies, and to Darwin and Rabaul.

Meanwhile, the UAP Country Party government seemed to be losing internal cohesion and popular support. The general election of September 1940 returned thirty-six government candidates and the same number of Labor members, so that the Menzies ministry depended entirely on the support of two Independents – one, A. W. Coles, a chain-store magnate, and the other, Alex Wilson, the representative of a small-farming area in Victoria. Like the British Conservative prime minister, Neville Chamberlain, Menzies was distrusted and despised because of his outspoken support for the policy of appeasing the Axis powers right up to the outbreak of war, but Chamberlain had been forced out of public life when France fell while "Pig-Iron Bob" had not. As the war situation grew worse, his leadership was questioned more and more sharply, not only by the country at large, but also by his own colleagues. At the end of August 1941, Arthur Fadden replaced him as prime minister, but otherwise the cabinet remained unchanged. In later life Fadden loved to compare his prime ministership with the same period of "forty days and forty nights" which Noah had spent battling with a sea of troubles. One of his worst hours was passed in the Sydney Journalists' Club on the occasion of the annual "ladies' night" party, the one night of the year when female journalists or guests were allowed into this then-exclusively male citadel. Fadden's secretary rang asking if the prime minister might join the party at about eleven o'clock. The club president was Syd Nicholls, the artist whose cartoon for *Direct Action* had earned Tom Barker a gaol sentence twenty-four years earlier. Nichols politely escorted Fadden into the room, assisted him to climb up and stand on a centrally placed table and then raised both arms in a vain attempt to obtain silence. Fadden was personally very popular with most journalists, but such was the unpopularity of his government that on this occasion the prime minister of Australia was booed to the echo and forced to abandon any hope of addressing the crowd.[2]

The government's position in Canberra was hardly much stronger. On 3 October John Curtin, the leader of the Labor opposition, moved a vote of no confidence. Coles and Wilson were disgusted by the personal jealousies in the government's ranks as well as by its apparent fumbling. They undoubtedly reflected faithfully the feeling of the majority of the people outside parliament when they crossed the floor to vote with Labor. The Curtin ministry was confirmed in office with a huge majority in both houses at the next general election in September 1943.

Ever since federation, Labor had claimed to be the party of national Australian patriotism, just as the anti-Labor parties had always laid more stress on the importance of generalised imperial, or British patriotism. It seems that the electorate recognised some validity in these two party images, for as the Japanese moved south it became painfully clear that the time-honoured concept of complete reliance on Britain might no longer serve. If the dreadful choice between defending Britain *or* Australia first had to be made, naturally there could be no doubt about the majority decision.

The new prime minister combined in his own person much that was characteristic of the Australian Labor movement. Born in Victoria in 1885, Curtin made his home in Western Australia from 1917 onward. Brought up in an Irish-Catholic family, he lost his religious faith as a young man when he embraced socialist ideals. Through the long workaday years of battling as a trade-union organiser and Labor journalist, through all the compromises and disillusionment which form such a large part of politics and of growing up, he never quite lost the vision he had seen in his youth. Quiet-spoken, thoughtful and unquestionably sincere, he was not, as Menzies was, an obviously impressive personality. Some thought him weak and vacillating. Yet he did more than perhaps any other single person to reunite his party and movement after

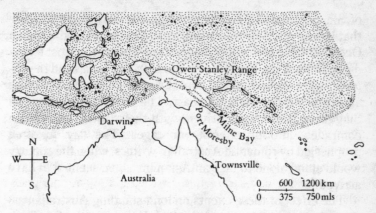

Figure 22   New Guinea/Solomons area showing maximum southern front line of Japanese in 1942

the splits and catastrophes of the depression years, and as prime minister during the darkest days Australia had ever known he gave firm and inspiring leadership. His political opponents sometimes derided him for having been a strong anti-conscriptionist with pacifist leanings during World War I, but more often they were inhibited by the fact that their own leader, R.G. Menzies, had resigned his commission in the Melbourne University Regiment on the outbreak of that conflict.[3]

The new government had hardly been sworn into office when the nation's fortitude was taxed to the utmost. The cruiser *Sydney* was lost with all hands in the Indian Ocean only a few hundred kilometres from Fremantle, Curtin's home town. On 7 December the Japanese made their sudden attack on Pearl Harbour. Thereby American might was enlisted on the side of the Allies, but at the time it seemed that, with much of the United States' Navy sunk in the sneak attack, Australia was more open than ever to an enemy invasion. Hong Kong, Borneo, the Philippines and Rabaul in New Britain – just to the north-east of New Guinea – fell to the Japanese. The Australian Eighth Division took part in the stubborn fighting retreat in Malaya, but it seemed that nothing could stop the enemy. Two months before the surrender of Singapore on 15 February 1942, the only major gesture that beleaguered Britain was then able to make in the Indian Ocean–Pacific area ended in disaster. Two of the most formidable ships in the Royal Navy, the *Prince of Wales* and the *Repulse*, were ignominiously sunk by vastly superior Japanese air power off the Malayan coast. The 15 000 Australians on Singapore Island were driven, with their British and Indian comrades, into prisoner-of-war cages. The day so often prophesied by romantic Australian writers, when the country would stand alone to face an Asian invasion, seemed to have arrived.[4]

The effect of these events on long-standing Australian assumptions cannot be overestimated. Ever since the first landing at Sydney Cove, most white people had taken it for granted in their hearts that Australian security was an indivisible part of British security and that Britain, particularly the British Navy, was naturally unconquerable. For a generation, Australians had been brought up to believe that the Singapore Naval Base was the impregnable pivot of Australian security *vis-à-vis* Japan. All this was swept away in a few terrible weeks. It has often been said that the Australian nation was born at Gallipoli. It is perhaps no less true to say that Australia came of age at Singapore. Whether she would have to face the Japanese alone during the next few critical months only time could tell, but it was certain that thenceforward she must be responsible for her own destiny in a way that had hardly occurred to most citizens in the past. Yet old habits die hard. During the Japanese advance in Malaya, two of the three Australian divisions fighting in the Middle East were hastily withdrawn to reinforce the Singapore garrison: but most of these diggers were still on the high seas when the fortress fell. Churchill demanded that they be diverted to bolster the defence of Burma and India – and his view of priorities was shared by most leading Opposition members in Canberra. Churchill seems to have been both surprised and angry at Curtin's inflexible insistence that these seasoned troops were needed to kill Japanese nearer their own homes.

It was against this background that the prime minister

made his historical appeal for American help. In some ways the words seemed shocking at the time, even to dyed-in-the-wool Labor people, but they were less shocking than the position Australia was in. The speech was overwhelmingly endorsed by public opinion:

> Without any inhibitions of any kind, I make it quite clear that Australia looks to America, free of any pangs as to our traditional links or kinship with the United Kingdom . . . We know . . . that Australia can go and Britain can still hold on. We are, therefore, determined that Australia shall not go, and we shall exert all our energies towards the shaping of a plan with the United States . . . which will give our country some confidence of being able to hold out until the tide of battle swings against the enemy.[5]

Naturally America was glad to have Australia as a base from which to mount and launch a counter-attack on the Japanese. Soon General Douglas MacArthur, escaped hero of American resistance in the Philippines, was established in Melbourne in supreme command of Allied forces in the whole Southwest Pacific area. His imperious style was not such as to appeal to most Australians, but none questioned his dedicated ability and his fitness for the post. That two men so different in nature and background as he and Curtin became friends was some measure of the stature of each. In spite of some friction, springing largely from the much higher rates of American military pay, US servicemen were naturally welcomed with open arms in Australia and the alliance worked uncommonly well.

Nevertheless, after the Pearl Harbour disaster, American strength could not be brought to bear overnight. For some months it seemed touch-and-go whether there would be a Japanese landing in force. The enemy took northern New Guinea and many of the Solomon Islands. Darwin, Broome, Wyndham and other Australian mainland ports were bombed. Ships were sunk within sight of the New South Wales coast by the Japanese Navy, and one night ferry passengers watched a lively exchange of gunfire in the middle of Sydney Harbour which had been penetrated by enemy midget submarines. At this period one keyed-up citizen, wakened and brought to the front door of his flat by an air-raid warden, was reported to have knocked out the latter with a right to the jaw before realising that he was not a member of a Japanese landing party.

The first sign of a turn in the tide came in May 1942, when a combined American–Australian fleet checked and drove back a Japanese naval force in an action that came to be known as the Battle of the Coral Sea. In June the American fleet won control of the Pacific by its decisive defeat of the Japanese at the Battle of Midway. Meanwhile enemy troops had crossed the precipitous Owen Stanley Range, mountainous backbone of New Guinea, and were approaching the main Australian base on the island's southern coast at Port Moresby, only a few hours' sailing time from the mainland. In August, at Milne Bay, near the eastern tip of New Guinea, a scratch force of Australians won the distinction of inflicting on Japanese land forces their first real defeat of the war. In a week of savage, hand-to-hand jungle fighting, the invaders were met, stopped and smashed. In the following month other diggers halted the enemy advance on Port Moresby and then, step by step, drove the Japanese back again over the Owen Stanleys. The war in the Pacific was far from won, but from this time onward an invasion of Australia seemed increasingly unlikely. By the end of the year the tide had turned on the other side of the world also. The Australian Ninth Division helped to smash German and Italian power in North Africa at the decisive Battle of El Alamein, while at the same time the Russian armies at bay routed the Germans at Stalingrad. From November 1942 onward, the Axis powers were on the defensive, and total Allied victory, however long and hard the road, was in sight.

At home in Australia, political and other events furnished in many ways a striking contrast with those of World War I. In politics the anti-Labor parties were weakened and discredited while Labor grew in unity and stature — just the opposite of what had happened twenty-five years earlier. Then the question of conscription for overseas military service had been the wedge which split the Labor Party and the nation, whereas during World War II the Curtin government imposed conscription with hardly a ripple of protest. True, Opposition members denounced the amendment to the *Defence Act* by which conscripts were required to serve overseas only as far away from Australian shores as the equator on the north and a roughly equivalent distance to east and west of the continent; but these boundaries covered the area where in fact most of the fighting in defence of Australia was taking place. On the left and within the government's own ranks, hardly a voice dissented strongly. Of course this wider measure of agreement was to a great extent imposed by the imminent peril of invasion. It would have been difficult even for doctrinaires to maintain that home defence ought to mean waiting until the enemy had actually landed on Australian soil. Minor reasons were the facts that those sections of the community traditionally opposed to conscription were also traditionally pro-Labor and so more willing to trust "their government" with sweeping powers, and that the Australian Communist Party's influence – by no means negligible in the trade unions during the war years when Russia was doing so much to bleed the common enemy – was of course solidly behind the war effort.[6]

Australians also accepted, with possibly less grumbling than such measures would have evoked in most free countries, a high measure of government direction in civil life. Essington Lewis, the extremely able manager of the country's greatest metal corporation, the Broken Hill Proprietary Company, was appointed director-general of munitions. Machine tools, precision optical goods, machine guns and even aeroplanes – all previously regarded as beyond the technological capacity of Australian industry – were soon being produced in large quantities. A Department of War Organisation of Industry diverted the use of all possible plants to war purposes, while such organisations as the Allied Works Council and the Civil Construction Corps conscripted labour for the building of airports, port facilities and other urgent tasks. Clothing and basic foods were rationed. Tobacco and liquor grew so scarce as to be almost unobtainable at times by civilians, while petrol rationing almost banished private cars from the roads. Many of these controls were established by the UAP government, but the war situation enabled Labor to use them more vigorously and to add others. Together they helped Australia's seven and a half million people to provision the million-odd who joined the armed services and to find food, and some equipment too, for the hundreds of thousands of American troops in the Southwest Pacific area. Towards the end of the war, the government also introduced a wide range of social benefits which included university scholarships for able young people and ex-servicemen and women, help for unemployed and sick people, free provision for all of certain life-saving drugs, and increased subsidies for hospitals.

The prime minister died in harness before the final victory and was succeeded by Joseph Benedict Chifley,[7] who had been treasurer in Curtin's cabinets. A year later, in the election of September 1946, Labor lost only six seats, and two of these were to independent Labor members, one a left-wing dissident and the other J.T. Lang, returning like a ghost from the past to badger the party he could no longer control. The Chifley government initiated a number of measures which were to have far-reaching effects on the whole pattern of Australian life. Ever since federation the Commonwealth had tended to gain power at the expense of the states, and this process had gathered momentum during the war – not least by the "uniform taxation" arrangements of 1942 under which the Commonwealth assumed exclusive power to levy income tax, some of which was handed back to the states in annual grants or "reimbursements". War also underlined the essential unity of the nation. Afterwards people were somewhat less concerned about state rights and more accustomed to look to Canberra for broad national initiatives.

Demobilisation of servicemen and women and their rehabilitation into civil life proceeded smoothly and quickly, amazingly so compared with the equivalent performance at the end of World War I. Many returned to their old jobs; for others subsidised training for trades and professions was provided. The war had practically ended the notion that Australia must forever remain a land of farmers and graziers. Land-settlement schemes catered for only a small minority of the demobilised diggers, but these men were given every reasonable help and were almost uniformly successful. Partly in order to accommodate the wave of ex-servicemen and women who wanted professional training, the Commonwealth government moved into the field of tertiary education. Old universities expanded their facilities, a new university opened in Sydney, and the Australian National University, conceived as primarily a postgraduate research and training institute, was founded in Canberra. Private home-building had almost ceased during the war. Commonwealth and state government agreements to alleviate this shortage were not so successful. For a time the term "squatter" came to mean not a wealthy grazier, but an ex-serviceman or woman forced to "squat", with or without a family, in almost any unoccupied building; but government action did help to keep the cost of housing lower than it would otherwise have been during the post-war housing famine. Perhaps the most imaginative scheme was that launched for developing the resources of the Snowy Mountains area near the border between New South Wales and Victoria. This giant undertaking was continued and expanded by the succeeding Menzies governments. When completed, millions of tonnes of water, which had run to waste annually in the Pacific, were used to supply much of Australia's needs for electric power. In addition, the water was diverted through tunnels so as to flow out on to the dry western plains of New South Wales for irrigation.

The greatest breaks with the past were made, however, in the fields of immigration and foreign policy. There had been much assisted migration throughout Australian history, but the scheme introduced by Arthur Augustus Calwell,[8] Chifley's minister for immigration, was unique both in its scope and in that it was sponsored so enthusiastically by Labor. The war had jolted everyone into realising that Australia would have to rely more heavily on her own resources for defence and for this, many thought, more Australians were needed. More people were not less important for a

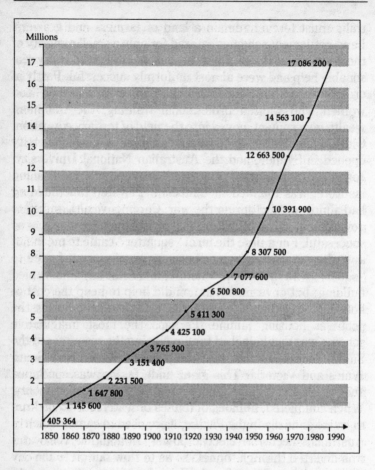

Millions

17 086 200

14 563 100

12 663 500

10 391 900

8 307 500

7 077 600

6 500 800

5 411 300

4 425 100

3 765 300

3 151 400

2 231 500

1 647 800

1 145 600

405 364

1850 1860 1870 1880 1890 1900 1910 1920 1930 1940 1950 1960 1970 1980 1990

Figure 23   Population increase 1850–1990

higher rate of economic growth and increased prosperity. Human decency also played some part in making people want to help displaced persons and other victims of the war in Europe. In the past Labor had opposed, or at best tolerated, assisted immigration on the ground that the government's first duty was to find work at reasonable wages for those already in the country. But there had been no appreciable unemployment since 1940. Jobs were more plentiful than ever immediately after the war and the Labor movement – possibly with some muted misgivings – decided to trust its own government to maintain full employment indefinitely. More surprising was the agreement of all political parties that about half of the immigrants might be European, but non-British, in origin, and most surprising of all, to anyone who knew the provincial xenophobia of Australians before the war, was the generally friendly way in which the newcomers were accepted. Abusive or contemptuous terms like "Dago" and "Reffo" (refugee) gave way, not just at an official level but in general usage, to "New Australian", though "Pommy" tended to stick more tenaciously to English immigrants, partly to distinguish them from other New Australians who, as an Irishman might have put it, were after all so much newer. Between 1945 and 1966, well over two million immigrants came to the country and the total population rose from 7.5 million to 11 million.[9]

For fifteen or twenty years after the war, most white Australians were apt frequently to congratulate themselves in public over the new immigration policy. They felt that it marked a complete break with past traditions and practices and demonstrated to the world how truly liberal and open their society had become. The rest of the whole world's inhabitants disagreed. Those few people in Europe, Asia, Africa and America who had heard anything at all about Australia knew of the "white Australia" policy and consequently regarded us as a racist pariah among nations, very like the Union of South Africa. It was not quite true. At no time in our history did the white conquerors enact laws which savagely punished human beings of a different skin-colour for loving each other; but most people who had grown up before the war continued to hate and fear brown, black and yellow people and to hold the "white Australia" policy in the sacred awe with which ancient Israelites regarded the ark of the covenant; and nearly all politicians agreed with them. Calwell himself, so genuinely liberal towards "new Australians" so long as they were white, was inflexibly opposed to admitting any of darker hue. Yet there had been some change in race relations. Calwell was a frequent guest of honour at national celebrations held by the Chinese communities in Sydney and Melbourne, and young white Australians, particularly those who were better educated, increasingly and demonstratively disowned the racial prejudices of their elders.

Even young people, however, showed little interest in Aboriginal rights at this time. After the war, so far as is known, Aboriginal people even in the remotest areas of the central Western Australian desert, of the Kimberley and of Arnhem Land were no longer massacred. Throughout the long years of Menzies' conservative rule (1950–66) they continued to be segregated as far as possible in reserves and on mission stations – and ignored. Most had no votes to trouble politicians and no rights, except special rights of the kind reserved for "protected" people, such as the right (and duty) of not drinking alcohol. "Fringe-dwelling" Aborigines continued to exist in ghettos on the outskirts of most country towns. They were prevented both by custom and terror from using public facilities on the same terms as white citizens. They could not, usually, use the same swimming pool or public bar or the same seats in a picture-theatre. Even in the more populous states like New South Wales and Victoria where they were entitled to vote, most feared to do so. In the last two or three years of the period covered by this chapter, some educated Aborigines in the capital cities began to protest, but for most of the time they hardly appeared on the stage where public events, the traditional subject matter of history, were enacted. It is not surprising that a conservative like Menzies tolerated this situation comfortably for sixteen years: he was probably not even aware of it. It is a little more surprising that a Labor leader like Evatt, with his concern for human dignity in other spheres, should also have been blind to so much lack of it at home.

Herbert Vere Evatt, Attorney-General and Minister for External Affairs from 1941 to 1949, had stepped down from the High Court bench in order to contest a Sydney suburban seat in the Labor interest. An intellectual and an idealist, he believed passionately in the importance of civil liberty at home and of the rule of law in international affairs. Some thought him insufficiently realistic for the hurly-burly of polit-

ical life, and others pointed to streaks of instability and of almost childlike vanity in his character. Yet his integrity was
unquestioned and his legal brilliance proverbial.[10] The latter
was the subject of one of those asides which occasionally
break the tedium of proceedings in the House of Representatives. Menzies, himself no mean lawyer, was "confessing", in
his loftiest and most ironic style, his "inability" to understand
the legal reasoning behind a Labor argument. "Never mind
Bob – Bert Evatt can," interjected E.J. Ward, member for
East Sydney and one of the very few men capable of ruffling
the Liberal leader's customary urbanity.

When at the end of the war the Indonesians revolted
against their Dutch masters, Evatt and the government sym-
pathised with the rebels and did nothing to hinder a continent-wide wharf-labourers' boycott of Dutch ships.[11]
Probably most Australians wished the Indonesians well,
though many Opposition supporters were scandalised at the
very idea of those whom some were old-fashioned enough to
call "natives" being helped to oppose "white men", no matter what the circumstances. On the whole, Australians encouraged Indonesian independence, partly from a genuine
belief in the natural right of every people to govern itself, and
partly too from motives of self-interest. Evatt was by no
means the only person to realise that the days of European
rule over Asia and Africa were numbered, that in the future
Australia would have to learn to deal with neighbouring
Asian governments, and that she would need all the Asian
friends she could get. Despite its implicit contradiction of the
"white Australia" policy – to which both Labor and anti-
Labor parties remained passionately attached – this liberal,
internationalist policy was warmly advocated by Evatt at the
early meetings of the United Nations Organisation. As the
candidate of a bloc of small and medium powers he was
elected president of the UN General Assembly in 1948.

The most controversial legislation of the time was the
Banking Act of 1947, which set out to nationalise the whole
banking system. In Chifley's view this was necessary as a
safeguard against the possibility of future depressions, but

Australia had in fact never been so prosperous and conservatives regarded the banking legislation as an almost revolutionary attack upon the most sacred shibboleth in their lexicon, private enterprise. The government also sought to nationalise air services, but both measures were ruled unconstitutional by the High Court. A government-owned airline, Trans-Australia Airlines, was set up in competition with private companies, however, and it, with the government-owned Australian overseas airline, Qantas, has maintained since a record of safety and efficiency second to none in the world.

At about the same time, Churchill's "iron-curtain" speech at Fulton, Missouri, gave impetus to the revived wave of anti-communist feeling which was sweeping all Western countries. In Australia, as elsewhere, people were tired of wartime restrictions and controls, some of which, like a modified form of petrol rationing, still survived. In the midst of prosperity and expansion a bitter coal strike caused power shortages, which on some nights plunged great cities into darkness. People were unpleasantly reminded of the wartime blackout. At the nadir of UAP fortunes in 1944, Menzies had taken the leading part in yet another reorganisation of the anti-Labor forces under the new (or refurbished) banner of the Liberal Party. He then promised to abolish petrol rationing and other troublesome restrictions on private enterprise, and to smash the influence of communism in the trade unions and elsewhere by making the Communist Party an illegal organisation. At the election of 1949, the Liberal and Country parties came back to power again with a comfortable majority. Within a few months, Australian soldiers were again fighting overseas, this time in Korea.[12]

Ruled for fifty years by Japan, Korea was divided at the end of World War II between a communist administration north of the 38th parallel of latitude and a capitalist one south of that line. Needless to say, the North Korean government was in effect a puppet of the Soviet Union, or to some extent of the newly communised People's Republic of China, while the South Korean government depended just as fully on the support of the United States. When fighting began in June 1950, the South Korean forces were nominally led by the United Nations Organisation, but in fact by General Douglas MacArthur, American hero of the war in the South-West Pacific and later commander of Allied Occupation Forces in conquered Japan. Some twenty nations contributed troops to the UN force in South Korea, but the Menzies government saw to it that Australia was the first to respond to American diplomatic pressure. Menzies, like most Austral-Britons, fondly believed that timely help to our great ally would ensure American protection of Australian interests in the future. Twelve years later, when President Sukarno of Indonesia annexed Netherlands New Guinea in the teeth of anguished Dutch – and Australian – protests, Menzies sought America's diplomatic support. The Americans unblushingly gave it to the Sukarno, but even this painful experience did nothing to shake the faith of Australian conservatives in American care for and loyalty to Australia. Most Australians, however, cared little about the Korean war just as they did later about confrontation with Sukarno, remaining much more interested in the anti-communist witch-hunt at home. True to its election promise, the new government in 1950 passed a Communist Party Dissolution Bill.

The bill gave power to declare the Australian Communist Party, and other bodies deemed to be affiliated with it, illegal organisations whose property should be forfeited to the Commonwealth. It also barred communists from employment in the Commonwealth government services and from holding offices in key trade unions, and it gave the government power to "declare" citizens to be communists. Contrary to the ancient principle of British law, the onus of disproving the charge was placed squarely on the accused or "declared" persons. In speaking to the bill in the House, the prime minister anticipated its passage a little by "declaring" twenty or so communist trade-union officers whose names had presumably been supplied to him by paid government spies. The fact that some were not communists, and that one was neither a communist *nor* a trade-union member, did not reassure the large body of moderate opinion which was strongly anti-communist but troubled by the idea of entrusting such arbitrary powers to any government. The bill was passed but immediately challenged in the High Court by the Communist Party and by some powerful trade unions such as that of the waterside workers. Labor was a little half-hearted in its opposition to the bill, partly for fear of being branded with guilt by association and partly because some Catholic Labor men were at least as illiberal on this matter as was the Liberal government. Nevertheless Evatt, in his private legal capacity, argued the case for the unions before the High Court, which found the bill unconstitutional in March 1951.

The government then decided to seek a constitutional amendment to give it the necessary power for passing its anti-communist legislation, and accordingly prepared for a nation-wide referendum on the subject.[13] At this point Chifley died suddenly and Evatt succeeded to the leadership of the Opposition. Despite the latter's zeal for a "no" vote, the referendum campaign was not fought strictly on party lines. Government members and practically all newspapers and radio commentators urged the electors to vote "yes", and some Labor men joined them – if only by their significant silence upon the issue; but as the campaign warmed up a good many prominent citizens not identified at all with party politics, including some who probably normally voted conservative, spoke out fearlessly on the "no" side. From his retirement in Perth, old Walter Murdoch said, "The government is asking for . . . the power to punish a man for his beliefs – or for what some spy alleges him to believe. It will be a sad day for Australia if she allows this spiritual poison to get into her system." On the same day the prime minister assured voters that, "Nobody other than a communist can, under any conceivable circumstances, be affected."[14] Almost everyone, whatever his or her hopes or fears, expected an overwhelming affirmative vote, but in the event the government's proposals were narrowly defeated. Needless to say, the vast majority of Australians were almost as strongly opposed to communism as were Americans at the same period; but they were apparently less ready to sacrifice traditional liberties in the name of opposing it.

Despite this defeat, Menzies immediately announced pettishly that the Commonwealth government, as an employer, would hire thenceforward only those whom it considered politically unobjectionable. Government offices were purged of communists, real or supposed, and government employment denied thereafter to any applicants considered politically unreliable by the government's secret police services. Yet these herculean efforts to scotch the communist menace seemed insufficient. With a federal election due by mid-1954 at the latest, public opinion polls showed an alarming swing towards Labor. On 6 April the *Sydney Morning Herald* wrote that the government would have to pull a couple of rabbits out of Mr Menzies' top-hat if it were to survive the election. Exactly a week later, cynics observed that the rabbits were already there. Menzies announced, in the absence of Dr Evatt, leader of the opposition, that Vladimir Petrov, a Russian diplomat and spy, had left his masters in the Soviet Embassy in Canberra and presented himself, together with a folio of Soviet spy documents, to the Australian spies in the Australian Security Intelligence Organisation. Petrov was granted political asylum and the prime minister set up a Royal Commission to inquire into the affair.

The Commission sat in the full glare of publicity in an atmosphere of hysterical witch-hunting which must have been more familiar to Petrov than to the natives of a democratic country. Preliminary proceedings, inspired "leaks" and unrestrained press speculation seemed to connect Petrov's spy network with the ALP and its leader, Evatt. No one was surprised when, two weeks and two days after the production of the rabbits, or perhaps the red herrings, the Menzies government was re-elected despite the earlier massive swing of opinion against it – and despite the fact that it polled only 47.07 per cent of total votes cast as against 50.03 per cent for the ALP.

For forty years people have argued passionately as to

whether the Petrov affair was just what it seemed – the defection of a Soviet spy – or a carefully set up political mare's nest designed by the government, or by ASIO on behalf of the government, to discredit the ALP at the 1954 election. Careful study of all the available evidence shows that it was most probably organised by a self-appointed group of conspirators, responsible to no one but themselves and bound by a solemn oath to secrecy. This group changed in personnel from time to time but usually included high-ranking Commonwealth public servants, especially from the Defence Department, and powerful air force, naval and military intelligence officers, including, certainly in the 1950s, Colonel Charles Spry, head of ASIO. Thus these guardians of Australian democracy could have used ASIO itself, probably without Menzies' knowledge, but certainly not without his gratitude, as an instrument for keeping him in power.[15]

Another fascinating glimpse of the activities of these seditious conspirators was provided by the Salisbury affair twenty-five years later. In January 1978 the South Australian Police Commissioner, Mr Harold Salisbury, was dimissed by the Labor premier of the state, Mr Don Dunstan, for having misled the government. The "special branch" of the South Australian police, like those of every other state, kept secret dossiers on thousands of citizens including Labor members of parliament, to some of whom, including the premier, it was legally responsible. Salisbury had given evasive, incomplete and misleading replies when asked about these matters. At a press conference three days after his sacking, he made the astonishing claim that he was "responsible to the Crown – directly to the Queen – or her representative in Australia" and not to the government which had appointed him. When reporters were nonplussed by this statement, Salisbury blundered on to explain that he had been "sworn to secrecy". No one then or since asked "to whom?" Presumably it could only have been directly to the Queen or her representative, to spies mightier than himself in the Australian network, or to the faceless persons banded together, in the reported words of Charles Spry in a conversation with Dr John Burton, head of the External Affairs Department in Evatt's day, in a conspiracy "to protect democracy from itself". An oath to any one such body would have been grossly illegal and subversive of the police commissioner's absolute responsibility to the Crown, through the government of the day and its first minister. It mattered not. At this stage of the affair no one even asked Pilate's question, what was the truth, though everyone, like the Judean governor, stayed not for an answer.[16] A year later Dunstan's health broke down and he retired from politics.

After what many saw as the tragic farce of the Petrov affair, the Liberal–Country Party coalition retained power with only relatively minor dramatic performances, and Menzies remained its unchallenged leader. No Australian prime minister ever ruled the country for anything like so long, or so continuous, a period. The reliable old anti-communist drum proved of considerable help in most of the succeeding election campaigns, but at the same time the government had profited by its earlier unhappy experience with the "anti-communist bill". It vigorously denounced communism but skilfully avoided any further head-on confrontations with the trade-union movement, such as had brought down the Bruce–Page government. The Liberals were also helped enormously by yet another Labor "split". From 1954 onward many right-wing people deserted, or were expelled from, the Labor Party to form a strongly anti-communist but separate group which finally came to be known as the Democratic Labor Party. The great majority of its members and supporters were zealous Catholics, although most of their co-religionists remained faithful to the official Australian Labor Party. From 1964 onwards, Menzies gained many Catholic votes, and fervid DLP support, by reversing a national policy that had been settled for nearly a hundred years: he reinstituted a form of state aid to church schools.[17]

Even without this help, however, the Liberals would probably have continued in office for most of the postwar period. Menzies was unquestionably the ablest politician in the country, and he combined with tenacity the ability to keep on learning from his mistakes. Under his leadership, the Liberals were not too proud to adopt, and successfully implement, some planks of their opponents' platform – full employment, for instance. During the Chifley regime, most Liberals felt, and some voiced, fears that really full employment for all who wanted work would have a disastrous effect on the economy. Without the competitive goad of fear, they believed, employees would work badly and national productivity would fall. Their theory was that a "small" or "moderate", but permanent, pool of unemployed – say 3 or 4 per cent of the workforce – was an unpleasant but necessary part of the free enterprise system for which the Liberals stood. In 1952, not very long after the Menzies government had returned to power, there was a brief recession during which unemployment rose to about 2 per cent. Public reaction was so strong that the government, to get everyone back to work, quickly imposed drastic import restrictions and other controls which would probably have been denounced as socialist measures if imposed by their opponents. After that, succeeding Menzies governments placed almost as much emphasis as Labor did on maintaining full employment. Nor was this mere lip service to catch votes. Almost full employment continued to be a fact, except for another brief recession nearly ten years later. The general election of December 1961 reduced the Liberal–Country Parties' usually comfortable majority in the lower house of 120 members to a majority of two. "Sound government" continued, without very much of the experimentation that might have been expected from Labor; but while expansion and full employment continued seemingly indefinitely, why change horses? Most people felt they had good reason to be content.

It was sometimes hard for Australians themselves to realise the extent of the development that took place in the decades following the war years. The war was the trigger rather than the cause of this enormous expansion, which continued under both Labor and anti-Labor governments. No earlier generation had "had it so good" – or so continuously. Australia continued to be the world's main supplier of wool, and

in the early 1950s overseas prices rose to the staggering figure of more than £1 per pound (or 500g) for the very best wool
– equivalent to perhaps $100 per kilogram in 1990 money
values; but the postwar period was remarkable precisely for
the great diversification of the economy. To wool, wheat,
meat, dairy products and orchard produce were added many
other crops. Some rice had been grown before the war, but afterwards there was a considerable surplus for export. Tobacco and cotton continued to be imported, but for the first
time it began to seem possible that this need not always be so.
Even coffee and cocoa from New Guinea began to appear on
the home market in significant quantities. For long before the
war most important metals had been mined in quantities
great enough to provide large export surpluses. After the
war, rich ores of nickel, aluminium and uranium were added
to the iron, lead, tin, copper, zinc, silver, gold and other metals already produced. The war also made Australians acutely
aware of the one vital raw material which they lacked – oil.
During the 1950s, generous government subsidies stepped
up the rate of search, and in the following decade rich strikes
were made in Queensland, Western Australia, Bass Strait
and elsewhere. In the late 1960s Australians dreamed of
being self-sufficient in oil, but reality in the 1970s saw local
production accounting for only about 70 per cent of consumption. It was some consolation that there was a large surplus of
natural gas for export.[18]

The discovery or development of new primary resources
was overshadowed by the much greater advance in secondary industries. Between 1940 and 1960 the number of factories more than doubled, the real value of manufactured goods
was multiplied by more than three, and the quantity of power
applied to secondary industries increased nearly four times.
Before the war durable consumer goods like cars, vacuum
cleaners, washing machines and refrigerators were mostly
imported luxuries which only the well-to-do could afford.
After it they became standard equipment for almost every
household, and the vast majority of these and other manufactured articles, like the new television sets, were made in Aus-

tralia. A healthy export trade in secondary products grew steadily. By 1966, relative to its population, Australia had one of the strongest and best-balanced economies in the world.

The new affluence and the technological changes on which it was based made life somewhat easier for Australian women at this time. The back-breaking labour of washing the family's clothes, sheets and towels had always been done by the "housewife", except in wealthy bourgeois families where it was done, more often than not in addition to labour for her own family, by an overworked and underpaid housewife from the poorer suburbs. By the 1960s a washing machine was standard equipment in all but the very poorest households. So were other labour-saving devices like electric irons, cooking appliances, vacuum cleaners, refrigerators and sewing-machines. So was a family motor car. Together these things went far towards making it possible for married women to get paid work outside the home and a steadily increasing number did so. That more did not was due first to the massive inertia of the traditional belief, still held firmly by most women as well as men, that "a women's place is in the home". Almost no one except communists and the "friends of communists" then demanded equal legal and social rights for women. Like Aboriginal people they were rigidly debarred by custom, if not by law, from drinking in most hotel bars and from working in some of the better-paid jobs. Like Aborigines, too, they were paid only a fraction of the white male wage for almost all kinds of work, and few indeed were the women who protested. In addition to all these barriers, there was an appalling absence of crèches, child-minding centres and children's health facilities. Finally, contraceptives were still quite inefficient. Women working in factories, business, politics or the professions were always likely to have their routines interrupted by unplanned and unwanted pregnancies. Small wonder that, though more women joined the workforce after the war, not a great many more did. For instance, when Annabelle Rankin (later Dame Annabelle Rankin) was elected to the Senate in 1946, she became the first Queensland woman sent to either house of the Commonwealth parliament.[19]

The great influx of European migrants improved, perceptibly if not dramatically, the status of Australian women. This it did by diluting quite rapidly some of the worst traditions of what was no longer such an aggressively male "frontier" society. It helped too to create a higher valuation of culture, in the narrower sense of the word, than was common in the Australian past. Life became much more urbanised, more complex, and more sophisticated. Between 1945 and 1965, for instance, the number of universities more than doubled and the number of undergraduate enrolments more than quadrupled. In painting, literature and other arts, more Australian work reached a mature standard which challenged comparison with work done anywhere in the world – and without any special pleading for regional values. Moreover, private citizens and public institutions began to patronise art to a degree scarcely conceivable before 1939. Instead of leaving for foreign parts where their work was appreciated, some leading intellectuals, artists and writers, like the great novelist Patrick White, even returned to live in the new Australia that appreciated *them*. In the early 1960s J.J. Cahill, Labor premier of New South Wales, did something, possibly the only thing, for which he will be gratefully remembered by posterity. He imported the Danish genius, Joern Utzon, to create that architectural masterpiece of the modern world which now soars and dreams over Sydney Harbour, symbolising the best aspirations of the Australian people.

The greatest painter of them all, Russell Drysdale, had stayed near the source of his inspiration, the Australian bush, particularly in Cape York Peninsula. He painted Aborigines long before most white Australians cared even to remember their existence. Kenneth Clark, probably the most eminent and catholic art critic alive in the 1980s, wrote of him: "No one except Drysdale gives the same authentic feeling of the resolute humanity, that has managed to exist in that terrible continent. Those who love Australia and the Australians as I do, will find their feelings reflected in the bold, sincere and deeply human records he has made of the landscape and its inhabitants, black and white." Despite competition from mass-produced overseas books, the local publishing industry expanded sufficiently to meet most of the new demands made upon it. Most citizens were happy enough in the knowledge that progress in all these fields did not involve any falling away from what they regarded as Australia's natural pre-eminence in tennis, swimming and other sports. Similarly, the New Australians introduced many new skills, fashions and foods without really challenging the ancient and excellent predominance of steak-and-eggs.

Nevertheless, there was a good deal of speculation about the extent to which the continuing wave of European migration was changing what Australians regarded as their basic national attitudes and goals. It was perhaps an indication of increasing maturity that not all of the speculation was apprehensive in character. For example, many prosperous citizens had long agreed with the multitude of visitors who declared that the average Australian was far too leisure- and pleasure-loving for either his own or the national good. Perhaps, thought these moralists, New Australians would work harder and for longer hours, so setting a good example to the government servants, the footballers, the surfers, the trade unionists, the life-savers, the coal miners, the students, the race-goers and the beer-drinkers — in fact, to the regrettably easy-going bulk of the population? Certainly a disproportionately large number of New Australians, by skill, perseverance and sheer hard work, built up large or small businesses of their own; and this helped to raise somewhat the general standard of business efficiency. More often than before it happened that a pair of shoes would be mended in a day or two rather than a week or two, or even that a building would be finished within a few weeks — rather than months or years — of the date stipulated in the contract; but by North American standards at least, Australian business methods still seemed inefficient.

On the other hand, most New Australians fairly readily absorbed, in trade unions and elsewhere, the old Australian conviction that a person should work to live, but should not live to work. Teachers agreed that the New Australian children were usually completely assimilated into the general community even when, as often happened, their parents were not. Those who feared or hoped for dramatic changes as a longer-term result of the massive immigration were probably wrong. American and Canadian experience of what were, proportionately, equally massive foreign migrations, suggests that sooner or later immigrants almost inevitably conform to the established ways of their new country – if not in the first generation, then in the second or third. And the sudden influx of new people, money and ideas into Australia was not relatively as great, after all, as was that during the gold-rush decade in the middle of the last century. Then most contemporaries thought that the whole nature of Australian life was bound to be transformed, but in fact it was not.

A good many older Australians were vaguely troubled by some of the other possible effects of the long-continued post-war boom – its effects not so much on themselves, of course, as on young people. After 1940, they pointed out, a whole generation grew up without experiencing at first hand depression, war or other hardships of former days which, in retrospect, seemed to have been so salutary. Boys and girls took it for granted that jobs would be available just as they assumed the sun would continue to rise in the east. If they wanted to go to university, and had the ability to do so, a wide range of government scholarships was ready to make it easier for them. Among lefterly senior citizens, these head-shakings were inspired partly by the feeling that there would be nothing like another good depression to make younger voters change their political allegiance. To this extent the forebodings suggested a certain fossilising of attitudes among Labor supporters, but it is also true that the policies of the two major parties tended to approach each other during the 1950s.

More often, the gloomy apprehensions merely reflected the well-founded conviction, not unusual among older people everywhere, that life was not what it had been when they were young. In fact the mental horizons of young people were not nearly as circumscribed as their parents' had been, and this augured well for the future. For years trade with America, Japan and other foreign countries had been increasing while the traditionally accepted trade with Britain had declined. People were growing more aware of the no longer so remote outside world beyond Australia's – and Britain's – shores. Young people were, or liked to feel they were, more sophisticated and cosmopolitan in outlook than their elders. Some of them seemed even to question the hallowed sentiments associated with the celebration of Anzac Day, while many vigorously queried the wisdom of the "white Australia" policy. Yet this same generation was equally often criticised by its elders for "playing it safe" and for conformism.

In truth it was the older generation which was being left behind by events. Nothing in recent history is so striking, and so important for humanity's future, as the rapid change which was taking place everywhere in race relations. In a backhanded way, perhaps, we may thank Hitler for it. In earlier wars men fought and died in the belief that their race or nation was innately superior to all other "lesser breeds without the law". During World War II, by their systematic and cold-blooded murder of many millions of men, women and children for the crime of not having been born into the "master race", the Nazis demonstrated to everyone the logical end of racist delusions. Allied propaganda was not slow to point the moral. In Australia as elsewhere, through every medium of mass communication, people were taught the truth about race. The Nazis had to be defeated, not because they belonged to a different and supposedly inferior race or nation, but because they preached and practised a scientifically false and ethnically monstrous doctrine of "racial superiority".

The effectiveness of the lesson was underlined by the speed with which almost all groups of African and Asian peoples, formerly ruled by European powers, won or were given national independence in the twenty years following the war. It was shown too by the United States' rapid movement towards real social and economic integration of its Negro citizens, and by the much slower movement in Australia towards assimilation of its Aboriginal non-citizens. Yet Australia, with her New Guinea dependency, still appeared before the world as one of the few surviving, old-style colonial powers, and she shared with South Africa the doubtful distinction of believing, or appearing to believe, in the principle of racial inequality. For, however Australians might explain the "white Australia" policy, this was inevitably what it meant in the eyes of most other nations.

Fortunately the true picture was not as damning as it seemed to most outside observers. During the war, thousands of Australian soldiers learned to value Asian friends in Malaya and the Indonesian archipelago. In 1951 the Menzies government took a leading part in launching the Colombo Plan, under which many thousands of Asian and African students were assisted to study at Australian universities. They were completely accepted as equals and friends by Australian students in a way that surprised many of the latter's parents and horrified some surviving grandparents. Indeed, however conformist they may have seemed in some other respects, if we judge by their actions, Australian undergraduates felt more strongly about racial equality than about any other political issue. Incidents such as those at Sharpeville in South Africa, or Birmingham in Alabama, usually evoked student demonstrations and resolutions in Australian cities and, since they creditably felt that charity should begin at home, undergraduates frequently embarrassed senior statesmen of all political parties with persistent questions about their attitude to the "white Australia" policy.

Of course, there was a large element of ingenuousness in the younger generation's attitude. Not all of them realised how easy it was to love all humans as brothers and sisters in a country which, partly because of the long-standing exclusion policy that they derided, had comparatively slight "race" or other minority problems. Some public opinion polls indicated a decisive change in attitudes. Those interviewed were told that people of certain nationalities (no Australian could have any doubt about what was meant) were prohibited from settling permanently in Australia. They were then asked if they were in favour of admitting at least fifty migrants a year from each of those countries. Between 1954 and 1959 the answers changed as shown in Table 4:[20]

Year	Keep out (%)	Let in (%)	No opinion (%)
1954	51	31	8
1956	51	42	7
1957	55	36	9
1958	45	44	11
1959	34	55	11

Table 4 Public opinion on migration, 1954–59

It should be emphasised that few or no Australians supported a policy of completely unrestricted and unplanned immigration. If, say, 2 million or so of India's 500 million-odd people were to have immigrated over a few years, the effect on Australian living standards and folkways would obviously have been enormous, while the effect on India's distressingly low living standards would have been negligible. It was the principle and practice of absolute exclusion on "racial" grounds which was offensive to Asians, Africans and Polynesians, and discreditable to Australians. Those who wanted to abolish the policy aimed at substituting a planned quota system such as those of the United States, Canada and many other countries. As Britain moved towards entering the European Economic Community, the importance of trade and friendship with Asian neighbours increasingly occupied the attention of Australian governments. More and more Australians were coming to believe that abandonment of the "white Australia" policy, at least in its historically rigid form, might be a necessary condition of survival as well as a moral imperative.

The vast majority of citizens had readily accepted the other, and more immediately vital, great change in external relations – those with the United States; but this did not mean that there were no tensions between the two countries. In the last century, when Great Britain was the most powerful country in the world, Australians generally took for granted their ultimate political and cultural dependence on her. Yet even though she was also their "mother country", they did not always love their dependent role. Indeed, as we have seen, Australian nationality sprang in large part from resentment at what many felt, with little reason, to be British domination. After World War II the United States largely took over Britain's role in the world, and in 1951 Australia recognised the changed reality by signing a treaty with New Zealand and the United States – the ANZUS treaty – which bound the signatories to consult and aid each other in wartime. After 1942 Australian security, in the ultimate analysis, appeared to depend just as much on the United States as it formerly had on Britain.

In 1954 Australia sought to underline this dependence on the Great Republic by joining with her in SEATO, the South-East Asia Treaty Organisation, which embraced also the United Kingdom, France, New Zealand, Pakistan, the Philippines and Thailand. The treaty bound the signatories to consult about measures to be taken in the event of an attack on any one of them, but no such consultation has ever taken place. The real aim of the treaty was embodied in a protocol which enabled member-states to join with the United States in fighting communism in Indo-China. Most Australians readily accepted government assurances that SEATO had strengthened them against Asian communism, and none had any tangible cause to doubt this until the American intervention in the Vietnamese civil war began ten years later. During 1963, for the first time, United States investments in Australian business and industry exceeded British investments. The influence of American films, gramophone records, magazines, books and television programs increased steadily, while that of British books and so on tended slowly to decline. In 1966, as the first step in converting Australia to the metric system, the traditional British currency of pounds, shillings and pence was replaced by dollars and cents.

Australians generally were virtuous enough to make a modest degree of happiness out of apparent necessity. They never forgot America's decisive role in the war with Japan. On the whole they liked and admired Americans and, as official spokesmen seldom wearied of repeating, the two countries had much more in common than Australia had with any other land outside the British-descended members of the British Commonwealth. With the possible exception of Canada, Australia was the most loyal ally America had. Yet many Australians also felt irked by their dependent role just as, like the Americans themselves, they previously had *vis-à-vis* the land of their forefathers. In Australia, as elsewhere, only a rather small minority of people thought very much about international relations. Those who did sometimes felt as exasperated over American exercises in "brinkmanship" and the doctrine of massive nuclear retaliation as they felt grateful for the, after all, hypothetical assurance of American protection. Similarly, many Australians resented the trend towards American domination of important sectors of the national economy, even while they recognised the need for more American capital investment to help in the development of their country. Americans, after all, took just as ambivalent an attitude towards British financial influence on the United States in the last century.

There was also something of a reversal of roles between right and left, *vis-à-vis* America. In the last century, Australian liberals and nationalists were generally pro-American. The United States presented to them an image of progressive and nationalist radical democracy; but for this very reason Australian conservatives tended to damn Uncle Sam as a shoddy, revolutionary, anti-British vulgarian. In the third quarter of the twentieth century, when the United States, with its vast power and world-wide responsibilities, had become more interested in preserving the status quo, the Australian left discovered an increasing affinity with welfare-state Britain, while the right tended to love the new America much more, though not to love the "old country" very much less. When Menzies left public life, these changes in the outlook of Australians seemed to gather momentum.

8 Going it alone
c. 1967–92

On 20 January 1966, R.G. Menzies retired after more than sixteen years of continous service as prime minister. The Queen had already honoured him with an exclusive knighthood, the Order of the Thistle. To this was soon added the even more exclusive title, unique for a colonial, of Lord Warden of the Cinque Ports. In 1973, long after his retirement, the imperial Japanese government conferred on him the Order of the Rising Sun (First Class) for his services to Japanese–Australian friendship. Critics and admirers agreed it was only fitting that the erstwhile "Pig-Iron Bob" should end his days loaded with overseas honours.

When at a Canberra dinner for the Queen in 1963, he had quoted the couplet:

I did but see her passing by
And yet I love her till I die

some had questioned his good taste, but none his sincerity. Before the bungled Anglo-French attack on Suez in 1956, he had allowed himself to be appointed chief spokesman to Egypt's President Nasser for the British, French and other governments deeply interested in the use of the canal. In one of his last speeches in the Australian parliament, he went a little out of his way to proclaim: "it is well known that I am British to my boot-heels". Indeed he was both deeply British and deeply conservative. During the first decade or two of this century, Australia and New Zealand were the most "advanced" democracies in the world. Intelligent travellers came here to study welfare state measures in much the same way as they now visit Sweden or Denmark or China to see possible shapes of the future.[1] By the time Menzies retired in 1966, Australia, in this respect, had fallen far behind Britain and many other European democracies. Full employment and unprecedented prosperity continued, but a growing number of people were questioning the out-of-date assumptions on which the Liberal–Country Party governments' domestic and foreign policies had rested for so long.

At the time of federation, belief in the innate and absolute superiority of British blood and institutions seemed, at least to most British people, merely common sense. By 1966, as we have seen, many white people in Australia, as elsewhere, had begun to wonder whether they had the right to guide, govern or coerce black, brown and yellow people "for their own good". During the long Menzies reign, the government did practically nothing to recognise the full humanity of Aboriginal Australians. Preparations for the independence of Papua New Guinea proceeded slowly and, it often seemed, unwillingly. South Africa's racist policies, condemned by world opinion, were supported by Australia to the point where Menzies was fondly christened "Oom Robert" – Uncle Bob – by the Afrikaaner nationalist press. The "white Australia" policy continued – in fact, if not in public proclamations – as the basis of our immigration arrangements.

With Menzies' departure from public life, there departed also the old white Australian assumption that Britain, still "Home" to many conservative people, was the centre of the whole world, not merely of the British Empire, recently renamed the Commonwealth of Nations. It was obvious to thoughtful Australians, if not at once to all politicians and public servants, that thenceforth we had increasingly to make our own decisions. Unthinking reliance on British advice or tradition would no longer serve. We had, however reluctantly, to begin learning to go it alone.

Among Menzies' last deeds as prime minister were two with long-term consequences he could hardly have foreseen. Late in 1964 his government passed an act by which liability to military conscription for overseas service in peacetime was imposed on young Australian males between the ages of 20 and 22. Then on 29 April 1965 he announced that his government had decided to send a battalion of diggers to help the growing American military intervention in Vietnam.

On Sir Robert's retirement, the Liberal Party immediately elected to replace him its deputy leader, Harold Holt. The 59-year-old "young Harold", as Menzies called him, had been his protégé and heir-apparent to the party leadership for many years. A fellow Victorian and prefect at his chief's old school, Wesley College, Holt had been a member of all cabinets since 1949 while other men, who might have posed a threat to Menzies' leadership, were persuaded to accept more secure positions elsewhere. Thus three able ministers for external affairs left politics: Percy Spender was sent as ambassador to Washington in 1951, eight years later becoming a judge, and then president, of the International Court of Justice at The Hague; R.G. Casey retired to the British House of Lords in 1960 and became Australia's governor-general in 1965; and Garfield Barwick became chief justice of the High Court of Australia in 1964. Holt had been an astute and successful minister for labour in several of Menzies' governments before being promoted to treasurer. Sociable, straightforward and something of a playboy in private life, Holt had more of the common touch and was less conservative than his old chief. He reshuffled some portfolios, but retained in office all members of the previous cabinet.

Nothing much seemed to have changed, but, despite Liberal–Country Party victories at the next two general elections, the conservative forces had lost internal cohesion and much electoral appeal. It seemed that the parliamentary Liberal Party could produce no leader with the political sagacity and commanding prestige of its old master. Sir John ("Black Jack") McEwen, the Country Party leader, might have saved the day for conservatism, but the Liberals would not countenance the idea of handing over the prime ministership to the junior partner in the coalition. So Holt was left to modify some of Menzies' old policies and to pursue others more vigorously. Like the next two prime ministers, Gorton and McMahon, but emphatically unlike Menzies, he looked to Washington, not London, as the centre of the universe and fount of all good things.

One of his first acts was to ease slightly the conditions under which non-European residents in Australia could be naturalised and, unlike Menzies, he made positive efforts to cultivate good relations with some Asian governments: yet at the same time he committed Australia even more firmly to total, uncritical support of America's "anti-communist" crusade in Vietnam and elsewhere. In March 1966 he announced that Australian forces in Vietnam would be increased from 1500 to 4500 men and that the relieving battalions would include conscripted national servicemen. A few months later, at a state dinner in Washington, he promised President Johnson that Australia would go "all the way with LBJ". Even among the majority of citizens who agreed with the government's foreign policy, many deplored the sycophantic tone of his remark. Menzies, they felt, would never have been so undignified; but there was worse to come.

Holt arranged for President Johnson to visit Australia a month before the general election of November 1966. Naturally Arthur Calwell, leader of the Labor opposition, and others charged that the first event was designed to influence the outcome of the second. Perhaps it did. The president's train included 400 American journalists and photographers, plus an unknown but great number of secret policemen, spies and security guards. The Australian poet Dorothy Auchterlonie satirically compared the visit with an imperial Roman triumph in tributary territory.[2] Vast and vociferous crowds choked the streets, sometimes bringing the presidential cavalcade to a halt. At one point Johnson turned aside from acknowledging the cheers long enough to put a patronising arm round the shoulders of the smirking Holt, whom he drew forward with the condescending words, "Look! This is your prime minister!" But not all the noise and grimaces were made by supporters of the war. The president's car was spattered with red paint symbolising blood, and more than once brought to a halt by hostile demonstrators lying across the roadway in the path of the procession. The Liberal premier of New South Wales, Robin Askin, earned some notoriety by loudly urging his chauffeur to "drive over the bastards!"[3] The community was deeply and bitterly divided.

For the Democratic Labor Party, the Liberal and Country Parties and most of their supporters, the issue was simple. The Australian way of life was based on private enterprise, "white" blood and Christian traditions. They held it to be self-evident that these things were threatened by international communism, particularly Asian communism, and that they could be defended only by almost unconditional dependence on a great "white" power. Therefore Australia must fight shoulder to shoulder with her "great and powerful" friend to contain communism in Asia, for only thus could she be assured of the protection of a grateful America in some future crisis. Labor supporters and a rapidly increasing number of young people, students, artists, intellectuals and even business people seeking profitable trade with communist countries, dissented vigorously. International communism, they believed, was a mythical monster, since events daily demonstrated tensions between the major communist powers, China and the Soviet Union, as great as any between either country and the United States. The Vietnamese "enemy" was as much nationalist as communist, and Vietnam and China had been enemies for millennia. In any case, by intervening against popular national movements in Asia, Australia was earning the enmity of her neighbours and so undermining her own long-term security. Finally, we and the Americans were clearly the aggressors in an unequal and unjust war condemned as such by practically the entire weight of world opinion. During the election campaign Calwell emphasised opposition to the war, and to conscription for overseas service, as central issues: yet he was an old-fashioned type of Labor man, more racist in his outlook than many of his Liberal or Country Party opponents. To young voters he seemed to belong to a past, provincial age, while Holt presented a much more sophisticated "swinging" image. The DLP warned that the "red" peril had become "yellow" also. All parties stressed the need for development of Australia's northern areas. In November 1966 the conservative coalition was returned to power with its greatest majority since 1949. The new House of Representatives contained sixty-one Liberal, twenty-one Country Party and forty-one Labor members.

With his stewardship thus endorsed, many looked to Mr Holt for new initiatives. Early in 1967 he gave his blessing to a move whereby the Senate took up the American practice of appointing select committees to inquire into specific problems. Political observers generally agreed that this step both produced useful results and helped to revitalise the second chamber. Then in May the government put to the people two referenda for amendments to the constitution. The first, which had long been shelved by preceding governments, sought Commonwealth power to legislate for Aborigines and to abolish apparent constitutional discrimination against them. It was easily carried: no other referendum in history has been assented to by every electorate in every state of the Commonwealth, though pessimists noted that the "no" vote was highest in those electorates containing a large number of Aborigines. The other referendum sought power to alter the "nexus" or constitutionally fixed ratio of approximately one to two, between the number of senators and members of the House of Representatives. To this question most citizens answered "no", as they usually have in Australian plebiscites.

The result of the referendum of 1967 marked the beginning of a new era in relations between black and white Australians. It did nothing immediately – or for some years afterwards – to improve the unspeakable conditions in which most Aborigines had long lived, but it did for the first time recognise them in law as full and equal citizens of the Commonwealth, and it showed politicians and other timid people that the great majority of white Australians regretted their ancestors' genocide of so many Aboriginal tribes, and so would support governmental measures designed to help Aboriginal advancement. From this time onwards more and more black Australians took part in public agitation for the basic human rights so long denied them. Tribal Aborigines in the north and west, reserve and mission-dwellers, "fringe-dwellers" near the country towns and partly assimilated people in the city slums all began to make their presence felt by the whole white community. Decent whites did what they could to help, as they always had done, but for every one Daisy Bates before 1967 there were a dozen after that year like "Nugget" (H.C.) Coombs, the greatest public servant Australia has known, who devoted his "retirement" to advocating Aboriginal land rights and the signing of a treaty between whites and blacks. Don Dunstan, Labor premier of South Australia, in 1976 appointed to the governorship of that state a distinguished Aborigine, Pastor Sir Douglas Nichols. More importantly, Labor governments in South Australia and New South Wales passed laws making it a criminal offence to discriminate against a person in any way because of his or her race. Up until 1990, however, no such laws had been passed by Liberal–Country Party governments in Queensland or Western Australia – where most Aborigines lived.

Despite the modest kudos it gained from having sponsored the "Aboriginal referendum", the federal government's standing was continuously underminded by internal divisions, by bitter disagreement with its Country Party component and above all by its increasing commitment to a doctrinaire and outmoded foreign policy. The British government announced the withdrawal of all but token forces from the Indian Ocean and Southern Asia, but this only strengthened Holt's belief that Australia's military presence in the area should be increased. On 17 October 1967, when it had already become obvious that American public opinion was swinging massively against the war, Holt announced that his government would send another 1700 men, a tank squadron and several more helicopters to Vietnam, bringing the whole Australian force up to about 8000 men. Two months later, on Sunday 17 December, he was drowned in the surf near Portsea in his native Victoria. His friend L.B. Johnson and other heads of state came to the memorial service. The prime minister had always kept himself physically fit, working hard and playing hard. He entered the surf alone on a wild day, watched by a woman friend on the beach, and was never seen again. Some thought it shocking that the leader of the government could ever be unaccompanied by a retinue of aides and security guards, but other Australians felt a measure of gladness, despite the tragic circumstances, that they dwelt in a country where even the prime minister might still live his own private life, at least at weekends.

As deputy head of the coalition, Sir John McEwen, leader of the Country Party, was sworn in as prime minister for a few weeks while the Liberal parliamentarians contended for the vacant leadership of their party, and so for the prime ministership. Partly because McEwen let it be known that Country Party members would not accept office under Holt's deputy leader, William McMahon, but partly for other reasons, the Liberals chose their Senate leader, John Grey Gorton, as Holt's successor and he duly replaced McEwen as prime minister on 10 January 1968. Subsequently he was elected to the Lower House as the member for Holt's vacant Victorian seat.

Born in Melbourne in 1911, the new prime minister was a product of Geelong Grammar School and Brasenose College, Oxford. As a fighter pilot in the Royal Australian Air Force during World War II, he had served with distinction in Britain, Singapore, Darwin and Milne Bay. He had been severely wounded and was to carry the scars for the rest of his life. His face, reconstructed by plastic surgery, expressed at once toughness, good humour and devil-may-care challenge. When to this were added his height of 6 foot 2 inches (or 188 centimetres in the metric mensuration being introduced at the time), his rather gangling gait, casual dress and easy manners, it is easy to see why he was nicknamed "Jolly John" and why he possessed far more electoral appeal than any of his party rivals. It is doubtful whether any of them could have mixed as easily with his fellow citizens in street or pub as Holt had done and Gorton was to do.

On a nationwide television program a few days after his election to the Liberal leadership, he consciously contrasted himself with Menzies by saying, "Well, you might say I am Australian to my boot-heels". And indeed he was a nationalist and a centralist, but it was precisely these qualities which before long were to destroy his standing, not with the voters, but with his own party. In Australian history it is the Labor Party which has generally stood for Australian nationalism, while the more conservative non-Labor parties have just as generally — and naturally — stood for loyalty to, and dependence upon, the "mother country", or its surrogate overseas. As the conservative scholar, Dr Frank Knopfelmacher, wrote after the following election of 1969 when the Gorton government's majority was cut dramatically:

> the party of ex-colonial loyalists with no mother country to be loyal to is in a state of moral crisis and political paralysis . . . there seems to be nothing to replace the old, shrewd, imperial-colonial patriciate of the Menzies era.[4]

This was true, but Gorton and his conservative successors were plagued by problems more intractable than their own state of "moral crisis" and "political paralysis". A few months after he came to power, a worldwide youth revolt was both signalled and symbolised by an abortive revolution in Paris in the northern hemisphere spring of 1968. Students at the Sorbonne and other European universities protested vigorously at centuries of intolerable neglect and bad teaching. One eminent history professor boasted of supervising the work of fifty-six PhD students — in one afternoon a week for approximately half of each year.[5] The students in Paris were joined by other groups of young people and then by trade union and radical political organisations. President De Gaulle surrounded the capital with army tanks and for a time it seemed possible that Paris would again lead the world into revolution. No such thing happened of course, but the "Paris Spring" did influence fashions and attitudes among young people all over the world. In Australia during the long Menzies regime and until 1968, young people voted on the average far more conservatively than their elders: after that time they voted far more radically.

Students at universities and colleges of advanced education led the youth revolt. Professors and lecturers, who for a generation had deplored the conservatism and conformism of their charges, were suddenly disconcerted by students who refused to sit for traditional examinations, conducted anti-war and anti-racist demonstrations and, worst of all, addressed their mentors familiarly by their first names as though they were equals. Thousands of young Australians who had grown up to take for granted full employment and a measure of affluence, began to ask what it was all for. Young men began wearing long hair and beards. Both sexes dressed in the same drab or colourful clothes, or in few or no clothes at all. Consumption of marijuana, rather than of alcohol or tobacco, became a popular symbol of sophistication and liberation. For some members of the new generation, these manners were fashionable, for others they were merely outward signs of a serious questioning of assumptions on which society seemed to rest.

Many of them came from comfortable, conservative, middle-class homes. Freed of the need that had bound their ancestors to worry about earning a living, they asked what was the point of affluence in a world where warfare, greed and injustice still seemed to be accepted by constituted authority as part of the natural order of things. Some merely "dropped out" of conventional patterns of living: but a great many challenged traditionally hallowed policies far more directly than previous generations of young radicals had done. Often sceptical of the value of political action, the "new left" believed passionately in "confrontation" politics. By physically demonstrating – in schools, universities, government offices and the streets – their disapproval of war, racial discrimination and authoritiarianism, many believed they would hasten the day of "revolution". Few observers shared this belief, but the "youth revolt" did demonstrably help to speed up the rate of change within the existing social structure.

At his first press conference on 17 January, Gorton declared that no more Australian troops would be sent to Vietnam and gave a "doveish" impression on the issue. However, when the Vietcong launched their Tet offensive at the end of that month, he declared that Australia would fight on with America to the end. Then some of his ministers made most bellicose statements about the bombing of North Vietnam on the very eve of President Johnson's announcement on 31 March that he had ordered a bombing halt in the North, and that he would not be standing for re-election. Gorton was told of the first decision only on the same day it was announced to the world, and he learned of the second when he heard it on the radio. He and his government were embarrassed and angered by this cavalier treatment at the hands of their great ally, yet they continued, not without some vacillation on the prime minister's part, to be "more royalist than the King" on the issue. In May, legislation to put more teeth in the *National Service Act* was introduced into parliament. The major result was to provoke more massive demonstrations of dissent by trade unionists, students, creative artists and others opposed to the war. Then Gorton was again angered by his distant patron in Washington.

On 1 November 1968, President Johnson announced the cessation of all military action against North Vietnam. This time the Australian government was apparently informed, though hardly consulted on its views, only about twenty-four hours before the public statement. The American ambassador in Canberra had previously invited Mr Gorton to call in at any time. At some time after midnight, and after attending a Canberra press gallery dinner as guest of honour, he did so, accompanied by his press secretary and a 19-year-old woman journalist. Others present were his private secretary, Miss Ainslie Gotto, his host the American ambassador and an American attaché. The visitors stayed for about two hours, practically the whole of which time was spent by the prime minister and the woman journalist in private conversation apart from the others. There was a great furore when the facts were made known early in the New Year by a Liberal back-bencher, Mr Edward St John. Some surmised that

Gorton's rudeness had been deliberate – that he had set out thus to make plain his displeasure with the Americans' way of doing things – but even these apologists conceded that his choice of means was an unfortunate one. Others agreed with the righteous Mr St John's statement in parliament, that the incident exhibited a "standard of conduct" totally unacceptable in the nation's leader. Most, however, to judge from public opinion polls, were favourably impressed by his casual and spirited behaviour.

By May 1969, when Mr Gorton made his pilgrimage to Washington, all had apparently been forgotten and forgiven once more. Like Holt on an earlier occasion, he seemed to be over-awed and confused by the physical embodiment of American wealth and power. At a White House dinner he promised President Nixon that Australia would "go a-waltzing Matilda" with her great and powerful friend, a remark which drew derisive criticism even from conservative sections of the Australian press.

Thus by the time of the October 1969 general election, Gorton's suitability for leadership of the Liberal Party was being questioned by more and more of its members both inside and outside parliament. Despite, or because of, his vacillations, he seemed less than wholly and uncritically committed to the American alliance, and his free-wheeling, impulsive, individual style of governing struck many of his colleagues as too high a price to pay for his electoral appeal. During the campaign his minister for foreign affairs, a Western Australian named Freeth, hinted at the possibility of opening discussions with Russia about collective security in the Asian and Indian Ocean regions. No non-Labor spokesman since World War II had ever dreamt of entertaining such a thought, though by 1969 Britain had prepared to leave the region and America showed some signs of doing likewise. Gorton seemed, though equivocally, to be endorsing Freeth's initiative. In addition to his other troubles, he had developed a curiously repetitive, qualified and convoluted style of speaking, which was as hard to follow as it was easy to parody. A month before the election this led the North Sydney branch of the Liberal Party to resolve:

> We are of the opinion that our party, which cherishes the right of all members to freely express their views, cannot afford to be led by one who neither expresses his views clearly, nor appears to accept the official platform.

When preferences had been allocated, the coalition government's majority was reduced from forty seats to seven. Freeth was among the defeated Liberal members. Gorton was narrowly re-elected as party leader, but from this time on it seemed clear that he would sooner or later be displaced. Indeed, the minister for national development, an old schoolfellow from Geelong Grammar, Mr D.E. Fairbairn, a few days after the election publicly refused to serve under Gorton in the new cabinet.

During 1970 the prime minister lost further ground in the party room by pressing for national control of Australia's sea bed. This was a matter on which the Commonwealth constitution had nothing specific to say, since no one at the time of federation could have foreseen that rich fields of offshore oil and natural gas would one day be discovered and exploited. The government introduced legislation to give the Commonwealth clear sovereignty over the sea bed to the limits of the continental shelf. Gorton strongly backed the proposals, but was opposed by the state governments, by many of his own back-benchers and by the right-wing group in his own cabinet. The bill was shelved. The non-Labor parties have generally, though not always when in office in the states, been stronger advocates of state rights than have their opponents. In connection with this issue, Sir Robert Menzies, the retired Liberal elder statesman, damaged his reputation as a constitutional lawyer by claiming that "federalism", or support for state rights, was what distinguished the Liberal creed from "socialism", or strong central government. Thus Gorton alienated the support of more and more of his own colleagues.

In January 1971 he and William McMahon, the deputy party leader and minister for foreign affairs, flew to Singapore to attend a Commonwealth prime ministers' conference.

However, they made the journey in separate aeroplanes, stayed on different floors of the same hotel and reportedly had no communication with each other, except at some plenary sessions of the conference. The minister for foreign affairs had the greatest difficulty in finding out what took place at heads of government sessions.

On 8 March Mr Malcolm Fraser, nicknamed "the Prefect" by his colleagues, resigned as minister for the Army, telling parliament next day that Gorton had been disloyal to him and that,

> the Prime Minister, because of his unreasoned drive to get his own way, his obstinancy, impetuous and emotional reactions, has imposed strains upon the Liberal Party, the Government and the Public Service. I do not believe he is fit to hold the great office of Prime Minister, and I cannot serve in his Government.[6]

This was the end. At a meeting of Liberal Party parliamentarians on 10 March, two back-benchers moved a motion of confidence in Gorton's leadership. Thirty-three members voted for and thirty-three against the motion. With creditable grace, Gorton gave his casting vote against and ceased to be leader of the party and the government. McEwen having withdrawn his ban, the meeting then elected McMahon as party leader with Gorton as his deputy. The new cabinet was announced on 21 March.

Born in Sydney in 1908 and educated at Sydney Grammar School and the University of Sydney, William McMahon was – except for the "Labor rats", Cook, Hughes, and Lyons – the only Liberal Party prime minister in our history who was not a Victorian. A graduate in both Law and Economics, he had earned a good reputation as treasurer in the Holt government and had competently handled other portfolios; yet he was not of the stuff of which leaders are made. Diminutive in stature and slightly built, he had sharp and yet mouse-like features which were a cartoonist's delight. Deafness handicapped him in parliamentary debates, but even more at press conferences or on the hustings. He was a good party man who, unlike his predecessor, set out to compose differences and smooth over difficulties; but it seemed that these qualities, which brought him to the leadership, were not those needed to exercise it effectively. Sharpness, tact and a perspicacious nose for the sources of power were not enough in his new role. His twenty-one months as prime minister were characterised by procrastination, indecisiveness and counter-productive efforts to please everybody, including the Democratic Labor Party, on the conservative side of the house.

The point is well illustrated by his appalling relations with Gorton. Having been instrumental in the deposition of the former Liberal leader, McMahon made him minister for defence in the new cabinet, but forced his resignation from office five months later on the stated ground that press articles by Gorton had breached "basic principles of Cabinet solidarity and unity". Gorton soon afterwards referred to the prime minister as "Billy the Leak". Next time the two men spoke, in May 1972, it was reported that McMahon approached Gorton in the House when the bells were ringing and said, "John, I'd like you to sit and talk to me during the division". "Go to buggery," replied the former prime minister. Questioned later about the incident, Gorton was reported to have said,

Well – it was a bit of a journalistic beat-up, but it was near enough . . . He put his arm around me. And I don't like that. I don't like anyone putting their arm around me. And some are worse than others.[7]

It seemed that each of the three Liberal successors to Menzies was doomed to be progressively less effective than his predecessor. During 1971 the bill to give the Commonwealth control of the continental shelf was again brought forward and again shelved, because of dissension within the coalition, as happened yet again in 1972. Following President Nixon's announcement of America's withdrawal of her land forces from Vietnam, McMahon announced that Australia would follow suit, but naturally he received little credit for an action which had palpably been forced on the government by events beyond its control. Then, like his predecessors in office, he was severely embarrassed by a sudden switch in American policy.

In July, E.G. Whitlam, leader of the federal Labor opposition, visited China, and had a public exchange of views with

Zhou Enlai, the Chinese prime minister. For twenty-three years, faithfully following the American lead, Australian governments had refused to recognise diplomatically the existence of the Chinese mainland regime. McMahon, not the man for bold initiatives, denounced the Whitlam visit in unmeasured terms, claiming that he had put "personal notoriety before the national interests". A few days later the world learned that President Nixon was about to visit Peking and that his personal envoy, Henry Kissinger, had been there making the preliminary arrangements at the same time as Whitlam; but this time the loyal Australian allied government had not been given even a hint of what was afoot until after the event. This untoward incident did not visibly inhibit McMahon when he made his pilgrimage to Washington only three months later. At a state dinner in the White House he surpassed his two predecessors in incoherence, if not also in obsequiousness. Menzies, one felt, must have writhed at the manner, if not the matter, of these performances.

In the winter of 1971, a racially selected South African football team, "the Springboks", visited Australia and almost everywhere provoked massive demonstrations by students, trade-unionists and others deeply opposed to racist policies. Mr Bob Hawke, president of the Australian Council of Trade Unions, promised that boycotts would prevent the tour from proceeding and Mr McMahon promised to use the Royal Australian Air Force, if necessary, to see that it did. The tour did take place and RAAF planes were not used, but a good deal of police violence *was*, particularly in Queensland, where the Country Party premier of the state, Mr Joh Bjelke-Petersen, declared a "state of emergency".[8]

McMahon contemplated calling a general election in the belief that his stand on "keeping politics out of sport" would win many votes, but events during the tour made this a doubtful hypothesis. With the approach of summer, plans were mooted for a tour of Australia by an all-white South African cricket team. This time, the prime minister sought advice from the Australian Cricketing Board of Control. Its chairman, Sir Donald Bradman, a national sporting hero and in private life a conservative stockbroker, replied firmly that politics should indeed be kept out of sport as was notoriously not the case in South Africa, and that Australian sportsmen could help their white and black brethren in that country only by banning tours of racially selected teams. The government quietly accepted this advice but its paternalistic and *laissez-faire* attitude to race questions caused it further trouble.

Black Australians, as we have seen, were no longer content to be left alone. Some of them, recently counted as citizens for the first time in 180 years, set up an "Aboriginal Embassy" in tents on the shaven lawns in front of Parliament House in Canberra. They swore they would stay there to embarrass the government until it granted them "land rights" or until a new government was elected. They did remain for many months until the government was reduced to the indignity of gazetting a special ordinance to give itself legal power to have them removed.

However, Mr McMahon's troubles were most threatening in the very area where he was supposed to possess expertise – the state of the national economy. Ever since the great depression of the 1930s, Australian voters had demanded of all governments the maintenance of full employment. In the belief that business prosperity depended heavily on consumer spending power, employers were often quite as sensitive on the subject, as were employees. Thus, when in 1961 unemployment had been allowed to rise briefly above 2 per cent of the workforce, the conservative coalition (then led by Menzies at the height of his powers) had barely avoided defeat in the December elections of that year. Yet unemployment figures rose towards the end of 1971 and by July 1972 exceeded 2 per cent. Though this was a wonderfully low unemployment rate by American, Canadian or British standards, it was certainly a politically disastrous one in Australia, and despite repeated emergency measures and a spate of optimistic government forecasts, the figure remained in this vicinity right up till the general election.

Harassed by Labor on their left, by their DLP and Country Party allies on the right, and at odds amongst themselves, many Liberals became desperate. The election could not be postponed beyond the end of the year and successive public opinion polls spelt their doom. Faced with such impressive prime ministerial ineptitude, many remembered Gorton's strengths and forgot the not inconsiderable weaknesses which had helped to put him out of office. On the first Tuesday in November 1971, when he appeared at the Melbourne Cup, he received from the members' stand a spontaneous ovation of the kind usually awarded by Australians only to successful horses, jockeys or athletes. A "Get Gorton Back" committe sprang up, but when it came to the sticking point most Liberal politicians felt, probably correctly, that yet another change in leadership with the elections only months away would do their prospects more harm than good.

McMahon deferred until the last possible moment both the date of the poll and its public announcement. Before and during the campaign he shunned press conferences and "live" television appearances almost entirely – at first sight a puzzling course of action, but one which many of his strongest supporters applauded, such was his apparent genius for making verbal blunders when giving an unprepared speech. On 2 December 1972, the people of the Commonwealth elected a Labor government to power for the first time in a quarter of a century. Nothing became McMahon's prime ministership like his leaving of it. Late on that Saturday night when the electors' verdict was quite clear, he bowed out before the television cameras with a degree of dignity not conspicuous in him on so many other great occasions.

There were many reasons for the Labor victory, not the least of which were the glaring incapacity of their opponents and the apparent threat of rising unemployment. Many people, too, felt that, after twenty-three years of non-Labor rule, it was time for a change of government to preserve the healthy functioning of democracy; and Labor capitalised on this feeling with the slogan "It's time". Another factor which favoured Labor's victory at the polls was the growth of the women's liberation movement. Neither the movement nor a much more tightly organised body, the Women's Electoral

Lobby, declared support for any political party but, because Labor was seen as the party of change and innovation, it undoubtedly gained a great many women's votes. More importantly, from this time onward women began to take a much more active part in all political parties, both inside and outside parliament. In 1981 the National Conference of the ALP, meeting in Melbourne, resolved that for the future at least 25 per cent of all state delegations to this supreme governing body of the party must be women and, more vaguely, that by the end of a ten-year period at least 30 per cent of Labor parliamentary seats should be occupied by women.[9]

Contrary to the dictum of the Biblical preacher, the women's liberation movement *was* something new under the sun. Since time began, women in nearly all cultures known to us were treated as second-class people, not fully human in all respects and certainly not equal, either in rights or capacities, to the mighty males. In Australia for 50 000 years, black women were exploited and abused – were in fact regarded as a form of property by the men of the tribes. For nearly 200 years white women were treated in much the same way, though men often disguised this fact from themselves by acting chivalrously towards women, that is, by patronising, condescending to, and making allowances for the supposedly innate deficiencies of the "weaker vessels". It is appropriate therefore that the book which launched the movement for the liberation of all women, and the recognition of their equality with men, should have been written by an Australian. In 1970 an expatriate Australian lecturing in English literature at the University of Warwick, Dr Germaine Greer, published *The Female Eunuch*.

There had of course been earlier books about women's place in the modern world, books like Simone de Beauvoir's *Second Sex*, and there has been a spate of books on the subject since, but none of them was as well written, as influential or as devastatingly accurate in getting to the heart of the matter as *The Female Eunuch*. None of those written earlier *could* have been, because Greer's was the first major work to follow the widespread use of contraceptive pills. In the late 1960s, for the first time in human history, by abolishing the terrifying fear of unwanted pregnancies, "the pill" made it possible for women to exercise their sexuality as freely and fully as men had always done. Germaine Greer urged women to do just that – and to enjoy the consequent growth in self-respect and self-confidence whcih is rapidly according them at least equality with the other half of humanity. Many Australian women were quick to join the movement and most, except the most conservative, were more or less strongly affected by it. By 1968 sociological surveys showed that most Catholic women were using the pill despite the stern exhortation to the contrary issued by the Pope in July. Bishop Muldoon of Sydney, in newspaper interviews, stressed that the Holy Father's words, though not infallible and therefore not absolutely mandatory in this instance, were "only one step removed" from infallibility. This subtle male theological exegesis prompted Michelle Cronin, "a Catholic mother of two little children" to write to the *Sydney Morning Herald* seeking clarification. It sounded, she wrote, "like being one step removed from being pregnant. As any woman knows, that is very, very different from being pregnant".[10]

At the 2 December 1972 poll, Labor benefited also from the fact that conservative policies on foreign relations, race and associated questions, above all on the Vietnam War, had been overtaken by events. The world situation, public opinon, even the "conventional wisdom" of the time had changed, but the stance of the parties supporting the government had not. On most issues the Country Party, and even more the Democratic Labor Party, whose support was crucial to the government, were far to the right of many Liberal members. For example, Australian governments for many years had managed to negotiate the sale of enough wheat and wool to communist countries, especially China, to keep many Country Party voters solvent, if not always prosperous; yet these same governments opposed official recognition of mainland China even after Nixon's embarrassing *volte-face*. The vast majority of white Australians, as shown by the 1967 referendum of this subject, had long believed that they and their ancestors were guilty at the very least of 180 years' culpable neglect of the Aboriginal Australian people:[11] not so the Democratic Labor party. During the election campaign, Senator J.A. Little put forward that party's view of the matter in terms that managed to be at once irrational, obscure and reactionary. He said:

> Nobody who has fairly considered the history of this country could say that the Australian aborigines, any more than the animal species of this disappearing continent before the white man came, would have survived through to this generation, had it not been for the intervention of the white people, bringing the knowledge and the skills of Europe with them which enabled them to tackle the deteriorating environment of this country and make of it what it is today.[12]

Labor promised that, if elected, it would abolish fees at universities and other tertiary institutions, and spend a great deal more money on primary and secondary education, while abolishing, or scaling down, financial grants to wealthy private schools. Thus the Labor Party, without sacrificing its trade union base, broadened its policies to attract support from large numbers of middle-class liberals (with a small "L") and young people, students, artists, nationalists, intellectuals, white-collar workers and professional people, and even a number of businessmen dissatisfied with the Liberals' management of the economy. More than any other person, the man responsible for this transformation was Edward Gough Whitlam, who had succeeded Arthur Calwell as federal leader of the Parliamentary Labor Party early in 1967. Son of a senior Commonwealth public servant, Whitlam was born in Melbourne in 1916, and brought up in Canberra and Sydney. Educated in both state and private schools, he graduated in Arts and Law from the University of Sydney, and served during the war as a flight-lieutenant in the Royal Australian Air Force from 1941 to 1945. After a brief but successful career at the bar, he entered the federal parliament in 1952 as a member for the safe Labor seat of Werriwa in Sydney's outer suburban area.

Whitlam was something of a classical and historical scholar. He read widely and used both the written and spoken word clearly and persuasively. He had a ready and devastating wit, as many an interjector found to their cost. An imposing 193 centimetres (6 feet 4 inches) in height, and with a commanding presence, he looked the part of a prime minister. Indeed, it was often remarked that he established a sort of moral domination in the house of representatives while he and his party were in opposition, especially during the McMahon government's tenure of office. His wife Margaret, daughter of a distinguished judge of the Supreme Court of New South Wales, was quite as intelligent as her husband and probably even better at relating to all kinds of people. Certainly no other Australian prime minister ever had such a publicly active and helpful spouse. With all these great gifts were joined two notable weaknesses. Like Menzies, with whom he was often compared by friend and foe alike, he too easily exhibited a broad streak of arrogance, or at best of unpleasant complacency. The other weakness was peculiarly his own. In rare moments of stress or frustration, he was apt to lose his temper, lashing out blindly at opponents with word and gesture and, for the moment, quite reckless of the consequences.[13] Thus in September 1965, as deputy leader of the opposition, he was speaking in the house to an amendment to a government repatriation bill. The Labor amendment sought to extend full repatriation benefits to Salvation Army personnel who had served in the armed forces. With questionable taste, Mr Whitlam challenged the then minister for external affairs, Mr Paul Hasluck, to deny justice to his Salvation Army parents by opposing the amendment. Hasluck replied, apparently too quietly for the speaker to hear him, "You are one of the filthiest objects ever to come into this chamber"; whereupon Whitlam threw the contents of a glass of water in the minister's face. Both men then complied with the speaker's demand for apologies.

Within a few hours of the time when the overall national electoral verdict became clear, Whitlam and his deputy leader, the Tasmanian Lance Barnard, were sworn in respectively as prime minister and minister for foreign affairs and as minister for defence, by the governor-general, Sir Paul

Hasluck. History does not record whether reference was made to parliamentary water sports on this occasion. Not until preference votes had been allocated and the final result determined in all seats could the Labor Caucus meet to select the full cabinet, which was sworn in on 19 December 1972, after what some sourly called the duumvirate had begun giving effect to some of Labor's election promises. A new wind, which most found invigorating but some alarming, blew through Canberra's corridors of power. It may be doubted whether there is a precedent in the history of British-style democratic governments anywhere for the promptitude with which the new government implemented so many of its campaign promises.

Within a month of election it had ended the lottery of conscription for military service and released gaoled draft-resisters, negotiated an exchange of ambassadors with China, abolished race or skin colour as a criterion of Australia's immigration policy, banned racially selected sports teams from our soil, begun planning a new deal, including the grant of land rights, for the Aboriginal people, revalued the Australian dollar upwards, set about the reform of the national health service and of the divorce laws, moved to support equal pay for equal work for women, increased unemployment monies paid to the state governments, banned the slaughter of the nearly extinct Australian crocodile and the export of its skin and of kangaroo skins, steeply increased subsidies to the arts, put the contraceptive pill on the medical benefits list and abolished what Mrs Whitlam happily referred to as the "entertainment tax" on it, and abolished the excise, first introduced by the Gorton government, on unfortified wine. It also abolished the conferring of knighthoods and other British titles, as the Canadians had done a generation earlier, and instituted instead the Order of Australia whose members were to take precedence over holders of all other decorations whatsoever. For a time many Labor supporters were almost equally amazed and delighted, while opponents were seemingly bemused, by the authority, the confidence and the speed with which the new government set about making up for its twenty-three years in the wilderness.

In the nature of things, this euphoric situation for Labor could not continue indefinitely. Not all members of the complete Labor cabinet, elected by caucus two weeks after the election, worked together as harmoniously as Whitlam and Barnard had done. There were signs, quickly suppressed, that after twenty-three years of implementing Liberal-Country Party policies, some senior public servants were less than happy and efficient in the service of their new masters. The situation was particularly bad in the Australian Security Intelligence Organisation (ASIO) − a secret police body supposedly responsible to the new attorney-general, Senator Lionel Murphy, and to the prime minister. On 16 September 1972, under the previous government, bombs had been detonated outside Yugoslav tourist agencies in Sydney and sixteen innocent bystanders had been seriously injured. The criminals were widely believed to belong to a Croat terrorist organisation, the Ustashi, which had collaborated with the Nazis during World War II, but the Liberal attorney-general, Senator Ivor Greenwood, vehemently asserted that his ASIO spies denied the existence of any Croation terrorist organisation whatever in Australia. Six months later, in March 1973, the Yugoslav prime minister was to visit us. Concern for his safety, and worry about ASIO's ability to see sedition on the right after so long a period looking for it on the left, increased Murphy's worries. Then he found that the head of ASIO had met secretly with other senior departmental heads and come to an agreement that no statement would be made by any of them in such a form as to contradict official statements made by a department under the previous government. Murphy would have been unpardonably naive not to suppress this grossly disloyal behaviour in the chief spy. Accordingly, with a party of Commonwealth police, he made an unannounced early morning visit to ASIO headquarters in Melbourne, seeking more evidence of its insubordinate and dubious manoeuvres. Murphy's attempt to enforce proper constitutional behaviour among his subordinates was painted by the news media as a wild-eyed attack on the "security services".[14] Douglas Anthony, deputy leader of the opposition parties, made in this connection the astounding statement that the security services ought not to be responsible to any politician or, presumably, to anyone but themselves. The whole episode was labelled by the media, "Murphy's raid". It was the first, but by no means the last, indication that some conservatives were prepared to tear up the constitution and to undermine democracy itself in their efforts to regain power.

The government's greatest constitutional problem was the fact that its members constituted only a minority of the upper house. Again and again the majority of Liberal, Country Party and DLP senators amended or rejected bills, embodying Labor legislation which had been explicitly promised in the prime minister's policy speech. One of these bills sought to establish a minerals and energy authority with power to exploit oil and other minerals in the national interest. Conservatives naturally saw this as an attack on the sacred principle of private enterprise. Two other rejected bills sought to set up a comprehensive national health service, to be financed from taxation, along the lines of the British and New Zealand health services established about a quarter of a century earlier. These bills were attacked by medical trade unions (professional associations), and rejected by Opposition senators on the same ground. The third group of bills sought to make the electoral system more democratic, or at any rate more equal, as promised in Whitlam's policy speech. Under the existing system the number of voters or persons in federal electorates could vary by up to plus or minus 20 per cent of the average figure. This had long meant in practice that on the average city electorates were very much larger than country ones – so much so that in some cases a city person's vote could count for little more than half as much as a country dweller's. In senate elections the position was worse. In 1901 there had been no federal capital territory, and only a handful of voters in the Northern Territory, and so the constitution made no provisions for them. By 1974 Canberra's population was about 160 000 and the Northern Territory's population was approximately half that number. To many it seemed anomalous, not to say undemocratic, that all these citizens should have no vote for the Senate and none in national referenda: yet the Opposition rejected bills designed to rectify the situation because it seemed likely that their enactment would be disadvantageous to the Country Party.

There was much talk of going to the people again through the medium of a double dissolution. Labor leaders felt confident, but in the end it was the conservative opposition parties which forced an election for both houses of parliament. After its defeat in the 1972 general election, the Liberal Party had lost no time in dismissing McMahon from its leadership; however, his successor, Mr Billy Snedden, at first seemed hardly more impressive. He apparently shared with most other opposition politicians the belief that the electorate wanted them back on the treasury benches. To a degree they appeared to believe their own rhetoric, as when they declared that the Labor government had antagonised the United States and other old friends by recognising China and withdrawing troops from Southeast Asia; but since the United States was itself engaged in the same manoeuvres, few voters were impressed.

So in April 1974 Her Australian Majesty's loyal opposition behaved more like a gang of fascist thugs than responsible politicians in a democratic country. They threatened to use their Senate majority to withhold supply to the government. Not even in the depths of the great depression, when the state of Australia was incomparably worse, had the opposition-controlled Senate even contemplated such a step. Many constitutional lawyers held that the fact that the Senate had never blocked supply during the whole seventy-four years of its existence established a binding precedent and proved that it had no power to do so. Yet Snedden's henchmen in the upper house carried the threat through to the point where Whitlam was virtually forced to seek a double dissolution eighteen months before an election should have been necessary. The immediate reason advanced was that the DLP

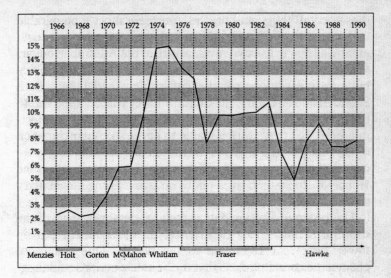

Figure 24 Inflation rate from 1966 to 1990

leader, Senator Gair, had just accepted from his political opponents, the Labor government, an appointment as Australian Ambassador to Eire. Of course, the government had hoped to gain another Senate seat as a result of Gair's resignation. Most people thought the incident reflected more discredit on the new ambassador than on the government, and that it certainly constituted no crisis of any sort, let alone one sufficiently serious to justify refusal of supply.

In any case, the incident was virtually forgotten during the ensuing election campaign. The prime minister again called on the governor-general, Sir Paul Hasluck, and asked him to dissolve both houses because of the Senate's failure to pass the electoral, health and minerals authority bills. Whitlam announced that the election would be held on 18 May. Labor appealed for "a fair go" on the grounds that the Senate had obstructed the will of the people. The Opposition parties concentrated on inflation, which had risen to the rate of 14 per cent per annum in the past year. Labor spokesmen replied that Australia's inflation rate was falling more rapidly than those in all but one of the fourteen most comparable "advanced" countries of the world, and that this improvement was due to the two revaluations of the Australian dollar, to the courageous 25 per cent tariff cut and to other salutary but unpopular measures the government had taken. Both Snedden and Anthony, the Country Party leader, appealed to the nation to return the country to its "right course" by electing them, but they were not able to agree so convincingly on other policy matters. When the tumult and the shouting were over, Labor was returned with the loss of only two seats in the House of Representatives and with twenty-nine out of sixty seats in the Senate.[15]

On the same election day, in a signal demonstration of the triumph of hope over experience, the government put no fewer than four referenda to the people. One sought to change the constitution so that the Senate elections could regularly be held on the same days as those for the House of Representatives. The second sought to give citizens of the Northern Territory and the ACT a vote in referenda and to allow constitutional changes to be made by a majority of all voters and a majority of voters in three of the six states, instead of four. The third sought to write into the constitution a provision that in federal and state elections all electorates should be approximately equal in population so that votes would be of approximately equal value, and that all houses of parliament should be directly elected by the people. The fourth sought power for the federal government to grant money directly to local government bodies, previously an exclusively state government function. As usual, all four questions were decisively negatived.

By mid-1975, the Labor government had brought about some important changes in Australian life which were likely to be enduring. The "white Australia" policy, at least in its historically rigid and insulting form, had been ended. Justice for Aboriginal Australians was unlikely ever again to be completely neglected as it had been in the past and Papua New Guinea had become an independent nation. Women's legal and social rights had been increased.

It was less likely that the abolition of tuition fees in tertiary educational institutions and the tax-funded, comprehensive national health service, Medibank, would survive future conservative assaults. A private members' bill, drafted by Lionel Murphy, and supported by most Labor, some Liberal and no Country Party members, had greatly simplified the divorce law. It recognised only one ground for divorce — irretrievable breakdown of a marriage. Political and "moral" (i.e. sexual) censorship had been almost abolished and the sniff of the wowser muted everywhere exept in Joh Bjelke-Petersen's Queensland. Finally, Australian foreign policy was unlikely to revert to the unquestionably subservient neo-colonial stance it had held for so long under the Liberals. The American alliance would continue; but future governments of any complexion were more likely to continue the nationalist Labor policy of cultivating good relations also with other powers, particularly those in Asia. Despite these achievements, the government's electoral support declined during the year as inflation and unemployment rates increased. In March the Liberals deprived Labor of its greatest electoral asset by deposing the disastrous Billy Snedden and installing Malcolm Fraser to lead them. A vicious press campaign smeared the government with allegations of corruption in its attempts to raise overseas loans. Not a penny had changed hands improperly, but much of the mud stuck to its target. Then many political gangsters on the conservative side of politics, to bring down the government they hated, began flouting the traditions, conventions and precedents on which democracy itself depends.

One Labor senator died and another, Lionel Murphy, retired to the High Court. By long-established convention they should have been replaced by party colleagues, formally nominated by the governments of their respective states. Instead, the premiers of New South Wales and Queensland disgraced themselves and their office by appointing "neutral" or anti-Labor senators to the temporary vacancies. The governor of Queensland, Sir Colin Hannah, flagrantly breached the ancient tradition that the Crown must be seen to be politically

impartial with a grossly partisan and quite gratuitous attack
on the federal ALP. Finally the LCP Senate majority again
broke precedent by deferring consideration of supply bills.
The government began to run out of money for essential services.

Under the vaguely defined provisions of the written constitution, the new governor-general, Sir John Kerr, could have
resolved the crisis in a number of ways. By all known rules of
precedent and tradition in Westminster-style government, he
should have resolved it on the advice of his prime minister. So
far from doing that, he actively deceived Whitlam and other
senior ministers as to his intentions, was seen to be conspiring with the Leader of the Opposition, and then dismissed the
Whitlam government on 11 November.

The manner of the dismissal suggests that the Queen's
representative harboured inner qualms about the legality, not
to mention the honourableness, of his own actions. Before ad-
ministering the *coup-de-grâce* from a prepared ambush, he
took great pains to get in writing the support of the Chief Justice of the High Court of Australia, the Right Honourable Sir
Garfield Edward John Barwick, like himself and so many
other prominent citizens, a product of Fort Street Boys' High
School. As the Liberal Party's MP for Parramatta from 1958
to 1964, Barwick had served Menzies in succession as Commonwealth attorney-general and minister for external affairs.
His elevation to the High Court was seen by some political observers as one more instance of Sir Robert's adroitness in
kicking rivals upstairs before they could challenge him for
the party leadership. By others it was seen simply as the fitting culmination to the career of an eminent jurist who would,
of course, magically put off a lifetime's political prejudice the
moment he put on his judicial robes.

On the day before the dismissal, this man lunched at Admiralty House with the governor-general, secretly and contrary
to specific advice given him by Whitlam. He was asked first
whether it was constitutionally proper for the governor-general to seek advice from the chief justice. Though this was a
political or historical query on which the Constitution has

nothing whatever to say, and was not a legal question, Barwick unhesitatingly answered, "Yes".

Kerr then asked Barwick whether his proposal to sack, without warning, his chief adviser the prime minister was consistent with his powers and duties under the Australian Constitution. Again the highest legal authority answered yes because, he said, "A government having the confidence of the House of Representatives but not that of the Senate, both elected Houses, cannot secure Supply to the Crown." This too was not a legal judgment, but a doubly political one. First, the government was still in fact securing supplies to pay government contractors, public servants and so on. Second, even if it had been true, inability to obtain supply from a recalcitrant upper house is no reason for resignation or dismissal of a prime minister. As Geoffrey Sawer, sometime Professor of Law at the Australian National University, wrote:

> On no previous occasion in Britain, Australia or any British-derived parliamentary system has the Monarch or a Governor-General dismissed a ministry having a majority in the Commons, Representatives or similar House, because that ministry has been denied supply by the Lords, Senate or similar House.[16]

Throughout their lunchtime discussion, both judge and viceroy assured themselves and each other that they were guided purely by legal, not political, considerations. Manifestly they were not.

The events of Remembrance Day 1975 were widely spoken of as "Kerr's Coup" and respect for the vice-regal office and its incumbent slumped disastrously. Opinion polls showed that most people strongly disapproved the Senate's blocking of supply, and Kerr's departure from the high traditions of his office. "Nugget" Coombs, the great public servant, and Patrick White, the literary genius, resigned from the Order of Australia since Kerr was its head. Not all Australians behaved with such dignity, however. The newly installed Liberal–Country Party government soon restored the distribution of British honours to Australian life. One of the first new knights created in 1976 was Sir John Egerton, previously for twenty years better known as Jack Egerton, president of the Queensland Trades and Labor Council. His notion of human dignity differed from that of Coombs and White and that held by James Cook two hundred years earlier. To receive his imperial bauble, he knelt subserviently, in the traditional manner, at the feet of the egregious Kerr.

It is ironic that all this frenetically larrikin behaviour by the conservative parties and the viceroy for whom at this time they and their leader, Malcolm Fraser, professed such profound respect, was quite unnecessary to their purpose – the grasping of power and perquisites for themselves. Throughout the year, unemployment had gripped well over 4 per cent of the workforce, a situation far worse than anything Australians had known since the great depression of the 1930s. At the same time the rate of inflation had climbed to an unprecedented 15 per cent per annum. Either figure alone would have been enough to secure the defeat at the polls of any Australian government elected since 1943. When at the general election following the coup, the Liberal–Country Party candidates promised to cure unemployment and inflation, they were returned to power with massive majorities in both houses.

Thoughtful people, including many who usually voted Liberal, were appalled at the irony of events. By ignoring 150 years of tradition and precedent, and choosing to act on the one possible interpretation of the written document which most favoured the conservative forces, Kerr had, in the words of one newspaper correspondent, "procured the prostitution of the Australian constitution". British and Australian legal tradition itself assumes that the popular vote, at an election subsequent to the dismissal of a government by the sovereign or her representative, either confirms or denies the legality of the vice-regal action. In fact, though most voters held Kerr's coup in abhorrence, they voted the Fraser government into power for quite other reasons.

One of the new Liberal–National Party government's first actions was to restore the superphosphate bounty, a subsidy to farmers which, in the last year before its abolition by

Labor, had been worth about $5000 to the new prime minister. Malcolm Fraser was the first of a new generation of prime ministers, too young to have been eligible for service in World War II. Born in 1930 into a wealthy Victorian Western District family and educated at Melbourne Grammar School and Oxford University, Fraser was nicknamed "the Prefect" by his political friends and "the crazy grazier" by his enemies. After the 1975 election, most people called him "Big Mal" or "Mad Mal". His long, thin, lugubrious face reminded many cartoonists and writers of "one of those po-faced, top-hatted idols on Easter Island". Tall, lean and disdainful in manner, he spoke with a pseudo-English upper-class accent that infuriated many ordinary people and ensured his continuing personal unpopularity with the electorate; yet the success of his policies ensured his continuing domination of his party and the country.

His cabinet made huge cuts in every kind of expenditure except defence and incentives to business and farming interests. In an apparent effort to recompense governors-general for the onerousness of their duties, salaries and expenditure incidental to the governor-general's office were increased in the Fraser government's first budget by an astounding 171 per cent. Funding of the most notorious secret police body, ASIO, which seemed to have helped in the coup, was also increased vastly.

By contrast, spending on less privileged sections of the community was cut heavily. Despite promises to the contrary, the Medibank health scheme was effectively dismantled. Real salaries and conditions in the public service worsened. Less and less government money was available for kindergartens, schools and universities, but more and more for the already wealthy private secondary schools. Those whose needs were greatest – Aborigines, the unemployed, the poor, the sick, the old, women and children – suffered most.

In spite, or because, of these drastic measures, the economy continued to be as sluggish as it had been under the Labor government. In fact the unemployment rate, 4.4 per cent when Fraser had been made prime minister by the governor-general in November 1975, was 5.8 per cent two years later in 1977. This record alone would have ensured electoral disaster for any Australian government before the coup, but most previous governments had not had to cope with inflation. According to figures supplied by the World Organisation for Economic Co-operation and Development, the inflation rate for 1977 had fallen slightly – to 13.1 per cent – but the government claimed that the true figure for the calendar year would be 9 per cent. In either case, the Liberal and National Parties could claim to have brought inflation under control, even at the cost of increasing unemployment. Fraser decided to call a general election a full year before it was due and before unemployment grew worse. In New Delhi in February 1975 Sir John Kerr had publicly said that a governor-general should not grant an election to a prime minister unless he could "be satisfied that Parliament [had], in fact, become unworkable". In view of this, would he, could he, asked some ingenuous citizens, grant a double dissolution to the government with a massive majority in both houses? Only these few were surprised when, despite his Delhi pronouncement, he obligingly granted a double dissolution that Fraser wanted purely for party political advantage.

On Tuesday 1 November 1977, *Gold and Black* won the Melbourne Cup. By tradition, not by force of any legal document, the cup was presented to the owner of the winning horse by the governor-general. Dressed ridiculously, as he always was in public, in a full morning suit and gleaming top hat, Kerr was driven once round the Flemington racecourse to acknowledge, as his predecessors had done for three-quarters of a century, the good-humoured cheers and banter of the crowd. Instead he was greeted by a storm of boos, jeers and hooting which rose in intensity until he reached the more refined air of the members' stand. There his progress was marked by a mingling of muted abuse and tepid applause. After the race, when he lurched down the steps of the grandstand to present the Cup, jeers and catcalls drowned out the applause, and much of Kerr's rambling, emotional and rather incoherent speech. To most of the six million people watching on their television screens it seemed painfully clear that the Queen's representative in Australia, the man whose prime function it was to embody the dignity of the nation, was querulously drunk. Next day, in the Upper House at Canberra, Senator Walsh (Labor) said:

> Any public servant who appeared, in discharging his duties in public, drunk would face disciplinary action . . . I wish to know what will happen to the Governor-General because of his disgusting drunken performance at Flemington yesterday.[17]

The deputy president of the Senate forced Walsh to withdraw his words, though he and all other speakers did not attempt to deny the truth of the Western Australian senator's statement. The prime minister, it seemed, no longer had any great respect for his benefactor, but having, like Shakespeare's Caesar, attained the upmost round, he scorned "the base degrees by which he did ascend". He terminated Kerr's appointment and sent him to a post as Australian Ambassador to the United Nations Education, Scientific and Cultural Organisation in Europe. But this well-paid sinecure was too much even for many Liberal politicans. A storm of public protest resulted in Kerr's being left in exile, like Joseph Furphy's hero, "unemployed at last",[18] but not unprovided for.

Five weeks after the most remarkable Melbourne Cup in our history, the federal election of 10 December 1977 resulted in a resounding victory for the Liberal–National Party coalition, which won eighty-six seats to Labor's thirty-eight. Those watching on television saw Gough Whitlam, with his customary dignity, announce his resignation from the leadership of the ALP. The government's huge majority had been confirmed, the prime minister's political judgment vindicated, and the country replaced firmly on what he kept calling the "right" and "appropriate" course. Most electors apparently shared his insouciance about the miseries of the unemployed, provided only that inflation continued to be reduced or at least controlled. However unpopular he personally might remain with the people, his standing and his authority within his own party and the coalition rivalled those of Menzies at the height of his powers. The new parliament was allowed to run its full term and Malcolm Fraser's leadership of the nation was again endorsed in October 1980. It is time to ask why. What positive benefits of his five years of government were perceived by the electors, to most of whom "the Prefect" sternly dispensed such nasty medicine?

It is important to notice first that the bitter physic kept on coming. For six years in real terms, that is in terms of the purchasing power of money whose value decreased in that time by almost half, every budget found less than its predecessor for all those areas of national life humane people thought most worthwhile. The real value of payments to the aged, the sick, to widows and deserted wives, to war veterans, the unemployed and others in need, fell year by year. So did the amount of money made available to schools, colleges of advanced education and universities with the inevitable result that redundant teachers, and students who left understaffed institutions without finishing their courses, helped to swell the ranks of the workless. Not only formal educational institutions were affected. The Whitlam government had spent as much money on direct and indirect subsidies to literature, painting, the other arts and research of all kinds as had long been spent on such things in Canada and other civilised countries. Year by year, Fraser's government cut back spending in these areas too and even on that sacred cow of national life, the CSIRO. Payments to tertiary students, artists and others were reduced annually – again in real terms – while more stringent means tests and other qualifying conditions reduced the number of beneficiaries. Free medical and hospital care, except for the very poor, was abolished, while the cost of these things rose steeply for everyone else. A wide range of community health centres, childcare services, women's shelters and rape crisis centres had been established during the three years of federal Labor rule: these curtailed their activities and sometimes closed altogether as the parsimonious government tightened the financial screws.

Boat-loads of anti-communist Vietnamese refugees, "the

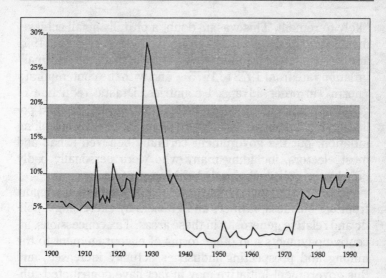

Figure 25 Unemployment since 1900

boat people", kept arriving at Darwin and other northern ports. This made greater than ever the need for organisations devoted to helping the assimilation of immigrants of different ethnic backgrounds, bodies like the Good Neighbour Council set up in Arthur Calwell's day, but less and less money was devoted to such purposes. Black Australians suffered most, as they had done for 190 years, from the latest conservative reaction among the whites. The Whitlam government had established a government department and a host of minor instrumentalities to advise and help Aborigines. These bodies were by no means exempted from Fraser's general policy of curtailing spending on all forms of social welfare.

Again, then, what benefits were perceived by the majority of Australians who continued to vote for the Liberal–National Party coalition, despite such massive provocation to a contrary course? Undoubtedly the main motive was control of inflation. Standing at about 15 per cent a year when Fraser was ushered into power in 1975, by the time of the 1980 election this figure had fallen to about 10 per cent – where it seemed likely to remain. This was no doubt a pitifully small achievement compared with the "normal" situation between 1955 and 1970, but it was impressive compared with the "normal" inflation rate from 1972 to 1975 – and with the contemporary "norm" in other advanced countries. Drastic reduction of government spending on everything except defence and police spying may have had little to do, in fact, with controlling inflation, but the government certainly believed it had and most electors, including many who were personally badly hurt by the policy, obviously believed so too.

Secondly the government retained its traditional support from big business, farmers and graziers by exercising a politic and relative generosity in these areas. Tax concessions, incentive payments and other forms of encouragement to the mining and prospecting industries actually increased, and this government initiative may in fact have contributed substantially to what was known as the resources boom during the Fraser years. Vast quantities of coal, iron, aluminium, oil, uranium and other ores were dragged out of the continent and shipped overseas, thus strengthening greatly the Australian currency and balance of payments position. Again the government, and most of the people who elected it, were certain that this boom was somehow good for Australia. Others protested that a great and rapidly growing part of the ownership of the mining industry was in foreign hands, and that it could not be good to give away most of the national estate to foreigners at bargain-basement rates. In July 1981, even the senior public servants in the treasurer's department were worried to discover that six billion dollars of foreign capital had been invested in Australia in the twelve months just ended, as against something over one billion in the previous year; but "Big Mal" was delighted with the praise just heaped upon him by his properly grateful American business hosts.[19]

Nevertheless, Fraser's performance abroad won him a kind of grudging respect even from those most opposed to all he did at home. Like Menzies and Whitlam, but unlike Holt, McMahon and Gorton, he conducted himself with dignity in public, especially during his obligatory pilgrimages to Washington. Furthermore, his foreign policy, unlike that of every previous conservative prime minister, was at least intelligible and even intelligent. Though he fully shared the paranoid delusions about the USSR of most "Western" leaders, he did not, as they did, lump all communist powers together as parts of a malign and monolithic force. On the contrary, one of his first actions after the 1975 election was to make a visit to mainland China to cement good relations with that country. Millions too respected his outspoken abhorrence of racist ideology. Detractors might suggest this attitude sprang from the fact that his mother was a Melbourne Jewess, or that he believed Russian communism would take over majority black African areas if the indigenous people did not; but there was no doubt of Fraser's passionate sincerity. He spoke freely of "the obscenity of racism" and at a Commonwealth conference in 1979, to the consternation of many who had voted for him, Fraser was instrumental in securing, peacefully, majority black rule for Rhodesia under its new name of Zimbabwe.

He did nothing, however, for the black people of Australia, particularly for those unfortunate enough to live in Queensland or Western Australia, states controlled during the Fraser years by Liberal–National coalitions. In the remote Kimberley district, for instance, though black Australians were no longer butchered by policemen as they had been only fifty years earlier,[20] they were still exploited, abused and sometimes disfranchised by the conservative state government. The Western Australian state election of February 1977 showed that, despite all the progress that had been made since the Aboriginal referendum of ten years earlier, the most vicious form of white Australian racism was still active among those who considered themselves the best people in the country. On polling day, the white Liberal cabinet minister, Alan Ridge, defeated the black Labor candidate, Ernie Bridge, by 1784 to 1691 votes. In May, Bridge appealed to the Court of Disputed Returns which, in due course, laid bare a story of Liberal Party fraud and intimidation which would have been quite incredible anywhere in Australia in 1977 –

except in Joh Bjelke-Petersen's Queensland and Sir Charles Court's Western Australia.

Before the election, Liberal supporters feared that the Labor candidate might win. So, at considerable expense, Ridge and the state Liberal Party, with the connivance of some government officials, sent five lawyers to the Kimberley electorate with instructions, in effect, to prevent as many black citizens as possible from voting. At some polling booths the Liberal lawyers bluffed local officials into accepting their interpretation of the meaning of the *Electoral Act*, a meaning which of course had the effect of denying the vote to many Aborigines. At other places the lawyers or their friends treated would-be Aboriginal voters to such vast quantities of alcohol that they could not walk into the polling booths. At still other places local white supporters of Ridge simply intimidated Aboriginal voters.

The most appalling part of the story is that, when the court had given its findings, neither Ridge nor any of the other Liberals who had conspired to subvert the democratic processes of their state was punished in any way. Not only that, but the government of Sir Charles Court immediately brought forward a bill to amend the *Electoral Act* in such a way as to rob many illiterate Aborigines of the vote altogether. Not all the conservative politicians in the house disgraced themselves. Four of six National party members crossed the floor to vote with the Labor members against the amendments. One Liberal, Dr G.T. Dadour, without casting his vote, left the Chamber with the moving words, "I know I have to live with myself for probably another 10 or 20 years". Then the speaker, Mr Ian Thompson, gave his casting vote with the "No's" to defeat the amendment. At the subsequent by-election, held under the old rules, Ridge was returned honestly to the seat,[21] but at the next general election of 1980 he was decisively defeated by the Labor candidate, Ernie Bridge, Aboriginal station owner, stockman and country music singer.

Despite the best efforts of those who regarded themselves as its best people, times were changing in the Kimberley district much more than was evident in the nation as a whole. By seeking to reform too much too fast, the Whitlam government had scared conservative voters and back-stage power-brokers out of their scanty wits. Swinging voters too had been badly frightened – if not by Labor efforts at reform, by the panic surrounding Kerr's coup. So people elected the Fraser government to give them, above all, not change or reform of any kind but respectability and stability; and for seven years the prime minister almost succeeded in his avowed ambition, to govern so quietly that political news would be replaced in the headlines by sporting intelligence. One of the few events to break the post-prandial political torpor of that time occurred in the last week of April 1980.

The nationally respected Melbourne *Age* reported on Saturday 29 April that the chief justice of the High Court, Sir Garfield Barwick, had, without declaring his interest, been sitting in judgment on cases brought to litigation by wealthy corporations in which Barwick's own private family company had shares. Mundroola Pty Ltd had been incorporated in 1946, apparently as a means of reducing Barwick's income tax payments by making over a large sum to his two children. In 1973 his wife owned 850 shares in the company, her son Ross, her daughter Dianne and her husband Garfield one each. An old friend of the already eminent QC, Mr Leslie James Thompson, held "4000 deferred non-voting and non-management shares". Thompson also became chairman of Ampol Petroleum and a director of Brambles Ltd and the "sugar, chemicals and mining conglomerate CSR", all companies in which Mundroola had made lucrative investments. In the fifteen-year period to 1980, Sir Garfield (as head of three- or five-judge High Court benches) heard six appeals from the three companies on matters ranging from personal injury damages to income tax assessments. The appellant companies lost four of the six cases and won two. No one ever alleged that the chief justice, in hearing the cases, had acted other than impartially, but the media and Labor members of parliament did ask persistently why he had not declared his interest or possible conflict of interest. Four years earlier he had, in another case, emphatically declared his agreement with the ancient rule of British Law that: "A judge should not sit to hear a case if in all the circumstances the parties or the public might reasonably suspect that he was not un-prejudiced and impartial." Over the weekend, many thought that the chief justice would be forced to resign, but he easily avoided that course by breaking another venerable rule of law — delivering judgment on his own case. He pronounced himself innocent of a misdemeanour of which he had never been accused. When parliamentary sittings resumed on Tuesday morning, the prime minister tabled a letter from Barwick which, with mind-boggling disingenuousness, stated, "I feel sure that no informed and fair-minded person would have honestly thought that my views might have been influenced by the fact that my adult children beneficially owned shares in the litigant company." As though God had spoken, the political tempest stilled. No one had the bad taste to ask why Sir Garfield's "parties [to the case] or the public" had silently been transformed into one "informed and fair-minded person", or why his long letter so resolutely refrained from mentioning even the appearance of any possible conflict of interest.

During the spring and summer of 1982–83, the auspices showed that Fraser's conservative coalition government seemed to be on its last legs. To an unusual extent it was hoist on its own petard. In 1980, to discredit its political enemies according to ALP spokespersons, the government appointed F.X. Costigan QC, a one-man Royal Commission, to inquire into the affairs of the notoriously corrupt Painters' and Dockers' Union. Costigan's report confirmed that indeed many petty and some murderous criminals were to be found among the union's members, but that their activities were sometimes directed by great, rich and powerful persons not hitherto suspected of criminal associations. Prominent among the latter were white-collar criminals who had con-spired to rob poor shareholders, to cheat the government of hundreds of millions of dollars in taxation and to enrich them-selves by nefariously ingenious schemes to circumvent the letter of the law regulating public companies. The most lucrative and widespread plan was known as the "bottom-of-the-harbour" scheme, though no one supposed that it was used only in Sydney. It worked like this:

A company that made great profits in a given financial year thereby rendered itself liable for the payment of a large tax bill. A single director, or close-knit body of directors who themselves owned the great majority of the company's shares, would then send the company to the bottom of the harbour. That is, they would transfer its assets to other companies, owned or controlled, through intermediaries, by themselves, so that when the tax bill arrived the original rich concern would have been reduced to a bankrupt, empty shell.

Costigan reported that "gross negligence" [or criminal collusion] in the crown solicitors' office had helped the number of identified deep sunken companies to increase from twenty-seven in 1973 to 1412 in 1982. In particular, the deputy Crown solicitor in Western Australia had, whether by negligence or design, delayed the launching of prosecutions for over two years. Another officer in Perth conducted a call-girl service using the Crown solicitor's office phone number in advertisements for clients. His more fastidious wife used their home address for that of over a hundred asset-stripped companies of which she had been made the nominal secretary. The government's embarrassment was compounded by the revelation that three senior officials of the Western Australian branch of the Liberal Party had been prominently engaged in the tawdry company-stripping business. They were Sydney Corser, a former chairman of the party's Finance Committee, Sir Victor Garland, formerly a cabinet minister who had been kicked upstairs to London as Australian high commissioner, and Denis Horgan, the current chairman of the Western Australian Liberal Party. The last named delivered the unkindest cut of all to his comrades. In an apparent effort to convince the viewers, or perhaps himself, that the law, not he and his fellow deep-sea divers, was wrong, he wept copiously on Richard Carleton's ABC television show.

Fraser sought to contain the political damage by denouncing the tax cheats' greed and promising to bring down retrospective legislation to recover the money from everyone who had gained in the past seven years from bottom-of-the-harbour schemes, but this merely provoked a more damaging split in the party. Many Liberals felt their three Western Australian colleagues had rightly earned praise, not obloquy, for engaging in such extraordinarily private and enterprising behaviour. The proposed legislation was amended and watered down by dissident coalition members until an almost toothless bill was passed with solid Labor support at the end of October; but by then the government's position had weakened so much that Fraser began to meditate calling an early general election before economic trends became worse still. W.G. Hayden, leader of the ALP since Whitlam's resignation in the wake of Kerr's coup, did not seem a dangerous opponent. Born in 1933 and educated at the Brisbane State High School, he was a police constable before being elected MHR for Oxley in 1961. Despite his Queensland police background, his integrity was absolute and unquestioned. He had done more than anyone else to rebuild the parliamentary Labor Party and enjoyed the universal respect of its members. It is not too much to say that even his political enemies liked the man. Perhaps he was too ordinarily decent for the jungle of party politics and lacked the cunning so necessary to ambitious politicians. Perhaps that is why his own party both rejected him as leader on the eve of the election and made him Governor-General long afterwards on 16 February 1989. In any case, Fraser sensed that the continuing rise in unemployment figures and the inflation rate were less threatening than the extraordinary popularity of the Labor member for Wills, R.J. Hawke.

Born in 1929 at Bordertown, South Australia, son of a Congregational minister and nephew of a Labor premier of Western Australia, Hawke grew up with the conviction that he was destined to become prime minister. With the Western Australian Rhodes Scholarship behind him, he returned from Oxford with that university's BA, LLB and BLitt degrees and the reputation of being a good cricketer and a great drinker. In 1958 he became resident officer and legal advocate to the

Australian Council of Trade Unions and then president of that body from 1970 to 1980. Throughout that decade, without being seen to produce any very tangible gains for those whose dues paid his salary, he became a leading charismatic figure on the national stage by settling, at the last minute, every serious strike in the country – largely on the employers' terms. Thus he entered parliament in 1980 as the darling of almost every floating voter, that 20 per cent of lower middle class and upper working class citizens who agree on nothing except that their hatred of strikes is a sure measure of their own virtue. It is hardly surprising that in March, three years later, he displaced Bill Hayden as leader of the parliamentary Labor Party and became prime minister. It happened like this.

After the "bottom-of-the-harbour" scandals, opinion polls showed that the conservative coalition was losing support. Another poll taken in July 1982 showed that 43 per cent of voters thought Hawke would make the best prime minister, 22 per cent thought Fraser and 12 per cent Peacock, deputy leader of the Liberals. Lionel Bowen, the Sydney suburban lawyer who was deputy leader of the parliamentary ALP, earned a left-wing ovation at a party conference by telling delegates that, as far as he was concerned, "charisma" was only a fancy brand of soap; but Hawke's amazing popularity with the public continued to increase. Because it seemed clear to the prime minister that his chances of retaining power could only get worse with time, on 3 February 1983, Fraser, with some difficulty, obtained the governor-general's assent to an early election. He probably did further damage to his prospects by announcing that the federal electoral rolls would close forty-eight hours later, a move which effectively disenfranchised thousands of new, mainly younger voters.

On the same day Senator John Button, ablest of the Labor politicians, and Bowen, one of the least distinguished, pressed Hayden to hand over the leadership to Hawke. Hayden complied, remarking acidly that in the existing circumstances even "the drover's dog" could not help but lead the ALP to victory. And so it proved. With consummate political skill Hawke promised practically nothing more specific than what was implied by the ALP's campaign slogan, "Bringing Australia Together". Backed in the House of Representatives by seventy-five Labor members to the fifty mustered by the conservative Opposition, the new prime minister was hailed by many as "the Messiah", by others as "the drover's dog" and by most, shortly after, as "Mr 70 Per Cent", an allusion to the fact that for nearly a year more than 70 per cent of those surveyed by the pollsters strongly approved of his prime ministerial performance.

So sweeping was the ALP's victory that Doug Anthony, leader of the National Party and deputy prime minister for many years of coalition governments, resigned from parliament and left politics a few months later. In the resulting imbroglio for leadership of the National Party, Ian Sinclair, member for New England and Anthony's deputy, was pitted against opponents who included a Queenslander urging extremely right-wing policies. Some months prior to this, when criminal charges of which he was later acquitted had been pending against him, Sinclair had publicly claimed that two prominent Sydney racing figures had told him at lunch that he could have the charges dropped by making a large donation to the funds of the New South Wales Labor Party. The ALP government of that state had promptly appointed Mr Justice Cross as a royal commissioner to inquire into Sinclair's allegation. Five days before the National Party leadership ballot was to be held, Judge Cross had reported that Sinclair's allegations were "simply untrue", and that "the Spanish Inquisition would not have convicted the Devil himself on the sort of defective answers and evidence Mr Sinclair gave to support his allegations". The member for new England, nevertheless, was elected leader of the National Party.

Under parliamentary privilege, when the House resumed on the last day of February, Sinclair attacked Judge Cross for denying him (Sinclair) "natural justice" and for "getting the evidence wrong". In the ensuing verbal brawl, Hayden, the new foreign minister, declared that Sinclair "had the personality and public morals of a cashiered sergeant-major from the New South Wales Rum Corps", and that while Cross had an unblemished career stretching over twenty-five years, Sinclair was "a malicious liar and a total stranger to the truth".[22]

Barely a month after the election of 5 March, and before parliament had met, people were regaled by the most polished and successful public relations campaign ever mounted by an Australian government. It was called the National Economic Summit, and it had been signalled by Hawke long before he achieved party leadership. During the second week of April a tripartite conference, chaired by the new prime minister, "bringing Australia together", met on the plushly padded green baize seats of the House of Representatives. Eight cabinet ministers, all state premiers and five or six other government representatives, about thirty big businessmen and delegates from employer organisations and a rather larger number of leading trade union figures debated national economic policies in a strangely theatrical spirit of comradely love and co-operation. With the predictable exception of Queensland's egregious premier, Joh Bjelke-Petersen, all participants agreed to a few pious expressions of good intentions. The twin problems of unemployment and inflation should be addressed simultaneously, not in tandem. In return for the unions' promise to exercise restraint in their wage demands, employers undertook to recommend that their companies' shareholders should accept lower dividends.

In the event, real wages and the number of strikes per annum did decrease significantly, but, not surprisingly, corporation profits and dividends did not. Neither did unemployment figures or the inflation rate. Gradually, painfully, it dawned on traditional Labor voters that "their" government intended to retain power by implementing coalition policies more efficiently (not to say ruthlessly) than the conservatives had ever been able to do. As millionaires like Alan Bond, John Elliott, Rupert Murdoch and Christopher Skase swallowed up thousands of smaller companies in a hundred takeovers, the rich became richer and the poor became poorer. Neal Blewett, Minister for Health, did establish the Medicare scheme, which paid 85 per cent of the basic medical costs of anyone not too proud to use it, but it was hard to identify any other measure clearly benefiting the many rather than the few. Smaller public hospitals were closed while the number of beds and services was cut back in many larger ones. Spending on education at all levels was scaled down even more savagely than it had been under the Fraser governments. Heavy fees were reimposed upon foreign students at Australian universities and a so-called "service-fee" of $250 a year was levied on all. Expenditure on pensions and other social services was cut dramatically. Public servants administering the dole to workless people were ordered to inquire more searchingly into the eligibility of recipients.

Most unemployed people were young, but the government also determinedly attacked the living standards of those who had come to the end of their working lives. For the first time in our history, lump-sum superannuation payments were taxed and a stringent means test was imposed on the old-age pensions of all over 70. A capital gains tax did nothing perceptible to the naked eye to reduce the wealth of the rapidly multiplying number of millionaires, but hit very hard the relatively trifling investments of employees, professionals and small-businesspeople. The same groups were hurt most by the fringe benefits tax; and while the government talked incessantly of income tax cuts, those that were implemented always, in real terms, benefited the very rich more than the average or poor citizen. All these hard-line, right-wing policies were strongly backed by the second most powerful man in the cabinet, the Treasurer Paul Keating, a flinty-eyed, street-fighter type of politician, and they were justified by exactly the same rhetoric as conservative governments had always used.

Restraint, especially in government spending, was the surest means of curing inflation and was good for what right-thinking people called "the economy" and what radical malcontents called big business. This was especially so when private investment was encouraged by tax reductions and other incentives. As Australian industrialists made more profits, they would hire more workers and so reduce unemployment. So much for the rhetoric. In fact Hawke and Keating found, as Fraser had done before them, that the only part of this pie-in-the-sky plan that actually worked was that the rich did usually get even richer. They should have been grateful, but weren't. Habitual conservative supporters can rarely bring themselves to vote Labor, even when it has manifestly done more for them than their own politicians did when in power; similarly, habitual Labor voters can rarely bring themselves to vote for the National or Liberal Parties, even when their own party has manifestly ignored ALP policy and sold them down the river. When Hawke called a premature general election on 1 December 1984 before his party's stocks grew even worse, the result was determined by the same middle-of-the-road, floating voters who had voted the year before for the party of him whom they had rightly perceived as Australia's champion strike-breaker. They sent the ALP back to power in Canberra, but with a sadly reduced majority. As Bill Hayden said to his great leader, the drover's dog had done it again but he was a bit clapped out this time.

After the election, as before it, public approval of the prime minister and his party continued to plummet. Under the misnamed policy of "pragmatism", the government encouraged massive foreign investment in Australian industries and did all it could to please banking and big business circles. Those ingenuous souls who had always believed that the ALP had something to do with idealism, with Chifley's "light on the hill", were appalled. To them it seemed that, more and more frequently, Hawke, Keating and Co. backed away from the implementation even of those longstanding Labor policies which would have been popular with the electorate. Thus they quickly gave back Uluru (Ayer's Rock) and its accompanying tourist development to the traditional Aboriginal owners; but thereafter, in metalliferous outback areas, Aboriginal interests appeared to come a bad second or third to those of multinational mining companies. In flat defiance of ALP policy and majority party sentiment, the government facilitated the mining, shipment and sale to the highest bidders of uranium ore from Roxby Downs and elsewhere. Even the party's resolutely anti-racist stance was compromised.

In March 1984, one of Australia's most distinguished historians, Professor Geoffrey Blainey, addressed the Warrnambool Rotary Club. His speech made headlines all over the country and weakened the politically bi-partisan approach to immigration which had ruled since the time of the Whitlam government. In essence, Blainey claimed that too many Asians, particularly Vietnamese, were coming to Australia and too few Britons and other Europeans.

Blainey's speech had the effect, though perhaps not the intention, of making racist views respectable. Thousands who shared them but had remained silent for a decade hastened by word and deed to propagate race hatred again. Among them were some members of the federal Opposition. On 8 May, one government backbencher, Lewis Kent, a Yugoslav by birth who had lived through the Nazi occupation, grew so warm that he climbed over the benches to assault some of the more provocative coalition speakers. Shouting "Dishonest racist bastards!" he was restrained and led out of the Chamber by the government whip. While no ALP spokesperson was heard to support the new anti-Asian drive, the government, very quietly, did change administrative practices in the Immigration Department so as to bring in more Europeans and fewer Asian settlers.

In August 1986, the re-elected government's popularity quickly plummeted when an opinion poll showed its approval at 40 per cent compared with 50 per cent of the Liberal-National opposition. A month earlier, even the approval rating of the prime minister, "Mr 70 Per Cent", had fallen to 38 per cent. Mainly because of a massive overseas trading imbalance, the value of the Australian dollar fell to US$57.15. Inflation and unemployment obstinately remained almost as high as they had been under Fraser in 1983. The treasurer, Paul Keating, complained truly but quite unavailingly in the *New York Times* that the Australian government was "getting all the right things done in the economy" yet was "getting kicked to death" by international trading conditions quite beyond its control.[23] Politically the government sustained more pain − if not more damage − from the kicks of some of its own members who ought not to have been beyond its control. In flat defiance of party policy, for the sake of $100 to $200 million in export income, cabinet allowed the resumption of uranium sales to France. Bob Hogg, senior adviser to Bob Hawke, resigned in protest and Senator Joan Childs observed sadly that the decision was "yet another example" of the government's failure to carry out party policy. Less convincingly, the deputy prime minister, Lionel Bowen, argued that those who wished to leave uranium in the Australian earth were helping the Opposition to turn "safe Labor seats into marginal ones". In fact, pacifists, reformers and "progressives" of all kinds felt betrayed by the government, but sadly sure that Opposition policies on such issues would be even more unpalatable.

To demonstrate their disillusion with the government, or perhaps with "the system" or life itself, some self-styled "feral women" camped on the lawns in front of Parliament House. When three Liberal women members of the Upper House and a brave (or foolhardy) male colleague, Senator David MacGibbon, approached, they were surrounded by the wild women who jostled and spat upon their visitors, humming the while like a swarm of bees. They also delivered what Senator MacGibbon called "a concerted attack to the front of my trousers". Labor Senator Michael Tate fared no better. A feral woman abused him for "invading women's space". When he suggested that the public gardens before the House were everybody's space, she "dropped her pants and urinated on the grass in front of him − like a dog marking its own boundary". The whole incident, no doubt, showed more about the capacity of zealots in any movement to discredit their own cause than about the state of federal politics, but it also underlined a growing nihilistic mood of disgust with all politicians and even with democracy itself.[24]

By the long, hot summer of 1986–87, it had become a truism to observe that the Hawke government was ruling the country in the interests of big business far more effectively

than those who trumpeted the importance of private enterprise had ever been able to do. This made life increasingly difficult for John Howard and Ian Sinclair, leaders of the Liberal
and National Parties. If voters in the general election due by
the end of 1987 were to perceive any difference between the
programs offered by the two major political parties, Coalition
rhetoric had to be moved a long way to the right. That in itself
has seldom presented insuperable difficulties to any politician, but leading Liberals argued publicly and embarrass-
ingly about how far to the right they should appear to have
moved. Many thought that leading National (Country) Party
figures had always stood as far to the right as it was possible
to be, but they had under-estimated the eccentricity (to use
the kindest word) of 76-year-old Sir Johannes Bjelke-
Petersen, National Party premier of Queensland since 1968.

On 1 November 1986, with the help of massively gerry-
mandered state electoral boundaries, his party won another
general election; not only that, but an absolute majority of
seats in Queensland's single-chamber parliament — more
than the Labor and Liberal parties combined. The Premier
was inspired with delusions of grandeur. If Queensland, why
not Canberra? From the far right this paladin of all the worst
nineteenth-century British notions suddenly launched an attack on his own political comrades in the federal sphere. Just
when there was a real chance for the conservative forces to
take power from the Hawke government, its most bigoted
enemy contemptuously denounced the Liberal Party and proclaimed his intention of replacing Sinclair as leader of the federal National Party.

Some thought him afflicted at last with senile dementia
and others that he was being secretly paid by the ALP to sow
confusion in the Coalition ranks, but in fact Joh's push from
the bush to Canberra was being funded, surprisingly openly,
by the "white shoe brigade", a group of about fifty wealthy
businessmen, some of them newly enriched by participation
in development projects in the swamps of the Gold Coast. At
one stage they boasted of having $25 million dollars pledged
to the campaign. It seemed that their semi-articulate cham-

pion had cause to be vaingloriously confident. In a telephone interview with the *Sydney Morning Herald* he spluttered from his Kingaroy peanut farm:

> I want candidates across Australia. We can get them, we can fund them and we can win. Sinclair? Isn't he a Liberal? . . . We will do a General Macarthur with him. We will get our own Joh candidates that will completely annihilate them [Howard and Sinclair].[25]

Joh's unguided intervention must have appalled the Coalition chiefs in Canberra as much as it delighted the Labor ones who could now sit back and watch the Opposition parties destroy their electoral credibility by passionate public disputation among themselves. Some sophisticated southerners, using the analogy of the Ayatollah Khomieni in Iran, dubbed Bjelke-Petersen "the Mad Mullah of the Deep North", but nothing seemed to shake his popularity with rural Queensland voters. He seems never to have doubted that Howard and Peacock, already locked in a continuing battle for the Liberal Party leadership, would be forced to hand over that of the Coalition to the Nationals. Only a madman could have believed further that Ian Sinclair, the ablest and most ruthless member of the Commonwealth parliament, could be forced under any circumstances to relinquish leadership of the National Party to the "Mad Mullah". In April 1987 a *Sydney Morning Herald* poll showed that Labor again had a commanding lead over the Opposition: 51 per cent to 42 per cent for the Liberal–National group. It was probably at this time that Labor strategists like Senator Graham Richardson began to think of calling the next federal election early. Controversy over the Australia Card provided the trigger.

This measure proposed to equip every citizen with a card recording his or her Taxation Department file number and other personal details which, the government argued, would make it easier to detect tax cheats and tax evaders. For that very reason, it seemed to some observers, the Opposition parties combined with the Australian Democrats in the Senate to block the legislation twice within three months, thus providing the government with a constitutional reason for calling a double-dissolution election, announced by the Prime Minister for 11 July. John Elliott, multi-millionaire and leader of the Liberal Party's extra-parliamentary organisation, fecklessly helped the Labor campaign with his suggestion that the Australia Card might usefully be issued to unemployed persons, pensioners and other ne'er-do-wells, but on no account to respectable people such, presumably, as himself. But the troublesome card practically disappeared from view during the six weeks of electioneering. Voters and those wooing them were preoccupied with the bizarre daily spectacle created by the "Joh for Canberra" campaign. Nearly half of all National Party Members of the federal parliament were Queenslanders fanatically committed to the belief that Joh, as leader of the far or lunatic right, would destroy the Hawke government they hated. This northern mafia forced Sinclair and the whole National organisation to end the coalition with the Liberals, thereby writing *finis* to conservative chances. It is hardly surprising that, though the ALP lost two seats and gained two elsewhere, it won four seats in Queensland and an increased overall majority in the House of Representatives. For the first time in history, a Commonwealth Labor government was re-elected to a third consecutive term in office. It seemed that what W.K. Hancock had characterised in 1930 as the "party of initiative" had become the acceptable party of government, helped thereto more by the political stupidity of its opponents than by any great virtues of its own.

Three months later the world was rocked by the greatest stockmarket crash since the great depression of the early 1930s. Panic selling began on Wall Street on 17 October and spread to London, Tokyo, Hong Kong and of course Australia. By the end of the month the market value of shares throughout the world had fallen on the average by more than one-third.[26] Paul Keating had long been hailed by many as the most skilful Treasurer in the Western world. He had "managed" the economy by abolishing controls as much as possible, in order to allow it to be managed by "market forces", that is to say, by the freest possible competition between capitalists. And it worked. The richest individuals and corporations became richer still as, with limitless credit pressed upon them by the banks, they "took over" or swallowed smaller companies, which had already swallowed smaller ones and so on *ad infinitum*. By enriching the greatest sharks, the process was seen to be enriching the whole country, for few noticed that the first result of a successful takeover was often to add to the unemployed pool workers made redundant by the new giant company's rationalising plans. Names like John Elliott, Robert Homes à Court, Laurie Connell, Christopher Skase and Alan Bond, unknown a generation earlier, became household words, while those who bore them were inflated by the media almost to folk hero status. In 1983 a trifling part of Bond's money had made it possible for Ben Lexcen and other talented Australians to wrest the America's Cup briefly from the New York Yacht Club. A celebratory party raged all night in the Royal Perth Yacht Club. The recently elected prime minister, Bob Hawke, had flown across the continent on time to congratulate the winners at daybreak. In 1987 Bond's name was emblazoned on a huge ovoid captive balloon floating in the polluted air above some Australian cities. Five years later he was made bankrupt and began serving a two-and-a-half-year gaol sentence for fraud.

The only prominent investor to emerge from the crash not only unscathed, but richer than ever, was polo-playing Kerry Packer, son of a previous America's Cup challenger, Sir Frank Packer of the Sydney *Daily Telegraph*. The rest were execrated by press and public as though their inordinate greed, abetted by that of the banks which backed them, had actually caused the crash. Overnight almost, the folk heroes were transformed by the media into scapegoats. But in truth no two economic experts could wholly agree on what had caused the disaster, still less on what the government should do to restore prosperity. Like the first black Australians who refused to utter the name of a dead kinsman, everyone agreed not to utter the word "depression", as though to do so might make the "recession" worse. For the past seventy years a few thoughtful people had pointed to the planned economy of communist states as the only way of avoiding cyclic booms and depressions brought about by the free play of market forces; but this no longer offered a credible alternative. Comrade Gorbachev, leading the dictatorship of the proletariat in the Soviet Union itself, had already begun to dismantle that country's centrally planned economy in favour of one driven by "market forces". So the recession continued for year after year with interest rates of between 15 and 25 per cent, rising unemployment and declining government expenditure on social services, particularly education. Government and Opposition agreed that this increasing hardship for the masses was the only way of reducing inflation, but by the end of 1990 the purchasing power of the Australian dollar was still decreasing by more than 8 per cent per annum.

It is good to record that public penny-pinching and private penury were not allowed to blight the Bicentenary celebrations of 1988. Inevitably these culminated in a re-enactment of the arrival of the first fleet of white invaders on Australia Day, 26 January. Original Australians had long proclaimed their view that this was an occasion for mourning, not joy, and many people feared that the official performances led by Prince Charles and the prime minister might be marred by violent Aboriginal protests. They need not have worried. On the great, sunny morning when so many hundreds of thousands of good-humoured people streamed towards Sydney Cove, it seemed all the policemen in Australia would have been lost among them and so quite unable to keep order even if they had been ordered to do so. Those who marched under the red, yellow and black Aboriginal flag[27] reported friendly gaiety just as evident as everywhere else and as it still was at night among the throngs who, from every harbourside suburb, watched the illuminations on the Sydney Harbour Bridge and in the sky. The harbour itself was covered with many thousands of boats ranging in size from home-made, one-child canoes to the long straight line of one or two thousand-tonne sailing ships which passed through the Heads, between the myriad moving smaller craft and under the Bridge.

So sparkling was the weather and so joyful the spirit of the people, that class, sexual, racial and even political divisions were forgotten. Collisions and accidents ducked many pleasure seekers but hurt none. Not far from Man-o-war Steps where the official speakers were in full flight, two white Australians in clothing suggesting the naval uniform of two centuries ago paddled a tiny bumboat beside the shore. Two black Australians dived into the water, dispossessed the invaders and ran up the Aboriginal flag in place of the "white" Australian one. Everyone, including the four principal actors, cheered and roared with laughter. Best of all, the whole spectacle, and the rare feeling for common humanity which informed it, were brought by the Australian Broadcasting Commission's television service to millions of viewers from Cape York to Cape Leewin. Many feared they might never see again such a demonstration of that unaffected egalitarian goodwill which optimists have liked to think is a distinguishing characteristic of the Australian people. On that day it was possible to hope that the nineteenth-century bushman's mateship might one day embrace the whole human race.

Voters always tend to blame economic recession on the party in power: which at this time meant the ALP everywhere except the Northern Territory, Tasmania and Queensland. Hard times, however, added little to the failing credibility of the long-lived National Party government of the last-named state, which had already sown the seeds of its own destruction. After the federal election, Sir Robert Sparkes, chairman of the Queensland National Party's State Council, who had been enthusiastic about Joh's "push for Canberra", naturally blamed him for its failure. By October 1987 the premier was made to realise that his once-loyal party comrades perceived him as an electoral liability, even in Queensland, but he clung grimly to power and place. In November he asked the governor to approve his sacking of five "disloyal" cabinet ministers and, it was reported, to call a new election. Advised by other ministers that Joh no longer had the support of his parliamentary colleagues, the governor properly refused. On 26 November, all forty-seven National Party MPs met in Joh's absence and elected Mike Ahern their leader, but it took them another five days to force their 76-year-old icon to resign from parliament and the premiership.

Even before the last climactic state election, the most self-righteous and religious premier Queensland ever knew had been touched by the shadow of future disasters. In 1986 in an out-of-court settlement of a libel action, he had admitted receiving from Alan Bond $400,000 which, the West Australian believed, was the equivalent of a bribe to be allowed to engage in business in Queenland; but no one then believed the Lutheran lay preacher capable of wrongdoing. The first allegations to be taken seriously were made during the election campaign by a National Party trustee, Sir Roderick Proctor, who publicly stated that the Bjelke-Petersen government was involved in "cronyism", Sir Roderick's euphimism for corruption. Before long, four senior public servants were gaoled for "misappropriating" money belonging to the government departments which they had helped to administer. So the quaint phraseology of the law avoided calling presumably respectable people thieves. Most prominent in Brisbane society were Judith Callaghan, executive director of the Queensland Day Committee, and her husband Allen, under-secretary of the Department of Arts, National Parks and Sport and sometime press secretary and adviser to the premier. Each purloined about $40 000 but, quaintly again, Judith was sentenced to only thirty months' gaol compared with four years for her spouse. Then ABC TV devoted its "Four Corners" program to long-standing allegations of corruption in the police force and newspapers alleged that a prominent member of the "white-shoe brigade", Mr Mike Gore, had received from the government a bridging loan of $10.16 million to help with his Sanctuary Cove development. At last, in Joh's absence and against his wishes, a cabinet meeting chaired by Deputy Premier Bill Gunn on 26 May 1987 commissioned Mr Tony Fitzgerald, QC to inquire into the augean stables which, many believed, were presided over by the Queensland premier.

Experience had made many Australians expect from Commissions of Inquiry little more than a whitewashing of those accused of any wrongdoing. The Fitzgerald Report, made public two years later on 3 July 1989, confounded the expectations of the most cynical. It revealed not only criminal behaviour by named government ministers and senior public servants, but, much worse, that the whole administrative structure of the state had been misused to further the political ends of the National Party. Criminal and political networks operated over a wide range of activities "including bribery, prostitution, the operation of sex parlours and brothels, tax evasion, illegal gambling, SP betting, the rorting of ministerial expenses, protection rackets, money laundering and, probably, drug running".[28] Most cabinet ministers were later charged with misappropriating public money for their own personal benefit as the Callaghans had done, but the grossly gargantuan "Big Russ Hinze, Minister for Everything" was shown to have accepted $1.8 million dollars from developers within weeks of cabinet approval of projects in which they were interested. A Supreme Court Judge, Mr Angelo Vasta, under investigation by Fitzgerald for perjury, was allowed by the Chief Justice of Queensland "to stand down from his duties voluntarily, with dignity". But corruption began, it seemed, at the top.

In 1976 the Bjelke-Petersen cabinet had inexplicably promoted a man called Lewis, over the heads of more than a hundred better qualified applicants, to the position of assistant police commissioner for the whole state. The then-Commissioner, Ray Whitrod, a man notorious among many of his colleagues for unassailable integrity, resigned in protest. Lewis then "automatically" became commissioner and was knighted soon afterwards. From his instantly acquired vantage point, Sir Terence presided over what Fitzgerald characterised as the corrupt "police culture" of the whole state. He also provided welcome advice to his benefactor on such matters as appointments to the cabinet, the judicial bench, the governorship of the state and how best to redistribute electoral boundaries to the advantage of the National Party. Even before the Inquiry's report was presented, Sir Terence was suspended from duty as Vasta had been; but this did nothing to divert attention from the ex-premier. Fitzgerald showed that Joh had instructed the Special Branch police to "get something on" designated political opponents, such as Liberal MP Angus Innes, Labor Opposition leader Keith Wright, and former state president of the ALP, Dr Denis Murphy. The ex-premier's belief that he had done nothing wrong merely reinforced what other revelations to the Inquiry showed: that the yokel who misruled Queensland for twenty years knew nothing and cared less about the traditions of Westminster-style democracy. "The greatest thing that could happen to the state and the nation," he declared in a gem of purest Johspeak, "is when we get rid of all media. Then we could live in peace and tranquillity and no one would know anything."[29]

Evidence to the Inquiry suggested, however, that he knew more than he was willing to admit about a safe in the anteroom to his office in Parliament House. The ex-premier explained that National Party supporters frequently dropped tens of thousands of dollars in cash into this treasure box and that neither he nor his staff "wanted to know" the names of the donors nor the amounts of money for which no receipts were issued. It seems to have been this pecadillo which later brought Joh into court to answer "one charge of official corruption and two of perjury". The former charge held that "on or about September 18th, 1986, being premier and treasurer of Queensland", Bjelke-Petersen "corruptly received from Singapore businessman Robert Sng $100 000 in cash on account of his ensuring that Historic Holdings Pty Ltd would be the 'selected developer' for the redevelopment of the Brisbane Post Office building and site".[30] At his trial in October 1991, Australia's best-known Lutheran lay preacher escaped conviction because the jury was unable to reach a verdict. But long before the case came to trial, the Fitzgerald Report had changed the course of Australian history. The state election of 2 December 1989, though fought on the old gerrymandered boundaries, was won by the Goss Labor Party with fifty-four seats to thirty-five for all other parties. The National Party's percentage of all votes cast was slashed from 39.6 at the previous election (called by some "Joh's last hurrah") to 24.

Electors decided that the National Party, with or without its Liberal partners, had been in power for too long for its own good or for that of Queensland; but voters sometimes reject a government for no real reason other than that they feel it is time for a change. So the long-lived Labor government of New South Wales had already been replaced by the Greiner-led Liberal–National coalition on 20 March 1988. In South Australia, Victoria and Western Australia, the ALP still clung to office, though only after savage in-fighting which in the last-mentioned state had ended only with the replacement of Labor's leader, Peter Dowding by Dr Carmen Lawrence, the first female premier in Australia. On balance, despite the Labor renaissance in Queensland, the auspices seemed clearly to favour the conservative parties as the 1990 federal election approached. Inflation, interest rates and unemployment remained unacceptably high and the recession promised to become worse before conditions could improve. Judging (or perhaps just gambling) that an early election would help his party, Hawke set its date at 24 March. Labor's campaign was again helped considerably by public brawling between the Liberal leader, Andrew Peacock, and his deposed predecessor, John Howard, and between both and the far-right national figures who had succeeded Joh Bjelke-Petersen and Ian Sinclair. Two of the ALP's own positive strategies probably had more to do with the party's success. First they saturated with direct propagandist mail those marginal seats which public opinion research suggested could be won. Second, as similar research showed that unprecedently large numbers of electors were determined to vote for the Democrats, Green (environmentalists) and other minority party or independent candidates, the ALP solicited their second-preference votes on the grounds that Labor's environmentalist record was demonstrably much better than that of the Coalition.

The gamble paid off when the ALP won seventy-eight seats in the House of Representatives against sixty-nine for the Opposition plus one independent. The vainglorious Robert James Lee Hawke had led his troops from their unprecedented third successive term of office into their fourth. With the exception of the fabulous R.G. Menzies, no political leader in the history of the Commonwealth parliament had ever done so much, but judicious observers felt sure that this was Bob's last hurrah. Immediately after the election, the Liberals replaced Peacock with John Hewson, sometime Professor of Economics, who bade fair once and for all to end the internecine warfare in the Opposition camp. Besides, by-elections and opinion polls continually showed that Australian voters were "sick of Labor" and steadily becoming sicker. Even in the poll on 24 March, Labor had lost votes and seats in every state except Queensland. But the main reason why the ALP's ten-year rule would be ended (if not before) by the election due in 1993 was the party's manifest abandonment – reversal even – of its traditional policy: using taxation and other government powers to reduce the income gap between rich and poor. One of Labor's brightest backroom boys, wine merchant Richard Farmer, analysed the Commissioner of Taxation's official statistics to show just how much wider the gap had grown in two Sydney suburbs during the first eight years of Labor administration:

> After-tax income in working-class Bankstown is up just 41 per cent while over in upper class Edgecliff it has grown 267 per cent.
>
> . . . Back in 1982–83, income tax in Bankstown was 20.4 per cent of taxable income and in Edgecliff 33.5 per cent. By 1988–89 the Bankstown rate was up to 24.7 per cent and that in Edgecliff down to 27.6 per cent.[31]

Before the end of the year, the tired government was presented with another problem. The ruthless Iraqi dictator, Saddam Hussein, brutally annexed the neighbouring oil-rich Arab state of Kuwait. The president of the United States, George Bush, swore to make war on Iraq if Hussein did not withdraw his troops and restore Kuwaiti sovereignty. He sent American land, sea and air forces to the area and obtained practically unanimous United Nations backing for his planned attack. Should Hawke "go all the way" with Bush as preceding prime ministers had done with President Truman in Korea and President Johnson in Vietnam? Or should he keep our forces at home on the ground that our vital interests and national integrity were in no way threatened by an Arab quarrel half a world away? Experts in the Foreign Affairs Department advised the latter course, but his instincts, he declared, pushed him toward the former.[32] In the past, support for the United States had always been justified by the perceived need to oppose communism, but the Soviet government had demolished the Berlin Wall and thereby written *finis* to any expansionist aims it may have nourished. It had also abandoned its support for Hussein and offered diplomatic support to the United States. No sane person could any longer pretend that "international communism" posed a threat to Australian territorial integrity. So Hawke compromised, sending three RAN vessels, but no land or air forces, to support American and Allied ships in the Persian Gulf. In a political sense his plan worked brilliantly. Thousands of tonnes of American bombs smashed Iraq in a few weeks. Australia was seen to have been a loyal United States ally and yet our victorious ships returned without the loss of one Australian life.

Public opinion on the whole approved, if tepidly, the government's handling of the situation, but the war's outcome did nothing to arrest the downward slide of the economy into the "recession" which the Treasurer claimed "we had to have" in order to make Australia more competitive in world markets. His strategy seemed to be working when, in April 1991, the balance of payments improved as exports exceeded imports for the first time in many years, and in May the annual inflation rate fell to 4.9 per cent, the lowest since 1962. So the Labor government, in Keating's New York words,[33] kept on "doing all the right things", but this time it was "being kicked to death" by pensioners, dismissed schoolteachers and other workless people – for, as the inflation rate fell, that of unemployment rose, in 1991 to more than 10 per cent. All the opinion polls spelt Labor's doom. It seemed that people were tired of the same old faces in the Canberra *opera-bouffe*. They wanted a new cast.

The only person in the government ranks apparently not rendered immobile by the situation was the man once described by some as the "world's greatest treasurer", Paul Keating. Since 1983 he had been seen by all, including himself, as the inevitable successor to the prime ministership. In the last weeks of the year, Senator Graham Richardson and other ALP "numbers men" began, not very covertly, to mobilise support for the change. There was no difference between the stated policies of the two men, but because Hawke's leadership was seen to be increasingly ineffective, a small majority voted for Keating at a caucus meeting a few days before Christmas 1991. It was not a vote in faith in the new leader's genius, but rather a measure of the desperation in Labor ranks. Just possibly, some members hoped (rather than thought) the jaded electors might be appeased by a change of leaders instead of a change of party. Keating had the political cunning to produce the appearance of a radical change. Fostering republican sentiment was ALP policy, but Hawke and all his followers had talked of republicanism, if at all, only softly as a possible future development. Keating used the Queen's visit in March 1992 to put republicanism on the contemporary political agenda. His wife Annita pointedly shook the royal hand instead of curtseying when the Queen visited parliament. Keating's speech of welcome stated that Australia was likely to go its separate republican way by the end of the decade. His remarks were delivered in such a way as to recall an earlier Australian's address to the Emperor of Japan, "With all respect you may conceive to be due you without degrading formalities . . ."[34] Many older people were outraged, but most opinion polls showed approval of the new prime minister's emphasis on Australia entering the third millennium as a republic. Yet it seemed as likely as ever that the National–Liberal coalition would be returned to power at the next election.

Notes

Abbreviations

Arch.Phys. *Anth.Oceania*	*Archaeology and Physical Anthropology in Oceania*
A.D.B.	*Australian Dictionary of Biography*
A.J.P.H.	*Australian Journal of Politics and History*
A.N.L.	*Australian National Library*
C.P.D.	*Commonwealth Parliamentary Debates*
H.R.A.	*Historical Records of Australia*
H.R.N.S.W.	*Historical Records of New South Wales*
H.S.	*Historical Studies*
J.A.S.	*Journal of Australian Studies*
L.H.	*Labour History*
Leg. Ass.	Legislative Assembly
Leg. Coun.	Legislative Council
M.L.	Mitchell Library
R.A.H.S.J.	*Royal Australian Historical Society Journal and Proceedings*
S.M.H.	*Sydney Morning Herald*
U.N.E.	University of New England
V. and P.	*Votes and Proceedings*

1 Black and white discoverers

1. Richard G. Roberts, Rhys Jones and M.A. Smith, "Thermoluminescence dating of a 50,000-year-old human occupation site in northern Australia", in *Nature*, vol. 345, no. 6271, 10 May 1990, pp. 153-56.
2. J.M. Bowler, R. Jones, H.R. Allen and A.G. Thorne, "Pleistocene

human remains from Australia: a living site and human cremation from Lake Mungo", *World Archaeology*, no. 2, 1970.

3. Cliff D. Ollier, "The geological background to prehistory in island Southeast Asia", in *Modern Quaternary Research in Australia*, Balkema, Rotterdam, vol. 9, 1985.

4. Rhys Jones, "East of Wallace's Line: Issues and Problems in the Colonisation of the Australian Continent", in P. Mellors and G. Striger, *The Human Revolution* (Edinburgh: University of Edinburgh Press, 1989).

5. For example, W.D. Jackson, "Fire, air, water and earth: an elemental ecology of Tasmania", *Proceedings of Ecological Society of Tasmania*, no. 3, 1968.

6. G. Singh, A.P. Kershaw and Robin Clark, "Quaternary vegetation and fire history in Australia", in A.M. Gill, R.A. Groves and I.H. Noble, *Fire and Australian Biota* (Canberra: Australian Academy of Science, 1979).

7. R.V.S Wright, "How old is Zone F at Lake George?", in *Archaeology in Oceania*, 21 (2), 1986, pp. 138-39.

8. D.J. Mulvaney, "Aboriginal Social Evolution: A Retrospective View", in D.J. Mulvaney and J. Golson (eds), *Aboriginal Man and Environment in Australia* (Canberra, 1971).

9. William Howells, *The Pacific Islanders*, London, 1973, ch. 6. Peter Bellwood, *Man's Conquest of the Pacific: the Pre-history of Southeast Asia and Oceania*, Auckland, 1978. A.G. Thorne, "The Racial Affinities and Origins of the Australian Aborigines", in Mulvaney and Golson, *Aboriginal Man*.

10. A.G. Thorne, "The Longest Link: Human Evolution in Southeast Asia" in James J. Fox (ed.), *Indonesia: the Making of a Culture* (Canberra, 1980).

11. A.G. Thorne and P.G. Macumber, "Discoveries of Late Pleistocene man at Kow Swamp, Australia", *Nature*, vol. 238, 11 August 1972. A.G. Thorne, "Mungo and Kow Swamp: Morphological variation in Pleistocene Australians", *Mankind*, no. 8, 1971.

12. R.M.W. Dixon, *The Languages of Australia*, Cambridge, 1980, Introduction and ch. 1; Thomas H. Sebeck (ed.), *Current Trends in Linguistics*, vol. 8, *Linguistics in Oceania* (The Hague, 1971), p. 721.

13. R.M.W. Dixon and Barry J. Blake (eds), *Handbook of Australian Languages* (Canberra, 1979), p. 2.

14. S. Bowdler, "Coastal Colonisation of Australia", in *Sunda and Sahul* "Aboriginal Social Evolution"; eds J. Allen, J. Golson and R. Jones (London 1977).

15. D.J. Mulvaney, "East of Wallace's Line"; D. Tryon, "Linguistic Evidence and Aboriginal Origins" in *Aboriginal Man and Environment*, pp. 344-80; Klim Gollan, Prehistoric Dingo, ANU PhD thesis, 1980.

16. Rhys Jones, "East of Wallace's Line", p. 34.

17. William Dampier, *Dampier's Voyages*, ed. A.E.M. Bayliss, (Sydney, 1945), pp. 143-44.
18. Donald F. Thompson, "Some Wood and Stone Implements of the Bindibu Tribe of Central Western Australia", *Proceedings of the Prehistoric Society for 1964*, December 1964, pp. 400-22.
19. M.J. Meggitt, "Indigenous Forms of Government among the Australian Aborigines", Paper read to meeting of Société Jean Rodin, Brussels, June 1962, pp. 7-8.
20. W.E.H. Stanner, *Whiteman Got No Dreaming: Essays 1938-1973,* Sydney 1973, pp. 23-27; but see Harry Lourandos, "Aboriginal Spatial Organisation and Population", in *Arch. Phys. Anth. Oceania,* 12, 3, 1977, and Noel M. Wallace, Appendix V, *Proposed Master Plan Ayers Rock* (Alice Springs, 1963).
21. George French Angas, *Savage Life and Scenes in Australia and New Zealand,* 2 vols (London, 1847), vol. 1, pp. 82-83.
22. A.P. Elkin, *Aboriginal Men of High Degrees* (Sydney, 1945) and M.J. Meggitt, "Indigenous Forms of Government".
23. John Haviland, in Dixon and Blake, *Handbook of Australian Languages,* p. 77; S.A. Wurm, *Languages of Australia and Tasmania* (The Hague, 1972), pp. 63-64; R.M.W. Dixon, *The Languages of Australia* pp. 107-8.
24. John Morgan, *The Life and Adventures of William Buckley,* (London, 1853) pp. 212-13.
25. M.J. Meggitt, "Indigenous Forms of Government".
26. Lieut. Breton R.N., *Excursions in New South Wales, Western Australia and Van Diemen's Land* (London, 1833), pp. 212-13. Cf. W.E.H. Stanner, *After the Dreaming* (Sydney, 1968), pp. 47-49.
27. C.C. Macknight, *The Voyage to Marege* (Melbourne, 1976).
28. "The Author", *The Picture of Australia* (London, 1849), pp. 206-8.
29. D.J. Mulvaney and J. Golson, *Aboriginal Man,* pp. 30-33.
30. C.P. Fitzgerald, "A Chinese Discovery of Australia?" in *Australia Writes,* ed. T. Inglis Moore, Melbourne, 1953.
31. For a detailed study of possible Portuguese discoveries in Australia see K.G. McIntyre, *The Secret Discovery of Australia: Portuguese Ventures 200 Years Before Captain Cook* (Menindie, SA, 1977) and O.H.K. Spate, "The Dieppe Connection", Seminar Paper, ANU, 1979.
32. I. McKiggan, "The Portuguese Expedition to Bass Street in A.D. 1522", in *J.A.S.,* 1 June 1977.
33. Jeremy Green, "The Carronade Island guns and Australia's early visitors", in *Great Circle,* vol. 4, no. 2, October 1982.
34. G.G. McCrae, "The ancient buried vessel at Warrnambool", in *Victorian Geographical Journal,* vol. 28, 1910-11.
35. Brett Hilder, *The Voyage of Torres* (St Lucia, 1980) and Sir Clements Markham, *The Voyages of Pedro Fernandez de Quiros 1595 to 1606,* 2 vols (Hakluyt Society, 1904).

36. For detailed studies of Dutch discoveries in Australia see R.H. Major, *Early Voyages to Terra Australis, Now Called Australia* (Hakluyt Society, 1859); J.P. Sigmond and L.H. Zuiderbaan, *Dutch Discoveries of Australia* (Adelaide, 1979); Gunter Schilder, *Australia Unveiled: the Share of the Dutch Navigators in the Discovery of Australia* (Amsterdam, 1976).

37. Sigmond and Zuiderbaan, *Dutch Discoveries*, pp. 84-5.

38. Schilder, *Australia Unveiled*, pp. 180-81.

39. Sigmond and Zuiderbaan, *Dutch Discoveries*, pp. 99-109.

40. C.M.H. Clark, *A History of Australia*, vol. 1 (Melbourne, 1961), p. 45.

41. The best and most detailed study of Cook's life and work is J.C. Beaglehole's multi-volume *Journals of Captain James Cook* (Hakluyt Society, 1974), vol. 4, titled *The Life of Captain James Cook*.

42. Quoted Beaglehole, vol. 4, p. 224.

43. Beaglehole, vol. 1, p. 273.

44. ibid., p. 309.

45. ibid., pp. 323-24.

46. vol. 2, *The Endeavour Journal of Joseph Banks*, p. 78.

47. vol. 1, p. 366 and E.H. Kodicek and F.G. Young, "Captain Cook and Scurvy", in *Notes and Records of the Royal Society of London*, 24, 1969.

48. vol. 2, p. 97.

49. vol. 1, pp. 387-88.

50. ibid., p. 399.

51. vol. 4, pp. 637-72.

2 Empire, convicts and currency

1. Alan Frost, *Convicts and Empire: a Naval Question 1776-1811* (Melbourne 1980), p. 77.

2. ibid., p.45.

3. A.W. Martin, *Henry Parkes: a Biography* (Melbourne, 1980), pp. 1-6.

4. J.L. and B. Hammond, *The Village Labourer 1760-1833* (London, 1913), p. 195 *et passim*.

5. G.A. Wood, "Convicts", *J.R.A.H.S.*, 8, 4, 1922.

6. Patrick Colquhoun, *A Treatise on the Police of the Metropolis* (London, 1800), pp. 437-40.

7. Frost, *Convicts and Empire*, pp. 3-49; A.G.L. Shaw, *Convicts and the Colonies* (London, 1966), pp. 38-57, 66; Geoffrey Blainey, *The Tyranny of Distance* (Melbourne, 1966), pp. 7-37, and Ged Martin (ed.), *The Founding of Australia: The Argument about Australia's Origins* (Sydney, 1978).

8. Frost, *Convicts and Empire*, p. 45.

9. Quoted C.M.H. Clark, *Select Documents in Australian History, 1788-1850* (Sydney, 1950), pp. 40-41.

10. Captain Watkin Tench, *A Narrative of the Expedition to Botany Bay* (London, 1789), p. 73; and *S.M.H.*, 15 December 1980.

11. Frost, *Convicts and Empire*, pp. 88-135.

12. *A.D.B.*, Vol. 2, "James Ruse".

13. A.G.L. Shaw, *Convicts and Colonies*, p. 148.

14. *H.R.A.*, Series I, 1, p. 14.

15. Lt. A. Bowes, *Diary*, MS, M.L., quoted John Cobley, *Sydney Cove 1788*, London, 1962, pp. 58-59.

16. Portia Robinson, *The Hatch and Brood of Time* (Melbourne, 1985); Helen Heney, *Australia's Founding Mothers* (Melbourne, 1978); Michael Belcher, UNE PhD thesis, 1982.

17. Lloyd Robson, *The Convict Settlers of Australia* (Melbourne, 1965), p. 78.

18. *H.R.A.*, 1, 7, p. 205.

19. W.H. Breton, quoted L. Evans and P. Nicholls, *Convicts and Colonial Society 1788-1853* (Sydney, 1976), p. 146.

20. James F. O'Connell, *A Residence of Eleven Years in New Holland* (Canberra, 1972), pp. 67-73; *Colonial Times*, 18 Feb. 1840.

21. Russel Ward, *Uses of History*, UNE Publication Unit, 1968.

22. *HRA*, I, 1, p. 13.

23. ibid., p. 24.

24. Watkin Tench, *A Narrative*, pp. 57-61.

25. ibid., pp. 89-102.

26. ibid., 111.

27. c.f. N.G. Butlin, *Our Original Aggression,* (Sydney, 1983), pp. 119-48.

28. John Turnbull *A Voyage Round the World in the Years 1800-1804*, 3 vols, (London, 1805) vol. 3, pp. 182-85.

29. See, e.g., James Mudie, *The Felonry of New South Wales* (London, 1837).

30. For this and following references to John Hood's views, see his *Australia and the East* (London, 1843).

31. David Collins, *An Account of the English Colony in New South Wales*, 2 vol, (London, 1798) ed. Brian H. Fletcher (Sydney, 1975), vol. 1, p. 64.

32. R. Therry *Reminiscences of Thirty Years' Residence in New South Wales* (London, 1963), pp. 57-59.

33. Charles Darwin, *Journal of Researches During the Voyage of H.M.S. Beagle* (London, 1889), p. 323.

34. Ken Macnab and Russel Ward, "The Nature and Nurture of the First Generation of Native-Born Australians", *HS*, 10, 39, Nov. 1962.

35. "An Emigrant Mechanic" (Alexander Harris), *Settlers and Convicts*, ed. C.M.H. Clark (Melbourne, 1953), pp. 12-13.

36. "The Author of Settlers and Convicts", *The Secrets of Alexander Harris*, ed. Grant Carr-Harris (Sydney, 1961), pp. 108-9.

37. *HRA*, I, 1, pp. 413-17.
38. J.C. Garran and L. White, *Merinos, Myths and Macarthurs,* (Canberra, 1986).
39. H.V. Evatt *Rum Rebellion* (Sydney, 1938); M.H. Ellis, *John Macarthur* (Sydney, 1955); G. Mackaness *The Life of Vice Admiral William Bligh*, 2nd edn (Sydney, 1951).
40. *HRNSW*, VI, p. 594; *Sydney Gazette*, 11 Mar. 1804; J.E. Gallagher, The Convict Rising at Castle Hill, BA Hons thesis, UNE, 1970.
41. Joseph Holt, *Life, 1826,* MS A2024, pp. 294-95, ML.
42. J.D. Lang, *Historical and Statistical Account of New South Wales*, 2 vols (London, 1834), vol. 2, p. 248; J.T. Bigge, *Report of the Commissioner into the state of the Colony of New South Wales,* (London, 1822), p. 91.
43. *ADB*, vol. 2, "William Redfern".
44. *HRA*, I, 8, pp. 1-27.
45. *HRA*, I, 10, pp. 220-24; and M.H. Ellis, *Lachlan Macquarie (Sydney, 1947).*
46. W.C. Wentworth, *Statistical, Historical and Political Description of New South Wales* (London, 1819), p. 64.
47. J.T. Bigge, *Report into Colony of NSW,* and *Report on Agriculture and Trade in New South Wales* (London, 1823). See also John Ritchie, *The Evidence to the Bigge Reports*, 2 vols., Melbourne, 1971; and Russel Ward, *Finding Australia* (Melbourne, 1987), pp. 411-13.
48. Matthew Flinders, in *The Farthest Coast*, ed. C.C. Macknight (Melbourne, 1969), pp. 49-72, esp. p. 65.
49. Quoted in *Friendly Mission: the Tasmanian Journals and Papers of George Augustus Robinson 1829-1834,* ed. N.J.B. Plomley (Tasmanian Historical Research Association, 1966), p. 1008.
50. K.M. Bowden, *Captain James Kelly of Hobart Town* (Melbourne, 1964).
51. J.W. Bull, *Early Experiences of Life in South Australia* (Adelaide, 1884), p. 5.
52. Archibald Campbell, *The Restless Voyage from 1806 to 1812,* ed. Stanley D. Porteous DSc (London, 1949), pp. 129-81.
53. Clement Hodgkinson, *Australia from Port Macquarie to Moreton Bay* (London, 1845), pp. 9-12.
54. E.J. Tapp, *Early New Zealand* (Melbourne, 1958).
55. *ADB*, vol. 1, "William Grant Broughton"; Alexander Berry, "Passages in the Life of a Nonagenarian", *SMH,* 24 Dec. 1873; William Broughton, MS *Letter* to Don Gaspar de Rico, 8 Apr. 1814, NL, Canberra; *HRA*, I, 8, pp. 92-4; *HRNSW*, VII, pp. 259-63, 312-15, 406-8; Geoffrey C. Ingleton, *True Patriots All* (Sydney, 1952), p. 54; J. Nicholas, *Narrative of a Voyage to New Zealand* (London, 1817), pp. 143-56; Dr Harold Royle of Armidale, married to a descendant of Betsy Broughton, generously shared with me his exhaustive knowledge of her part in the *Boyd* massacre.

56. *HRA*, I, 2, pp. 236-37.
57. Peter Cunningham, *Two Years in New South Wales*, London, 1827, ed. David S. Macmillan (Sydney, 1966), p. 206.
58. J.T. Bigge, *Report into Colony of NSW*.
59. Peter Cunningham, *Two Years in NSW*.
60. J.D. Lang, *Historical and Statistical Account*, vol. I, p. 366.
61. W. Burton, "State of Society and Crime in New South Wales", in *The Colonial Magazine and Commercial-Maritime Journal*, vol. I, 1840, p. 437.
62. R.D. Barton, *Reminiscences of an Australian Pioneer* (Sydney, 1917), pp. 170-71.
63. See note 16 above.
64. Ken Macnab and Russel Ward, "Nature and Nurture".

3 New settlements and new pastures

1. Roger Therry, *Reminiscences of Thirty Years' Residence in New South Wales,* ed. JM Bennett (Sydney, 1974), pp. 18-26.
2. *RAHSJ*, 22, pp. 371-74; 12, p. 86; and 14, pp. 232-44.
3. Russel Ward (ed.) *The Penguin Book of Australian Ballads* (Ringwood, 1964), pp. 36-38.
4. J.V. Barry, *Alexander Maconochie of Norfolk Island* (Melbourne, 1958); *idem, The Life and Death of John Price* (Melbourne, 1964).
5. James Stirling to Governor Darling *HRA*, III, 5, pp. 808-11; Geoffrey Blainey, *The Tyranny of Distance* (Melbourne, 1966), pp. 82-88.
6. ibid., pp. 88-95, and *HRA*, I, 12, pp. 194, 218.
7. Bourn Russell, *Journal of the Ship 'Lady Rowena', 1830-32, with later annotations*, MS 3532, ML.
8. *ADB*, vol. 1, "Hamilton Hume" and "W.H. Hovell"; H. Hume, *A Brief Statement of Facts in Connection with an Overland Expedition from Lake George to Port Phillip in 1824,* Sydney, 1855; W.H. Hovell, *Reply to 'A Brief Statement'*, Sydney, 1855.
9. *ADB*, vol. 2, "Charles Sturt"; Edgar Beale, *Sturt, the Chipped Idol* (Sydney, 1980); D. G. Brock, *To the Desert with Sturt: A Diary of the 1844 Expedition*, ed. K. Peake-Jones (Adelaide, 1975); J.H.L. Cumpston, *Charles Sturt* (Melbourne, 1951); Keith Swan and Margaret Carnegie, *In Step with Sturt* (Sydney, 1980).
10. T.L. Mitchell, *Three Expeditions into the Interior of Eastern Australia*, 2 vols, London, 1838, vol. 2, p. 158; *ADB*, vol. 2, "Sir T.L. Mitchell".
11. *ADB*, vol. 1, "E.J. Eyre"; and Geoffrey Dutton, *The Hero as Murderer* (Melbourne, 1966).
12. *ADB*, vol. 2, "F.W.L. Leichhardt"; Daniel Bunce, *Travels with Dr Leichhardt* (first published 1859) (Melbourne, 1979) and A.H. Chisholm, *Strange New World* (Melbourne, 1955).
13. ibid., and Gordon Connell, *The Mystery of Ludwig Leichhardt* (Mel-

bourne, 1980); and E.M. Webster, *Whirlwinds in the Plain: Ludwig Leichhardt* (Melbourne, 1980).

14. C.H. Currey, *Sir Francis Forbes* (Sydney, 1968); J.J. Eddy, *Britain and the Australian Colonies 1818-1831* (Oxford, 1969).

15. A.C.V. Melbourne, *Early Constitutional Development in Australia,* ed. R.B. Joyce (St Lucia, 1963), pp. 1-269, J.M. Ward, "The 'Blended' Legislative Council in New South Wales", in his (ed.) *New South Wales — Autocracy to Parliament 1824-1856* (Sydney, 1976).

16. Alan Barnard, *Visions and Profits* (Melbourne, 1961), p. 20; *ADB*, vol. 2, "William Charles Wentworth".

17. House of Commons, *Report of Select Committee on Transportation 1837-38;* N. Townsend, "The Molesworth Enquiry: Does the Report fit the Evidence", in *Journal of Australian Studies*, no. 1, June 1977.

18. A.C.V. Melbourne, *Early Constitutional Development*; J.M. Ward *"The Blended Legislative Council"*, and K. Buckley, "Gipps and the Graziers of New South Wales", in *HS* 6, 24 May 1955.

19. R.T. Appleyard and Toby Manford, *The Beginning: European Discovery and Early Settlement of Western Australia* (Nedlands, 1979), p.38 and *passim*.

20. James Stirling to Governor Darling, *HRA*, III, 6, pp. 551-84.

21. G.F. Moore, *Diary of Ten Years . . . in Western Australia* (London, 1884), pp. 236-37, 239-43.

22. F.K. Crowley, *Australia's Western Third* (London, 1960).

23. Lord Birkett (ed.), *The New Newgate Calendar* (London, 1960), pp.126-35.

24. P. Bloomfield, *Edward Gibbon Wakefield, Builder of the British Commonwealth* (London, 1961); P. Burroughs, *Britain and Australia: 1831-1855* (Oxford, 1967).

25. Douglas Pike, *Paradise of Dissent: South Australia: 1829-57* (London, 1957).

26. Geoffrey Dutton, *Founder of a City: the Life of Colonial William Light* (Melbourne, 1960), p. 288.

27. Samuel Sidney, *The Three Colonies of Australia* (London, 1852), pp. 307-8; J.W. Bull, *Early Experiences of Life in South Australia* (Adelaide, 1884), p. 245.

28. *HRA*, I, 21, p. 127.

29. Marnie Bassett, *The Hentys* (Melbourne, 1961).

30. J. Bonwick, *William Buckley* (Melbourne, 1961); John Morgan, *The Life and Adventures of William Buckley* (Melbourne, 1967) (first published Hobart, 1852).

31. Hugh Anderson, *Out of the Shadow: The Career of John Pascoe Fawkner* (Melburne, 1962); C.P. Billot, *John Batman* (Melbourne, 1979).

32. Margaret Kiddle, *Men of Yesterday . . . 1834-1890* (Melbourne, 1961).

33. S.G. Foster, "The Concession of Responsible Government to New South Wales", in J.M. Ward (ed.), *The Blended Legislative Council*.

34. D.W.A. Baker, *Days of Wrath: a Life of John Dumore Lang* (Melbourne, 1985).

35. For comparisons of the effects of the Australian and American frontiers see Russel Ward *The Australian Legend* (Melbourne, 1958), and H.C. Allen, *Bush and Backwoods* (Michigan State, 1959).

36. Carter Goodrich, *The Economic Record*, November 1928, pp. 206-7.

37. Anthony Trollope, *Australia and New Zealand* (Melbourne, 1876), p. 69.

38. Watkin Tench, in *Sydney's First Four Years,* ed. L.F. Fitzhardinge (Sydney, 1961), p. 245.

39. James Macarthur (Edward Edwards), *New South Wales: Its Present State* (London, 1837), p. 27.

40. John Hood, *Australia and the East* (London, 1843), p. 163.

41. All figures include districts which later became part of Queensland, but exclude the districts of Port Phillip and the penal stations of Norfolk Island and Moreton Bay. The figures for 1841 exclude the 2130 persons on board colonial vessels at sea, and those for 1851 include the "reputed County of Stanley" with other counties within the boundaries of location.

42. This phrase was coined by Vance Palmer in his *Legend of the Nineties* (Melbourne, 1964).

43. Frank Fowler, *Southern Lights and Shadows* (London, 1859), p.107ff.

44. Francis J. Grund, *Aristocracy in America* (New York, 1959), p. 30.

45. *HRA*, III, 1, pp. 238, 242-43, 282.

46. G.H. Chomley, *Tales of Old Times* (Sydney, 1903), p. 48; Brian Harrison, The Myall Creek Massacre, BA Hons thesis, UNE, 1966; James Steele, *Early Days of Windsor* (Sydney, 1916), p. 135.

47. An Emigrant Mechanic (Alexander Harris), *Settlers and Convicts,* ed. C.M.H. Clark, (Melbourne, 1953), ch. XX.

48. Harris, *loc. cit.*

49. Michael Cannon, *Who's Master? Who's Man?* (Melbourne, 1971), p.145.

50. Margaret Kiddle, *Caroline Chisholm* (Melbourne, 1950), p. 49 *et passim*.

51. Jean Woolmington, Early Christian Missions to the Australian Aborigines: a Study in Failure, PhD thesis, UNE, 1979.

52. G.A. Price, Genesis of the Robertson Land Acts of 1861: a Study of the Evidence in the Liverpool Plains, MA Hons thesis, UNE, 1963.

53. H.S. Russell, *The Genesis of Queensland* (Sydney, 1888), pp. 166, 171.

54. Percy Clarke, *The 'New Chum' in Australia* (London, 1886), p. 262; Russel Ward, "The Australian Legend Revisited" in *HS*, 18, 71, October 1978.

55. J.M. Ward, "The Blended Legislative Council"; *idem, Earl Grey and the Australian Colonies, 1846-57* (Melbourne, 1958); S.J. Dyson, Opposition to Transportation Movement in Van Diemen's Land, 1845-1853, LittB thesis, UNE, 1981. S.G. Foster, "The Concession of Responsible Government".

56. J.N. Rawling, *Charles Harpur: an Australian* (Sydney, 1962).

57. Frank Cayley, *Flag of Stars* (Adelaide, 1966), esp. pp. 57-65.

58. *ADB*, vol. 2, John West, and S.J. Dyson, Opposition to Transportation.

59. Alan Martin, *Henry Parkes: a Biography* (Melbourne, 1980), pp. 55-59.

60. *ADB*, vol. 4, William Henry Groom.

4   Diggers, democracy and urbanisation

1. S.G. Foster, *Colonial Improver: Edward Deas Thomson 1800-1879* (Melbourne, 1978), p. 116.

2. Thatcher, MS, *Script* for Diorama of goldfield life, La Trobe Library.

3. G.C. Mundy, *Our Antipodes* (London, 1855), p. 566ff.

4. Geoffrey Serle, *The Golden Age* (Melbourne, 1963), p. 86.

5. William Howitt, *Land, Labour and Gold* (London, 1855), vol. I, p.236.

6. Personal information from Mrs M.H. Armstrong, a granddaughter of Tommy Marx.

7. Geoffrey Serle (ed.), *The Eureka Stockade* (Melbourne, 1963) (first published 1855).

8. *HS, Special Eureka Supplement*, December 1954, pp. 50-80.

9. Len Fox, *The Strange Story of the Eureka Flag* (Darlinghurst, 1963).

10. G.C. Bolton, *A Thousand Miles Away: A History of North Queensland to 1920* (Brisbane, 1963), pp. 51-60.

11. Ross Fitzgerald, *A History of Queensland from the Dreaming to 1915* (St Lucia, 1986), pp. 236-56.

12. A.H. Markham, *The Cruise of the Rosario* (London, 1873), pp. 111-16.

13. D.B. Waterson, "Thomas McIlwraith", in Denis Murphy, Roger Joyce and Margaret Cribb (eds), *The Premiers of Queensland* (St Lucia, 1990), pp. 118-41.

14. K.A. Austin, *The Lights of Cobb and Co.* (Adelaide, 1967); L.G. Churchward, *Australia and America 1788-1972* (Sydney, 1979), pp. 54-55.

15. Ian Mudie, *Riverboats* (Adelaide, 1961); G.L. Buxton, *The Riverina 1861-91* (Melbourne, 1967); *ADB*, vol. 3 "Francis Cadell" and vol. 6 "William Richard Randell".

16. Craufurd, D.W. Goodwin, *Economic Enquiry in Australia* (Durham, N.C. 1966), pp. 265-98.

17. Colin Roderick (ed.), *Henry Lawson: Collected Verse,* 3 vols (Sydney, 1967), vol. 1, p. 57.
18. Geoffrey Blainey, *The Tyranny of Distance* (Melbourne, 1966), pp. 175-205.
19. ibid., pp. 206-27; and *SMH*, 28 August 1852.
20. Russel Ward and John Robertson (eds), *Such Was Life: Select Documents in Australian Social History vol. 2, 1851-1913* (Sydney, 1980), pp. 219-21; and *ADB*, vol. 6, "Sir Charles Todd".
21. N.G. Butlin, *Investment in Australian Economic Development, 1861-1900* (Cambridge, 1964); and Bruce Ryan, "Metropolitan Growth" in Richard Preston (ed), *Contemporary Australia* (Durham, N.C., 1969).
22. *Schools of Arts and Colonial Nationality: A Lecture* (Sydney, 1861).
23. *loc. cit.,* p. 98.
24. See p. 102 above.
25. *Narrative of a Voyage to New South Wales* (London, 1822), p. 92.
26. Bruce Ryan, "Metropolitan Growth", and *ADB* vol. 3, "Sir William John Clarke", vol. 4, "Sir Simon Fraser"; vol. 6, "Sir Frederick Thomas Sargood" and "David Syme".
27. Geoffrey Blainey, *The Rush that Never Ended* (Melbourne 1963).
28. Geoffrey Serle, *The Rush to be Rich* (Melbourne, 1971), p. 235.
29. John Gale, *History of . . . the Federal Capital Territory* (Queanbeyan, 1927), pp. 118-19.
30. Pakington to Fitzroy, 15 December 1852; *V. and P. Leg. Council of NSW, 1853, Vol. 1.*
31. Cyril Pearl, *Brilliant Dan Deniehy* (Melbourne, 1972).
32. *Letters from Australia* (London, 1869), pp. 50, 133.
33. J.D. Lang, *Emigration: . . . in Reference to . . . Settling . . . a Numerous, Industrious and Virtuous Agricultural Population*, (Sydney, 1833).
34. For a complete text of this song, see Russel Ward, *The Penguin Book of Australian Ballads* (Ringwood, 1964).
35. *ADB*, vol. 6, "Sir John Robertson"; Colin Roderick, *Henry Lawson*, p. 233.
36. Edward Shann, *An Economic History of Australia* (Cambridge, 1948), p. 233.
37. *SMH*, 7 May 1861.
38. Douglas Pike, *Paradise of Dissent* (London, 1957), pp. 249-82, 353-91, 421-41.
39. Russel Ward and John Robertson, *Such Was Life*, pp. 230-34.
40. Keith Amos, *The Fenians in Australia 1865-1880* (Sydney, 1988).
41. *ADB*, vol. 3, "Robert O'Hara Burke": A.M. Moorehead, *Cooper's Creek* (London, 1963); and T.J. Bergin, The Burke and Wills Expedition MA thesis, UNE, 1983.
42. *ADB*, vol. 6, "John McDouall Stuart" and Douglas Pike, *John McDouall Stuart* (Melbourne, 1958).

43. Ray Ericksen, *Ernest Giles: Explorer and Traveller 1835-1897* (Melbourne, 1978); Ernest Giles, *Australia Twice Traversed*, 2 vols (London, 1889).

44. Keith Willey, *When the Sky Fell Down* (Sydney, 1979), p. 220.

45. [George Carrington], *Colonial Adventures and Experiences* (London, 1871), pp. 150-53.

46. *SMH*, 21 November 1861; *ADB*, vol. 2, "Horatio Spencer Wills" and vol. 6, "Thomas Wentworth Spencer Wills".

47. Cf. Russel Ward, *The Australian Legend* (Melbourne, 1958), pp. 157-63.

48. *ADB*, vol. 3, "Sir Redmond Barry" and vol. 5, "Edward Kelly"; John McQuilton, *The Kelly Outbreak* (Melbourne, 1979); Graham Seal, *Ned Kelly in Popular Tradition* (Melbourne, 1980); John Molony, *I Am Ned Kelly* (Ringwood, 1980).

5 Radicals and nationalists

1. Vance Palmer, *The Legend of the Nineties* (Melbourne, 1954), p. 9.

2. e.g. John Rickard, *Class and Politics* (Canberra, 1976); R.W. Connell and T.H. Irving, *Class Structure in Australian History*, (Melbourne, 1980); *cf.* V.G. Childe, *How Labour Governs* (London, 1923).

3. R.N. Ebbels, *The Australian Labor Movement 1850-1907* (Sydney, 1960), p. 222.

4. Geoffrey Blainey, *The Rise of Broken Hill* (Melbourne, 1968); Brian Kennedy, *Silver, Sin and Sixpenny Ale: a Social History of Broken Hill 1883-1921* (Melbourne, 1978).

5. W.C. Wentworth, *Australasia: a Poem* (London, 1823), p. 22.

6. Quoted B.R. Wise, *The Making of the Australian Commonwealth 1889-1900* (London, 1913), p. 117.

7. Cyril Pearl, *The Three Lives of Gavan Duffy* (Kensington, 1979).

8. J.F. Mason Catholics and the Labor Movement in NSW, 1890-1960, LittB thesis, UNE, 1963.

9. Quoted B.R. Wise, *the Making of the Australian Commonwealth*, p.204.

10. Bernard Smith, *Australian Painting 1788-1970* (Melbourne, 1971).

11. Quoted R.N. Ebbels, *the Australian Labor Movement*, p. 121.

12. F.P. Donovan, Australia and the Great London Dock Strike 1889, BA Hons thesis, UNE, 1968.

13. *V. & P. Leg. Ass. NSW*, 1894, vol. I, p. 2.

14. Mary Durack, *Kings in Grass Castles* (London, 1959).

15. Geoffrey Blainey, *The Rush that Never Ended* (Melbourne, 1973), pp. 161-98.

16. David W. Carnegie, *Spinifex and Sand* (Ringwood, 1973) (first published 1898), p. 399.

17. John Rickard, *Class and Politics;* Robin Gollan, *Radical and Working Class Politics: a Study of Eastern Australia 1850-1910* (Melbourne,

1967); Stuart Svensen, *The Shearers' War: the Story of the 1891 Shearers' Strike* (St Lucia, 1989).

18. *The Riverina Herald*, 28 August 1894, quoted R.N. Ebbels, *The Australian Labor Movement*, pp. 146-48.

19. Robin Gollan, *Radical Politics*, pp. 129-35.

20. Albert Métin, *Socialism Without Doctrine* (trans. Russel Ward) (Sydney, 1977) (first published 1901).

21. W.C. Windeyer, *Ex Parte Collins: A Judgment* (Sydney, 1889); Ray Markey, "Women and Labour 1880-1900" in Elizabeth Windschuttle (ed.), *Women, Class and History* (Melbourne, 1980).

22. *SMH*, 6 April, 1981.

23. Solomon Encel, Norman Mackenzie and Margaret Tebbutt, *Women and Society: an Australian Study* (Melbourne, 1974), pp. 222-25; Coral Lansbury, "The Feminine Frontier: Women's Suffrage and Economic Reality", *Meanjin*, 31, 3, 1972; and Baiba Irving, "Women in Australian Politics", *Refractory Girl*, Summer 1974-75.

24. Frank J. Hardy, *Power Without Glory* (Melbourne, 1950); Niall Brennan, *John Wren: Gambler* (Melbourne, 1971); Hugh Buggy, *The Real John Wren* (Melbourne, 1977).

25. C.S. Blackton, "Australian Nationality and Nationalism: the Imperial Federationist Interlude 1885-1901", *HS*, 7, 25, 1955.

26. Richard Hall and John Iremonger, *The Makers and the Breakers: the Governor-General and the Senate vs. the Constitution* (Sydney, 1976).

27. B.R. Wise, *The Making of the Australian Commonwealth*, p. 356.

28. D.C. Murray, quoted B.R. Wise, ibid., p. 5.

29. J.A. La Nauze, *The Making of the Australian Constitution* (Melbourne, 1972).

30. B.R. Penny, "The Age of Empire: an Australian episode", *HS*, 11, 41, 1963; J.W. McQualter, Australian Patriotism and the Sudan Contingent of 1885, BA Hons thesis, UNE, 1966.

31. Russel Ward, " 'Breaker Morant' and Australian Nationalism", published in *University of Northern Territory Planning Authority Bulletin*, 1981.

32. ibid., and see Margaret Carnegie and Frank Shields, *In Search of Breaker Morant* (Armadale, 1979); F.M. Cutlack, *Breaker Morant* (Sydney, 1962); L.M. Field, *The Forgotten War* (Melbourne, 1979); Lieut. George Witton, *Scapegoats of the Empire* (Sydney, 1893) (first published 1907).

33. See e.g. Bruce Mansfield, *Australian Democrat* (Sydney, 1965).

34. J.A. La Nauze, *Alfred Deakin: a Biography*, 2 vols (Melbourne, 1965).

35. M.V. Moore, Unequal and Inferior: the White Australia Policy, BA Hons thesis, UNE, 1962; Russel Ward, *Nation for a Continent* (Melbourne, 1977), pp. 1-40; Myra Willard, *History of the White Australia Policy to 1920* (Melbourne, 1967).

36. D. Catts, *King O'Malley: Man and Statesman* (Sydney, 1957).

37. Robin Gollan, *The Commonwealth Bank of Australia: Origins and Early History* (Canberra, 1968).
38. T.W. Tanner, *Compulsory Citizen Soldiers* (Sydney, 1980); John Barrett, *Falling In* (Sydney, 1979).

6 War and depression

1. John Welfield, The Labor Party and the War, 1914-15, BA Hons thesis, UNE, 1965; *CPD, House of Representatives*, 14 October, 1914, pp. 147-49.
2. See pp. 80-81, above.
3. David Kent, *Overland*, Nos 84, 85.
4. Letter from "a Native", *SMH*, 10 November 1863; Geoffrey Serle, *John Monash* (Melbourne, 1982).
5. L.F. Fitzhardinge, *William Morris Hughes*, vol. I (Sydney, 1964) and vol. II (Sydney, 1979).
6. E.C. Fry (ed.), *Tom Baker and the I.W.W.* (Canberra, 1965); Ian Turner, *Sydney's Burning* (London, 1967); *idem, Industrial Labour and Politics* (Canberra, 1965).
7. F.B. Smith, *The Conscription Plebiscites in Australia 1916-17* (Melbourne, 1965); J.M. Main, *Conscription: the Australian Debate 1901-1970* (Melbourne, 1970); Roy Forward and Bob Reece (eds), *Conscription in Australia* (Brisbane, 1968).
8. Geoffrey Serle, 'The Digger Tradition and Australian Nationalism', *Meanjin*, 24, 2, 1965.
9. L. Lett, "Sir Hubert Murray . . ., *RAHSJ*, 34, 3, 1948; M. Tate, "Australia and Self-Determination for New Guinea", *AJPH*, 17, 2, 1971.
10. G.L. Kristianson, *The Politics of Patriotism* (Canberra, 1966).
11. H.F. Willcock, Moderation in Western Australian Politics 1890-1936, LittB thesis, UNE, 1961.
12. Earle Page, *Truant Surgeon* (Sydney, 1963); J.B. O'Hara, The Entry into Public Life of Sir Earle Christmas Grafton Page 1915-1921, BA Hons thesis, UNE, 1969.
13. Don Aitkin, *The Country Party in New South Wales* (Canberra 1972); B.D. Graham, *The Formation of the Australian Country Parties* (Canberra, 1966).
14. C. Edwards, *Bruce of Melbourne* (London, 1965); *Anstey Papers, ANL.*
15. V.G. Childe, *How Labor Governs* (Melbourne, 1964); R.A. Gollan, *Revolutionaries and Reformists* (Canberra, 1975).
16. Personal information, the late Bill Harney.
17. Geoffrey Blainey, *The Tyranny of Distance* (Melbourne, 1966).
18. C.B. Schedvin, *Australia and the Great Depression* (Sydney, 1970).
19. John Robertson, *J.H. Scullin* (Perth, 1974); Zelman Cowen, *Isaac Isaacs* (Melbourne, 1967).

20. Irwin Young, *Theodore: His Life and Times* (Sydney, 1971).
21. Miriam Dixson, *Greater Than Lenin? Lang and Labor 1916-1932* (Melbourne, n.d. (1974)).
22. Keith Amos, *The New Guard Movement 1931-1935* (Melbourne, 1976); Eric Campbell, *The Rallying Point* (Melbourne, 1965).
23. P.R. Hart, "J.A. Lyons, Tasmanian Labor Leader", *LH*, 9, 1965 and *idem*, "Lyons: Labor Minister — Leader of the UAP.", *LH*, 17, 1970.
24. J.K. Galbraith, *The Affluent Society* (Cambridge, Mass.) 1958.
25. Stan Moran, *Reminiscences of a Rebel* (Sydney, 1979); Victor Williams, *The Years of Big Jim* (Perth, 1975).
26. Russel Ward, " 'Frontierism' and National Stereotypes", *Canadian Historical Association Report*, 1964.
27. Egon Kisch, *Australian Landfall* (Sydney, 1969) (first edidtion London 1937).
28. C.D. Rowley, *The Destruction of Aboriginal Society*, vol. 1, Canberra, 1970 and G.T. Wood, *Report of the Royal Commission . . . into Alleged Killing of Aborigines in East Kimberley* (Perth, 1927) (*V.&P.* of W.A. Leg. Ass.).
29. M.C. Hartwig, The Coniston Killings, BA Hons thesis, Univ. Adelaide, 1960.

7 War and affluence

1. K. Perkins, *Menzies, Last of the Queen's Men* (Adelaide, 1968); Cameron Hazelhurst, *Menzies Observed* (Sydney, 1979).
2. Events witnessed by writer.
3. A. Chester, *John Curtin* (Sydney, 1945); Lloyd Ross, *John Curtin* (Melbourne, 1977).
4. Charles Bateson, *The War with Japan* (Sydney, 1968); John Robertson, *Australia at War 1939-45*, (Melbourne, 1981).
5. *SMH*, 29 December 1941; John J. Dedman, "The Return of the AIF from the Middle East", in *Australian Outlook*, 21, 2, (August 1967).
6. Alastair Davidson, *The Communist Party of Australia* (Stanford, 1969).
7. L.F. Crisp, *Ben Chifley* (Melbourne, 1957).
8. A.A. Calwell, *Be Just and Fear Not* (Melbourne, 1972).
9. J.L. Martin, *Refugee Settlers* (Canberra, 1965); and C.A. Price, *Southern Europeans in Australia* (Melbourne 1963).
10. Kylie Tennant, *Evatt, Politics and Justice* (Sydney, 1970); A. Dalziel, *Evatt the Enigma* (Melbourne, 1967); Carl Bridge, "Herbert Vere Evatt", pp. 242-47 in *The Greats* ed. Leonie Kramer and Russel Ward (Sydney, 1986).
11. Rupert Lockwood, *Black Armada* (Sydney, 1975).
12. R.J. O'Neill, *Australia in the Korean War, 1950-53*, 2 vols (Canberra, 1980).

13. L.C. Webb, *Communism and Democracy in Australia: the 1951 Referendum* (Melbourne, 1954).
14. Brian Fitzpatrick, *The Australian Commonwealth* (Melbourne, 1956), p. 254.
15. *Transcript of Proceedings of Royal Commission on Espionage 1954-55* (NSW Govt Printer, 1955); *National Times*, 3-8 September 1973; N. Whitlam and J. Stubbs, *Nest of Traitors* (Brisbane, 1974); Cedric Ralph, *The Petrov Commission Unmasked* (Melbourne, 1973).
16. *AJPH*, 24, 3, 1978; *Australian*, 20 January 1978.
17. T. Truman, *Catholic Action and Politics* (Melbourne, 1959); Paul Ormonde, *the Movement* (Melbourne, 1972).
18. *Reserve Bank of Australia: Statistical Bulletin*, August 1979.
19. Waveney Brown, *A Woman of Distinction* (Brisbane, 1981).
20. Kenneth Rivett (ed.), *Immigration: Control or Colour Bar* (Melbourne, 1960).

8 Going it alone

1. See e.g., Albert Métin, *Socialisme sans Doctrines*, Paris, 1901 (English edition, trans. Russel Ward, Sydney, 1977), and W. Pember Reeves, *State Experiments in Australia and New Zealand* (London, 1902).
2. "The Second Coming", *Meanjin*, 26, 1 Autumn 1967.
3. *Australian*, 25 July 1968.
4. ibid., 31 October 1969; Alan Trengove, *John Grey Gorton* (Melbourne, 1969)
5. Personal information from Prof. J.B. Duroselle, Sorbonne, 1971.
6. CPD, *House of Representatives*, 9 March 1971, p. 684.
7. *AJPH*, 18, 3, 1972.
8. Stewart Harris, *Political Football* (Melbourne, 1972).
9. *SMH*, 29 July 1981.
10. ibid., 3 August 1968.
11. See p. 302 above.
12. *Sunday Telegraph*, 29 October 1972.
13. Laurie Oakes and David Solomon, *The Making of an Australian Prime Minister* (Melbourne, 1973).
14. *Cf.* pp. 284-85 above, and Richard Hall, *The Secret State: Australia's Spy Industry* (Sydney, 1978).
15. *AJPH*, 20, 3, 1974.
16. Geoffrey Sawer, *Federation under Strain* (Melbourne, 1977), p. 145.
17. *CPD, Senate*, 1-4 November 1977, p. 1965.
18. The opening words of *Such Is Life*.
19. Brian Toohey in *National Times*, 19-25 July 1981; and see Len Fox, *Multinationals Take Over Australia* (Sydney, 1980).
20. See p. 261 above.
21. Colin Tatz, *Race Politics in Australia* (Armidale, 1979); *Nation Re-*

view, 8-14 September 1977; and ibid., 29 September-5 October 1977.
22. *AJPH*, 30, 3, 1984.
23. *New York Times*, 28 July 1986.
24. *AJPH*, 33, 2, 1987.
25. *SMH*, 9 February 1987.
26. *Age*, 27 October 1987.
27. Including some of my children and grandchildren who witnessed the miniscule naval engagement described below.
28. *AJPH*, 36, 2, 1990.
29. "Australian Magazine" in *Weekend Australian*, 11-12 November 1989.
30. *Weekend Australian*, 3-4 November 1990.
31. Peter Harcher in *SMH*, 8 March, 1991.
32. *The Australian*, 30 January 1991.
33. See note 23 above.
34. See p. 92 above.

Index